HUNTING BIG-GAME TROPHIES

A North American Guide

HUNTING BIG-GAME

A North American Guide

An Outdoor Life Book

TROPHIES

by Tom Brakefield

OUTDOOR LIFE

Sunrise Books / E. P. Dutton & Company, Inc.
New York

Times Mirror Magazines, Inc.
BOOK DIVISION

Editor and Publisher John W. Sill
Executive Editor Henry Gross
Associate Editor Neil Soderstrom
Art Director Jeff Fitschen
Production Manager Millicent La Roque
Editorial Assistant Pat Blair

The editors wish to thank the following for their assistance: James C. Rikhoff, chairman of the Editorial and Historical Committee of the Boone and Crockett Club; Wm. H. Nesbitt, coordinator of the North American Big Game Awards Program; and Colonel James W. Hirzel, executive secretary custodian of the Association of American Rod and Gun Clubs, Europe.

Library of Congress Catalog Card Number: 75-31060
ISBN: 0-87690-214-X

Manufactured in the United States of America

For Greg and Scott.

May they be able to enjoy the glory
of the outdoors as much as I have.

Contents

Preface

The average hunter goes into the hills or the woods to hunt for large game for a variety of reasons. Some of these may include curiosity, a desire for travel and excitement, an urge to temporarily return to a more basic existence, or a simple longing for more solitude and privacy than one can find in the cities. The success or failure of the hunt is usually judged by the size of the bag or by whether there was a kill.

But as the hunter increases his experience and competence, he increases his enjoyment in direct proportion. And the *nature* of that enjoyment also changes. All of the individual "reasons" for hunting become melded into a simple but compelling love for the wild places and the marvelous creatures that live there.

The more accomplished and sophisticated the hunter becomes, the more fully he appreciates all aspects of the hunt. There are subtle factors of great value such as the tinkle of horsebells before sleep, the fragrance of balsam on a crystal day, the invigorating pre-dawn shock at the ice-rimmed wash basin, the contentment of exhausted men at day's end who share similar feelings as to what is important in life. No longer is his enjoyment of the hunt so dominated by the exciting, but all too brief, moments of the climactic stalk and kill.

Our hunter has become more selective of the game he takes and more perceptive about his experiences. He becomes one who "kills to hunt rather than one who hunts to kill," as the mellow phrase has it. He takes pride in his earned competence. He knows how to select and work properly with professional guides and outfitters. He knows which areas and what times to hunt for different game. He can spot, evaluate and approach game in a workmanlike fashion. Though he has opportunities to kill one or more heads of game, he lets them go while continuing to search for the older, larger and wiser heads that exceed any trophies he has yet taken.

As the years roll by, he finds his life enriched by friendships he would not otherwise have made and by his discovering resources within himself that he would never have known if he had led a purely urban existence. He develops collateral interests in outdoor literature, firearms, ballistics, the wildlife sciences, outdoor photography, and the early history of his country and his sport. He kills less. But he makes no apologies for killing. For he realizes that man is still an aggressive eyes-front predator whose opposable thumb was put to early use to help him wield and fashion weapons. He knows that hunting, quite to the contrary to much of the senseless nattering heard today, is one of the most natural and healthy pursuits of mankind. He knows that man's natural aggressions, which are but lightly overlaid with a few brief years of civilization, can be channeled more constructively and enjoyably upon the hunting field than in practically any other fashion.

He comes to know and love animals in a deeper sense than the addle-headed abstractionist who calls himself a total preservationist ever will. Every hunt, barring serious illness or accident, becomes a "success," whatever the bag. He realizes that every hunt affords so many trophies, the most precious of which are intangible and thus can never be put on a wall. And he knows that the true value of a physical trophy on the wall is determined by many considerations in addition to mere size and dimensions. In short, he has matured into a "trophy hunter."

This is a book of considerable length and substance. And, like any other project of substance, it could never be solely the product of one man's mind and experiences. So many people have, directly and indirectly, helped me to fashion this book that it becomes a formidable task to indicate even a partial list.

First would have to come the outdoor writers, both of today and yesteryear, here and abroad, who have helped refine and sharpen whatever basic insights and interests that I may have possessed at the beginning. A very incomplete list of early writers would have to include such giants as F. C. Selous, Theodore Roosevelt, Charles Sheldon, W. A. Baillie-Grohman, William Hornaday, Sir Samuel Baker and a whole generation of intrepid British army officers who hunted the world over and, generally, weren't half-bad writers. A most incomplete list of more recent writers would have to include Jack O'Connor, John Jobson and Warren Page — fine sportsmen and fine writers whose work has influenced for the better a whole generation of American hunters.

There are also guides and outfitters, the professionals, who have generously and gladly shared their experiences and knowledge with me over the years. Many were contacted for up-to-date information in preparing this manuscript and, to a man, they responded promptly and fully in spite of busy schedules and other commitments. John Holmes, Sam Sands, Roy Seward, Jack Atcheson, Gene Holmes, Andy Dennis, Rocky Seward, and far too many others to list here were of inestimable value. So were some of America's senior hunters, such as Elgin Gates and George Parker, who afforded opinions, information, and photographs.

In this book I have been as specific as possible in indicating where and when to hunt trophies of the various big-game species that can be hunted and imported. No man, or group of men, can hunt every valley and check out every exception that proves each rule. Though the advice and information provided by the men listed here was of immense value, any mistakes are solely my responsibility.

Hopefully I may be excused a couple of very personal and very important mentions here. My stepbrother, John McCartt, is one of the finest sportsmen I know. A good field man and a knowledgeable student of hunting, he's the best guy I know to share a tent with or just some of Scotland's finest while yarning long into the night about trips past. No man ever had a better brother.

Outdoor writing is something of a strange and arcane craft. Many elements have to mesh, and personalities must jibe for a book of this nature to ever reach publication. From the time he received my first truncated draft proposal for this book until the final manuscript was in, John Sill, the editor and publisher at Outdoor Life Books, was unflaggingly enthusiastic and helpful. And that included the stretches of road with the potholes and bumps as well as the long downhill straights. Neil Soderstrom, my editor, has patience, persistence and — above all — perception in abundance. Editors like these two men leave any book the better and any writer the richer.

Lastly, and maybe most importantly, are the many hunters that it has been my good fortune to hunt with, meet while traveling, or communicate with by phone or mail. These men, sharing with me both their enthusiams and their opinions, have also helped to shape this book and me, as well.

It is my wish that this book entertain and instruct. America needs an ever larger crop of informed and alert sportsmen who can protect our hunting heritage and pass it on to those still to come. We need men who can explain and defend the sport in both law and spirit. If this book contributes in some measure to that end, I will be abundantly gratified.

Tom Brakefield

HUNTING BIG–GAME TROPHIES

A North American Guide

Trophy Hunting Today

1

Trying to pin down universally acceptable and meaningful definitions of "trophy" and "trophy hunt" is like trying to pinch quicksilver. As when defining "high society," one's definition is inevitably colored both by his own experiences and the times he lives in.

Some examples? Defining a trophy inevitably gets into numbers — dimensions and measurements — though there are other elements involved also. A bighorn sheep hunter in the 1920s, who had the time and money to spend 45 to 60 days on each hunting trip into almost virgin territory, might well have defined a trophy as a 45-inch ram. Such animals hardly exist outside national parks today, and to cleave to the definition of a half century earlier is ludicrous. In the 1940s and 1950s the bighorn hunter might well have felt that a 38- to 42-inch ram was a real "trophy." Thirty-eight inch bighorn sheep are still taken, but only rarely. Then how big must a trophy be to be a trophy? This is, at best, difficult to say.

There are also differing opinions as to the spirit and ethics that should underlie a trophy hunt. Most hunters would agree that a man who backpacks into rough country on his own and lives off his pack and the land for two or three weeks to spot, follow up, and cleanly kill an outstanding head has undertaken a hunt in the best sense. If that same hunter passes up many smaller heads, knowing he could return home empty handed, he's managed to uphold a very high ideal. Furthermore, most would agree that the fellow who flies into sheep country by night, steadfastly refuses to do much climbing or walking, and finally pays his guide to stalk for him and shoot the first small ram they see has conducted a sadly grotesque parody of a trophy hunt.

But there's a wide stretch of country between these two extremes. Most hunters would agree that employing a guide in unfamiliar country is sporting and acceptable. And most would applaud the good fortune of a hunter who had developed a special comradeship with a guide during previous hunts that caused the guide to "save back" for his friend a head he had spotted with another hunter.

But what if the hunter is wealthy and before the season opens posts a massive reward for anyone who spots and then notifies him of a head of a certain size? The wealthy hunter then drops everything and flies up immediately. Within a day or two of the call, our "hunter" is 5,000 miles from home and 200 yards from his prize. One shot and he collects. And then the guide collects! This practice is a bit sticky and, though perfectly legal, it is in my opinion low-standard trophy hunting. (However, I do feel that a reasonable tip to a guide for good service, and for being an agreeable camp and field companion, is certainly in line with the best traditions of the sport.)

An exclusive province of the nobility, early European hunting was a ritualized affair that employed large retinues and often resulted in sizable kill figures. Sporting? Those were different times.

Perhaps it would illuminate matters to trace the evolution of trophy hunting to the point that it now occupies in North America.

Man was an eyes-in-front, weapons-fashioning hunting animal before he discovered agriculture. Even in the dimmest of prehistoric times, undoubtedly, special note was taken of unusually large animals slain in the chase, as well as of freakish or malformed animals. As man entered the "civilized" era in Europe and in the Middle East, ever larger and denser populations were supportable through agriculture. Hunting became the province of royalty and the landed classes. Hunting on a mass scale as we know it in America simply did not exist.

And how those noblemen loved the chase! To the dismay of his clerics, one German count in Hesse insisted upon striking the mention of "daily bread" from the Lord's Prayer and rephrasing the entreaty to "Give us our daily hart (red deer stag) in the pride of grease (fat and ready for the rut)." The great hunters of that era found time to note only details of the chase in their personal diaries. Apparently nothing else seemed worth recording. On the fateful day of July 14, 1789, in Paris, which witnessed the storming of the Bastille, Louis XVI went hunting and only noted laconically, "Killed nothing." Later that year, on the 5th of October, after the maddened hordes had thrown themselves upon Versailles, Louis who'd been hunting nearby, made this diary entry: "Shot at the gate of Chatillon, killed 81 head, interrupted by events; went and returned on horseback." "*Events*"? Now that's absorption in the hunt!

Roughly during the period of 1400 to 1800 when European hunting was still the exclusive province of nobility and before growing human population resulted in land-use conflicts with game, some truly fantastic game bags were accumulated. The nobility went afield with vast and luxuriant retinues of drivers, beaters, weighers and recorders. The success of the "trophy hunt" was adjudged more on the gross size of its bag than on any other factor. Painstaking records were kept over the years on the sizes of the largest animals and on the number of animals slaughtered (there is no other word for it).

Toward the end of this innocent era of some four centuries, a noticeable decline was occurring in both the quantity of the bag taken and the size of the largest animals — an unmistakable sign of the conflict accelerating between increasing human populations and the game. For instance, in Saxony (in present-day Germany) during the 70-year reigns of Elector John George the First (1611–1656) and his son Elector John George the Second (1656–1680), these two men bagged over 110,000 deer of all types between them! And that didn't include 54,200 wild boar, 6,067 wolves and over 50,000 other animals. This was in spite of the fact that ten years of terrible havoc was wrought through the same area as a part of the Thirty Years War. Without the warfare, the "bag" would have undoubtedly been a lot larger.

Among these animals some unbelievable red deer were taken. In one authenticated instance, a 61-stone, 11-pound (854 U.S. pounds) monster was taken. In another less well authenticated instance, a 900-plus-pound goliath was noted. These are simply fantastic sizes for the red deer, an animal which is considerably smaller than our elk. A later descendant of Saxony's Georges, Duke Earnest II of Saxe-Coburg-Gotha, ruled from 1837 to 1886 and hunted the same area as avidly as his ancestors. During this 49-year period he managed to take only 3,283 red deer as compared with the 79,070 red deer his forebears took in their 70-year hunting marathon. Apparently times were getting tougher.

Enormous heads were taken during this era. The Moritzburg Castle, near Dresden, East Germany, houses one of the great collections of red deer antlers, all taken prior to 1725, many taken prior to 1576. In the dining hall 65 sets of antlers are on display, eight of which outrank the world record head for modern times. In another hall hang 42 nontypical heads, among which is the famous 66-point head. It does not, however, show 66 well defined tines. (By the old laws of hunting, any point, or "offer," from which the leather thong of the hunting horn could be hung was counted. And in Germany and Austria one always spoke of a head as if it had an even number of tines. The so-called 66-point head has 33 "offers" on one side but only 29 on the other.)

Of the great typical heads in the collection, one is truly fantastic. Though it has "only" 24 points, it is without question the largest pair of red deer antlers ever taken. The outside, tip-to-tip spread is an incredible 75⁶/10 inches. And the weight, with a very small section of skull bone, is an unbelievable 41½ U.S. pounds. Unfortunately, little is known about how and exactly when this great head was taken. Although there is an assumption that the kill was prior to 1586.

The antler weight of over 40 pounds after better than 350 years of drying is stupendous. For comparison, a nice heavy 6-point bull elk's antlers that I took in Alberta in 1968 weighed 19 pounds-and-change only two weeks after he was shot. World-

These two drawings show the two most famous red deer heads in the collection at the Moritzburg Castle, near Dresden, East Germany. The nontypical 66-point rack, above, was taken in 1696. It weighs about 12 lb. 2oz. The 24-pointer, below, was taken prior to 1700. It is the largest set of red deer antlers on record. With an inside spread of 41 inches and an outside spread of 75$^6/_{10}$ inches, it weighs a phenomenal 41 lb. 8 oz.

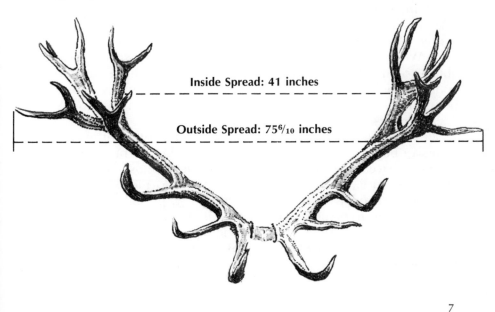

Inside Spread: 41 inches

Outside Spread: 75$^6/_{10}$ inches

wide, any round-antlered deer with a rack of over 40 pounds is a creature of wonder and awe.

Roughly, during the period 1825 through 1940, we saw the advent of the "British Officer" era in worldwide trophy hunting. Then England ruled the seas and much of the world, and when the lads left the playing fields of Eton and Harrow, it was usually to explore, subjugate, garrison and even minister to "the heathen" — all usually with a gun in hand and a desire for sport.

The emphasis on bag size decreased as this upper-middle-class sport replaced the old nobility-only pastime on the continent. Rather, the accent was on collecting strange and unusual animals (sometimes described for science for the first time in the process) as well as animals of large size. The big cats of India and Africa, the pachyderms, the antelopes, and the oddities were avidly sought. By today's standards of one animal to the hunter, the bag sizes were still quite prodigal, but they were modest indeed compared to those of earlier eras.

Around 1925 came the wealthy American sportsman, privately financing his own hunting rather than picking it up as a side benefit of his military duty. These men sought the single largest specimen of each species. Bag sizes decreased still further, and absolute emphasis was placed on securing the very largest heads and trophies — this to the last 1/8th of an inch and the last score point.

This North American trophy hunting era had its fullest flowering during the 1950s and the early 1960s, and it produced some very fine hunters, some of whom are still hunting avidly. These men were very fortunate in that they came along after World War II when rapid transportation first came available on a large scale and yet while human populations were still considerably smaller than today. Then too, the game was often better managed in the old African colonies than in today's "democracies" of the "Third World."

Starting about 1960 the emphasis changed still another time — or so I believe. The enormous growth of both American and worldwide wealth and the growth of credit systems teamed with ever faster and cheaper transportation to enormously increase the number of trophy hunters afield. Especially in North America but in other places as well, trophy hunting truly became a mass sport. A group of the best educated, most well-read hunters logically evolved away from the "shoot anything" level of hunting into the more demanding, quality-conscious pursuit of trophies.

However, with less game and more hunting pressure, it is very doubtful that the best heads of most species will be bettered significantly or even, in some cases, matched. Thus, though the basis for a "trophy" still remains large size and attractive conformation, the absolute emphasis on size has diminished a bit. Trophy hunting on this large and growing level must be looked upon as a total sport which takes into account, along with the ultimate size of the head, a great number of other considerations.

The mark of a good trophy hunter now is shown in many ways. How well does he know his guns? How well can he shoot them? Does he know his animals so that, even though guided in unfamiliar territory, he contributes to the hunt rather than being "put" into position to shoot the designated animal? How intelligently and conscientiously does he do his "desk work" in order to keep up with the best trophy hunting areas, the availability of special trophy seasons, the planning of hunts to meet special requirements or opportunities?

The sportsman who *actively* participates in planning the hunt and hunts in a sporting, ethical fashion is the real trophy hunter of today. This man is after the uncommon head but measures his satisfaction on a broader and more substantial scale than merely that of inches of antler or horn. This man saddles his own horse, carries his own gun, and has the willpower and knowledge to turn down average heads that he has already bettered. He has the grace to thank God and the others around him who help him when he fells his trophy. This man knows enough and cares enough to experience the full irony of the bitter and the sweet that comes to every thinking hunter who has finally, after so long and so much work, taken the magnificent animal that he had his heart set on. This is today's trophy hunter—a sportsman in the best sense of the word and ultimately the best hope for intelligent conservation and game management in the troubled years ahead.

How to Get Started

2

Most trophy hunters show a love of the outdoors and its wonderful wild creatures at a fairly early age. From there it's a short step into deer hunting. But after having taken several small and unimpressive heads, this hunter usually feels an urge for better trophies. Thus he evolves, perhaps unconsciously, into a selective trophy seeker who sets for himself the more challenging task of locating and taking the older, warier game.

I can well remember my situation as I first began to get somewhat more "serious" about my hunting—and I believe mine is pretty representative. I found that, though at one time I had regarded myself very knowledgeable and well equipped, I really was not and had much to learn. And how fascinating and interesting it is to do just that. Would that all "homework" were as enjoyable as this was—and still is!

Getting yourself ready for trophy hunting breaks down readily into a number of categories.

Background Reading

To hunt well you must know your quarry: what it eats, where it lives, how it depends on its senses for survival, all the bits of natural history that add up to its strengths and weaknesses. Thus you should read thoroughly into the natural history of the species that you are most interested in. This should include the classics of yesteryear from such great naturalists as Ernest Thompson Seton, Stanley T. Young, Edward A. Goldman, Olaus and Adolph Murie, as well as more contemporary works of authorities such as Leonard Lee Rue III and Roger Caras.

Where to locate these books and articles? One good source is a book list or catalogs from book sellers specializing in outdoor titles. Many of these outlets advertise in the outdoor magazines, and one of the largest and most helpful is the Pierce Book Shop out in Winthrop, Iowa 50682. Fred Pierce will be happy to send you a free catalog.

A trip to your local library will unearth more sources for good natural history material — both books and periodicals as well as scientific monographs. Most libraries will also stock indexes to helpful publications available from the U.S. Government Printing Office at reasonable cost. Also, state fish and game departments may well have research papers or studies on specific species available at a nominal cost. The "hunt" for information on the animals and locales becomes exciting in its own right. And hunting, like any other hobby or pursuit, becomes more and more enjoyable and more productive as you feel your own competence increasing.

You'll probably also find that you want to read more about the hunting of a specific animal as well as about the animal itself. Here, the great hunting yarns of yesteryear from Charles Sheldon, Teddy Roosevelt, William T. Hornaday, John C. Phillips and a host of others will help you gain a better perspective on the grand traditions of American sport hunting and how it has evolved and changed over the years.

This harking back to the earlier years of American hunting quite frequently leads into an enjoyable browsing of the great foreign works of yesteryear. Here you can learn more about the "British Officer" school of the sport that flourished from roughly 1825 to 1935 in all parts of the world, but primarily in India and Africa. William Charles Baldwin, Frederick Courteney Selous, W. A. Baillie-Grohman, Sir Samuel White Baker, and a host of other intrepid British explorer-adventurer-sportsmen authors furnish exciting off-season reading that serves to broaden one's perspective on (and enjoyment of!) the American brand of sport hunting. To read something like Baillie-Grohman's superb *Sport in the Alps,* published in 1896, and learn all about the surprisingly rich sport hunting that persisted in Europe until the turn of the century is to glean new insight into North American mountain hunting. Many of these foreign authors, mostly Englishmen, also wrote about hunting American gamefields around the turn of the century, and their views are worth examining. (Baillie-Grohman's marvelous *Camps in the Rockies* tells of the fine bighorn sheep this grand old-time hunter shot in 1879. The head is still listed in the 1971 edition of the Boone and Crockett Club's *North American Big Game*.)

Of course the series of hunting books published by the Boone and Crockett Club over the years are excellent resources. These include the periodically issued record books with articles of general interest and books on hunting and conservation. They introduce you to some of the great names of American sport hunting and enhance your sense of hunting traditions.

Though a few of these old-time books are available in reprint form, most must be secured through antiquarian book dealers specializing in out-of-print books. Many of these book dealers advertise in the leading magazines. Two of the largest are Hank Siegel's Anglers and Shooters Bookshelf in Goshen, Connecticut 06756, and Howard and Janet French, 284 Redwood Drive, Pasadena, California 91105. Both usually have several thousand titles on hand, and if you're interested in a book they don't have, they'll be glad to "search" it out for you.

Since wild game is a dynamic and renewable resource, hunting is a constantly changing sport. Various species experience "boom and bust" cycles that often result from changing land-use patterns and game management objectives. This means that the best trophy hunting areas change periodically. Thus, *current* hunting books by the leading authorities can help you keep informed. I can think of no better single source than the Outdoor Life Book Club for a broad choice of the best and most informative works on hunting and guns. The well versed hunter must always keep up with the continually evolving "state of the art" of firearms, scope sights, ammunition and components and various related equipment. This reading not only helps you become a more effective hunter but, along with its tips on photography, also helps you stretch the sport into a year-round pastime rather than just a fall flurry.

Another good, informal way of learning is to meet other hunters through the local sportsmen's clubs, sporting goods dealers, or taxidermists. Hunting is a marvelous hobby that immediately diminishes the importance of age differences, economic statuses or other social distinctions among outdoorsmen. And hunters can learn from each other constantly. If you have a buddy who has hunted a particular area you're interested in or owns the gun or piece of gear you're thinking about purchasing, then you're ahead of the game. So, develop your "network" of hunting friends. Some of these friendships will last a lifetime.

Your Physical Condition

You may find that more demanding hunting challenges supply the incentive to lose unwanted pounds, stop smoking, eat a more balanced diet or do any one of a number of things that can reduce medical bills and extend life expectancy. So it has been with me and most of my friends. This is one positive feature of hunting that no wife can disagree with.

Obtaining Equipment

You must also accumulate the necessary gear and equipment. My advice is to read thoroughly into the subject and then buy the best quality of the gear that fulfills your needs. You will undoubtedly need a good sleeping bag, several types of boots and shoes, as well as general outdoor clothing and hardware. It's far cheaper in the long run to buy the best and take care of it during a lifetime than to constantly replace cheap shoddy equipment that lets you down in the field—when you need it most. Here again, the personal experiences of hunting friends can be invaluable in helping you to select the right gear.

Also helpful is a battery of "wish books" or catalogs from the leading outdoor mail-order houses. These help educate you,

As these leather goods attest, the well equipped trophy hunter must have a sizable array of gear. It's wise to buy the best quality you can afford.

and they make fascinating fireside reading during long winter evenings. You'll find addresses for these mail-order houses listed at the back of this book.

You must know your firearms and related hardware. Books from the Outdoor Life Book Club can keep you well informed in this area, and the *Gun Digest* is of particular value here. It annually surveys the firearms industry and enticing offerings better than any other publication. The Outdoor Life Book Club's address is 44 Hillside Avenue, Manhasset, N.Y. 11030.

Psychological Preparation

There's an old proverb that runs something like this: "To the stupid man all things appear simple, to the smart man all things appear complicated, to the *wise* man all things appear simple again." In the beginning it's easy to delude yourself into thinking you know more about animals and hunting than you really do. Later, as you immerse yourself in the sport, it's easy to overreact in the other direction and start feeling that you know nothing and will never be able to learn enough to be really competent.

Most competent woodsmen, naturalists and hunters eventually end up with a quiet confidence in their own abilities and knowledge, while realizing that there is always something new to be learned and that you can learn from the most unexpected people or sources. This open-minded approach to the sport, avoiding categorical thinking when studying animals and hunting, is ultimately the single most important factor in helping you become ever more proficient.

The Evolution of a Trophy Hunter

In the past, a hunter generally started out after whitetail deer or mule deer. The first step up, especially for the eastern whitetail hunter, was usually a pronghorn hunt in Wyoming or Montana. (Sometimes this was a pronghorn-mulie combo hunt; though changing season dates and game regulations have made this more difficult to schedule.) Next up the ladder was often an elk hunt. After that came hunts for moose and caribou, then usually goat, and finally for those most desired and expensive of trophies, sheep and grizzly. Black bears were usually taken along the way as "bonus trophies," incidental to the other hunting.

These bushplanes, a beaver (left) and an otter (right), provide the lifts for hunters meeting for the first time on an unnamed lake in the Yukon.

This pattern still generally holds true for today's trophy hunter, but there is evidence that the emphasis is changing a bit. Pronghorn are doing well and are still widely available, but *trophy-size* mule deer have become much more difficult to take, and the hunter will have to get used to the idea of spending more time and money afield when after a big mule deer. Bull elk have also become much more difficult and expensive to secure, and this has changed their economic relationship to moose and caribou. Historically, most hunters have been willing to pay more for the latter two animals probably because they are basically non-U.S. game while the elk isn't. Yet it is now much easier to take a good trophy-sized moose or caribou, and do it at less cost if you know what you're doing, than it is to take a comparable, 6-point bull elk. This is a relatively recent turn of events, and many hunters will have to adjust their thinking when planning hunts for these three biggest deer.

Goat are still a fine trophy and they are still reasonable in cost to hunt. They are located primarily in British Columbia and in the southeastern Alaskan panhandle, but for goat you should plan to be in excellent physical condition. Sheep and grizzly are enormously expensive trophies and become more so every year. The best bet here is to save up enough money to allow you to take a long hunt into the best game country, and then you will probably be successful — and satisfied. Even cut-rate hunts for these two premier trophies are very expensive — doubly so if you don't score and don't enjoy the hunt!

Desk Work

It's impossible to overemphasize the importance of being well informed on current big-game population trends. Some areas do not produce big heads due to the lack of minerals, the genetic strain present in a specific population, a temporary overpopulation that results in stunted animals and racks, or heavy annual harvests that simply don't allow the animals chance to live long enough to become trophy size. Although some of these areas may be among the best in which to score on an unimpressive animal, it is useless to hunt them for big trophies, because the trophies just aren't there.

Probably 51 percent of a trophy hunter's chances for success depends on the decisions he makes before he leaves home. Where to go, when to go, how to hunt and what to take all play a far more significant role in true trophy hunting than in anything-that-comes-along hunting. This is especially true with the more heavily hunted animals, such as whitetail, elk, and mule deer for which your chances of scoring with a really big head are very small.

Desk work prior to the hunt takes care of at least half the battle — finding a top-notch outfitter with weather-tight camps in good hunting country.

Retaining an Outfitter or Guide

3

Not too many years ago a "guided hunt" automatically meant a far northern hunt for the exotic species or it meant a wealthy hunter. Many southern and eastern hunters trekked to the mountain states and eastern Canada on a straight do-it-yourself basis. There was far less hunting pressure then, and most states and provinces didn't require a guide for nonresident hunters.

Things have changed considerably since about 1960. Hunting pressure has greatly increased, and the costs of nonresident hunting licenses are skyrocketing all out of proportion to national inflation. Here many western states and provinces frankly attempt to discourage nonresident hunters from coming in ever-increasing numbers each year.

No matter what big-game trophy you're hunting or how you're doing it, getting an outsized prize has become an expensive proposition. And that's not limited to the larger, deep-wilderness game like sheep and grizzly. Very seldom is it possible to drive to trophy mule deer or elk hunting. The big old-timers, the ones with those coveted outsized antlers, usually live way back in or way up high (or both!) and require horses, specialized seasonal camping equipment, and expert guides.

Regarding state requirements that all nonresident hunters be accompanied by resident guides, the pendulum periodically swings one way and then the other among the states. Over the years, one by one, practically all of them began to require a guide for nonresidents. This trend was caused by a variety of reasons. For one thing, the requirement obviously brought more money to backwoods hamlets which were usually about as short on industry as they were long on game. For another, the states got tired of pulling multitudes of visiting hunters off various mountaintops or out of various wilderness areas after they had managed to get lost in the big, unfamiliar territory.

Not only were these rescue operations expensive and time consuming to mount, occasionally they weren't in time to prevent tragedy. So, the trend was toward a requirement that duly licensed local guides accompany nonresident hunters. The Canadian provinces followed the same path, mostly for the same reasons. At the current time, most eastern states don't require that a guide accompany visiting hunters because these states don't have the influx of visitors that the western states do. Nor do the eastern states — except in certain state or national forests — have enough wilderness to make getting lost as serious a predicament. However, it wouldn't surprise me to see some eastern states imposing limited guide requirements for certain areas and certain types of hunts.

There is currently some movement away from the guide requirement among the big hunting states. Montana and Wyoming have, at the time of this writing, removed their guide requirements. Alaska, which now requires that guides accompany hunters after some big-game species but not others, is rumored to be doing away with all automatic guide requirements. However, I do not foresee a similar trend developing in the various Canadian provinces. If anything, the provinces may go the other way, with regulations that lower guide-hunter ratios and impose other restrictions as well.

So, although the majority of the best trophy hunting areas on the continent do require that a nonresident be accompanied by a licensed guide, there are many areas that do not. Thus you, the trophy hunter, have an option as to how you'll hunt in some areas. Whether a guided or a nonguided hunt is best for you depends on a number of factors, such as these: What game are you after and where do you want to hunt it? How much backwoods experience and competence do you have? How much time and money are available? And what are your personal preferences?

Whatever you plan to hunt and wherever you plan to hunt it, two general guidelines apply:

1. Check the current hunting regulations as to whether a guide is required for nonresidents. These rules can change from year to year. And so can other basic regulations which you should also familiarize yourself with.

2. When interpreting and applying other basic considerations of your hunt, be completely honest with yourself. Always keep in mind your objectives, resources and limitations. (Sometimes things appear entirely different in the field than they do at home.)

Here are the basic considerations that should, to some degree, affect your decisions.

Per Diem Fee

Outfitted and guided hunts are expensive. Of that there is no doubt. And yet, the guide himself isn't getting rich off these hunts. A stone sheep hunt in northern British Columbia, that will set you back $175 to $200 per day, pays the guide some $25 to $30 per day. Thus he earns only $525 to $630 for three weeks of difficult, often grueling, work on a 7-day-a-week job. Want to try it for a while?

On a Montana mule deer and elk combination hunt where two hunters share a guide and each hunter pays $100 per day, the guide will pocket about $35. On an Alaska brown bear hunt that runs $200 to $250 per day, the guide will bank $40 to $45 per day. A good cook in the same camp will make $30 to $35 — and be worth it twice over!

Outfitting is far more complex and sophisticated than most hunters imagine. It calls for many skills, including horse doctoring.

Tentage, tack and other gear receive punishment on wilderness hunts. A good outfitter must continually maintain and replace his gear.

On a guided and outfitted hunt, you're paying for food which you would have to pay for in any event. You're also paying for a way into the wilderness—by horse, bush plane, tracked vehicle or whatever.

On a nonguided hunt you still have to get "in" or else content yourself with road hunting. And along roads you'll usually encounter hordes of hunters and maybe a few scared juvenile animals that didn't have enough sense to clear out. You'll also have to pay to get your camping outfit into the good hunting area. And, even if you have a rather complete camp rig, you'll still probably have to buy or rent some special-purpose items.

And whether you are guided or not, you'll need hunting licenses as well as any personal gear that you may need to buy or replace (new boots, rifle case or scabbard, packframe or rucksack, etc.).

So, out of the total cost of the guided hunt, which may appear astronomical, the actual cost of the guide may only amount to 10 to 20 percent of the hunt, and many of the other costs may be built-in and difficult or impossible to avoid, however you hunt.

Length of Hunt

Any good trophy hunt usually takes a bit longer than a "shoot-anything-that-comes-along" excursion. Obviously. And yet, if you should decide to cut transportation costs by driving a long distance with buddies to the jumping off place, that means you've probably reduced actual hunting time. Thus, to maximize hunting time, you'll want to keep camp chores to a minimum. And yet, if you must do all the cooking and general

Among many other tasks, a good camp staff will take professional care of all trophies and meat.

Before selecting an outfitter, inquire about food and cooking. A good full-time cook improves a camp. Generally, guides make poor cooks. And if they must do the cooking, it's usually at the expense of hunting time.

camp chores, you'll find they cut deeply into the prime hours of the day: early and late.

If you ever take the time to calculate your actual *net hours hunting* on a two- or three-week trip, you'll be somewhat shocked, I assure you. It's a shame to spend large chunks of those few precious hours afield doing all the menial camp chores. I like to camp as much as the next man; taking care of yourself in the woods in a workmanlike fashion brings a satisfaction all its own. However, on the longer expeditions that are further afield for more exotic game (and that costs a pretty big buck, however they are done), I want to hunt—not camp!

To be able to stay out until dark and then arrive at camp completely spent and exhausted and have someone greet you with a hot meal is a priceless advantage. That last hour or 90 minutes you are able to spend afield is worth 5 or 6 hours in the middle of the day, in terms of increasing your chances for a good trophy. Ditto for the morning hunting. If you can get that extra hour or so of sleep and still get out to hunt before daylight, you'll at least double your morning chances.

If several of you decide to camp and hunt together on an extended do-it-yourself hunt, it's often better if you take turns cooking and doing chores. In this case it's best if the cook for each day doesn't even try to hunt. Rather, he should spend the whole time cooking, cutting wood, working on any heads or meat in camp, washing himself and his clothes, and preparing dinner so it's ready as soon as the weary hunters return in the evening.

Sure, the cook then misses a whole day's hunting, but as a result everyone else hunts more effectively and the cook for the next day inherits a tidy, shipshape camp. Meanwhile, the day's cook is refreshed by a light day with some rest, a bath, and fresh clothes. And he knows he'll be able to rise to a hot breakfast in the morning and stay out until dark in the evening because tomorrow's cook won't be trying to hunt. This way, if four of you are in camp, each man sacrifices one-fourth of the hunting time. I would never want to hunt more than four out of the same camp on a true trophy hunt — better that it be two or three if no horses are involved. Of course, the cook can keep his eyes open in camp and glass the surrounding hillsides for a "bonus" trophy.

Knowledge of an Area

If you have hunted a general area once or twice before and if you're familiar with the game you're after, then a nonguided hunt may well be the way to go. This is especially true if you have one local in camp or if you've been able to obtain info from the local game warden, someone in a sporting goods store, or others as to how the game is moving and where kills have been made.

On the other hand, if you're without a guide in new country and after game you've not hunted before, you can waste the whole hunt getting oriented before finding that you are hunting the wrong area or the wrong way. That can be heartbreaking. You can spend a bundle this way too, even though you "saved" some cost by not retaining an outfitter or guide. And you might not collect a trophy animal. The true trophy-size animals will constitute only about 4 to 5 percent of the herd, and they will be the smartest, wiliest, hardest to reach animals. I've been on bighorn sheep hunts on which we saw 250 to 300 sheep and never saw a legal ram, much less a true trophy.

If you are hunting a new area and animal, at least consider going "first class" with a guide the first year. Then, if you get to know the country well enough and feel reasonably confident of your chances, you may want to return with some buddies for your own independent hunt the following season. Even professional outfitters and guides, when they hunt on unfamiliar ground, invariably retain a guide to help orient them and improve their chances. Trophies don't come easy (usually) and you can use all the ethical advantages you can get.

Your Enjoyment

Fortunate indeed is the hunter who has a good guide and who establishes the right personal relationship with him. The guide can, depending upon the circumstances, double or triple the hunter's chances of bringing home a good trophy. The visiting sportsman is usually new to the area, and quite often the game is new to him. On the other hand, the right kind of guide is comfortable in his home country, and he probably knows the game better than he does most of his in-laws. No wonder a good guide can make the odds zoom upward in the hunter's favor.

Better yet, if one of these stellar guides cottons up to the visitor, he can help him see the glory of the outdoors with perceptions that took a lifetime of outdoor living to develop. With the guide's patient help, the hunter will see many interesting terrain or historical features. Also, the guide can help insure that you are "seeing," and not just "looking at," the outdoor world. That can add a whole new dimension to the hunt as an experience that at least equals the actual climactic kill. Thus, working the right way with the right kind of guide can actually double the thrill of a hunt.

Good companionship afield and the opportunity to learn from a man of different background and yet similar interests are definite pluses on any hunt. But it can work the other way, too. A hunter can get hooked up with a surly or incompetent guide who lessens both his chances and his enjoyment of the hunt. However, these cases are in the great minority. Most guides are in that profession because they love the outdoors and like hunting with the right kind of visiting sportsmen. They're sure not guiding to get rich or because it's such an easy, comfortable way to make a buck!

The Guiding Scene

The guiding scene has changed some in recent years. Many of the better guides are getting older. A surprising number of the younger guides, in the southern 48 states anyway, are easterners who have recently emigrated to the mountain states. In Canada and Alaska many of the younger guides are construction men who have a hard time finding work at that time of year (too cold) or servicemen from the big Alaska military bases who, after being mustered out, are getting to do some journeymen hunting of their own while guiding in an area that they are familiar with.

In the past, most of the guides were woods-wise trappers, ranchers, woods rats or—occasionally—prospectors. There simply weren't many other types in the back country. That's changed now. The oil and mineral surveys, hydroelectric devel-

Some outfitters economize on wages by employing beginners as guides and wranglers. It pays to check on an outfitter's reputation, especially if his hunt carries an overly attractive price tag. Shown here, an experienced hand prepares a cape for shipment.

opment and construction, and enlarged military installations in remote areas have brought many new people into the backwoods areas of the U.S. and Canada. Most of them don't have the depth of experience that the old-timers did, and many of the newer guides aren't the equal of the grizzled old veterans. Don't charge them all off in that category though. Some of the best younger guides are real pros and on a par with the fabled names of yesteryear.

The racial mix of guides is changing, too. If someone nailed my boots to the floor and made me guesstimate, I'd figure that Canada had approximately 40 percent Indian and 60 percent White in their mix of registered guides. In Alaska it might run 20 percent Indian and 80 percent White; while in the southern 48 it would be almost 100 percent White. Interestingly enough, this mix appears to be changing noticeably with the percentage of Indian guides decreasing as more and more Whites move north and west to escape the pollution-ridden cities. At the same time more and more Indians move south and east for better job and educational opportunities.

There are all sorts of guides and outfitters. Basically, an outfitter is somewhat similar to a movie producer, while the guide is more like a movie director. The outfitter is responsible for furnishing all the food, provisions, camping gear and transportation; and he also handles the booking, either directly with the hunters or through a booking agent. The guide is responsible for furnishing his own personal gear, performing work around camp as directed by the outfitter or head guide and, of course, actually guiding the hunter afield. As I've said before, there's more to good guiding than just showing the hunter game.

There are all sorts of hybrids and spin-offs on the two jobs we just described. Some outfitters — often smaller operators such as ranchers, farmers or trappers — will also guide. Usually they and maybe a son and a close friend will take a limited number of hunters out each year as a sideline. There are also outfits that may not fall exactly into either category but most closely resemble outfitters. These operators (many of them quite reliable and inexpensive) will "spot pack" the hunters and their gear into an area and then come back for them and their trophies at a designated time, usually 7 or 10 days later. These operators are largely limited to the Rocky Mountain states in the U.S., and they often offer a variety of hunting packages.

They may only furnish the packstring transportation in and out, or they may also furnish everything from food to tents. They can pack you in to an established camp, or they can pack you in and let you set up your own camp. They can leave one man with you as a general factotum and cook. Of course, each additional service up the scale costs more money. These services provide a flexible opportunity for the hunters with the gear and the know-how to take advantage of them. About 90 percent of this type hunting is for elk or trophy mule deer.

On a completely outfitted and guided hunt, the ideal packstring for serious trophy hunting consists of two hunters, two guides, a cook and a wrangler. Up to four hunters *can* hunt out of a camp, depending upon the game population, the terrain, the time frame, and the number of trophies sought. It's best that each hunter have his own guide; though some moose, caribou, elk or deer hunts work well with two hunters to the guide. Again, the decision should be based on the abundance of game and the trophy objectives.

The "guided" hunts for elk and deer in which some cut-rate outfitters shoehorn 4, 6 or even 8 hunters into hunting with one guide, and have twice that many hunters in camp, are not trophy hunts by any stretch of the imagination. At their best, some of these operations may be fair meat hunts. And, at their worst, they're just a social gathering and running poker party in the woods. Usually, little or no game is seen as that motley infantry column wends its noisy way over hill and dale.

Though guided hunting offers many advantages, the nonguided option (when available to nonresidents) can save some coin, yield fine trophies, and provide memorable experiences—with the added satisfaction that comes with self-sufficiency. And there are some guided hunts can be overpriced and underproductive.

Yet it's important not to be misled by the siren song of "saving money" when planning your big hunt. I have seen far too many "money savers" that still cost a lot of money, were no fun, and resulted in no trophies, while they used up a year's precious vacation time.

The choice is up to you. But consider all the factors before making it.

In Many Ways King: Whitetail

4

The whitetail deer is in many ways king of the world's big-game animals. That's quite a statement but the whitetail has the credentials to back it up. With a continent-wide herd population fluctuating in the vicinity of 13 million, he's undoubtedly the world's most populous big-game animal. The African wildebeest has probably 10 million or so in its clan — with the zebra numbering perhaps half that many and the Thomson's gazelle and the impala following with lesser amounts. Our own mule deer, including blacktails, number around 3 to 4 million, and caribou run somewhere between 1 and 2 million in North America, with Eurasian populations undoubtedly raising this considerably higher but still leaving it far short of the whitetail.

The whitetail fields these enormous numbers primarily in the most industrialized country on earth, with its largest concentrations falling in some of the most densely populated and industrialized states. No other animal is pursued by as large a number of sport and trophy hunters, most of whom are far better equipped and more knowledgeable than any other large group of hunters in the world. For an animal to maintain such numbers and thrive in this sort of environment is nothing short of miraculous. It means that the animal can adapt to a wide range of forages, terrains, and climates. It means that he possesses effective defenses — in this case keen physical senses and speed in flight. Furthermore, it means that this animal is highly intelligent — that he is able to *learn* in order to continually adjust to environmental changes resulting from massive technology that sometimes runs amok in this country.

One of the oldest and tritest statements in wildlife and outdoor writing is that "there are now more deer in the U.S. than when Columbus landed." That's really not so surprising when

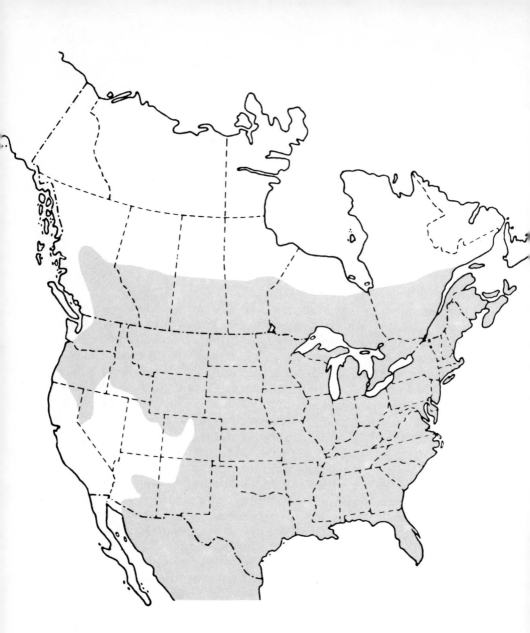

Whitetail/Coues Deer Ranges

This shows the overall range of whitetails. Coues deer, a miniature subspecies given separate trophy awards classification, is found only in Arizona, southern New Mexico and northwestern Mexico. Official measurers can readily distinguish between an immature whitetail rack and that of a mature Coues trophy based on antler development and conformation.

habitat is considered. Before the white man, the enormous eastern U.S. deciduous forest covered the major whitetail range with a dense growth that was, except for relatively small natural burn areas, almost completely mature or "climax" in character.

A climax forest makes for poor deer range since it lacks the vital understory and new growth that furnishes the animal's favored browse. The white man changed all that with his axe and his plow. The land was cleared, both by design and by accident (forest fires). The larger predators that were bothersome to man's livestock were in many areas eradicated. Now conditions were improved for whitetails. So, bearing in mind that under ideal conditions a healthy deer herd can double its size in only 3 to 5 years, it's no wonder that whitetails increased dramatically.

What is remarkable is that the animal has been able to largely maintain and, in some cases, continue to increase these numbers. Though some eastern states have seen reductions in their whitetail populations in recent years, the animal continues to expand its range, moving farther west and, as logging increases, farther north. The wily, highly adaptable whitetail appears to have initially penetrated newer regions that most resembled its classical eastern haunts, such as the Missouri River bottomlands and the "breaks" of eastern Montana. But then it moved into still other areas that were often more open and higher in elevation than the preferred eastern habitat.

Intelligent and sophisticated game management — financed completely by hunter dollars and not general revenues — has played a vital role in this success story. And sportsmen owe undying gratitude to the many skilled, dedicated and largely unsung technicians in wildlife science and game management fields who have helped bring this about. However, this simply would not have been possible, no matter how well financed and scientific in character, if the basic "product" — the deer itself — weren't a uniquely robust and adaptable animal. Measured on this same scale with the whitetail, all too many other animals have been found wanting. Among them are some of the finest trophies in the world such as the grizzly bear, the bighorn sheep and the caribou.

The Quarry

Some thirty subspecies of the whitetail deer populate the North American continent from the bottom of Central

America well up into Canada. Some of these subspecies differ greatly in size. For example, the tiny Key deer of southern Florida weighs only 70 pounds or so. But for our purposes, we can assume that the average, healthy whitetail adult buck weighs from about 125 to 175 pounds live and stands 36 to 40 inches at the shoulder. (That's at the top of the back.)

There are reports of tremendous whitetails that weighed 400 pounds and more, but the average deer is considerably smaller and is usually greatly overestimated in size, even by sportsmen who should know better.

I well remember my first sight of wild whitetails, as a lad in the swamps of southern Alabama. I had been on my morning stand for several hours and was daydreaming about practically everything in the world but deer. A silent gray flash that I barely caught out of the corner of my eye roused me from this reverie into buck-fever D.T.'s to the third power. Initially, though, my first reaction was that some farmer must have lost his goats. They were so *small!* Even though I had read everything on deer hunting that I could get my hands on, I kept looking for an animal that would measure about chest-high on me, not one that was barely belt-buckle high. And so it is with most sportsmen; they tend to expect an animal the size of a small cow rather than a creature about the size of a large German shepherd.

Deer are gifted with good physical senses. As is common with heavy-cover animals, the whitetail's sense of smell is probably his most acute sense. However, it also hears and sees well. Though like all other mammals, the whitetail sees no colors, its eyes are extremely sharp and pick up any movement.

These sharp and well balanced physical senses have played a major role in the whitetail's adaptability and survival, but other factors have perhaps been more important. The whitetail is apparently an intelligent animal with the ability to learn. He long ago learned to become almost completely nocturnal in those areas of heavy human populations. Thus we have seen the advent of the new "super" whitetail in the East.

These are large, healthy animals living in close proximity to man and surviving as much on the farmer's grains and fruits as on natural forage. They can fill their stomachs in about an hour of browsing in these ideal food circumstances, and they do so usually before dawn and shortly after nightfall. These animals will live and prosper in ridiculously small woodlots, often mere patches of trees in a small area of "rough" between farm fields. A whitetail is a creature of habit, strictly nonmigratory, and he'll usually not stray over a mile from the spot where he was born during his entire life.

That other quality that the whitetail possesses in unique abundance might be called "nerve." The animal will lay up in thick cover and almost let hunters walk over him before flushing. I would estimate that a *good* deer hunter only sees one deer out of 10 that see him; a novice would probably see one in 30 or 40. When the whitetail does flush though, it appears that he is heading for the state line nonstop. Actually he'll only run a few hundred yards, often until he is barely out of sight. Again, with that savvy intelligence of his, he has learned that by running he can blunder into other hazards. So he either watches his back-trail or skulks away — sometimes circling to get a vantage on the hunter.

Hunting vs. "Trophy Hunting"

Deer are hunted by so many different people in so many different places that there is an enormous variety of hunting methods involved. Whitetails are hunted by driving, by still hunting, by hunting from both ground and tree stands, and with dogs — to name a few. There are different kinds of drives, different methods of still hunting and using dogs, different types of ground stands and tree stands. This *general* hunting of whitetail deer is, each year, the subject of a wave of books.

There is no animal in North America or in the world for which *trophy* hunting and *general* hunting diverge so much in one respect: that is, the importance of "desk work" in helping you to find your big trophy before you leave home or the hunting camp. Once you are in the field, hunting big bucks and general hunting are often rather similar. True, you should be afield before daylight and ready to shoot as early and as late as is legal in your area under the general assumption that the older, wiser deer are less apt to be abroad and moving during daylight hours. Also, it's a good notion to seek out the very highest, roughest and most overgrown areas because those wily old bucks with the outsize headgear will usually use the terrain and cover to best advantage.

The denser the cover, the better the buck can hide himself and the more difficult it is for anything to sneak up on him. Although "high" places in the East may not be as radically different from "low" places as they are out West, the added

OFFICIAL SCORING SYSTEM FOR NORTH AMERICAN BIG GAME TROPHIES

RECORDS OF NORTH AMERICAN BIG GAME COMMITTEE

BOONE AND CROCKETT CLUB

RETURN TO:
N. A. B. G. Awards Program
1600 Rhode Island Ave. N. W.
Washington, D. C. 20036

Minimum Score: Deer
Whitetail: Typical 170
Coues: Typical 110

WHITETAIL and COUES DEER

KIND OF DEER

DETAIL OF POINT MEASUREMENT

SEE OTHER SIDE FOR INSTRUCTIONS	Supplementary Data		Column 1	Column 2	Column 3	Column 4
	R.	L.	Spread Credit	Right Antler	Left Antler	Difference
A. Number of Points on Each Antler						
B. Tip to Tip Spread						
C. Greatest Spread						
D. Inside Spread of MAIN BEAMS — Spread credit may equal but not exceed length of longer antler						
IF Inside Spread of Main Beams exceeds longer antler length, enter difference						
E. Total of Lengths of all Abnormal Points						
F. Length of Main Beam						
G-1. Length of First Point, if present						
G-2. Length of Second Point						
G-3. Length of Third Point						
G-4. Length of Fourth Point, if present						
G-5. Length of Fifth Point, if present						
G-6. Length of Sixth Point, if present						
G-7. Length of Seventh Point, if present						
H-1. Circumference at Smallest Place Between Burr and First Point						
H-2. Circumference at Smallest Place Between First and Second Points						
H-3. Circumference at Smallest Place Between Second and Third Points						
H-4. Circumference at Smallest Place between Third and Fourth Points or half way between Third Point and Beam Tip if Fourth Point is missing						
TOTALS						

ADD	Column 1		Exact locality where killed
	Column 2		Date killed By whom killed
	Column 3		Present owner
Total			Address
SUBTRACT Column 4			Guide's Name and Address
FINAL SCORE			Remarks: (Mention any abnormalities)

36

I certify that I have measured the above trophy on_____ 19 _____

at (address)_____City_____State _____

and that these measurements and data are, to the best of my knowledge and belief, made in accordance with the instructions given.

Witness: _____ Signature: _____

Boone and Crockett Official Measurer

INSTRUCTIONS

All measurements must be made with a flexible steel tape to the nearest one-eighth of an inch. Wherever it is necessary to change direction of measurement, mark a control point and swing tape at this point. To simplify addition, please enter fractional figures in eighths. Official measurements cannot be taken for at least sixty days after the animal was killed. Please submit photographs of trophy front and sides.

Supplementary Data measurements indicate conformation of the trophy, and none of the figures in Lines A, B and C are to be included in the score. Evaluation of conformation is a matter of personal preference. Excellent, but nontypical Whitetail Deer heads with many points shall be placed and judged in a separate class.

A. Number of Points on each Antler. To be counted a point, a projection must be at least one inch long AND its length must exceed the length of its base. All points are measured from tip of point to nearest edge of beam as illustrated. Beam tip is counted as a point but not measured as a point.

B. Tip to Tip Spread measured between tips of Main Beams.

C. Greatest Spread measured between perpendiculars at right angles to the center line of the skull at widest part whether across main beams or points.

D. Inside Spread of Main Beams measured at right angles to the center line of the skull at widest point between main beams. Enter this measurement again in "Spread Credit" column if it is less than or equal to the length of longer antler.

E. Total of lengths of all Abnormal Points. Abnormal points are generally considered to be those nontypical in shape or location.

F. Length of Main Beam measured from lowest outside edge of burr over outer curve to the most distant point of what is, or appears to be, the main beam. The point of beginning is that point on the burr where the center line along the outer curve of the beam intersects the burr.

G-1-2-3-4-5-6-7. Length of Normal Points. Normal points project from main beam. They are measured from nearest edge of main beam over outer curve to tip. To determine nearest edge (top edge) of beam, lay the tape along the outer curve of the beam so that the top edge of the tape coincides with the top edge of the beam on both sides of the point. Draw line along top edge of tape. This line will be base line from which point is measured.

H-1-2-3-4. Circumferences - If first point is missing, Take H-1 and H-2 at smallest place between burr and second point.

* * * * * * * * * *

TROPHIES OBTAINED ONLY BY FAIR CHASE MAY BE ENTERED
IN ANY BOONE AND CROCKETT CLUB BIG GAME COMPETITION

To make use of the following methods shall be deemed UNFAIR CHASE and unsportsmanlike, and any trophy obtained by use of such means is disqualified from entry in any Boone and Crockett Club big game competition:

    I. Spotting or herding game from the air, followed by landing in its vicinity for pursuit;
    II. Herding or pursuing game with motor-powered vehicles;
    III. Use of electronic communications for attracting, locating or observing game, or guiding the hunter to such game.

* * * * * * * * * *

I certify that the trophy scored on this chart was not taken in UNFAIR CHASE as defined above by the Boone and Crockett Club.

I certify that it was not spotted or herded by guide or hunter from the air followed by landing in its vicinity for pursuit, nor herded or pursued on the ground by motor-powered vehicles.

I further certify that no electronic communications were used to attract, locate, observe, or guide the hunter to such game; and that it was taken in full compliance with the local game laws or regulations of the state, province or territory.

Date _____ Hunter _____

This chart is reproduced with permission of the Boone and Crockett Club, which, together with the National Rifle Association, co-sponsors the North American Big Game Awards Program. (Another chart is used to score nontypical heads.)

elevation does discourage the lazier road hunters who don't want to walk and thus decreases pressure a bit. Also, the added height means that as the ground warms up in the morning and the thermals begin to rise, the deer can wind climbing intruders.

Stand hunting, especially on tree stands, is a very effective way of hunting any deer if the stand is located well. This is especially true for trophy bucks that are often in dense cover and are just too wary and gritty-nerved to be approached or flushed out. Sometimes letting the big fellows come to you is the only way to get them. Here it's best to locate a tree stand at junctions of well traveled trails between bedding areas and the animal's feed and water. However, all of these points apply to hunting any buck. The key to trophy whitetail hunting is to research and investigate thoroughly to locate those areas that still harbor *big* bucks. These big buck areas are practically never the big-volume producing areas within a state. Where the harvest is heavy, the bucks simply don't live the five years and more needed to produce the largest racks.

Given superior genetic strain, outstanding feed opportunities, and the right minerals in the soil for outstanding antler development, whitetails can grow very nice racks in three years. And some may sport large headgear in their second year; though the heavily hunted areas usually don't allow many bucks to live even that long.

My home state of Pennsylvania is a good example here. Over the years, the state has produced both bumper crops of whitetails and also a fair share of big bucks. However, in recent times the hunting pressure has become intense, as it has in other "big" eastern and midwestern deer states. And though the hunting in general is still quite excellent, this is not the place to go for the big one. The bucks just don't live long enough. Sure, some nice big deer come in each year. But when you consider the number of hunters and the amount of hunting hours, it's clear that a hunter's chances of bagging a really big buck are almost infinitesimal. With the exception of some special areas the "big" deer states are generally not the places for the trophy hunter seriously seeking an outsized head.

Thus I've concluded that a big whitetail is harder to come by than any other trophy. There are so many killed each year that, mathematically, any sportsman's chances of taking a really noteworthy head are small indeed. Also, the hunting pressure is so intense in many areas that fish and game departments are, of necessity and rightly so, forced to manage for quantity rather than trophy quality when setting season and bag limits. However, there are still huge outsized whitetails to be had — with big old buster bucks still dying of old age. But diligent research and desk work can help you locate the areas that still harbor the older and larger bucks.

Where to Go

These areas that harbor big bucks come and go rather quickly. Hunting pressure increases or is regulated downward for one reason or another. So, the quest to keep posted on top trophy areas is a never-ending one, especially when after white-tails because no hunting is more changeable. However, there are some particularly attractive areas to consider. Some of these places have, for years, been relatively big producers of nice heads, while others are of more recent vintage.

By far, Texas has the largest state herd of whitetail, some-thing over three million. The density has become so great, in fact, that many of the best whitetail ranges are now over-populated. This results in decreased body and antler size. How-ever, the border area, especially around Laredo, produces some very large racks. The population is not so dense there. So "general" hunting is not as favorable, but this is a good big-buck area. Among other factors, the area's rugged, semi-desert en-virons have helped keep general hunting pressure relatively modest, and thus a fair number of deer live long enough to grow those coveted antlers.

The region around Rapid City, South Dakota, and that around Sundance, Wyoming, across the state border, have con-sistently produced nice whitetail heads through the years. And they still do so. Saskatchewan produces some enormous white-tail racks. A number of these heads are on display in a small sporting goods store north of Minot, North Dakota, and they simply left me breathless. Their long-sweeping and heavy main beams, topped off with splendidly long tines, are what most trophy hunters see only in dreams, seldom if ever in the field.

Saskatchewan game officials have periodically closed whitetail hunting to U.S. sportsmen. But when they do allow it, the areas in the extreme southeastern part of the giant province, some-what north and east of Weyburn and Estevan, can hardly be bettered as big-deer producers anywhere on the continent.

Missouri has a large herd of whitetail. But with about a quarter-million permits awarded each year, the hunting pressure is very heavy. Hunter success hovers around 15 percent, which is fairly low even by whitetail standards. However, some very large heads have been taken in Missouri in recent years. Illinois is relatively lightly hunted for whitetail, with only about 60,000 permits awarded each year. But Illinois, too, produces some rather large heads. Unfortunately, Illinois deer hunting is generally limited to residents only. Certain counties in Ohio, often in the southwestern portion of the state, produce a surprisingly large number of big heads, considering the rather small herd (about 70,000) and the relatively light hunting in this urban state (about 100,000 permits). There is a very low 7 percent hunter-success rate.

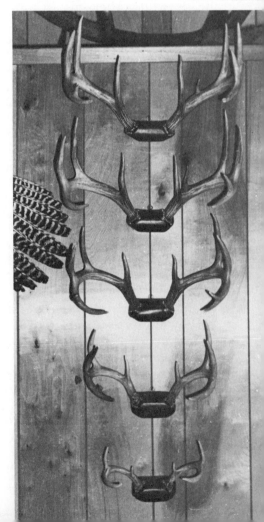

These five sets of antlers were dropped in successive years by the same buck. The first set refutes the popular notion that first antlers are always spikes or even "forkhorns." Racks don't attain trophy size until at least the third set. The spread on the top rack here goes over 23 inches.

The author rates the buck, above, as the finest whitetail he has ever seen. The widest inside spread is about 22 to 24 inches. The long tines are impressive, but their uneven number would penalize the head in scoring.

The big whitetail at right shows good symmetry and a spread of about 21 inches. Long brow tines, like these, seldom appear on any but the oldest bucks.

Even the young buck, below, with medium-light 8-point rack, would be a decent trophy in the hard-hunted East, where few bucks live to see their fourth winter. This buck would be about three years old.

Some nice whitetail are showing up in Montana, not all of them in the eastern portion of the state. Ditto in southern British Columbia. To pinpoint best areas it is necessary to correspond with the fish and game departments, primarily to locate names and addresses of local biologists and game wardens in trophy-producing areas from whom you can secure detailed, *current* information.

Alabama has an enormous herd of over 500,000 deer that are not exactly being overharvested. It is true that genetically these deer run smaller than their northern cousins. Yet they are not as intensively hunted either. This allows more bucks to live longer. And the generous bag limit of one buck per day during the long three-month season allows the hunter to take several trophies while trying for a big one.

Pinpointing Trophy Pockets

Whitetail hunting is, with the partial exception of a few areas like those around Rapid City, South Dakota, and Sundance, Wyoming, largely a do-it-yourself proposition rather than a professionally guided and outfitted one. Thus, it's a good idea to write fish and game departments of the various states to ask their opinions as to the best general areas for big trophies. Also request names of people or organizations within those areas that can furnish more detailed information.

Local game wardens, state or federal biologists, and even local sheriffs are often good sources. Chambers of commerce, sporting goods stores, and motels can be good sources. But beware of self-interest that may bias the advice from commercial enterprises. Sometimes you can secure names of local farmers or ranchers who will act as informal "guides" for a modest payment or even at no charge, just because you strike up a hunter-to-hunter friendship through the mail or over the phone.

Texas and Alabama rely largely on hunting clubs that lease exclusive hunting rights in various areas for most of their big game. Texas has literally no free, open-access hunting that the easterner is used to. However, it is often possible to secure the names of hunting clubs and their officers and begin corresponding with them. They will usually let the visitor hunt with them for a very modest fee, often free because nonresident deer hunters from far away are a bit of a novelty and club members are anxious to trade tips and anecdotes. A dog hunt for deer in south Alabama, where dogs are the only practical means of stirring deer out of the thick cover, is far from the unsporting and callous hunting that some eastern hunters assume it to be. And an experience on this unique type of hunt, in late December or January after the eastern hunters own state deer season has closed, is well worth the trip south.

The key to locating these often small, localized trophy hotspots is to find and question as many local sources as possible. It's possible to question diligently — in a friendly, easygoing fashion, without being "sweaty" about it. Cross-check your answers from one respondent to another. Most often you will be dealing with opinions and adjectives rather than concrete numbers and facts. So earnest cross-checking can help you avoid a fruitless trip or insure that you get maximum opportunities in the locale you select.

Guns for Whitetails

The whitetail is not an overly large animal, nor is he particularly difficult to kill, and he is often shot at close range. So devastating knock-down power isn't usually called for. Cartridges in the class of the .30/30, the .32 Special, and the .35 Remington have killed millions of whitetail deer cleanly.

There seems to be a trend toward slightly more powerful "brush buster" calibers. This has caused the resurrection of the .45/70 and, to a lesser degree the .33 Winchester, and has occasioned the use of the .44 Magnum in rifles. (Yes, I'm aware that these cartridges, except for the .33, have less muzzle energy on paper than the .30/30; however, many gun experts would argue that, considering their larger calibers and far heavier bullets, they are somewhat more "powerful" at close-in whitetail ranges.)

Also, many eastern whitetail hunters are using .308 Winchesters, .30/06s and even flat-shooting mountain calibers like .270s and .243s. Here, there is always the chance for a longer shot down a power line right-of-way or across to another ridge, and there is economic good sense to using one rifle for both eastern and western shooting. The old theory that a heavy, slow centerfire bullet would "buck brush" *significantly* better than smaller, lighter, flatter shooting bullets has largely fallen into disrepute. All centerfire rifle cartridges move out rather smartly and, with few exceptions, throw relatively light bullets. The difference between 2200 and 2800 feet per second is one of degree, not

These two heads evidence the different "look" of the Coues deer (left) and the basic Virginia whitetail. Even though the large Coues rack is almost as heavy as the large and sweeping whitetail rack, its spread is lesser, with the main beams characteristically hooking sharply toward one another rather than moderately or not at all, as is standard among whitetails. Also Coues bucks are thinner necked and smaller faced than whitetails of the same age.

of kind. And though some collisions with brush *immediately in front of the deer* might somewhat favor the "brush busters," the difference is tough to measure, at best.

And being thoroughly familiar with a single rifle has another advantage: Namely, it allows confident, rapid shooting, which is often more important for whitetails than for any other big game. This may well outweigh the theoretical advantages of "bucking the brush" with a special rifle. However, most hunters are probably like me, always looking for the slightest reason to try out a new gun or cartridge. I freely and happily admit to being a bit "impractical" in that sense!

Hunting the Coues Deer

This elegant little desert whitetail inhabits southern Arizona, southwestern New Mexico and northwestern and western Mexico (not Baja though) and bears roughly the same relationship to the "standard" whitetail that the blacktail does to the "standard" mule deer. That is, the Coues, though given separate trophy classification in the records, is actually a subspecies of whitetail and not a separate species. Since the Coues deer are rather small, since their racks could not compete against regular whitetails on a raw score basis, and since their range is clearly defined and separate from the other whitetail types, the Boone and Crockett Club has awarded them separate trophy classification.

Though Coues racks are small, they make elegant little trophies. The world's record Coues scores 143 points. The world's record whitetail goes 206⅝, and the minimum to make the book for whitetail is 170—more than 30 points higher than the Coues record. However, it is surprising how heavy-beamed and massive some of these small Coues racks are, when compared proportionally to whitetail racks.

The Future

The outlook for general whitetail hunting throughout most of the North American continent ranges from "good" to "excellent." The whitetail—like the squirrel, cottontail rabbit, wild turkey and some others—has thrived mightily during the civilized era. With any reasonable care and priority management, whitetails should continue to be abundant.

However, the outlook for *trophy* whitetail hunting, *for any given individual,* will generally worsen. As the years roll by and millions more deer are harvested, the sheer mathematical probability of taking a head that would place among the best of them becomes miniscule. Also, as hunting pressure continues to accelerate and game management for quantity becomes universal, there will be fewer and fewer areas where substantial numbers of bucks live long enough to grow the really outsized trophy racks. That doesn't mean that good heads will cease to come in. Far from it. The world's record may well be broken at any time. But the *incidence* of really large heads, which is another thing entirely, should decrease.

This leads me to make a rather novel proposal. Perhaps it would be wise for certain states, especially the heavily combed "big" deer states in the East, to set aside special trophy-hunting areas. These would probably be pockets of relatively rough,

Any whitetail hunt can double as both a trophy hunt and just a good time outdoors. Here Alabama hunters skin out the morning's kill. Note the uncommonly heavy amount of fat on these deer.

self-contained country where the hunting pressure could be kept light in order to allow the growth of *big* bucks.

Hunting of these "trophy areas" would be restricted to holders of special permits obtained through a drawing. In this way, western states have been carefully regulating such marginal species as goat, moose and sheep. These limited permits would have to be rather expensive if they were to finance the special overseeing and control monitoring necessary to maintain the trophy areas properly. The permits could be issued either in lieu of or in addition to the general state-wide license, depending upon the exact objectives and size of the trophy program. My inclination is that these special permits should be offered in addition to the general all-purpose deer license and that they should be used during a special "trophy season" that would run a week or ten days prior to the general state-wide hunt.

Since state fish and game departments are responsive to hunter requests, hunter petitions for this kind of Trophy Program could get results. Admittedly, this would slightly restrict the quantity harvest, but overall it would have an insignificant impact. Also, the chances of securing one of the special permits might be small, and drawing a permit wouldn't guarantee a *big* buck. The special-permit hunter could shoot any size buck that came along, if he decided to use up his permit that way. However, the permit would provide a chance at an outstanding head, right in the hunter's home state. And since the hunter's only added expense would be the special permit, costs would be reasonable.

For their part, the fish and game departments might want to transplant certain genetically superior deer to the area so that, along with reduced harvests which produce older bucks, the hunter's chances for *big* heads would be still further improved. This is an unorthodox idea, but as volume hunting reduces the take of big heads, perhaps trophy programs will gain acceptance. Even if the hunter never drew a permit, just trying for one each year would be an event. As in the case of "just knowing the grizzly are there," the chance at the "big one" would add another element of interest to each deer season.

In any event, there's no reason for despair. Whitetail deer are a very special trophy and whitetail hunting in this country has a very special significance. If, like me, you feel that *any* nice, adult buck whitetail is a unique "All American" trophy with a special status of his own, then you'll be afield with renewed excitement and anticipation each fall, whatever the chances may be of getting a really big head!

Easy No Longer: Mule Deer

5

Until the late 1960s it was relatively easy for any knowledgeable sportsman to take a nice mule deer buck with an outside spread upwards of, say, 30 inches. I don't mean to imply that bucks this size were hanging around most western street corners waiting to be bumped off. But if the hunter diligently pursued his "desk work" to locate the good areas and if he allowed enough time and was in reasonably good physical condition, he was almost assured of taking a nice head. Not so anymore.

Mule deer hunting in general is changing, and so is hunting for the trophy bucks. Any wild creature is the product of its environment and living conditions. Bighorn sheep that are super-wary, when "hard hunted" tame down to become the most confiding and easiest to approach of animals in national parks where they are not molested. Ruffed grouse, the bird that can drive most eastern hunters to the brink of despair is, in many spots out West where he is rather lightly hunted, a relatively dull witted citizen who can often be approached almost as closely as the spruce grouse, ptarmigan and other birds not exactly noted for their furtiveness. It all depends on how much exposure the bird or animal has to man and what that exposure is.

Throughout the years, mule deer have been noted in song and story as not being very wary. A very common and successful ploy often used on a hightailing buck was to yell loudly so that he would stop to stare at the hunter momentarily before disappearing over the ridge. This gave the hunter a standing shot and often meant venison in the stewpot. All this is changing, too.

Mule deer are coming of age, for better or for worse, as a game animal. They are basically an open country, mountain animal and possibly they will never fully develop the skulking, sly ways of the woods-loving whitetail. But they are sure changing their old ways.

No longer is it relatively common for a mule deer buck to spring up in front of a hunter and then stop to look him over, still well within gun range. Now, especially in the case of mature bucks, the deer may just let the hunter walk right by him (much in the fashion of a cagey old Pennsylvania whitetail). Or, when he does jump up and run, he moves out at flank speed with none of the hesitation or indecisiveness that used to be more common.

Mule deer are being much more intensively hunted, and this means far fewer bucks are living to the ripe old age of five years or more, the time needed to allow their headgear to reach true trophy proportions. At something over three million animals (including the blacktail subspecie) the mule deer is easily the second most populous big-game animal in North America. So, we are not exactly running out of mule deer. What we are running out of though is those areas that used to be rather lightly hunted and therefore had their full share of bragging size bucks — about 5 percent of the total mule deer herd, usually.

Yet most sportsmen have not fully recognized this changing fact of life, and they balk at spending the time and money now often necessary to take a really good mule deer buck. The hangover is still with us from the older era, when a 5-day hunt usually was more than enough time to garner in a nice buck. It's difficult to convince a man that he should allow two weeks and consider late-season or early-season hunts, as well as be prepared to climb higher than he often would when sheep hunting. It's difficult, that is, until the hunter has tried for a big mule deer for a few years and learned for himself.

In fact, interestingly enough, most hunting consultants and others who book hunters on trophy hunts, probably have more trouble with elk and mule deer hunts than with any others. If they spend the time and money, most sportsmen will have a very good chance to collect good trophies on such species as moose, caribou and Dall sheep. The same sportsmen also generally realize that they may well spend plenty of time and coin and *not* return home with outsized bighorn, whitetail, or grizzly trophies.

The two species for which reality often diverges the furthest from popular opinion are elk and — increasingly — mule deer. Most hunters expect to take a good mule deer if they do the right things. And, their chances are still rather good if they are hunting in the right areas. But it's far from a lead-pipe cinch.

Mule deer, like whitetail, are being intensively harvested, and fish and game departments are of necessity managing for quantity production rather than quality when setting season and bag limits, and when ascertaining how many licenses or permits will be allowed.

The Quarry

Mule deer stand 40 to 42 inches high at the shoulder. And although the very largest whitetail and mule deer bucks are just about the same size, the average good mulie will stand about 2 to 4 inches higher at the shoulder than a comparable whitetail buck. The mule deer will also be longer and heavier, weighing 175 to 200 pounds rather than 135 to 175 pounds, and stretching 6 to 6½ feet in length rather than 5 feet to a tad over 6 feet. The mule deer is named for his large ears which resemble those of a mule. These ears, on a good buck, will average 8 to 9 inches in length from the opening or on the under side. And the ears, rather than the body, are very handy to use as references when estimating trophy quality. Besides the ears, the biggest difference in appearance between the mule deer and the whitetail is the large forked or "bifurcated" antlers. The whitetail's antler points all extend from a common beam rather than a fork. Also the mule deer has a prominent black forehead patch.

There is only one species of mule deer but, in a hunting sense, the "blacktail" has long been considered a separate proposition. Blacktails range along the coast from northern California to Alaska (where they are called Sitka blacktails) and they are substantially smaller bodied and smaller antlered than the "basic" mule deer. These blacktails run about the same in height as a comparable whitetail buck but they are usually a bit shorter in length and thus blockier in build. It is my impression that a blacktail would weigh about the same or a bit less than a similar-size whitetail. The blacktail was once regarded by some authorities as a separate species. But though the blacktail now has long been accepted as being the same species as the mule deer farther east, the Boone and Crockett Club has wisely continued the blacktail's separate trophy classification—this in fairness to those hunters seeking the smaller blacktail.

The farther north the blacktail ranges, the smaller he runs in trophy size. In the 1971 record book, 8 of the top 15 blacktail heads come from California, with 6 from Oregon, and 1 from Washington. British Columbia doesn't show up until 34th

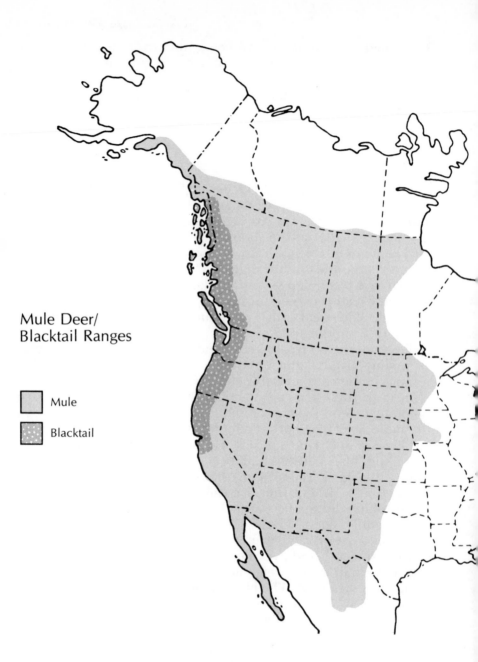

Mule Deer/
Blacktail Ranges

Mule

Blacktail

This shows approximate taxonomic ranges and also boundaries for trophy scoring. The trophy boundaries for blacktail are intended to reduce the chances that animals of heavier-antlered, mixed strain might be mistaken for relatively pure blacktails. (Mule deer and blacktails may not always be huntable in all portions of the ranges shown here.)

place, and there isn't an Alaskan head listed among the entire 226 trophies.

Guns for Mule Deer

Mule deer are not especially tenacious of life — not difficult to kill. They are basically an open country animal, which means that a flat-shooting rifle is in order and, if you are climbing the heights for a big trophy head, rifle weight becomes a factor. It has been my experience that where mule deer range together, the deer will often be as high or higher than sheep. Hunting big wily bucks requires that you be in good physical condition.

If mule deer will be the rifle's largest target, a rifle in the .243 to .257 Roberts class is adequate. These flat-shooting, light recoiling guns can be made into compact mountain rifles that are a joy to carry, especially appreciated after mid-afternoon if you're hunting afoot. The .270 can't be topped for mule deer. Flat shooting and providing no recoil or muzzle blast problems for the majority of hunters, this cartridge teamed with a flat-shooting spitzer-pointed 130-grain bullet is the classic mule deer round. And it does offer a bit more knock-down power than the lighter shells.

The .30/06 with 150-grain loads and the 7mm Mauser with 139-grain bullets are also good mule deer killers, though not quite as flat-shooting as the .270 and its twins. The 7mm Remington Magnum is very flat-shooting, but the extra power isn't needed unless you're also hunting heavier game such as elk. This gun will, of necessity, need to be longer barreled and heavier than the nonmagnums.

Although a mule deer isn't particularly difficult to lay down — like any other animal shot badly in the ham or stomach and madly pumping adrenaline — he can absorb a surprising amount of punishment and carry on. Whether it's mule deer or moose you're after, where you hit them is — within reason — far more important than what you hit them with.

Where to Go

The top 15 mule deer heads in the 1971 record book are from all over the West; 5 from Colorado, 3 from Wyoming, 2 each from Idaho and New Mexico and 1 each from Oregon, Arizona and Utah. Mule deer, since they are hunted so intensively, are very difficult to pinpoint as far as trophy availability. As with the whitetail, trophy availability is a very changeable factor with them. Also, like the whitetail, *the number of big heads must be considered in relation to both the total size of the deer harvest and the approximate total man hours of hunting in a given area.*

Generally, the best area for outsized trophies is not the best all-round or most densely populated area. And nowhere is this guideline truer than when you are trying to locate a big white-tail or mule deer. Montana has some nice trophy-producing areas; among them I would list the Tobacco Root Mountains (near Sheridan) and the Madison and Bridger mountains (north of Bozeman), and the area around Drummond. Wyoming has historically produced good heads, with the northern part of the state generally yielding more, especially in the north-western sections. Colorado has more record heads than any other state but, with both a large resident hunting population and a tremendous influx of visitors each year, this is not quite as impressive, relative to hunting hours spent afield. However, there are certainly good trophies to be had there, and my own preference would be around the Ute Reservation in the south-eastern part of the state. New Mexico has produced some enormous heads in recent years in its northwestern section around Chama and the Jicarilla Apache Indian Reservation.

When hunting for trophy mule deer in *any* area, the same basics apply. Get as far away from the road and other hunters as possible. Climb as high as you can into the roughest country —this with one slight exception. I have found that in some areas, surprisingly good mule deer bucks can be found near small ranches, much the same as some outsized, old whitetail bucks are found around farmyards and other "civilized" places.

Certainly the basic rule is "go high into rough country." But, I have kicked out just enough nice mulies around small (usually high) ranches to make ranch environs an interesting, off-beat possibility that I don't overlook. I'm not sure whether this is the beginning of an adaptive trend in which a certain number of big old mulies will learn to survive in close, skulking in proximity to man by going almost 100 percent nocturnal as the whitetail does or whether my experiences have just been happenstances. I do know it has netted me some nice bucks that I would otherwise have overlooked.

Estimating Trophy Heads

Mulies are an ear-rated trophy, meaning that ear/antler comparison is the single most effective way of gauging from a front, or quartering, or rear view. Although a big mulie's ears will usually be about 8 to 9 inches long if stuck out straight from his head, they're actually longer by a couple inches or so if you measure down the back of them. But the back-of-the-ear length is not their *apparent* length. At the angle an alert deer holds them, they'll usually span about 20 to 21 inches. Thus, any deer with a rack wider than his ears is starting to get interesting. If his *inside main beam* spread is wider than his ears, chances are you may really have something. Greatest or outside spread, although it is what most hunters mean when they refer to "spread" is not scored. This is listed as "supplementary data."

In the strict records scoring sense, the perfect trophy heads are 5-pointers rather than 7-pointers. This is because, under the Boone and Crockett system, points in addition to the five normal points are considered abnormal and are actually subtracted from the total score. Naturally, if you prefer the added mass of additional points, you might justifiably consider the 7-pointer a superb personal trophy.

Symmetry is very important and an even, balanced head with approximately the same measurements per side and 4 *long* points (plus brows) per side is what to look for. A quick glance at the official scoring chart for mule deer will show you that the scoring of the antler points in a strict sense is somewhat different than that which is handiest in practical field terms. For scoring purposes the main beam is measured from the burr at the base to the tip of the lower point on the first antler branch. However, when the hunter has to quickly size up a head in the field, especially if it's in silhouette, he invariably estimates the "lengths of the Y's," that is the two forks on each side. It's an unconscious but almost universal approach.

In those terms your Y's should be at least 8 or 9 inches deep for trophy consideration, and it's better that they be 10 or 11 inches long. Of course the total length of main beam and the heaviness of the antlers will also enter in and influence the final score. But long, symmetrical points are the key to most outstanding mule deer heads. Mule deer heads can be "narrow and high" or "wide and low" and the look of the two is a matter of personal preference. However, the "narrow and high" heads often are tops in scoring. (These sometimes only look a bit narrow because the points are so long and thus make them appear to be narrow.)

RECORDS OF NORTH AMERICAN BIG GAME COMMITTEE

BOONE AND CROCKETT CLUB

RETURN TO:
N. A. B. G. Awards Program
1600 Rhode Island Ave. N. W.
Washington, D. C. 20036

Minimum Score: Deer

| Col. Blacktail: | Typical — 130 |
| Mule: | Typical — 195 |

MULE and BLACKTAIL DEER

KIND OF DEER:

DETAIL OF POINT MEASUREMENT

SEE OTHER SIDE FOR INSTRUCTIONS		Supplementary Data		Column 1	Column 2	Column 3	Column 4
		R.	L.	Spread Credit	Right Antler	Left Antler	Difference
A. Number of Points on Each Antler				////////	////////	////////	////////
B. Tip to Tip Spread				////////	////////	////////	////////
C. Greatest Spread				////////	////////	////////	////////
D. Inside Spread of MAIN BEAMS	Spread credit may equal but not exceed length of longer antler				////////	////////	////////
IF Inside Spread of Main Beams exceeds longer antler length, enter difference				////////	////////	////////	
E. Total of Lengths of all Abnormal Points				////////	////////	////////	
F. Length of Main Beam				////////			
G-1 Length of First Point, if present				////////			
G-2 Length of Second Point				////////			
G-3 Length of Third Point, if present				////////			
G-4 Length of Fourth Point, if present				////////			
H-1 Circumference at Smallest Place Between Burr and First Point				////////			
H-2 Circumference at Smallest Place Between First and Second Points				////////			
H-3 Circumference at Smallest Place Between Main Beam and Third Point				////////			
H-4 Circumference at Smallest Place Between Second and Fourth Points				////////			
TOTALS							

ADD	Column 1		Exact locality where killed	
	Column 2		Date killed By whom killed	
	Column 3		Present owner	
	TOTAL		Address Zip	
SUBTRACT Column 4			Guide's Name and Address	
FINAL SCORE			Remarks: (Mention any abnormalities)	

I certify that I have measured the above trophy on _____ 19_____
at (address) _____ City _____ State _____
that these measurements and data are, to the best of my knowledge and belief, made in accordance with the
instructions given.

Witness: _____ Signature: _____
                                                           Boone & Crockett Official Measurer

INSTRUCTIONS

All measurements must be made with a flexible steel tape to the nearest one-eighth of an inch. Wherever it is necessary to change direction of measurement, mark a control point and swing tape at this point. To simplify addition, please enter fractional figures in eighths. Official measurements cannot be taken for at least sixty days after the animal was killed. Please submit photographs of trophy front and sides.

Supplementary Data measurements indicate conformation of the trophy, and none of the figures in Lines A, B and C are to be included in the score. Evaluation of conformation is a matter of personal preference. Excellent, but nontypical Mule Deer heads with many points shall be placed and judged in a separate class.

A. Number of Points on Each Antler. To be counted a point, a projection must be at least one inch long AND its length must exceed the length of its base. All points are measured from tip of point to nearest edge of beam as illustrated. Beam tip is counted as a point but not measured as a point.

B. Tip to Tip Spread measured between tips of main beams.

C. Greatest Spread measured between perpendiculars at right angles to the center line of the skull at widest part whether across main beams or points.

D. Inside Spread of Main Beams measured at right angles to the center line of the skull at widest point between main beams. Enter this measurement again in "Spread Credit" column if it is less than or equal to the length of longer antler.

E. Total of Lengths of all Abnormal Points. Abnormal points are generally considered to be those nontypical in shape or location.

F. Length of Main Beam measured from lowest outside edge of burr over outer curve to the tip of the main beam. The point of beginning is that point on the burr where the center line along the outer curve of the beam intersects the burr.

G-1-2-3-4. Length of Normal Points. Normal points are the brow (or first) and the upper and lower forks as shown in illustration. They are measured from nearest edge of beam over outer curve to tip. To determine nearest edge (top edge) of beam, lay the tape along the outer curve of the beam so that the top edge of the tape coincides with the top edge of the beam on both sides of the point. Draw line along top edge of tape. This line will be base line from which point is measured.

H-1-2-3-4. Circumferences — if first point is missing, take H-1 and H-2 at smallest place between burr and second point. If third point is missing, take H-3 half way between the base and tip of second point. If the fourth is missing, take H-4 half way between the second point and tip of main beam.

TROPHIES OBTAINED ONLY BY FAIR CHASE MAY BE ENTERED IN ANY BOONE AND CROCKETT CLUB BIG GAME COMPETITION

To make use of the following methods shall be deemed UNFAIR CHASE and unsportsmanlike, and any trophy obtained by use of such means is disqualified from entry in any Boone and Crockett Club big game competition:

    I. Spotting or herding game from the air, followed by landing in its vicinity for pursuit;
    II. Herding or pursuing game with motor-powered vehicles;
    III. Use of electronic communications for attracting, locating or observing game, or guiding the hunter to such game.

I certify that the trophy scored on this chart was not taken in UNFAIR CHASE as defined above by the Boone and Crockett Club.

I certify that it was not spotted or herded by guide or hunter from the air followed by landing in its vicinity for pursuit, nor herded or pursued on the ground by motor-powered vehicles.

I further certify that no electronic communications were used to attract, locate, observe, or guide the hunter to such game; and that it was taken in full compliance with the local game laws or regulations of the state, province or territory.

Date _____ Signature of Hunter _____

This chart is reproduced with permission of the Boone and Crockett Club, which, together with the National Rifle Association, co-sponsors the North American Big Game Awards Program. (Another chart is used for the scoring of nontypical mule deer heads. There is no awards category for nontypical blacktails.)

This young mule deer buck is relatively light-antlered and shows only modest tines. But few sportsmen after their first mulie would pass him up.

The spread is decent on this mule deer buck, but the lack of mass and the short, almost vestigial, points of the lower "Y" leave him a just personal, rather than a record-book, trophy.

This massive blacktail head, taken by Elgin Gates, ranked 40th in the 1971 record book. Note the sweep well beyond the ears and the uniformity of corresponding tines. The odd point on the rear of the right antler cost score points.

A quick glance at the tabulated measurements of top heads in the record book will show that many of the inside spreads are relatively narrow; that is, in the 17- to 24-inch range. Certainly these heads are very large and handsome and only "narrow" in the sense that as many mule deer as are harvested each year, some extremely wide heads do come in.

These two bucks show the difference between an "extraordinary" and a "decent" trophy. Though no sportsman in his right mind would "pass" on the big fellow, the normal tines are not especially long — considering the mass — and the abnormal tines would penalize the score in the "typical" category.

How to Hunt Them

The mulie is the westerner's "everyman's" game, similar to the whitetail for the easterner. Thus, the basic method of hunting over the years has been to hunt afoot after driving in, often by 4-wheeldrive, as far as possible. This is still the most common method but, as hunting pressure intensifies, it is less and less effective for the big heads. Thus, mule deer hunting in a trophy sense, has come to somewhat resemble elk hunting in that horses are becoming more and more important. Horses allow you to get in far away from the road and other hunters and to cover more ground once there. This implies longer and more expensive hunts rather than the weekend to 5 day jaunts where the hunter is limited to a day's walk around his pickup or car.

While it's true that a man in top physical condition can usually outclimb and outhunt a horseback hunter in really rough country, for the vast majority of us a horse means we can climb higher and top more mountains. That means more country glassed and a far better chance to locate those big fellows.

Late season trophy hunts are often a good idea, but you'll be surprised at how long these relatively small animals can hang tough before moving down to you out of the high country. One year in Montana's Sun River country we just weren't seeing any decent bucks. We hunted higher and higher though it was the very end of November and deep snow lay in the high country. Finally we topped out, far above the bighorn sheep which had already started moving down or were already down in the valley floors, and then we started seeing bucks. It was brutally cold and the undrifted snow was often 8 to 10 inches deep, far deeper in drifts. We could hear avalanches all around us, this due to the amount of snow and the steepness of some of the peaks. Yet the deer had not even started to move down! Even the elk were moving in some areas but not these far smaller but hardy deer. I would hardly have believed it if I hadn't seen it myself.

Mule deer are attractive animals and though the chances of getting a real buster are slimmer than ever, chances are good that the confirmed whitetail hunter can collect a set of mule deer antlers that outshine those of all the whitetails he's ever taken.

Prince of the Plains: Pronghorn

6

The pronghorn is a very attractive and readily available trophy — often, along with mule deer, the first trophy of another type taken by whitetail hunters. He is a dapper little fellow with an almost exotic appearance by North American big-game standards. A unique animal in many ways, he's also strictly an "all American" in that he exists only on our continent. And unlike many of our other major big-game trophy species, he does not trace his direct ancestry back to Eurasia.

The pronghorn, though often called an "antelope" because of his general resemblance to some members of that family, is actually the only surviving member of an entirely different family. As such, he sports a number of unique biological characteristics. He's the only animal in the world that regularly sheds his *horns* (not antlers) each year. Also of special interest to trophy hunters, he's the only horned animal in the world with branching, or forked horns. (That's where the "prong" in the popular name "pronghorn" comes from.)

Those little hooked, jet-black horns are highly attractive. And, along with the pronghorn's distinctive reddish-tan coloration which is set off by areas of black and white on the face and neck, the horns make him a very attractive — and unusual — game head. It has been my experience that pronghorn horns, along with those of mountain goats, probably shrink relatively more than any other horned North American game. Thus, the successful pronghorn hunter may well "lose" more of his trophy to the natural drying process. Also, pronghorn horns often smell rather strongly and unpleasantly for some weeks while drying.

The hair on a pronghorn is extremely stiff and bristly, and it is about the easiest pelage of all North American big game to damage or injure. Extreme care should be taken when handling pronghorn capes and body skins.

The animal should be field-dressed and caped or skinned as soon as possible after the kill. Salt the cape or skin liberally and evenly, making sure that you miss no spots. All stains should be daubed off or soaked out of the cape before they have a chance to dry and set.

The hair on a pronghorn is hollow and filled with air to increase its insulating properties and guard the beast against the considerable windchill factor that is often present on the high, windy plateaus that he calls home. The hair is somewhat similar to caribou hair in that respect, but it is far stiffer, coarser and more subject to damage. Handle it carefully. Avoid putting any weight on top of the skinned-out hide. Avoid sharp folds in the hide if it is to sit a while before being delivered to the taxidermist. And keep it out of the direct sunlight while it is drying. All of these comments apply to the proper care of any trophy hide in the field, but with pronghorn they are doubly important. Many a pronghorn cape has been inadvertently ruined by handling that would have been perfectly acceptable had it been that of a mule deer or whitetail.

How to Hunt Them

The first pronghorn hunt that an eastern whitetail hunter makes is often a strange and disquieting experience. Pronghorn are our one remaining true plains animal that furnishes a reasonably broad-based hunting opportunity. As a plains animal they rely almost completely on their eyesight and speed for safety rather than on the skulking concealment of which the wily old whitetail buck is a past master.

Along with sheep and goat, pronghorn have the sharpest vision of any North American big game. Their eyesight is often compared with that of an 8x binocular, which may be about right for stationary objects. But I have found them to be more keen-eyed than goat and sheep in detecting moving objects; here I've found their visual resolving power to be considerably better than 8x. Pronghorn have been tested and found to be able to resolve a small object in motion as far away as four miles. I don't know of any man with 8x binoculars who can equal that feat.

Not only are pronghorn sharp-eyed. They also possess peripheral vision which, if possessed by a man, would make him the best basketball guard of all time. (Notice how large their eyes are in proportion to their total face.) Their eyes protrude from their head, making them a bit bug-eyed (but not unattractively so), and they can actually see backward as well as forward. Keep that in mind if you tend to relax your guard a bit when sneaking up "behind" a pronghorn. An angle of approach that would work perfectly well with deer or elk (provided they didn't hear or wind you, of course) is usually doomed to failure with Mr. Vista-Vision. Pronghorn also hear and smell surprisingly well for an open country animal. What's more, they *trust* these two senses a bit more than goat or sheep. That factor is equal in importance to the actual acuteness of the senses themselves.

The pronghorns other primary defense mechanism is his blinding speed. Though much has been made of this, it is truly awesome when observed for the first time. The animal can hit a top speed of 70 miles an hour for short bursts. But to me, what is even more fantastic is the fact that he can run for rather long periods at 40 to 50 miles per hour. The "top speeds" given for most animals are always based on burst speed, and that's as misleading as quoting a man's speed as what he can do over a 50-yard dash. That an animal can *maintain* a 40- to 50-mile-per-hour speed boggles my mind. This ability requires far more than powerful legs and strong muscles. There must also be an enormous capacity to take in oxygen — and then the circulatory power to deliver the air/blood mix to the muscles in order to sustain the energy. The pronghorn accomplishes his miracle by running with mouth wide open and tongue lolling crazily out in order to inhale a maximum amount of oxygen. Then his oversized lungs and heart enable him to "process" this air and speed it to his muscles in adequate volumes.

All of these biological factors result in a type of hunting with an entirely different "feel" to it. The animals stand out in plain view and make no attempt to hide or run away — as long as they feel they are safe distance away.

Thus, for the first time the eastern heavy-woods hunter can actually see his game all around him and, if he's in the right place at the right time, see it in abundance. This is very novel and also a bit disquieting. The animals stand there and solemnly stare back, counting the whiskers on the hunter's face at 600 yards and better. They have a built in rangefinder that allows them to calculate the "danger zone" of a modern rifle with the accuracy of a computer-checked, ballistics drop table.

This means the hunter should do two things. First, although

first-day hunting is usually a good idea for any game, for pronghorn it is doubly important. During the first hour of opening day, the game may let hunters approach to within 350 to 400 yards. Also, pronghorn are, along with caribou, blessed or cursed with the strongest curiosity of our big-game species. When they haven't been shot at or bothered for a year, this curiosity often works to the hunter's advantage.

Once, on opening morning in Wyoming some years ago, I blew a crawling stalk on a big buck that I'd estimated at 16 inches, maybe a bit better. (Later he actually taped 15¾ and 15⅞ inches.) The animal spotted me and took off as though he had important business in Colorado. Disgustedly I hauled my much skinned and abraded carcass up into a more comfortable sitting position, slammed my hat into the ground, and mumbled some harsh remarks about that big buck's ancestry.

Idly, I noticed that the big fellow was making a big half circle as he disappeared into one of the innumerable washes in the area. I sat there and tried to figure out what to do next, before all the precious opening-morning time ran out. A few minutes later I put the glasses up to scan the area where I thought the big buck would come out of the wash again before disappearing into the distance. Nothing. No powder-puff rump, with erectile hairs signaling other pronghorn to beware. But as I put the glasses down, I noticed a strange apparition some 75 yards in front of me and a bit to the left. A big pronghorn head was sprouting out of the busy plain, large horns and big face visible down to about six inches under the chin and staring straight at me with all the solemnity of missionary addressing the faithful.

I blinked, and blinked again, and he was still there. Shakily I brought the scope sighted rifle up, racked it over to 7 power and blinked again. No doubt about it. It *was* a big pronghorn — *my* big pronghorn, in fact. Carefully I wormed into the sling and assumed a sitting position that was almost benchrest-steady. Holding the crosshairs right at the very lowest part of the animal that was visible (since the bullet would be about two inches high at that range), I managed to drill the animal cleanly right under the chin. He evaporated. I ran over and found him stone dead a few feet below the lip of the wash where he had been standing.

That animal had literally committed suicide, duped into doing so by his own fatal curiosity. He had run along the wash. And when it branched into a "Y," he had elected to follow it back my way to get a better look at that strange phenomenon making those funny motions and those funny noises. My hunting prowess had little or nothing to do with the taking of that outstanding trophy. The fact that hunting season was only about an hour old had everything to do with it. Within another hour or so that buck wouldn't have made the same mistake. I had evidently been the very first person to chivy him around a bit in a year, and the old fellow was curious—too curious.

This well known curiosity was exploited by the 19th century hunters when they waved-up, or tolled-in, pronghorn. This was done by crouching (to cover the man silhouette a bit) and waving slowly a hat or white rag tied onto a stick. I've tried this on animals I didn't want to shoot, and though I've had some stop and stare at it and even drawn some in a bit closer, I've never been able to pull a nice buck well into shooting range doing this. I have done so, quite successfully, with big caribou, however.

In addition to getting out on opening day, the other thing an aspiring pronghorn hunter should do is to practice his shooting and stalking. On average, pronghorn are shot at longer ranges than any other North American game. This is due to the animal and the terrain that he inhabits. There is more abuse in pronghorn shooting (shooting running animals at ridiculously long ranges) than any other type of hunting. If one included all of these circus shots, the average pronghorn shot probably runs over 400 yards. If you discounted these and only included those shots that were roughly "legitimate," the average shot would probably still run 250 to 300 yards.

Any range routine to get ready for pronghorn hunting should include a very high proportion of practice beyond the 200- and even 300-yard marks. Much of this can be from the prone and sitting positions because the pronghorn hunter can use these positions, rather than offhand, more frequently than for most other game. If you are consistently holding your shots in an 8-inch circle out around 300 yards, you're in business. Though your initial long-range practice can be over known distances purely for the mechanistic accuracy practice, you should eventually graduate to long-distance practice at unknown ranges. Range estimation is more important in *legitimate* pronghorn hunting than elsewhere. Almost all cartridges begin to sag a bit out beyond 300 yards. So knowing how much to hold over and when not to shoot at all can be very critical.

In addition to being able to shoot accurately and knowing your load trajectories all the way out, you should also plan on doing the best-possible job stalking. Good stalking and patience generally net out to about the same thing. Most good stalkers will take the extra time to do it right. This means the extra time starting the stalk from a very long range or a completely hidden vantage point; the extra time to go slow enough so that motion and sound aren't exaggerated; the extra time to move along with few or none of the curiosity-salving but pronghorn-losing "look sees." If you find that you are stalking to the preselected shooting point and the animals have moved or fed out of range, but still aren't alarmed, then you know you're doing it right. Some would regard this unsuccessful stalk as wasted time. Not I. This is just one of the breaks of the game when pronghorn hunting.

Often, if you can get a buddy to help, you can enjoy the best of both worlds. Sometimes you can circle around behind, and downwind from, the pronghorns while a buddy keeps them diverted from the other side at a long distance away. If your friend can get a bit of elevation, you can often see him even though the pronghorn between you are still invisible. He can signal you where they are, which direction they're moving and how fast or when to abort the whole stalk. This way you don't have to watch the animals and run the risk of being spotted. Also, his presence can keep them diverted and help focus their attention away from your direction. After you collect, you can then spot for your buddy, helping him with the spookier, later-in-the-day animals.

How Not to Hunt Them

Though I have no figures to prove it, I would estimate that more wounded pronghorn are wasted, relative to the number taken by hunters, than any other game animal. All too many callous, unthinking hunters like to pile into a jeep and take off after pronghorn. Then when they spot a band, running at top speeds and at ridiculous ranges of 600 yards and better, they'll open fire—emitting the racket of a military skirmish.

I don't know why they do it. Some of it is undoubtedly due to laziness—an unwillingness to work for game on a long stalk. Also, especially with the advent of the cigar-size super magnums in the last few years, many apparently feel an infantile urge to fire off the old super-whomper-stomper at unbelievable ranges just to see what will happen. I guess they feel they're plinking at animated beer cans rather than firing at live animals that are among our most splendid game and should be treated as such.

When these "sports" resort to this kind of hunting they invariably accomplish two things. They wound the animal rather than killing it cleanly, and they usually hit the wrong animal — most often about two or three animals back of the one they were shooting at. A running pronghorn out at 600 yards or so covers tremendous distances before even the fastest of bullets can arrive. And people just aren't used to leading animals 40 to 60 feet!

Perhaps my words sound harsh, but I have had to finish off far too many grievously wounded pronghorn hit by this type of shooting. Because the "hunter" didn't want to use up his precious permit on the doe or small buck hit by mistake, these animals were left to die a painful and tragic death. Pronghorn are tough, plucky little fellows. For their 100- to 120-pound size they are surprisingly tough to lay down, and many can survive to suffer all too long with one or even two legs shot completely off.

Such shooting antics not only waste valuable game and sport but they also serve to fuel the ever present anti-hunting clique in its strident demands to do away with all sport hunting. Sure, the trigger-crazy boob is in the minority. I wouldn't call him a sport hunter, much less a trophy hunter. He's more an armed juvenile delinquent. But he's the one everyone remembers — not the hundreds of well behaved gentlemanly hunters who accord the game the respect it deserves with a clean and sporting kill.

The ironic thing is that this kind of shoot-'em-at-one-mile approach not only isn't necessary, it's less fun than hunting right. It isn't necessary because, though the pronghorn's high plains home is noted for being largely treeless and devoid of major cover, there is a surprising amount of cover for the enterprising hunter to use. Those seeming level-to-gently-undulating plains are actually surprisingly rough when you investigate the terrain closely. There are all sorts of sagebrush bushes, some quite large, as well as ravines and washes ranging from the very small those big enough to drive a trailer truck through unseen. Using these terrain features, as well as the gentler folds and swells in the general topography, the hunter can sneak up on his quarry. He may not be able to "bee-line it" straight toward the game at all times, and the indirect route may take extra time. But with skill and patience, most pronghorn can be approached unaware to within a reasonable 200- to 250-yard shooting range.

Also, this kind of long-distance spotting to locate the game

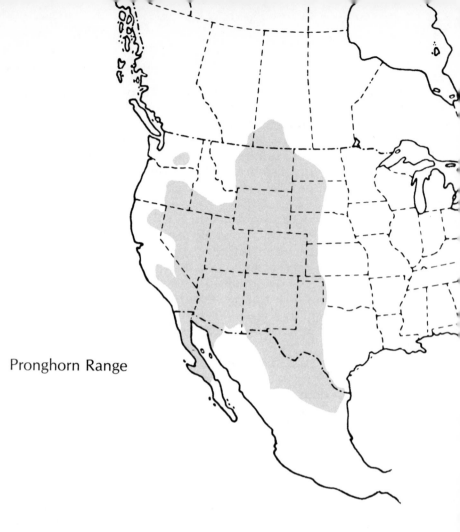

Pronghorn Range

Pronghorn may not always be huntable in all portions of the range indicated and may be absent entirely in many parts.

before it spots you, combined with careful stalking or outwitting by means of a buddy as decoy/diversion, adds much spice to the hunt. If you agree with me that there is much more to any hunt than the climactic kill itself, then you'll also agree that this kind of sporting method is actually *more fun* than indiscriminate long-distance shooting.

Where to Go

Estimates for the pronghorn population prior to the settlement of the West run as high as 20 million, making it second only in numbers to the bison on our continent — and possibly in the world — for a single large animal species. This changed radically with the settlement of the West. Pronghorn are not used to vertical obstructions, and to this day most will not jump a fence even though they and their ancestors have been exposed to these contraptions for over a century now. Rather, pronghorn scoot under or through a barbed wire fence, often at a full run. To see them do this, with hunks of fur flying 30 or 40 feet, is an arresting sight to say the least.

The fencing of the West, with much of it put under cultivation, much decreased the available pronghorn habitat. Also, the planned destruction of the bison greatly reduced the pronghorn's numbers because bison kept the grasses eaten well down so that the sagebrush and other brush that the pronghorn favors could thrive in some areas. With the buffalo gone the grass grew high, choking out much of the preferred pronghorn feed; and though pronghorn do eat some grass, it is a minor part of their diet. Shortly after the turn of the last century, their numbers were down to less than 20,000 continent-wide. But the large-scale introduction of cattle partially alleviated the sagebrush feed shortage. Now, as a result of wise game management, the pronghorn numbers between 300,000 and 350,000, with most of these animals residing in the states. Alberta and Saskatchewan have relatively small herds.

Wyoming is THE pronghorn state. Its herd is estimated at 180,000 — or better than half of the total population. Wyoming's annual legal harvest of 34,000 is also about half of the total reported continent-wide, legal harvest. So, with six of the top twelve heads in the 1971 Boone and Crockett record book coming from Wyoming, the state's overall trophy production seems to conform to mathematical probability (neither exceptionally good nor bad) for the herd size. Hunter success ratios run around 85 percent for the 40,000, or so, pronghorn permits awarded each year. Thus, due to sheer numbers of permits and animals available, Wyoming is by far the best bet for the nonresident. And with the 85 percent success ratio, Wyoming is the best bet for filling that tag. For the biggest Wyoming trophies I would look to the southern part of the state, and near the town of Red Desert.

Montana is securely entrenched in second place, also due to the size of the herd. Though Montana game officials don't make state-wide herd estimates for pronghorn, the harvest of about 20,000 each year is more than the total from all other states and provinces, excepting Wyoming. In Montana the

**RECORDS OF NORTH AMERICAN
BIG GAME COMMITTEE**

BOONE AND CROCKETT CLUB

RETURN TO:
N.A.B.G. Awards Program
1600 Rhode Island Ave., N.W.
Washington, D. C. 20036

Minimum Score
Pronghorn: 82

PRONGHORN

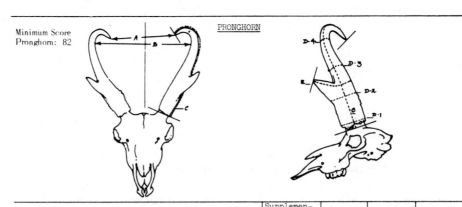

SEE OTHER SIDE FOR INSTRUCTIONS	Supplementary Data	Column 1	Column 2	Column 3
		Right Horn	Left Horn	Difference
A. Tip to Tip Spread				
B. Inside Spread of Main Beams		//////	//////	//////
IF Inside Spread of Main Beams exceeds longer horn length, enter difference.		//////	//////	
C. Length of Horn				
D-1. Circumference of Base				
D-2. Circumference at First Quarter				
D-3. Circumference at Second Quarter				
D-4. Circumference at Third Quarter				
E. Length of Prong				
TOTALS				

ADD	Column 1		Exact locality where killed
	Column 2		Date killed By whom killed
	Total		Present owner
SUBTRACT	Column 3		Address
			Guide's Name and Address
			Remarks: (Mention any abnormalities)
FINAL SCORE			

I certify that I have measured the above trophy on   19
at (address)   City   State
and that these measurements and data are, to the best of my knowledge and belief, made in
accordance with the instructions given.

Witness:_____ Signature:_____

A 1M 7 62   Boone and Crockett Official Measurer

72

INSTRUCTIONS

All measurements must be made with a flexible steel tape to the nearest one-eighth of an inch. Wherever it is necessary to change direction of measurement, mark a control point and swing tape at this point. To simplify addition, please enter fractional figures in eighths.

Official measurements cannot be taken for at least sixty days after the animal was killed. Please submit photographs.

Supplementary Data measurements indicate conformation of the trophy.
None of the figures in Lines A and B are to be included in the score.
Evaluation of conformation is a matter of personal preference.

A. Tip to Tip Spread measured between tips of horns.

B. Inside Spread of Main Beams measured at right angles to the center line of the skull at widest point between main beams.

C. Length of horn is measured on the outside curve, so the line taken will vary with different heads, depending on the direction of their curvature. Measure along the center of the outer curve from tip of horn to a point in line with the lowest edge of the base.

D-1. Measure around base of horn at right angles to long axis. Tape must be in contact with the lowest circumference of the horn in which there are no sierrations.

D-2-3-4. Divide measurement of LONGER horn by four, mark BOTH horns at these quarters even though one horn is shorter, and measure circumferences at these marks. If the prong occurs at approximately D-3, take this measurement immediately above the swelling of the prong.

E. Length of Prong – Measure from the tip of the prong along the upper edge of the outer curve to the horn; thence, around the horn to a point at the rear of the horn where a straight edge across the back of both horns touches the horn. This measurement around the horn from the base of the prong should be taken at right angles to the long axis of the horn.

* * * * * * * * * * * * * *

TROPHIES OBTAINED ONLY BY FAIR CHASE MAY BE ENTERED IN ANY BOONE AND CROCKETT CLUB BIG GAME COMPETITION

To make use of the following methods shall be deemed UNFAIR CHASE and unsportsmanlike, and any trophy obtained by use of such means is disqualified from entry in any Boone and Crockett Club big game competition:

I. Spotting or herding game from the air, followed by landing in its vicinity for pursuit;

II. Herding or pursuing game with motor-powered vehicles;

III. Use of electronic communications for attracting, locating or observing game, or guiding the hunter to such game.

****

I certify that the trophy scored on this chart was not taken in UNFAIR CHASE as defined above by the Boone and Crockett Club.

I certify that it was not spotted or herded by guide or hunter from the air followed by landing in its vicinity for pursuit, nor herded or pursued on the ground by motor-powered vehicles.

I further certify that no electronic communications were used to attract, locate, observe, or guide the hunter to such game; and that it was taken in full compliance with the local game laws or regulations of the state, province or territory.

Date_____ Signature of Hunter_____

This chart is reproduced with permission of the Boone and Crockett Club, which, together with the National Rifle Association, co-sponsors the North American Big Game Awards Program.

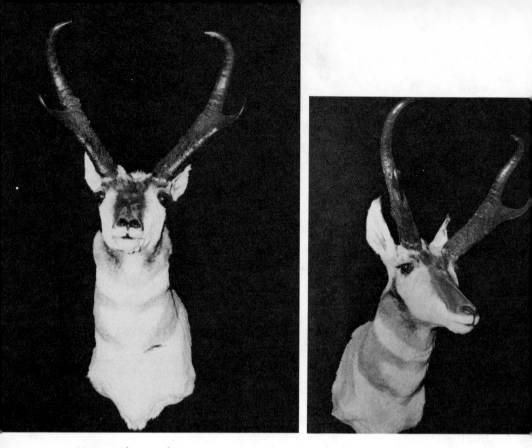

Here are front and quartering views of a tremendous Arizona pronghorn shot by Elgin Gates in the 1950s. Scoring 84⁶/₈ points, this head still ranked 67th in the 1971 awards. Note that the nearly 17-inch-long horns are at least four times longer than the 4-inch-long ears. Heaviness and the long prongs add important points to the score.

hunter success ratio runs 80 to 85 percent. With about 4,000 to 4,500 permits awarded to nonresidents each year, the visitor also has a good chance.

In fact, for *big* pronghorn, I would look to Montana more than Wyoming, especially to the areas slightly north and east of Miles City in eastern Montana. On a recent trophy hunt in that area, an experienced hunter-friend of mine saw fifty bucks that he estimated at 14½ to 15 inches or better. Those are nice trophy bucks. And the only 17-inch pronghorn that I've seen mounted was shot in this same area by taxidermist Jack Atcheson, a fellow from Butte. The big buck went well over 17 inches and that is simply huge. Atcheson's Taxidermy has mounted over 3,500 pronghorn over the years, but aside from the one Atcheson shot himself, only *five* heads have come through that went 17 inches or better. When you figure that this isn't just six heads out of any 3,500 but out of 3,500 that were 99.9 percent bucks and heads that people thought good enough to be mounted, you can appreciate how rare a 16-inch head is.

Ironically, though I am recommending eastern Montana as the best area for large heads, there isn't a single Montana head in the top dozen in the book, and the first Big Sky head doesn't turn up until 30th place. So, why do I recommend Montana? Simply this. The other states that have produced some very large heads over the years have very small herds. And the possibility of a nonresident securing a legal pronghorn permit runs from thin to none.

In spite of having only a rather small herd of about 7,200 animals, Arizona has produced some very large trophies over the years. Three of the top 12 heads (including First Place, a monster shot back in 1878) come from Arizona. However, the kill runs only about 600 to 800 animals per year (about a 55 to 60 percent hunter success rate), and only 15 to 20 of the highly prized pronghorn permits go to visitors. Thus, unless you happen to live in Arizona, look elsewhere for any reasonable chance at trophy pronghorn.

Colorado has a nice herd of some 35,000 animals and an annual harvest of 4,000 to 5,000 animals. The hunter success rate is an attractive 80 to 85 percent. Also, Colorado has produced the Number 2 head, a rather short-horned ($15^1/8$/$15^2/8$-inch) monster that scores $91^4/8$ and ties another old 1899 Arizona head. This big trophy was shot in 1965. However, the next Colorado head is well down the list, tied for 90th place, in fact. Colorado is a very populous state by western standards and the pronghorn, as are whitetails in some of the big eastern whitetail states, are pretty well shot-over before most have a chance to get old enough to grow the big hatrack-size horns. Though 6,000 to 7,000 pronghorn permits are awarded each year, the demand is such that usually less than 100 go to nonresidents. So, when you consider the harvest size and the man-hours spent hunting, Colorado trophy production hasn't been outstanding. Also, it is very difficult to secure a nonresident tag.

Idaho has produced some nice heads. Though it has a large enough herd to harvest between 1,000 and 2,000 head per year, the 2,000 or so resident permits are usually oversubscribed about 4 to 1. So the state awards only about 50 to 100 nonresident tags a year. Oregon and New Mexico have also produced some outstanding trophies, but they award even fewer permits.

Estimating Trophy Heads

As with goats, pronghorn ears are the most helpful reference when sizing up the horns. Both animals are "ear rated" rather than "body rated." The spread on pronghorn horns is, like the goat's, extremely variable. Therefore, spread is not counted as part of the score but is entered as "supplementary data."

Mass of the horn, determined by various circumferences as well as prong length, is at least as important as the horn length. But it is almost impossible to accurately gauge the horn mass on most animals. The animals are usually glassed at rather long range. And to attempt a horn-mass estimate, you would almost have to use a spotting scope rather than binoculars. Such painstaking estimation would also increase chances that you would spook the herd. Also, you would have to have an almost "picture book" side view and be fortunate enough to have the beast stand in that position for several minutes. If you are that lucky and find that the apparent width of the horn is considerably wider than the apparent width of the ear (which will be turned at a somewhat different angle), then you have a good heavy-horned head.

Horn length is a more practical estimating factor, but there are some foolers to beware of. Always concentrate on noting how much of a "hook" there is at the end of each horn. Horn length and *apparent* horn height off the top of the head can vary tremendously. The big head I mentioned earlier that I took on a lucky day, was one of those "fooler" heads. When I first put the glasses on him I thought I had an honest-to-goodness 17-inch head because there was so little hook and the horns stood up so high and straight (small spread). The more I looked the more I scaled down the horns, but I still thought they'd go over 16 inches. The head's a heck of a trophy at the near 16-inch mark but it fooled me to the end because of that narrow spread and those short hooks. From the front those horns just looked too high.

The apparent height of a big buck's ear above the top of his head will run about 4 inches, though the ears are actually longer. Thus, if you see horns that run closer to 4 times than 3 times the length of the ear, you've got something interesting. The prongs on the horns may begin high or low on some heads. So it is difficult to estimate overall horn length by guessing at the length of horn above the prong. But a good long prong adds important points to the score.

Most sportsmen fortunate enough to secure pronghorn permits will usually get game, the hunter success rates being what they are. The keys are locating the big ones, estimating them reasonably accurately, and knowing "how good is good" when trying for them.

Ideally the pronghorn hunter should arrive in his designated hunting area in time to scout it for one or two days before the season opens. The idea is to locate the bands ·with some *big* bucks so that you can try for them during the "easy" hunting of the first couple of hours on opening morning. Also, if you haven't hunted pronghorn before, it's wise to secure the services of a guide, or local rancher, or someone more experienced in viewing and evaluating heads. Be sure to look at, estimate and check yourself on as many mounted pronghorn heads as possible before making your hunt—even if you've hunted pronghorn before. If it's been some time since you've been "thinking pronghorn," you may well have lost much of your eye for them, and it's a good idea to hone it up before leaving for the hunt. ·

What size head should you shoot? When is a trophy a trophy or a TROPHY as pronghorn heads go? Well, as with a trophy of any other animal, a lot of this depends on you. Important factors include how much time and money you have to invest in the hunt; whether it's your first pronghorn; how big a pronghorn you've already taken; and other personal considerations.

The most common size adult bucks harvested by nontrophy hunters run around 12½ inches in horn length. I would not recommend taking one of less than 13 inches. A 14-inch head is nice though not really outstanding. For some reason the pronghorn heads really thin out at about 14½ inches in horn length. That seems to be the great line of demarcation, with far, far fewer heads over it than under it. At 15 inches, you have a very nice head that, if heavy enough, has an off chance at making the book. You won't see a lot of heads over 15 inches.

A 16-inch pronghorn is a very exceptional trophy—the equivalent of a big 7-point bull elk or a 42-inch ram. Some men hunt pronghorn all their life and never even see a 16-inch buck. As I mentioned before, in mounting over 3,000 pronghorn heads, Jack Atcheson has only handled six that were over 17 inches in length. I have never seen a head this large on a live or recently killed animal, and I've seen only one mounted head this large. When you see a 16-inch or 17-inch pronghorn head, as with all really outstanding game heads, you *know* immediately that this is an exceptional trophy. Estimating isn't very difficult for a head of this caliber. Just try to quiet those shakes down enough so that you can hit him before he decides to decamp!

Guns for Pronghorn

What is needed for "goat" (as many pronghorn-country natives call him) is a high-velocity, flat-shooting rifle. Though he's a plucky little fellow, he *is* little. So tremendous power isn't required. The ability to shoot straight at long ranges is. The .243, 6mm. Remington, .25/06, and .240 Weatherby are all fine pronghorn hulls. Though the .257 Weatherby, .270, .284, .280 and numerous others are also fine choices, they offer more power (and muzzle blast) than is needed.

To my mind an ideal pronghorn rifle is one of the heavy-weight "varmint specials" shooting a .243-class cartridge rather than a .22 centerfire (however powerful). There are several single shots available that offer "medium-heavy" and heavy-weight barrels, and these make sporty rifles for this type of hunting. This is not particularly arduous hunting and a heavy gun with a bulky extra-high-power hunting type scope, or even with one of the still bulkier target scopes, works no real physical hardship on the pronghorn hunter. And the heavy gun is usually more accurate and hangs much better in the hand in the gusty, windy arena in which most pronghorn are taken. And I do think that the single-shot feature adds a bit of sportiness to the hunt. Also, it discourages those often disastrous, second long-distance shots at running animals. When that first shot has to count, usually it does.

Though diligent practice and good range routines count in preparing for all types of hunting, they simply cannot be over-emphasized when you want to get ready for pronghorn. Practice at those long distances of 300 yards and better. Practice your range estimation as religiously as your actual shooting. Know your gun and load. Know your trajectory. And if you think you're good enough for the extra-long-distance shots out around 400 yards and better, check your *actual* load drop at those ranges yourself. Don't rely on standardized drop tables at these ranges. A slight variance of your load to the one plotted on the standard table often isn't so slight at a quarter of a mile!

Wind drift is often a significant factor in pronghorn hunting and hitting. That's why somewhat heavier bullets (if not too heavily constructed) are a good idea in these small to medium calibers. The increased weight and better sectional density help to partially offset the insidious effects of wind over the travel distance of the far shot. However, be sure that you don't use a bullet too heavily constructed for the light-boned prey, a bullet that drills a neat hole cleanly through your quarry and then uselessly expends 90 percent of its energy on the landscape behind.

Be sure to do some long-range practice at your shooting range on windy days. Make a point of it. Try to estimate wind drift, always realizing that it may be a bit different out at 400 yards than it is where you are shooting from. At least be wind *conscious* and try to deal with it as well as possible by practicing in windy conditions and becoming generally familiar with the wind-drift tendencies of your selected loads.

Optics

For pronghorn hunting and trophy assessment, you need the very best in optics: binoculars, spotting scopes and rifle scopes. More than one hunter has shot a buck he wasn't happy with primarily because he didn't estimate him accurately before beginning a long arduous stalk and then, though with misgivings, he shot him because he didn't want to "waste" the difficult stalk. Well-selected optics help to prevent this.

For binoculars I lean to the 8x and stronger. The 10x models are fine in the top quality roof prism models that are compact enough, even at that power, and that resolve well at that high power. For a rifle scope I prefer a minimum of 6x and feel better with one of the big 3x-9x variables. I don't favor zooms in most spotting scopes for this kind of highly detailed work; though some of the better and more expensive makes are very good indeed. A 20x or 30x spotting scope is good with a spare 45x eyepiece to use for ultra-fine work, when conditions allow.

He's a fine little trophy, this all-American plains dandy of ours and we're fortunate indeed to have him with us in good huntable populations. But he should always be stalked and shot with the respect that he deserves.

Eight Foot at the Shoulder: Moos

7

Moose are huge animals. If you've ever packed one out on your back, as I have several times, that's an experience you'll never quite forget. Antlers, on the largest far northern trophy bulls, may approach or even exceed 80 inches in spread and may weigh up to 90 pounds. This makes for a massive and highly impressive trophy.

Worldwide, there are seven subspecies, or races, of moose. All inhabit the northern hemisphere. Two of the three races living outside of North America (the European and the Manchurian) are smaller than our smallest, the Shiras (Wyoming) moose. The other foreigner, the Siberian, approaches but doesn't quite rival the greatest deer that ever trod the earth, the enormous Alaska-Yukon moose.

A full grown moose stands taller than a big horse, and he looks like nothing so much as a giant Missouri mule perched way up on stilts. He's an ungainly fellow with high humped shoulders and a deep, bulky body set up on long legs. The awe-inspiring yet somewhat grotesque face is set on a short, heavy neck and it will certainly never win any beauty contests. The huge overhanging nose, the smallish eyes and the gigantic ears (larger than a mule's) all conspire to make him homely on a super scale.

However, his lack of comeliness doesn't detract a bit from his value or attractiveness in a trophy sense. Though he doesn't have the exotic good looks of some of the larger African antelope, or the regal bearing of the elk, or the elegance of the caribou, he is so big and powerful and he carries such giant antlers that he must be regarded as one of the world's outstanding trophies. Better yet, he's a rather intelligent animal, gifted with keen ears and nose; reflecting the fact that he originally evolved as a deep woods animal. And he is "game" in every sense of that word.

Although moose in the lower 48 United States seldom exceed 1,000 to 1,200 pounds live weight and 72 inches in shoulder height, their huge cousins farther to the north grow considerably larger. Moose are primarily animals of the Boreal Region, inhabiting not only the Hudsonian and Canadian portions of this farthest north region but also thriving, during certain parts of the year, even in the Arctic Zone.

In the 48 contiguous states, their distribution is generally confined to those higher elevation areas where the Canadian Life Zone extends south. With a few exceptions in Alaska itself, the farther away from the equator, the larger the moose — and moose rack.

I'll never forget the first moose I ever shot. Though only average to good by Alaska standards, this giant wore the coveted 60-inch-plus rack. And he dwarfed the large 6-point bull elk that I had killed in years gone by. After shakily measuring his rack and snapping the trophy pictures, I set about measuring him. When I picked up his front leg in order to work it up into the shoulder socket to get a true shoulder height — rather than "cheating" it by extending the leg — I was astounded at the weight of the leg. And not just the leg! The *foot* was substantial in weight as I later discovered when I took the two front feet off and packed them out to have bookends made of them.

By the most conservative measurement, this big bull stood 80 inches at the shoulder — that is, at the top of his hump, he was the height of a big basketball center! The largest Alaska moose approach 8 feet in shoulder height. A big bull's antlers will tower some 12 feet off the ground when he is standing fully erect, head up. Mine measured 110 inches in length. This measurement was "around the curve" rather than "between the pegs" because the animal wasn't lying straight. (You don't "straighten" downed moose; you don't even pick their heads up!) A really big bull can exceed 10 feet in length. That's big by any standards.

Trophy Categories

Though taxonomists generally recognize four subspecies of North American moose, the Boone and Crockett Club only accepts three classifications, for the Awards Program, which the

Club now jointly sponsors with the NRA. The Club lumps *Alces alces americana* and *Alces alces andersoni* together as being "Canada" moose. All moose taken in Canada, except those in the Yukon which are included in the "Alaska-Yukon" category, are included in their single designation.

Through the years this has generally been a practical and workable approach. But as increasingly more sport and record-book trophy hunting has been done in the westernmost part of the country in the last 20 years or so, this approach has become somewhat questionable. Lumped in with the larger western *andersoni* trophy animals, the eastern *americana* heads today don't have much of a chance to qualify for the records. I suggest that an "Eastern Canada" category be set up to include all moose taken legally and by fair chase in Ontario, Quebec, Labrador, Newfoundland, Nova Scotia, New Brunswick and Maine — roughly coinciding with the range of *americana*. (Though Maine now prohibits moose hunting, its herd size is larger than those in western "moose states," and the herd would continue to thrive with properly controlled hunting.)

This new category would offer some advantages. For one thing, as more and more moose are taken by trophy hunters over the years, the minimum score requirement is inevitably raised higher and higher in order to keep the lists down to a manageable length. Eventually the minimums become so stratospheric that it becomes almost impossible for the serious sportsman to have much of a chance to make the record book no matter how intelligently he plans and how diligently he works at it. This is somewhat the situation with whitetail and mule deer already.

Also a fourth category of moose for trophy purposes would *legitimately* allow more eastern sportsmen to qualify for the honor. I say legitimately because, as mentioned, it appears that the farther west and north one travels, the larger the moose are. Thus, though far more moose have been taken in eastern Canada throughout the last 100 years, only three of the first ten moose in the 1971 record book would fall into the "Eastern" category that I have suggested. And all of these were shot prior to 1915! Only five would qualify from the East in the top twenty heads.

Now that considerable sport hunting is taking place in the central and western provinces, it would appear that the *andersoni* trophies from this area will dominate the lists ever more overwhelmingly in the future. The splitting up of the "Canada" classification would tend to make the competition both more broad based and more equitable.

Getting a Moose

Moose are not particularly armor plated or hard to kill. They are such large animals that they are very difficult to knock right off their feet, though I did it once. I had just descended a lonely, unnamed peak in the Alaska Range. After I picked my way through the dense timber thicket scalloping the base and running out onto the rather flat, bare river valley leading to the next peak, I saw a good 60-inch bull slouching his way upvalley.

This fellow was obviously high in the rut, looking rather tired

This shows boundaries of ranges for trophy scoring. Though "Canada class" moose are not huntable in Maine and Michigan, they are being hunted on a limited basis in northern Minnesota.

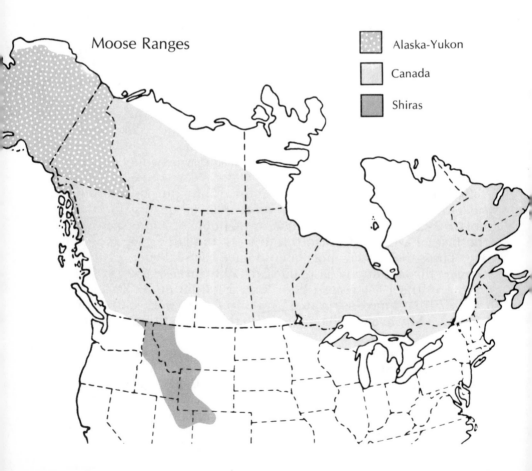

Moose Ranges

Alaska-Yukon

Canada

Shiras

and woebegone and casting a potent scent that only a lady moose could tolerate, much less love. However, he had a nice rack and since we needed meat, I determined to take him, knowing that with proper handling he would still be plenty good on the table. After a 300-yard sneak, I ended up in a position where he would quarter right past me, hardly a hundred yards out and right out in the middle of a sand and gravel bar area. There his nearest cover would be over 200 yards away. This was the kind of situation often depicted on outdoor magazine covers, which, alas, occurs for the hunter all too rarely.

Since I had plenty of time, I assumed a solid sitting position and watched the big fellow approach me through the 3x9 Leupold riflescope. The 7mm Remington Magnum was steady as a rock as the moose picked his way toward me, every hair on his neck and brisket visible. When he finally passed about 90 yards away, I decided to shoot. I had always heard that a moose cleanly shot through the hump will drop like a poleaxed steer, and this was an ideal opportunity to find out with no chance of the game getting away.

The "big 7" boomed and sped its 150-grain pointed Core-Lokt on the way. The results were dramatic to say the least. The huge animal literally dropped in his tracks with a resounding crash that raised dirt and dust six feet in the air.

As I walked over to him, he didn't stir. Though I finally shot him again to put him out, he never struggled to get up nor even lifted his head, which should be expected with downed moose, even those mortally wounded. Moose are so large that they hardly ever die immediately, no matter how well hit.

Immediately upon being hit, he was knocked off his feet and folded up like a rickety card table. He didn't move a foot after impact. Many stories to the contrary, big-game animals are seldom knocked right off their feet without moving in their tracks, no matter how well hit or with what size gun. I've only done it one other time and that was with a nice British Columbia mountain grizzly which I drilled neatly between the eyes with the same gun.

There's a very apt saying: "Moose hurt a lot." This means that practically any well hit moose will lie down shortly after being hit, if not immediately pressed hard. This usually occurs within 200 or 300 yards and is in distinct contrast to the behavior of elk, which run for miles until they die on their feet. Thus, it's generally a good idea to let a well hit moose have a few moments to think things over and lie down before trailing him up, after the shot.

Categories Reconsidered

There is little difference in physical appearance among the three classes of moose recognized for record purposes except gross size considerations. Although the smallest, the Wyoming — or Shiras — moose, does tend to be a bit lighter in color than the others, they all resemble each other in both body and antler conformation much more than the various kinds of caribou. Although the three types of moose do intergrade and there are usually no phenomenal size differences where they do, there is a great difference in size when each of the three types is appraised at its largest or optimum size. Here's the way they stack up in a trophy sense:

Moose Classification	Min. Score to Qualify	World Record Score	Spread of World Record Head	Where Killed
1. Alaska-Yukon	*224 pts.*	*251 pts.*	*77⁴/₈in.*	*Mt. Susitna, Alaska*
2. Canada	*195 pts.*	*238⁵/₈ pts.*	*66⁵/₈in.*	*Bear Lake, Quebec*
3. Wyoming (Shiras)	*155 pts.*	*205⁴/₈ pts.*	*53in.*	*Green River Lake, Wyoming*
4. West-Canada (proposed by author)	*195 pts.*	——	——	——
5. East-Canada (proposed by author)	*175 pts.*	——	——	——

As you can see, there is a marked difference in size among the three trophy classes. Incidentally, though the magnificent head that now leads the entire "Canada" class was killed in Quebec, and is thus in my proposed East-Canada category, that doesn't gainsay splitting the "Canada" class in two. This record head was killed way back in 1914, and eastern heads today are generally much smaller than those taken in the West.

Let's review each of the three current records classifications to assess both the general hunting viability of each and, more particularly, the best trophy opportunities in each case.

1. Alaska-Yukon Class. As the name indicates, only moose from these two areas are admitted under this classification; though I wonder if that might not change in the future. Two game zones (numbers 12 and 19) in the western reaches of the giant Northwest Territories were thrown open to nonresident hunters in the mid-1960s, and this virgin, pristine land has been only lightly hunted by trophy hunters since. Probably no more than 150 or so make the trip each year. This is some of the wildest, most isolated real estate on the planet, and it has not yet been scrutinized thoroughly by the various experts in the wildlife sciences. In a word, I don't think anyone truly knows much about the situation in this lonely area.

The moose from these two NWT game zones in the MacKenzie Mountains are taxonomically lumped with *andersoni* rather than the larger *gigas* to the west. Thus are currently included with the "Canada" class rather than the "Alaska-Yukon" class in the records book. Some very large animals indeed have begun to come out of these areas. And by *large,* I mean 240 points or more!

After more history is gathered on kills made in this area, it may be that Boone and Crockett will want to reconsider the classification of these animals. In any event, as long as they are included in the "Canada" group and compete with farther-south trophies, this is a good place to qualify for the record book if the sportsman is in good condition and is willing to look over some heads. Most of the hunting here is by fly-in and then backpacking. So if you want to try this, be sure you're in good physical condition before you set out.

Alaska is a moose hunter's paradise. This huge land harbors an estimated 150,000 of the big deer, many of them large size indeed by standards farther south. A 60-inch moose is a nice head almost anywhere, though spread isn't everything when assessing a moose trophy. But there are certainly more 60-inch heads in Alaska than anywhere else, and it's not uncommon to see several of them on the same hunt in the better trophy-moose-producing areas.

With the exception of those in the southeastern panhandle, moose are largest in southern Alaska. The Kenai Peninsula, the Alaska Peninsula, the Talkeetnas immediately north of Anchorage, the Chugach immediately east of Anchorage, and the southwestern reaches of the giant Alaska Range all produce enormous trophy-size moose. There was a time when the best hunting for big moose was on the Kenai Peninsula. Then, due to heavy hunting pressure, this changed so that the prime area was the Alaska Peninsula, especially the west side.

The Alaska Peninsula itself has been heavily combed for big heads. And though there are many trophy heads left in that area, some of truly enormous size, the hunting is not what it used to be for the very largest heads. The east side of the

Dressing and butchering a big bull moose is a formidable task for a beginner. For this, it's best to have experienced help on hand.

peninsula is probably as good or better than the west because the west is easier hunting and thus has been combed a good bit harder. Best times are late September and early to mid-October when the big bulls are high in the rut and traveling constantly in their incessant quest for lady moose.

Moose hunting doesn't run on the cheap side in Alaska, especially if you are working with a first-class outfitter in a prime trophy area — which, of course, is the best way to do it if you're after real trophy heads. Moose, when hunted alone or in conjunction with caribou, will generally cost in the neighborhood of $150 to $200 for a 7-, 10- or 12-day hunt. The price varies depending upon the length of the hunt; longer hunts are usually a bit cheaper per day, all else being equal — such as area, accommodations, and time of year. Late season hunts can be a bit cheaper, but the weather is colder and more uncertain.

Moose can also be hunted as a part of the general "3 Animal" hunt (usually for caribou, moose and sheep) or "5 Animal" hunt (for moose, caribou, sheep, grizzly, black bear). These hunts which also offer the more expensive "glamor" trophies (grizzly and sheep) are usually more expensive per diem and involve more moving around, which adds to the outfitter's expenses.

Plan on spending $200 to $300 per day for one of these unforgettable hunts. Chances are, if you're hunting with a top outfitter who has a number of camps in prime areas, you'll spend closer to $300 than $200 for your hunting.

Though the moose trophies tend to run a bit smaller in the Yukon, some very nice heads are taken each year. The top Yukon moose in the 1971 Boone and Crockett book occupies 22nd place and barely misses the coveted 240-point mark by a mere $2/8$ of a point. Truly a trophy of a lifetime! As with caribou heads, the fact that the Yukon has been less hunted by trophy hunters is partial reason why Alaskan heads so dominate the list. I am sure that the Alaska heads are larger and that the animal reaches his optimum size there. But in the future, the Yukon heads should begin to show up a bit better than they do now.

Usually the larger heads come from the southern and south-central areas of this vast Yukon Territory. Moose hunting is good. And though there is no official population estimate, the big deer are abundant. Hunting for them is usually on horse-back rather than by plane and foot as in most Alaskan moose hunting. Yet some of the more expensive Alaskan outfitters do offer tundra buggies and various other all-terrain-vehicle (ATV) methods of going after moose. There is little or no moose-only trophy hunting here as in Alaska or British Columbia. Practically all moose are taken as part of a general mixed-game hunt.

The rates for these 14- to 21-day, mixed-game hunts run a bit cheaper than in Alaska, usually ranging from about $125 to $200 per day depending upon the situation. Alaska's recorded kills between both resident and nonresident hunting (excluding unreported native kills) runs around 9,000 moose per year. In the Yukon the figure is about 1,000. To me, it looks as though the Yukon moose certainly aren't being overharvested. The big ones should still be there and dying of old age in many areas.

2. *"Canada" Class.* This category, as the name implies, covers all moose taken anywhere in Canada except in the Yukon. Best chances to make the book occur either in the games zones 12 and 19 of the MacKenzie Mountains of western Northwest Territories or in a small spur of extreme northwest-ern British Columbia up in the Atlin area. This latter area includes moose that are actually taxonomically of the larger *gigas* (Alaska-Yukon) type even though, for convenience of rec-ord keeping, Boone and Crockett draws the line at the border between British Columbia and the Yukon and thus groups them with the smaller "Canada" moose.

As a general rule, the farther north and west you go in Brit-ish Columbia, the larger the caribou. And the farther north and east you look (with the exception of the spur around Atlin), the larger the moose. Thus, many large moose are found around the Muskwa and Prophet river areas. The classic caribou grounds around Cassiar and Dease Lake have, over the years, yielded moose high in the record book, too.

Though I have not been able to secure any sort of population estimate for moose in British Columbia, the number is undoubtedly tremendous, probably larger than that of Alaska. Over 15,000 moose are usually taken each year on recorded kills alone, and this figure approaches 20,000 periodically. The herd must be large indeed to stand this sort of cropping.

Central and southern British Columbia also offer decent moose hunting, though the heads aren't as large as those of the northcountry. Rates for moose hunting in British Columbia vary all over the lot. As you would suspect, hunting in the northern wilderness part of the vast province is more expensive. Rates per day range from $175 to $250 and more if moose are taken as a part of a general all-the-trimmings mixed-game hunt which also features a good chance at sheep and grizzly. British Columbia offers a greater variety of hunting arrangements than any other major North American big-game field.

Their moose-only or moose-and-caribou-only hunts can run from a low of $100 per day (slightly less in the southern and central parts of the province). But here, you're into late hunts, hunts without horses, or hunts with several hunters per guide. Per diem prices run up to $150 or more for the best of trophy moose hunting in the far north where you've got a good chance for a record book head. The thrifty trophy hunter bent on the northern stretches should not overlook the attractive possibility of lower-cost moose hunting in late-season, occurring in late October and into November.

The weather is usually brutally cold during the late season. However, you'll probably run into fewer storms and thus lose less hunting time due to storms than during the fall-into-winter transition of the early part of the season. The northcountry is truly lovely in its mantle of snow as the deep cold of the near-arctic winter envelops it. I think the sportsman who visits the northcountry only during the deceptively short and mild late summer and early fall season is missing something. The true nature of the land is revealed better during the winter, with the bonus that wolves are much easier to see and shoot on these hunts. That's a nice bonus trophy in any sportsman's book.

Be prepared for the deep cold of one of these late hunts. Though it may vary from year to year and from area to area, you should be prepared to withstand and function well in cold that plummets the mercury to the minus 20 or 30 degree mark, sometimes even colder. Before setting out, have your teeth checked by a dentist because this kind of cold often seems to encourage painful tooth or ear problems. Also be sure that you will be able to keep your ears and hands warm; here several extra pairs of mittens serve far better than "cold fingered" gloves.

Alberta has a tremendous herd of moose estimated at some 140,000 animals. Harvesting is relatively heavy but still well within the normal reproductive capability of the herd. Though two of the top five moose heads in the "Canada" category came from Alberta (taken in 1947 and in 1960), this is not necessarily the area that I would go to for a record book head. However, there are still a good many large bulls taken, especially in the west-central and northwest portions of the province. Costs run about the same or slightly less than those for British Columbia.

Saskatchewan has a large moose herd that has supported annual reported kills of some 7,000 to 9,000 animals. But in recent years this has dropped a bit to the 4,000 to 6,000 range. Hunter success ratios generally run high — 50 percent and better among both residents and nonresidents. And surprisingly, two of the top heads in the book came from this province, little explored by American sportsmen. These heads, Number 3 and Number 5 in the book, were both taken in 1959, and for the reasonable costs of $60 to $100 per day (depending on accommodations, area, hunters per guide, and so on), a sportsman could do worse than to try this area and sample some of the almost-virgin fishing still available in many of the far-northern lakes. This is a wild, uninhabited part of the province, this northern quarter of Saskatchewan. And while it lacks the grandeur of the mountain country farther west, it nevertheless harbors some of the largest and purest lakes in the world. It has a lovely, wistful beauty all its own.

Most of the same comments may be made about Manitoba that apply to Saskatchewan. The estimated moose herd here is some 45,000. But only about half as many moose licenses are sold, and only about a third to a half as many animals are taken. The animals don't run quite as large here as you move east, but some nice heads are taken each year. One of the reasons that the highest Manitoba head in the book occupies 57th place is that this region has received little or no attention from trophy hunters in past years. Practically all the U.S. sportsmen trekking north into this land are meat hunters or only "trophy hunters" of the most casual sort, merely looking for a "nice" bull.

Again, I would not necessarily select Manitoba to try for a record book head. But the hunting is relatively inexpensive here and if a sportsman is knowledgeable and willing to look over a few heads, chances are he can take a decent moose.

Ontario has a large herd of some 125,000 animals. But considering the tremendous area of moose-inhabitable ground involved, even by Canadian standards, the moose population is not quite as dense as in some areas farther west. Ontario is hunted rather hard for moose and has been a classic moose hunting area for U.S. sportsmen for many years. Generally some 65,000 to 80,000 moose permits are sold each year with around 20 percent of them going to U.S. hunters.

The kill will generally run around 12,000 to 14,000. By western Canadian standards, this tallies out at a relatively low hunter success ratio of about 27 to 30 percent. We are now moving from the range of *Alces alces andersoni* (the northwestern moose) into the range of *Alces alces americana* (the eastern moose). (The taxonomic differentiation is based on some relatively minor cranial differences.)

I think it can be conclusively demonstrated that fewer really large trophies are being taken from Ontario and Quebec than from the more westerly provinces. It's difficult to say how much of this is due to the fact that the western animals are somewhat larger to begin with and how much is due to the more intensive harvest in the east, with fewer bulls living to the ripe old age of 7 to 10 years when the prime antlers are borne.

In spite of the fact that several large heads ranking high in the record book come from Quebec and Ontario—and *Maine!* —I would not try for a record book head in these eastern areas if I could hunt farther west. I wouldn't try, that is, unless the "Canada" moose category were split in two by the Boone and Crockett Club as I suggested earlier in this chapter—thus affording the eastern hunters a fairer chance of taking a qualifying head.

This is not to downplay the general moose hunting in Ontario in the least, though. The hunting is reasonable with 7-day hunts available for as little as $350 to $500 if you'll furnish much of your own food and gear, stay in "housekeeping" cabins, and hunt on a lightly guided basis of several hunters per guide. The chances are less, especially for a trophy bull, than on a western hunt, but then the hunt costs only about one-fourth to one-third as much and is much closer to home for the

Horses, canoes, or all-terrain vehicles are a godsend on most moose hunts. A big rack will weigh 50 to 80 pounds. And a green hide, which tans into a nice buckskin or hair-on rug, can easily weigh 100 pounds. Add to this a quarter-ton of meat, and you've got some freight to move.

East Coast sportsman. And this reduces travel time and expense.

Quebec moose hunting is rather similar to Ontario's except the numbers are lower. They have an estimated 75,000 head with almost as many hunters after them. And with a kill running about half of Ontario's, Quebec's hunter success ratio is considerably lower, generally running around 15 percent. Of course both of these hunter success ratios include many residents who are casual moose hunters. The serious nonresident hunter employing competent professional help could expect to have much better probability of success than the 15 and 30 percent figures I've noted. However, this better probability is for *any* moose and not for an outstanding trophy. Best areas to hunt in these two provinces would be Sioux Lookout in Ontario and the Atibi Region in Quebec. Costs to hunt in Quebec often run a bit higher than in Ontario, and the widespread dependence on French among natives can cause minor communications problems if you're not familiar with rudiments of the language. Though usually you can pick up enough to communicate essentials with a guide who knows at least some English. Quebec does have a certain charm and ambience all its own, due to its Gallic culture.

As long as we're talking about the eastern or *americana* moose, it's appropriate to include a word about Maine's herd. There are now about 14,000 moose in northern Maine, probably more than good game management practices would dictate relative to the carrying capacity of the range. There has not been an open season on the big deer since 1934, and unfortunately this is being continued more due to political considerations and misplaced sentiment than to scientific game management principles, this through no fault of Maine's Department of Game.

Maine's herd of 14,000 could stand a sizable harvest—this statement supported by the fact that the herd is undoubtedly as large or larger than those of the "moose states" in the West, such as Montana, Wyoming and Idaho. There should even be enough game to allow limited nonresident hunting which would provide exciting larger-than-deer sport to eastern sportsmen. And, though I would not recommend this area as the place to secure a record book head, it's interesting to note that the 9th and 10th place "Canada" heads came from Maine, though back in 1900 and 1880, respectively. With no hunting over the years and some old, oversized bulls undoubtedly dying of old age in the herd, there should be some very nice heads up there.

Labrador, New Brunswick and Nova Scotia are of little or no interest to the nonresident moose hunter because they allot little or no moose hunting to visitors.

Newfoundland has a sizable moose herd variously estimated at between 50,000 and 80,000 animals. Moose were introduced to the island around the turn of the century. Since then they have thrived mightily—practically taken over the place. Alas, the native woodland caribou haven't fared so well, whether due to indirect competition with moose, as some continue to believe, or not, as the Wildlife Division continues to state.

Newfoundland is combed hard for moose with some 25,000 or more moose licenses of all types being sold each year and around 10,000 to 12,000 animals being harvested for a 40 to 50 percent hunter success ratio. Newfoundland is relatively close by for the eastern hunters. But of late authorities have been raising the "nonresident alien" license costs for Yanks to really stratospheric heights.

This is not the area to pick up a record head. Though, with

this many animals killed each year, naturally a few nice heads do come in. The highest ranking head from Newfoundland in the record book is a fairly modest 164th place with a score of 197²/₈ and carrying a spread of 55²/₈ inches. I do not believe that the moose get very large here even at optimum size and, of course, the fact that the area is hunted so intensively means that few animals live long enough to reach the trophy bearing years of seven to ten.

3. Shiras, or Wyoming, Class. This third category which encompasses the Shiras moose killed in the few western areas allowing hunting is not of much interest. The moose is basically a far north animal and those herds that do precariously exist in the U.S. must be regarded as nothing more than a bit of a curiosity — albeit a nice one.

The place to see goodly numbers of moose and large moose is north of the border, in their more natural range. Since a moose's attractiveness is largely tied up with its sheer size — raw bulk and mass of both body and antler — I can't find it in my heart to get very excited about a junior-size edition of the animals farther north. Since the average sportsman generally only mounts one or maybe two moose heads — unless he has an unused barn to hang them in — it doesn't make sense to settle for small heads. Another factor is that a good taxidermist will charge anywhere from $200 to $400 to put up a first-class shoulder mount on a big moose — the price determined mainly by the size of the head and the amount of repair work necessary. And that doesn't even include the "incidentals" of packing, crating and shipping which come to substantial amounts of coin.

Shiras moose are generally lighter in color and less well antlered than the other races. The world's record head of this type only scores 205⁴/₈ points and has a spread of 53 inches. Many feel that on the average hunt any Shiras head with more than a 40-inch spread is a good one.

And most feel that a head of over 45 inches is big enough to break out the ceremonial brandy. All too often when Shiras heads of between 45 to 50 inches are taken, they are rather spindly, signalling, as with all moose, that the optimum spread is being approached at the cost of other desirable trophy characteristics such as palm width, brow palm width and mass and number of points.

I have never killed a Shiras moose nor do I plan to. Most that I have seen have led a rather well managed and well regulated life and thus appear to have all the "wildness" or "gameness" of a barnyard heifer. However, generalizations are always dangerous and somewhat incorrect when applied to nondomestic animals, and I'm sure there are Shiras that are, in some places or at some times, a more sporting proposition than I have observed.

Trophy Standards. Here are my notions as to what constitutes good and outstanding point scores in each of the three currently recognized classifications.

Type of Moose	Good Trophy	Outstanding Trophy	Record Head
1. Alaska-Yukon	*205*	*215*	*224*
2. Canada	*175*	*185*	*195*
3. Shiras	*135*	*145*	*155*

Similar figures for my proposed "East-Canada" classification could be arrived at by subtracting 20 points from each of the three above figures for the existing "Canada" category.

Estimating and Evaluating Trophies

Moose are among the most difficult of all trophies for me to estimate. And I find that to be a fairly common situation both among sportsmen in general and among outdoor authorities. All full grown bulls are so *big* in body size and mass that they dwarf even their huge antlers. Moose are simply so gigantic in scale that they tend to throw the eye off in a fashion not experienced when assessing smaller species.

This very size also tends to work against many trophy hunters who are only mildly serious in their quest for a moose trophy. All the moose look so big, even if the hunter has taken elk or caribou—much less if he's a deer hunter after his first larger-than-deer game—that he tends to settle for the first "nice" one that he sees. That's a shame because that first "nice" one practically never is nice. The only way to judge moose or any other trophy is to compare them against their own kind and not be overawed and rushed into a shot because he looks so blasted big and well antlered compared to a Pennsylvania whitetail or a Montana mulie. Unfortunately, many guides tend to "conspire" with this "first *nice* moose" approach. Why not?

The client seems happy and it gets them off the hook. He got his game and it's no bark off the guide's tree if, some months later the hunter compares his antlers with others and becomes more sophisticated on the subject—with the result that the hunter becomes very unhappy about having taken the first halfway decent head he saw rather than waiting a bit.

Actually, as far as literal number of measurements and considerations in scoring, moose heads are a simple affair. Only 14 different considerations (13 if no abnormal points are present) are involved in scoring. This is fewer than for any other antlered or horned game on the Boone and Crockett scoring system and far less than the maximum of 41 considerations involved with caribou scoring and 39 with elk or whitetail deer. And yet, even though scoring moose heads is a pretty simple affair I must re-emphasize that you should observe as many moose heads as possible before going on a trophy hunt in order to "up scale" your eyes for the perspective required for reliable field estimation. Unfortunately, the shoulder mounts of moose only hint at the enormous body size. But estimating and then checking out the scores of mounted heads still remains the best single way to train yourself to estimate moose heads accurately.

Spread is probably overemphasized more with moose than with any other antlered trophy. There are several reasons for this. First, the conformation of the unique moose antlers themselves is such that, by extending almost straight out from the head on each side, they lend themselves to a "spread" emphasis. Also, talking "spread" is a handy shorthand when discussing moose size that saves a lot of verbiage and time. I do it all the time myself.

And yet spread can be very misleading at times. The true measure of a fine moose head is its *total mass,* of which spread is only one characteristic—not even the most important one in the opinion of many. Moose antlers don't have the sweeping good looks of a nice elk rack nor the many-pointed splendor of a big caribou rack. But they do have an almost unbelievable bulk and mass. I think that using the weight as an additional scoring characteristic might improve the method of scoring moose trophies. Of course, this would have to be supervised to assure uniform weight of skull plate. Several international scoring systems other than Boone and Crockett do include weight, and nowhere would weight be more appropriate in scoring North American game than for moose antlers.

All too often the extremely wide moose antlers are spindly and uninspiring, all the development having gone into spread

RECORDS OF NORTH AMERICAN
BIG GAME COMMITTEE

BOONE AND CROCKETT CLUB

RETURN TO:
N. A. B. G. Awards Program
1600 Rhode Island Ave. N. W.
Washington, D. C.   20036

MINIMUM SCORE
MOOSE: Alaska-Yukon 224
       Canada   195
       Wyoming 155

MOOSE

KIND OF MOOSE

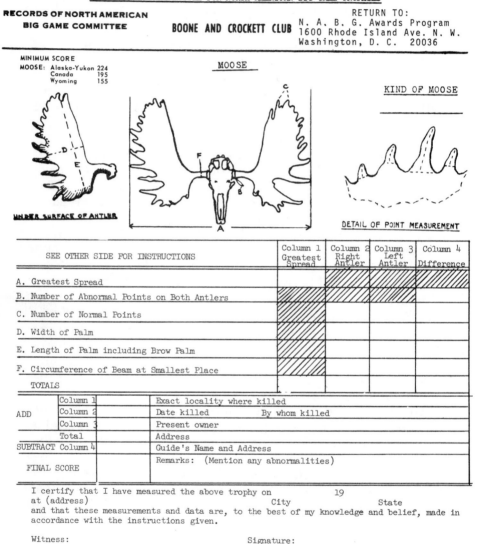

UNDER SURFACE OF ANTLER

DETAIL OF POINT MEASUREMENT

SEE OTHER SIDE FOR INSTRUCTIONS	Column 1 Greatest Spread	Column 2 Right Antler	Column 3 Left Antler	Column 4 Difference
A. Greatest Spread				
B. Number of Abnormal Points on Both Antlers				
C. Number of Normal Points				
D. Width of Palm				
E. Length of Palm including Brow Palm				
F. Circumference of Beam at Smallest Place				
TOTALS				

ADD	Column 1		Exact locality where killed
	Column 2		Date killed By whom killed
	Column 3		Present owner
	Total		Address
SUBTRACT Column 4			Guide's Name and Address
FINAL SCORE			Remarks: (Mention any abnormalities)

I certify that I have measured the above trophy on   19
at (address)   City   State
and that these measurements and data are, to the best of my knowledge and belief, made in
accordance with the instructions given.

Witness: Signature:

Boone & Crockett Official Measurer

INSTRUCTIONS

<u>All measurements</u> must be made with a flexible steel tape to the nearest one-eighth of an inch. Wherever it is necessary to change direction of measurement, mark a control point and swing tape at this point. To simplify addition, please enter fractional figures in <u>eighths</u>.

<u>Official measurements</u> cannot be taken for at least sixty days after the animal was killed. <u>Please submit photographs</u> of trophy front and sides.

A. <u>Greatest Spread</u> — measured in a straight line at right angles to the center line of the skull.

B. <u>Number of Abnormal Points on Both Antlers</u> — Abnormal points are generally considered to be those non-typical in shape or location.

C. <u>Number of Normal Points.</u> Normal points are those which project from the outer edge of the antler. To be counted a point, a projection must be at least one inch long and the length must exceed the breadth of the point's base. The breadth need not be computed from the deepest adjacent dips in the palmation. The length may be measured to any location -- at least one inch from the tip -- at which the length of the point exceeds its breadth.

D. <u>Width of Palm</u> — taken in contact with the surface across the under side of the palm, at right angles to the inside edge of palm, to a dip between points at the greatest width of palm. Measure width of palm from mid-points of edges of palm.

E. <u>Length of Palm including Brow Palm</u> — taken in contact with the surface along the under side of the palm, parallel to the inner edge from dips between points at the greatest length of palm. If a deep bay is present in the palm, measure palm length across the open bay if the proper line of measurement crosses the bay.

F. <u>Circumference of Beam</u> at Smallest Place — needs no explanation.

* * * * * * * * * * * * *

TROPHIES OBTAINED ONLY BY FAIR CHASE MAY BE ENTERED
IN ANY BOONE AND CROCKETT CLUB BIG GAME COMPETITION

To make use of the following methods shall be deemed UNFAIR CHASE and unsportsmanlike, and any trophy obtained by use of such means is disqualified from entry in any Boone and Crockett Club big game competition:

    I. Spotting or herding game from the air, followed by landing in its vicinity for pursuit;

    II. Herding or pursuing game with motor-powered vehicles;

    III. Use of electronic communications for attracting, locating or observing game, or guiding the hunter to such game.

* * * * * * * * * * * *

I certify that the trophy scored on this chart was not taken in UNFAIR CHASE as defined above by the Boone and Crockett Club.

I certify that it was not spotted or herded by guide or hunter from the air followed by landing in its vicinity for pursuit, nor herded or pursued on the ground by motor-powered vehicles.

I further certify that no electronic communications were used to attract, locate, observe, or guide the hunter to such game; and that it was taken in full compliance with the local game laws or regulations of the state, province or territory.

Date_____ Signature of Hunter _____

This chart is reproduced with permission of the Boone and Crockett Club, which, together with the National Rifle Association, co-sponsors the North American Big Game Awards Program.

This is a very large Alaska-Yukon moose with a spread over 60 inches. He shows good, but not spectacular, palms and nice brow palms.

and much of this coming from overlong points sticking too far out from the skinny, undersized palms. When I made my first Alaskan trip I shot a good moose with better than a 60-inch spread. I was pretty excited about him until, at the end of the trip, I returned to base camp and saw a couple of tremendous moose that other hunters had taken. There was one sweeping head with a 73½-inch spread taken by a grand guy, a Connecticut doctor in his 50s taking his long awaited "trip of a lifetime." This one, exceeding six feet in spread, is big even by the best Alaskan standards.

But sitting next to this fine trophy was another rack that completely dominated it. Though only 65 inches in spread, this rack was a grand moose, a true monarch of the *Alces* tribe. Giant palms cupped themselves into unbelievably wide and heavy bases for the massive but not overlong points. The brow palms were tremendous, dwarfing mine which had "spreads" themselves of 23 inches and 24½ inches—no mean width for *brow* palms. The gigantic brow palms on this head had 6 and 7 points respectively (mine had 4 on each side) and both exceeded 30 inches in spread. Spread of brow palm is not a scoring factor and it has nothing directly to do with how many points a head will score. But it is a handy secondary way I use of gauging and comparing the mass of really big heads. Of course the size of the "body" of the brow palm, the evenness and weight of the points and other factors also affect the overall attractiveness of the brow palms.

I picked up the two antler racks. The wide one was hefty indeed, probably weighing around 70 pounds even with its narrow, spindly palms and skinny brow palms that almost looked to be glued on as an afterthought by mother nature. The big head must have weighed a good 90-plus pounds; though sadly we had no scales to check this. Two good moose heads — one rather wide and unusual and the other a trophy of a lifetime, a moose that would dominate any trophy room.

I rough-scored the bigger of the green heads at a bit over 240. I figured that even after drying this one would be well up in the books. Since I didn't see this head in the latest record book, I doubt that it was measured officially.

Incidentally, the head was taken by a besotted Spanish duke, over with an entourage of lackeys, handmade double-barreled .375 H&H magnums (which he also used as sheep rifles but that's another story) and enough booze to keep the Bulgarian army blotto for weeks. Our friend had wandered outside his tent one day to answer nature's undeniable call when he saw the huge beast hardly 100 yards away. A short but unsteady trip back to the tent to secure his highly gilded weapon and several shaky shots (a moose is tough to miss broadside at that range unless you really work at it) and our royal sport had a fantastic trophy.

When the other hunters and guides returned that evening, exhausted after a long, tough day of climbing and walking, they could hardly believe their eyes. Such is trophy hunting, my friends!

There are several things to guard against when estimating moose heads. Long points coming well off the palms tend to make a rack look larger than it is. The points add to the overall spread by their long length but often indicate that rather than the spread being wide the palms are just narrow. Somewhat shorter but very heavy points more often indicate a heavier, "balanced" head that may be as wide or wider in total spread and much higher scoring due to the far wider palms.

Another thing that tends to throw me off is that most moose antlers look larger to me when viewed from the side than from the front. Their giant mass is more in evidence from the side. Also, when sizing up a moose rack from the side, don't get carried away until you take a look at the other side. It may not measure up to the first side or it may be very uneven, costing you many points in the "difference" column on the Boone and Crockett score sheet.

When appraising a head from the front, I try to evaluate how wide and heavy the palms are as well as how wide the total spread is. I know that the wider and larger the rack is, the more it tends to "lay back" rather than "stick up" when looked at from the front. The real breaking point tends to come around the highly important 55- to 60-inch spread range (more short-hand, to be sure). As most heads *legitimately* reach this spread they tend to "lay down" markedly when viewed from the front, but all this of course depends to a degree on the relative eleva-tions of the moose and the viewer. Beyond 60 inches most good heads are significantly "flatter." So, if your moose rack sticks way up from the ears rather than canting back a bit, chances are

This is another very good Alaska-Yukon bull just coming out of velvet in late August. His spread goes well over 60 inches. The many points, excellent palms and huge brows make him a strong candidate for the records.

you need to let him grow a bit. Also, check to see if your antler palms, when viewed from the front, tend to curve back toward each other at their ends, rather than continuing to diverge.

The greatest spread of a moose rack is classically pictured as occurring between the one or two longest side points immediately above the brow palms, but this is not always the case. Many times the widest spread can come way out the palms, if the palms continue to diverge rather than converge as they extend.

When viewed from the side, a really nice moose in the 60-inch-or-better class should have antlers that both lay down rather than stick up and that seem to come about halfway back on his body. It is necessary for them to both lay down and to carry the magic 5-foot-or-better spread in order for them to approach the middle of his back.

The main thing when estimating moose is to take your time and don't be rushed into a snap decision because the *animal* looks big. All of them do. But the antlers are what is scored, not the animal's body size.

Moose are rather trusting animals where not hunted or harried. However, they soon learn to be more suspicious, and many of the Alaskan and north Canadian areas where most trophy moose shots were taken at 50 to 75 yards in times gone by, now more often require 150 to 200 yard shots. So, when you're after a prize moose that will occupy a central place of honor over the fireplace or in your trophy room take your time. (Because they're so *big,* moose heads usually are centered with other smaller heads grouped around.)

Take your time both when you evaluate the head and when you decide to shoot him. Then approach your downed bull carefully. With one spasmodic toss of that huge head, he can turn you inside out, whether by accident or design.

The Most Elegant Game: Caribou

8

For many years I've had a love affair with caribou. And why not? Of all the marvelous big games species on this fauna-rich continent, they are undoubtedly the most elegant in our cast of North American trophy game. Their powerful slab sided bodies — stuffed round as a sausage when they are in their pre-rut fat — are predominantly seal gray in color and, at their best, are accented with a flowing white mane. But their real glory and the thing that makes them a trophy hunter's delight, is their astonishingly large antlers. And not only are these antlers *big*, but they come in a bewildering variety of "standard" shapes and configurations. No other deer — or horned animal, for that matter — exhibits such a wide variety among its typical heads. This naturally adds to the trophy interest since it would be possible for a hunter to collect three, four or five of the big heads and not really duplicate any of them.

It is well known that trophy-size adult caribou bulls carry the largest antlers relative to their body size of any deer in the world. A big bull will stand 50 to 60 inches high at the shoulder and, at his best, will have antlers that may even exceed that shoulder height in beam length, and match or nearly match it in spread. Only a very rare Alaskan moose, standing 80 to 90 inches at the shoulder with antlers that may have a spread of 70 to 80 inches can even begin to match either feature. And that's primarily due to the unique shape of moose antlers, whereby spread is maximized, as opposed to the more common shape of antlers on all other deer species. Nor can elk or red deer equal caribou proportions, even at their optimum.

The first time a trophy hunter is exposed to big adult caribou bulls, he usually suffers a temporary loss of equilibrium. Eyes that are used to scanning and estimating whitetail and mule

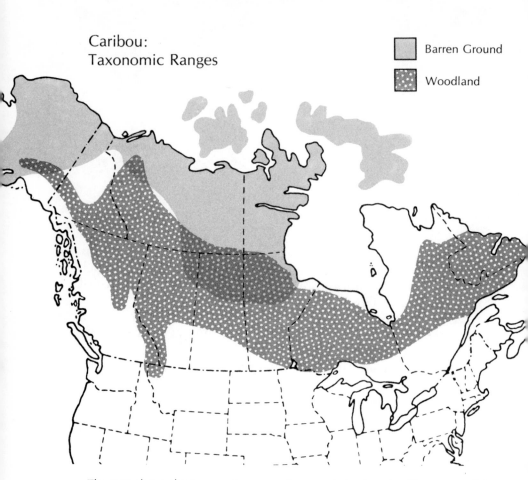

Caribou:
Taxonomic Ranges

Barren Ground

Woodland

The map shows the two most commonly accepted — though still controversial — "types" of caribou in the taxonomic sense. The chart below indicates political boundaries of the four "types" recognized for trophy purposes.

Caribou: Trophy Ranges

Locale	Barren Ground	Mountain	Q-L	Woodland
ALASKA	X			
YUKON	X			
N W T	X			
MANITOBA	X			
SASKATCHEWAN	X			
ONTARIO	X			
BRITISH COLUMBIA		X		
ALBERTA		X		
QUEBEC/				
LABRADOR			X	
NEWFOUNDLAND				X

Caribou have enormous hoofs, far larger than the heavier-bodied elk. These big hoofs carry the caribou over boggy tundra. This hoof and dew claw track splays to nearly 10 inches and was made by a medium-large Osborn bull.

deer heads, or even elk heads, boggle at the sight of animals weighing only about half as much as a large bull elk and yet carrying antlers that may be every bit as wide in spread and as long. Also, the shovel or shovels (brow palms), the spread of large bez (second points) and the impressive palmation in the antler tops all add together to make a somewhat more exotic and imposing rack than that of even a prime 6-point bull elk.

It is invaluable training for the trophy hunter to spend as much time as possible before the hunt sizing up mounted heads, estimating them and then measuring and scoring them out. It's also valuable practice to make estimates based on photos of large heads when you can verify the scoring "basics" such as beam length, spread, length of specific points. This helps you to develop an "eye" for each species. This exercise is particularly valuable for any species that you haven't hunted, and for caribou it's essential. Otherwise, you can end up shooting a head that you shouldn't. They all look so big to the untrained, untutored eye. I have even seen guides fooled by caribou heads. Or sometimes a hunter may be so bedazzled that he insists on taking the head against the guide's advice.

Caribou are the most graceful of all the large deer, striding along in that spongy, effortless gait that is a joy to watch. Ironically, for this elegant locomotion they depend on outsized, circus-clown feet. The foot of a 350-pound bull caribou may be wider and almost twice as long as that of a 650- to 700-pound bull elk. These big feet are part of a supreme adaptation to the harsh far northern environment where caribou thrive best. And the feet help the animals to easily swim the many large bodies of water and cross the many muskegs and bogs that they encounter on their endless migrations.

Caribou are circumpolar animals. Most taxonomists classify all the caribou and reindeer types that inhabit northern North America and Eurasia as a single species, *Rangifer tarandus*. However, when you get down to the more refined level of subspecies, or races, caribou are a taxonomist's delight — and a layman's nightmare — because of the jumble of conflicting claims as to how many different "legitimate" types there are. Suffice to say that all caribou are called just that in North America, while their European and Asian brethren, whether wild or domesticated, are known as reindeer.

Our caribou is a considerably larger, more vigorous and better antlered animal than any of the Eurasian reindeer types, though the two will readily interbreed if mingled together — to the detriment of the caribou gene pool! Caribou have never been domesticated on any scale and the largest of any that I have heard of is a remarkable bull taken in 1968 from an introduced herd on Adak Island that weighed some 700 pounds. For a caribou, that is simply enormous because the generally quoted maximum weight runs 400 to 450 pounds. Yet I have killed one that I'll believe to my dying day weighed an honest 500 pounds; he was a big Osborn bull from the northern British Columbia Cassiars. It is not uncommon for introduced herds to reach fantastic sizes, when initially turned loose in prime territory. A similar event occurred when elk were introduced onto Afognak Island off the south Alaskan coast; a few of the enormous bulls taken weighed an estimated 1300 to 1500 pounds! Unfortunately for the trophy hunter, the antler growth is not on the same scale with the bodies of these outsized specimens.

Hunters are a down-to-earth and practical lot. The Boone and Crockett Club's policy of recognizing four separate caribou types for record keeping purposes is as realistic and accurate as any. And it's better than most. Their rationale is basically geographic, and though it is somewhat arbitrary and contradicts majority taxonomic thought in a few instances (as any reasonable system would have to), it works well. One example of a contradiction is that while most taxonomists place the giant Osborn caribou of northern British Columbia in the barren ground caribou group, the Boone and Crockett system, since it draws the line at the British Columbia and Yukon border, considers the Osborn to be in the mountain caribou group. However, this is no major tragedy and establishing boundary lines among the major trophy classifications to conform with major provincial boundaries serves to simplify record keeping greatly and bring order out of what otherwise might be chaos. An attempt at a too-elaborate scheme would be unwieldy and confusing; so basically the four classifications are these:

1. Barren Ground Type: trophies from Alaska, the Yukon NWT, Manitoba, Saskatchewan, Ontario.
2. Mountain Type: trophies from British Columbia and Alberta
3. Woodland Type: trophies from Newfoundland
4. Quebec-Labrador Type: trophies from Labrador and northern Quebec

Caribou are the most spectacular of trophies but they aren't the wiliest, most intelligent game animal around. In fact, they are downright dumb. Or at least by all the yardsticks one would reasonably use to assess animal intelligence (general alertness, attention span, apparent ability to count, etc.), they don't come out as college material. Moose and elk, especially the latter, are far cannier animals.

Most caribou, except for the woodland type in some instances, are found in mountain country or on vast open barrens. Mountain animals, such as the sheep and goat, and plains dwellers, such as pronghorn, are noted for their extraordinarily sharp eyesight. The caribou is the exception to that rule, though he inhabits those same two environments. (The tundra is actually a vast desert plain, with little or no precipitation.

The caribou's eyes are rather dull when compared to those of other big-game animals. And based on my limited experiments of edging directly up to caribou, slowly and with no lateral movement, they appear to have even more limited depth-perception than other similar large herbivores. Eyes-front carnivores have considerably superior depth-perception necessary for them to accurately chase and strike their prey. In fact, it seems to me that the caribou doesn't see as well as the moose even though the latter evolved as an inhabitant of dense woodland areas and is not particularly noted for its keen eyesight; though during this era the moose has ventured high up into the mountains.

Antlers on a young bull like this one astound neophyte caribou hunters conditioned to mule deer and whitetails. Such a head often appears good enough to shoot until the hunter sees some large bulls.

Caribou don't appear to have any outstandingly sharp senses as compared to their peers. Their small ears aren't nearly as sensitive as those of the moose or elk, and their sense of smell, while reasonably good, doesn't approach that of the bear or moose. Caribou are inordinately curious animals, rivaled only by pronghorn or unhunted sheep in that respect. It is frequently possible, in the less inhabited parts of their range anyway, to hide the man-silhouette by kneeling and "wave them up" by swinging extended arms to and fro slowly, much as the old-time market hunters did with the then unsophisticated pronghorn. If you want to try this trick, make sure the wind is right.

The short attention span of caribou is apparent when they bolt upon getting your wind and then, more times than not, forget why they bolted as soon as they lose your wind and circle back toward you to check things out all over again. I've had any number of bulls, some of real trophy caliber, do this three or four times until they finally got it through that thick skull of theirs that I was up to no good. Or else, more likely, they just forgot all about me and wandered off to be bemused by something else. Caribou definitely aren't as smart as elk or whitetail, nor are they as wary as hunted populations of sheep or prong-horn.

Nor are caribou noted for any outstanding vitality when shot, as are goat and elk. Although I've never knocked one right off his feet or almost right off his feet as I have with some other species, I've never had one travel over 50 yards after being hit.

So, having said all that, why do caribou captivate me so? Part of it is their magnificent good looks. Anything *that* beautiful is a delight to observe in the wild and a gorgeous addition to the trophy room. For another, their grace and elegance of move-ment add to their overall attractiveness. When I think of the elk, the adjective "regal" comes to mind. For moose, it's "power-ful." With the caribou, the word has to be "elegant."

Still another salient point for the trophy hunter is the cari-bou's tremendous variety of antler shapes, all beautiful and impressive. When you see one goat or pronghorn, you've pretty well seen them all. (I'm talking here about typical heads, not freaks or nontypicals.) Sheep vary a bit more, especially in body and horn color among the four basic types, and there is some variation in horn configuration. Moose don't vary a lot among the various types except in gross size and somewhat in forma-tion of the brow tines. But no trophy rack varies more than the caribou's, and the fact that many of these variations are some-what predictable among the four types means that an increas-ing number of trophy hunters may want to collect good speci-mens of all four types to illustrate these variations.

Three types of caribou (barren ground, mountain and Quebec-Labrador) still have rather large populations and thus are attainable by almost everyone seriously interested. The relatively high travel and hunting costs associated with the first two types and the difficulty of drawing a permit for the wood-land caribou, with the $500 license if you do, add just enough difficulty to the enterprise to make matters interesting. Since caribou live in the far reaches of the continent, remote from civilization, the main task is to find them. Once you locate these always-on-the-move migratory animals, stalking and shooting are generally not overly difficult. So depending upon where you live, a fair amount of travel cost may be associated with hunting them.

Another part of their allure is indefinable. They live in such harsh, forbidding environments so far away from the regalia of man and his civilization that the sight of a big bull caribou, wild and free, is so romantically *wild* that it is equaled by few other hunting scenes.

Having gone to some length to indicate how dim and unwary most caribou are most of the time, I should add that I've never had a really big bull come easy. Though caribou can actually get in your way when you are hunting other game and often trot right up to you or let you approach them rather closely, it seems that once you spot and set out after one particular big bull, things never work that conveniently.

I waved up and shot my first big barren ground at an easy 150 yards. But I should add that that was only after five strenuous days of chasing the same damnably elusive bull up and down half a dozen mountains bordering that same valley. Caribou are constantly on the move, and a walking caribou will quickly outdistance a running or trotting man in the mountains. It's simply amazing how quickly they eat up the ground with that deceptively casual looking shuffle that they employ when not alarmed. My biggest Osborn bull came only after a tough three-hour climb that was rougher than 90 percent of sheep stalks and steep enough to satisfy most confirmed goat hunters. Caribou are often found high on the mountains, up above sheep and almost as high as goats. Though they don't actually traverse or inhabit country as rough as goats do, at times *you* may have to in order to intercept them for a shot.

Antlers

Let's talk about those different types of antlers. There are some characteristics that readily relate to the four different types, by type, and we'll cover them after reviewing the four in detail. Then, there are other variations that can crop up almost at random, on any of the four types.

On most typical heads, one antler carries an extended "shovel" (brow tine) that is palmated. And the other antler generally carries a prong that is parallel to the shovel and may or may not be as long, but it is not palmated like the shovel. In some instances this prong will be almost completely missing. In other cases the highly prized "double shovel" will be evident and some experts have estimated that this occurs only on one in every 10,000 animals. Whether this ratio has any empirical basis or is just a conversational license, there is no doubt that a true double-shovel bull is very rare. (Some hunters tend to generously bestow the term to a head with any second upswept or very slightly palmated brow prong. But the true double-shovel head should have an "honest" second shovel at least 3 or 4 inches in depth — better that it run 5 or 6 inches.)

These front and side views of the same barren ground bull show a good "lower story" consisting of double shovels (with heavy primary shovel) and nice bez formations. The main beams are only moderate in length and have weak tops. That is, the tops are spindly rather than palmated, they show few points, and they lack *two* long top points on each side (preferably over 20 inches each). Though this head is not a record, it is moderately good, with good double shovels. For the hunter who has already collected a good caribou head but never a double-shovel bull, this fellow would pose a dilemma. (The diagram below shows the probable way judges would designate this bull's top features.)

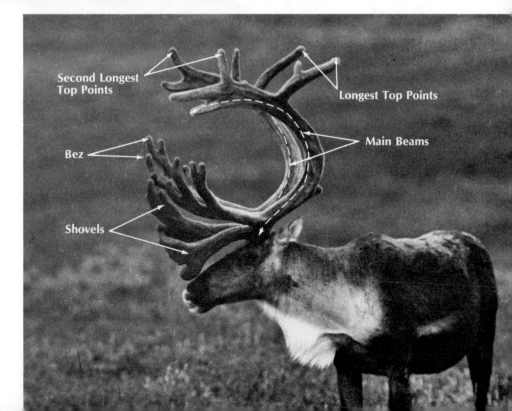

Second Longest Top Points

Longest Top Points

Main Beams

Bez

Shovels

**RECORDS OF NORTH AMERICAN
BIG GAME COMMITTEE**

BOONE AND CROCKETT CLUB

RETURN TO:
N. A. B. G. Awards Program
1600 Rhode Island Ave, N. W.
Washington, D. C. 20036

MINIMUM SCORE: Barren Ground - 400
Mountain - 390
Quebec-Labrador - 375
Woodland - 295

CARIBOU

KIND OF CARIBOU

DETAIL OF POINT MEASUREMENT

SEE OTHER SIDE FOR INSTRUCTIONS	Supplementary Data	Column 1	Column 2	Column 3	Column 4
		Spread Credit	Right Antler	Left Antler	Difference
A. Tip to Tip Spread		/////	/////	/////	/////
B. Greatest Spread					
C. Inside Spread of MAIN BEAMS — Spread credit may equal but not exceed length of longer antler			/////	/////	/////
IF Inside Spread of Main Beams exceeds longer antler length, enter difference		/////	/////	/////	
D. Number of Points on Each Antler excluding brows		/////			
Number of Points on Each Brow					/////
E. Length of Main Beam		/////			
F-1. Length of Brow Palm or First Point		/////			/////
F-2. Length of Bez or Second Point		/////			
F-3. Length of Rear Point, if present		/////			
F-4. Length of Second Longest Top Point		/////			
F-5. Length of Longest Top Point		/////			
G-1. Width of Brow Palm		/////			/////
G-2. Width of Top Palm		/////			
H-1. Circumference at Smallest Place Between Brow and Bez Points		/////			
H-2. Circumference at Smallest Place Between Bez and Rear Point, if present		/////			
H-3. Circumference at Smallest Place Before First Top Point		/////			
H-4. Circumference at Smallest Place Between Two Longest Top Palm Points		/////			
TOTALS					

ADD	Column 1		Exact locality where killed	
	Column 2		Date killed	By whom killed
	Column 3		Present owner	
	TOTAL		Address	
SUBTRACT Column 4			Guide's Name and Address	
FINAL SCORE			Remarks: (Mention any abnormalities)	

114

I certify that I have measured the above trophy on _____ 19 _____
at (address)_____ City _____ State _____
and that these measurements and data are, to the best of my knowledge and belief, made in accordance with the instructions given.

Witness: _____ Signature: _____
Boone and Crockett Official Measurer

INSTRUCTIONS

All measurements must be made with a flexible steel tape to the nearest one-eighth of an inch. Wherever it is necessary to change direction of measurement, mark a control point and swing tape at this point. To simplify addition, please enter fractional figures in eighths.

Official measurements cannot be taken for at least sixty days after the animal was killed. Please submit photographs of trophy front and sides.

Supplementary Data measurements indicate conformation of the trophy.

None of the figures in Lines A and B are to be included in the score.

Evaluation of conformation is a matter of personal preference.

A. Tip to Tip Spread measured between tips of Main Beams.

B. Greatest Spread measured between perpendiculars at right angles to the center line of the skull at widest part whether across main beams or points.

C. Inside Spread of Main Beams measured at right angles to the center line of the skull at widest point between main beams. Enter this measurement again in "Spread Credit" column if it is less than or equal to the length of longer antler.

D. Number of points on each antler. To be counted a point, a projection must be at least one-half inch long and this length must exceed the breadth of the point's base. The breadth need not be computed from the deepest adjacent dips in the palmation. The length may be measured to any location -- at least one-half inch from the tip -- at which the length of the point exceeds its breadth. Beam tip is counted as a point but not measured as a point.

E. Length of Main Beam measured from lowest outside edge of burr over outer curve to the most distant point of what is, or appears to be, the main beam. The point of beginning is that point on the burr where the center line along the outer curve of the beam intersects the burr.

F-1-2-3. Length of Points. They are measured from nearest edge of beam on the shortest line over outer curve to tip. To determine nearest edge (top edge) of beam, lay the tape along the outer curve of the beam so that the top edge of the tape coincides with the top edge of the beam on both sides of the point. Draw line along top edge of tape. This line will be base line from which point is measured.

F-4-5. Measure from the tip of the point to the top of the beam, then at right angles to the lower edge of beam.

G-1 Width of Brow measured in a straight line from top edge to lower edge.

G-2 Width of Top Palm measured from rear edge of main beam to the dip between points at widest part of palm.

H-1-2-3-4. Circumferences – If rear point is missing, take H-2 and H-3 measurements at smallest place between bez and first top point.

* * * * * * * * * * * * *

TROPHIES OBTAINED ONLY BY FAIR CHASE MAY BE ENTERED IN ANY BOONE AND CROCKETT CLUB BIG GAME COMPETITION

To make use of the following methods shall be deemed UNFAIR CHASE and unsportsmanlike, and any trophy obtained by use of such means is disqualified from entry in any Boone and Crockett Club big game competition:

    I. Spotting or herding game from the air, followed by landing in its vicinity for pursuit;

    II. Herding or pursuing game with motor-powered vehicles;

    III. Use of electronic communications for attracting, locating or observing game, or guiding the hunter to such game.

            * * * * * * * * * * * *

I certify that the trophy scored on this chart was not taken in UNFAIR CHASE as defined above by the Boone and Crockett Club.

I certify that it was not spotted or herded by guide or hunter from the air followed by landing in its vicinity for pursuit, nor herded or pursued on the ground by motor-powered vehicles.

I further certify that no electronic communications were used to attract, locate, observe, or guide the hunter to such game; and that it was taken in full compliance with the local game laws or regulations of the state, province or territory.

Date _____ Signature of Hunter _____

This chart is reproduced with permission of the Boone and Crockett Club, which, together with the National Rifle Association, co-sponsors the North American Big Game Awards Program.

Traveling up the rack, the next formation is the bez (second point). These fall into two rather common types and one rare type present only on a few very large heads. The bez can either be a single long beam coming off the main beam and having points extending from it, or it can flare out into a "hand" with "fingers" extending from the "palm." In some rare cases a very large bull with an enormous bez can have a long central beam, with some palmation that carries a major upper or lower branch with points extending off both.

Above the bez a rear point may jut off the back of the main beam. These points may be entirely absent or, in unusual cases, they may extend 6 to 8 inches back behind the beam. Three inches is about the norm. In the top section of each antler, the main beam generally sweeps forward and flattens or palmates with numerous top points, some of them possibly carrying secondary points. On other heads, the main beam sweeps upward. In this second type, the first and usually longest top point juts forward. It has been my experience that these "swept upward" tall racks are in the minority in all four subspecies but occur most often in the mountain (and Osborn) type. Usually these high heads don't carry the palmation and spread of the swept-forward type, but the main beams may be very long indeed and usually wear many points.

Guns for Caribou

To date I've killed all my caribou with either the .270 (130- and 150-grain bullets) or the 7mm Remington Magnum (150-grain bullets). However, this was because I was always on mixed-game hunts and out after bigger and tougher game as well as caribou. My brother and various other hunters that I know have readily disposed of all manner of caribou with .243's, 6mm's, 25/06's and such. The main thing with caribou, and any other game, is where you hit them, not what you hit them with. Every year thousands of caribou are dispatched neatly with .222-class rifles in the hands of economy conscious far northern Indians and Eskimos.

I'm certainly not recommending the .222 class of cartridge for nonresident trophy hunters. The native is at home and can pick and choose his shots at leisure. He often is purposefully avoiding the big bulls for more tender fare. The visiting trophy hunter is in the area for a limited time and after one of a few big bulls. Thus, he may have to take a far longer, chancier shot at a less advantageous angle in order to get the right animal.

Caribou Types

Let's survey the four types of caribou recognized for scoring:

1. Barren Ground Caribou. This is the most populous type, with Alaska carrying a herd of some 600,000 and northern Canada adding in another 350,000 to 400,000 in the sprawling northwestern barrens. (The northeastern barrens are the home of the newly recognized Quebec-Labrador type.) The big Grant caribou of Alaska is probably the largest race of the barren ground type, with big bulls achieving a maximum weight of some 350 to 400 pounds. The biggest barren ground I've taken to date carried antlers 51½ inches long and weighed just about 400 pounds. The saddle of pre-rut fat over his backsides measured a full 2⅝ inches in thickness, and his sleek hide fairly rolled as he bounded off a few yards after my killing shot.

The very largest barren grounds are found down on the Alaska Peninsula, though some very large bulls indeed are taken from the Kenai Peninsula and certain other parts of Alaska. As a general rule most Alaskan game species run larger in the more southerly portions of that giant state, and caribou are no exception. Every year big bulls come out of the Alaska Range, the Wrangell's and the general area surrounding Anchorage.

But if I wanted a record-book barren ground bull, I'd head for the Ugashik Lakes/Iliamna Lake area of the upper Alaska Peninsula around September 15 to 30, for the rut. The caribou move up the peninsula toward the mainland during the rut and congregate around Ugashik Lakes. If your timing is good, you'll see many, many animals, and among them will be some simply enormous bulls. Iliamna Lake also harbors many fine trophy caribou with most of them migrating in from the north during the rut.

If you are ever fortunate enough to hunt these areas at just the right times, the sight of these large numbers of big caribou moving relentlessly along during their fall migrations is something that you will treasure the rest of your days. Guided hunting for them doesn't come cheap in Alaska, with costs running $150 to $225 per day, and averaging out toward the upper end of that range rather than the lower. Many of these hunts are

This is a fine, but not outstanding, barren ground bull. The inside spread goes over 40 inches. The main beams sweep better than 50 inches. And the single shovel is decent. But the bez are undistinguished and the tops lack the number of points to make this a record-class head. Yet this is a classic barren ground — long sweeping antlers, wide spread, weak top palmation, and main beams lacking great mass. (The main beams look more massive than they are because of velvet.)

general game excursions where the hunter is hunting several different areas of Alaska for 3 to 5 species of game. However, for caribou only, 7 to 10 days should be allowed. The weather can sour overnight and knock you out of several days hunting quite easily. Also, though you may see a lot of animals and a lot of shootable bulls, you must get within rifle range. And since you are hunting on foot and the caribou are forever moving along at a pace that soon outdistances even a running hunter, getting within range is no easy trick. This is a special problem for the serious trophy hunter who glasses his bull carefully in order to estimate the quality of the head rather than just banging away at a "big" one. Most of this hunting is fly-in and then walk.

Current Alaska game regulations do not require that nonresidents have a guide for caribou; so it is possible for you to bring or rent (at a steep cost) a camp outfit and have it flown in with you for a do-it-yourself hunt. This can save you a lot of money. But it's strictly for seasoned woodsmen and hunters. This is rough, wild country and accidents can easily occur, especially to the unskilled.

Also, if you don't know the area, you can easily get lost or hunt the wrong sections rather than those that would enable you to spot a maximum amount of game. Doing all the chores yourself also robs time from the hunting. An expensive hunt that is successful is better than an unsuccessful cheaper hunt that still uses up your annual vacation and costs a significant amount of money for transportation and licenses. Each hunter must assess his own objectives, capabilities and resources and decide which hunting method is best for him.

By contrast, the twenty-two outfitters licensed to operate in the Yukon almost universally hunt by horse rather than by the Alaskan method of flying in and hunting afoot or from various tracked or other all-terrain vehicles. The rates here are somewhat cheaper at $125 to $200 per day. But, like everywhere else, they increase noticeably each year with no end in sight. There are very few caribou-only or caribou/moose-only hunts here as offered in Alaska or northern British Columbia. Almost all the caribou hunting (at least up until now) is a part of the general mixed game hunt for four or five species. Though the Alaska Peninsula has to be my top choice for big trophies, the best caribou hunting in the Yukon is very good indeed, almost matching the best in Alaska and exceeding many Alaskan areas in both availability and trophy quality.

Alaska undoubtedly has the larger trophies in some instances, but the fact that the Yukon placed only two heads in the top 20, and none in the top 10, in the latest record book is partially attributable to the face that far fewer caribou have been harvested there over the years by trophy hunters. Alaska generally harvests around 3,500 caribou annually by licensed hunters, while the kill in the Yukon is barely a third of that. Additionally some 30,000 caribou are taken annually by unlicensed Alaskan Indians and an unknown amount are taken by Yukon Indians. Caribou still provide subsistence food and materials for many people in the far north.

Two areas in the extreme western end of the giant Northwest Territories were opened to nonresident sport hunting for the first time back in 1964. Very few sportsmen have hunted this remote backwater of the continent, probably no more than 150 per year on average. Most hunting is on foot, though some outfitters have tried jet boats, horses or even pack dogs. I have the impression that the largest caribou from this area don't quite match the best in the Yukon and Alaska, though some fine heads do come out each year. There has been such a short history of sport hunting here though that it is difficult to be categoric.

Northwest Territory hunting is an expensive proposition, running upwards of $200 per day and about equaling Alaskan costs and somewhat exceeding Yukon averages. Here, as in the Yukon, caribou hunting occurs exclusively as a part of general, mixed-game hunts of 15 to 21 days in duration. There are no caribou-only or caribou/moose-only hunts offered here to my knowledge. If you hanker to tread some of the most remote, the wildest, ground left in the world, this might be for you.

There has been very limited barren-ground hunting in Manitoba, Saskatchewan, and Ontario.

The population of barren ground caribou is highly cyclical, evidencing periodical peaks and crashes. By and large this subspecies is increasing and has been doing so for the last 20 years. And though the population is well below the peaks prevailing some 75 years ago, the hunting outlook is bright.

Barren ground racks are characterized by long, sweeping main beams and large shovels. The beams generally do not run as heavy nor is the palmation as pronounced as in bulls of comparable quality of the mountain and woodland types. (As I've said, caribou do vary enormously; so all of these remarks about the *general* character of antlers from the four trophy types admit to many exceptions!) Many believe this animal to be the finest trophy of all. A big bull can carry 50-inch, and better, antlers with a spread exceeding 40 inches. Though that's an impressive trophy, one giant bull shot in the Ugashik Lakes area of the Alaskan Peninsula in 1968 carried antlers with both main beams measuring over 68 inches. It is now third in the record book.

2. Mountain Caribou. The Boone and Crockett Club recognizes all caribou shot in British Columbia and Alberta as belonging to this type. Alberta harvests some 500 per year by licensed hunters (resident Whites and nonresidents) while B.C.'s licensed hunter harvest is around 1600. The Indian kill is undoubtedly larger in both areas. Alberta doesn't have a large resident herd, probably totaling no more than 3,000 or so year-round animals, but their herd does receive periodic infusions of animals migrating southward from the Yukon and the Northwest Territories. I have not been able to locate any reliable estimate of British Columbia's resident herd, but it is undoubtedly far larger than Alberta's since B.C. has much more suitable habitat.

British Columbia plans to introduce a quota system, that is, hunting by permit drawing or other numerical limitation. But as this is written, exact details are not yet available. I am assuming that caribou will not initially be covered under the new program but will continue to be hunted with only season limits and one-to-the-hunter limits. British Columbia caribou hunting is universally a horseback proposition and the costs, if taken as part of a mixed-game hunt, run $150 to $250 per day on average. However, various B.C. outfitters do offer certain moose-only and caribou-only hunts at lower rates. Many of

The author here poses with his big Osborn mountain caribou in the Cassiars of northern B.C. This head demonstrates that caribou antlers don't always conform to their "type" as the author explains in the text. These sweeping beams of over 54 inches and light, unpalmated tops conform more to the barren ground type than to mountain type. But the heavy beams and double shovels do fit the expected Osborn conformation.

these are late-season hunts in late October and into November.

The late-season-caribou hunts, if you can stand the fearsome cold, often yield better trophies than many of the earlier hunts, and the rates may run only $100 to $150 per day. Some B.C. outfitters offer special rates for father-son hunts and other package deals. If big caribou are what you're after, by all means check into these various late season and promotional type hunts not generally available when sheep and grizzly are also hunted. Alberta hunting can run from $100 to $200 per day, depending on the length of the hunt, the territory to be hunted, the accommodations and the other game (if any) offered. For caribou only, a 7- to 10-day hunt is involved while moose-and-caribou usually means 10 days but can stretch to 12 or 14 days. The mixed-game hunts are a minimum of 15 days and most run 18 to 21 days.

Some argue that the woodland type is the largest bodied of all the caribou. That may be so but my vote would have to go to the giant Osborn caribou of the Cassiar Mountains in northern B.C. I have killed only two of this type but both were large and one was simply enormous. He was the largest bodied caribou the outfitter or any of the guides in camp had ever seen and he dwarfed my largest barren ground. I believe he weighed an honest 500 pounds on the hoof. The big antlers ran $51\frac{1}{2}$ and $54\frac{1}{2}$ inches in beam length and were fully as heavy in gross antler material as that of the largest elk that I have ever taken, though not as heavy as some of the elk antlers I've seen.

Although the largest mountain caribou antlers tend, as a group, to be much heavier and more palmated but not as sweeping as the best barren ground racks, this was one of the many exceptions I've mentioned. The beams were certainly heavy, but there was little or no top palmation. And 54 inches is certainly "sweeping" in anyone's book! (The main beams on the world-record barren ground and mountain heads only run $51\frac{5}{8}$ and 52 inches, respectively, though some heads lower on the lists are longer.)

To ice the cake, the big fellow wore the prized double shovels, and both of them were decent in size. I have the distinct impression that double shovels occur more frequently among mountain caribou than among barren ground. I've seen only one double shovel in all the barren ground hunting I've done (and all camps). But *six* doubles came into camp on my last mountain caribou hunt. A random quiz among other hunters appears to bear this out, though my "poll" certainly has no statistical validity. True double-shovel bulls are a rarity and a prized trophy in any case.

Most *big* mountain caribou bulls tend to run in the low to mid 40s in main beam length, while the comparable quality barren ground would run in the high 40s and low 50s. Also, though the top heads from both types in the latest record book don't indicate an enormous difference in inside spreads, I believe the average, large barren ground bull will generally carry more spread, pushing past the coveted 40-inch mark on inside spread far more frequently. However, I should mention that the world-record mountain caribou head does sport an enormous 57⅜-inch spread. This huge head has topped all challengers for over 50 years now and is unique in several other respects. Only six other mountain caribou in the record book approach within a foot of it in spread, and only one of those edges to within 6 inches of it.

My experiences, and those of other dependable observers whom I know, indicate that the big Osborn bulls are more alert and difficult to approach than most barren ground bulls. I've never been able to wave up a single mountain caribou, although I've done so frequently with barren grounds, many of them being big bulls, too. Mountain caribou appear to be more alert, warier and harder to approach. They're still not elk or bighorn sheep by a long shot, but they usually take far less time to make up their beautiful heads to get out of there. And once they do, they most often do it with little of the dalliance and indecision that often characterizes the barren grounds as they back and fill and bumble around trying to remember what it was they were fleeing from moments earlier.

All caribou – whatever the trophy type, subspecies, or race – go completely "bonkers" during the rut. But when the animals are not influenced by the "moon of madness," the comparisons I've mentioned generally hold true. Incidentally, "mountain" caribou don't tend to frequent mountains any more or less than "barren grounds" do. Both names are a convenient shorthand to help discriminate between the two, and are not based on exclusive ranges.

The place to go for the largest mountain caribou racks is the Cassiar Mountains of northwestern British Columbia. The racks do not run nearly as large farther to the east. Historically the Dease Lake area, the Spatsizi Plateau and Coldfish Lake are inextricably linked to huge caribou. Some really fine heads have also come in, still farther to the north and west from around Atlin Lake. Even in this top-quality caribou country, you should allow yourself a 10-day hunt in order to compensate for bad weather and to give you a chance to be selective. That's during the rut and for caribou only. Two weeks would be better. But if you add in moose or goat or are hunting before the rut, fourteen days or more would be mandatory.

3. Quebec-Labrador. This Boone and Crockett classification is very recent in origin. And it's purely hunting rather than taxonomic in rationale, since the animal is obviously a barren ground. However, due to the large geographical separation between the two and the recent advent of sport hunting for the Quebec-Labrador type, the Boone and Crockett Club made the commendably practical decision to distinguish between the two for record keeping purposes. There are a number of outfitters up on the Ungava Peninsula who offer hunts averaging 5 to 7 days and costing from $600 to $900. These are fly-in and walk hunts. The more expensive ones usually have the best camp locations relative to the migration routes, meaning that you should be able to look over more heads and be more selective. Some also often include some salmon fishing as a bonus.

These animals run about the same in body size as the barren grounds farther to the west and they most closely resemble them in antler characteristics. In fact, they are "even more so." By that I mean that the Quebec-Labrador antlers tend to be even more long-beamed, and they have spreads as wide or wider than those of the Alaskan-Yukon animals. I believe that they also tend to run to lighter beamed racks. The biggest Quebec-Labrador racks usually aren't quite as high as a comparable barren ground rack, both because their spreads are often wider and because they usually sweep farther back, thus not rising as high into the air.

Quebec has somewhere between 60,000 and 100,000 of these fine trophy game animals, depending upon whose estimate you accept. Hunting is good and the chances of taking a good trophy are excellent for the man who will work hard by walking those extra miles and who will discipline himself to look over a lot of heads before shooting. Be sure to select a camp and outfitter whose location and hunting methods will enable you to look over a maximum amount of game.

Sport hunting of this herd was only opened a few years ago. The existence of a herd this size appears to have been a late blooming surprise to the Quebec authorities. So there simply has not been enough harvesting to indicate what the maximum size of the bulls may be. However, it's fascinating to note that the all-time high scoring caribou head of *any* type is a monster Quebec-Labrador type that at 474⁶/₈ points outscores the leading barren ground and mountain heads by more than 10 points and exceeds the world's record woodland head by more than 50 points. Shot in 1931 by an Eskimo, this fantastic trophy was formerly classified as a barren ground, but it has fought off all comers of any type to remain the leading head for the whole species for over 40 years now.

This brand of caribou hunting is doubly attractive because it is not yet prohibitively expensive and it is only a few hours by air from the crowded eastern cities. I believe that more and more hunters from the East will want to add one of these marvelous heads to their trophy collections.

4. Woodland Caribou. In terms of antler size, the woodland caribou carries the smallest rack of the four general hunting classes. This is borne out by the comparison of the current world records and minimum qualifying scores.

Classification	World Record Score	Minimum Qualifying Score
1. Barren Ground	463⁶/₈	400
2. Mountain	462	390
3. Quebec-Labrador	474⁶/₈	375
4. Woodland	419⁵/₈	295

The island of Newfoundland is now the only place where any meaningful hunting for woodland is still available.

This has led the authorities there to place a rather high $500 price tag on the permits, drawn by lot. The island's herd runs about 16,000 to 18,000 animals, which is down considerably from the populations of a half century ago. By the authorities' own estimates, Newfoundland has the range for over 30,000 caribou. But apparently there has been some difficulty in building the herd back up. Moose were introduced to the island around the turn of the century, and now with moose numbering some 70,000 to 80,000, they practically overrun the place. However, the authorities claim that there is no meaningful competition, direct or indirect, between the two and that the population explosion in the moose herd has nothing to do with the depletion of caribou herd. The authorities have also recently raised their moose licenses to $350, not far from the $500 caribou price tag.

Frankly, the trophy quality of both the Newfoundland moose and the caribou is rather inferior. The moose rack is among the smallest of its species and the caribou (or "stag") rack is the smallest of all the four huntable caribou. The animals are rather big bodied but the racks tend to have far less sweep and spread than those of others in their clans. Though on the best bulls, the antlers are reasonably heavy and well palmated.

Almost all caribou hunting is a cinch bet to avoid striking out completely. However, your chances of a whitewash (no game) are greater here than in any other meaningful caribou hunting areas. Costs run about the same as, or slightly more than, they do in northern Quebec — except for that $500 license! Though some fine outfitters and guides operate here, others don't have the best of reputations.

Whether the provincial authorities, rather cavalier increase in the license costs will be good for them or for the animals in the long run is an open question. In the meantime, quite frankly, unless you have secured outstanding examples of all three other varieties and are just in a snit to round out the four, at these costs you can probably find better ways to spend your hard-earned dinero.

Trophy Standards. My own ideas as to what constitutes a good trophy and an outstanding trophy for each of the four types of caribou are as follows:

Subspecies	Good Trophy	Outstanding Trophy	Record Head
1. Barren Ground	350	375	400
2. Mountain	350	375	390
3. Quebec-Labrador*	350	375	375
4. Woodland	250	275	295

Since the Quebec-Labrador type caribou has not been hunted very long for sport and since there are few entries in the book relative to all the other trophy categories, the current minimum is rather low. But this is understandable since the fewer heads that come in from a particular species, the lower the minimum. This assures at least some representation in the records. Sometime later, as more heads come in, the minimum inevitably goes up. I definitely feel that it will escalate considerably for the Quebec-Labrador caribou. First, it will probably jump to 400 to be on a par with the barren ground minimum. Still later, I believe that it will be set even higher than barren ground, probably 10 or 15 points, because it may well work out that the largest Quebec-Labrador heads will outscore all others. That has certainly been the case with the all-species record shot by Zack Elbow, and I think that will prove to be the case for the category as a whole. The current method of scoring caribou rewards sweep (beam length, spread, length of top points) more than it does mass (beam circumference, top palmation, shovel palmation). And these Quebec heads are the most "sweeping" type of all.

Thus, I have set the "good" trophy in this category within only 25 points of the current record book minimum rather than 40 to 50 points below it as with the others. The "outstanding" trophy here is a record book qualifier, whereas the "outstanding" head in the other three categories is some 15 to 25 points below record book qualification. Right now the Quebec-Labrador category is probably about the easiest one in which to make the record book. As more heads come in and the minimum requirement eventually is raised, this will change.

Estimating and Evaluating Heads

Caribou heads are the most complex trophies of all to score under the Boone and Crockett system. Thus many observers feel that these heads are the most difficult trophy of all to estimate in the field. Caribou heads have as many as 41 characteristics, or factors, which may enter into the scoring, depending upon the conformation of the head. The nearest rivals in complexity, among typical heads, are the whitetail and the elk, with a maximum of 39 possible scoring factors in each case. However, there is far more possible variance in the scoring features of most of the caribou than in those for whitetail and elk. With heads of the latter two animals, size is relatively more important than with that of the caribou. But this is not to imply that symmetry is unimportant in the scoring of elk and whitetail heads or that large size isn't the basis of *any* record book head.

Since there are so many measurements that enter into the scoring of most caribou heads, symmetry of the two antlers is very important. It significantly affects the scoring. One caribou that I shot had a rack that ran over 50 inches in beam length and carried double shovels. Yet it was outscored by 23 points by a much smaller rack carrying 42- and 43-inch beams. My huge rack must have weighed a full 5 pounds heavier in raw antler material, it was so much larger. But the smaller rack—what I call a "magnum" head because it squeezed every bit of scoring possible out of the amount of antler material—had much

This is the kind of undistinguished bull that is often taken in good caribou country over the strong objections of the guide. This bull's single shovel is small, his bez spindly, his back points short, his main beams short and lightweight. The top points don't promise to be outstanding when fully developed.

longer top points, more palmation, longer bez and better shovels. Its spread was also somewhat wider, and it had reasonably long back points, while my big trophy had none. To top it off, this little "magnum" head lost only a fraction over 6 points in scoring due to asymmetry of the two antlers. That's the least asymmetry loss I've ever actually seen and scored myself on a caribou head. And I've only heard of one other head on which the loss was that small.

When I size up a caribou head, the first thing I look for is length of top points. I believe those four points are the key to a record book head. (The caribou scoring system takes into account the length of the two longest top points on each side.) All four of them should be over 20 inches and rather even when paired with points on the other side. And normally the longer pair must be 24 inches or more for record contention.

The next most important features are beam length and bez length. Two main beams that run 50 inches each are going to score 12 points higher than another head with 44- and 45-inch beams. (The second head would lose the extra inch on the 45-

inch side due to asymmetry.) Bez lengths can run 19 inches on each side rather than say, 14 and 16 inches. That would make a difference of 10 points in score. However, because of their curvature, bez lengths are very difficult to estimate accurately in the field. There is no other referent feature on the animal that can serve as a reliable comparison, though it's useful to ensure that beam length approximates shoulder height. Nor do the bez points usually stick out quite as straight as the shovel. Thus bez curvature must be allowed for. Of course spread is important, and it adds much to the general attractiveness of a head.

Sometimes it helps to see two or more animals together. Other times it may throw you off. Even though the younger bull's top points are rather good, considering his small rack, he is so undeveloped that he makes the older bull appear to be better than he is. Neither should be shot.

But on most big heads, spread doesn't vary more than 5 to 7 inches, with the inside spread running from about 35 to 42 inches. True, there are exceptions to this, but inside spreads of substantially more than 42 inches on a caribou rack are rare indeed.

What about double shovels and their effect on scoring? Aren't they significant? There's no doubt that double shovels are rare and they add additional interest, attractiveness, and *points* when they are present. However, the rare second shovel is usually smaller (less wide, fewer points) than the first. Also, I suspect that *if* a big double-shovel bull were carrying one shovel rather than two, that single shovel would often be considerably larger than the larger of the two he carried. However, this is just speculation on my part.

I believe one advantage that does accrue to a head carrying double shovels is that the shovels greatly increase the chances for overall symmetry. Although official scoring does not deduct points for the difference between the shovels (and rightly so), and thus does not penalize a head if it only carries a single shovel, it does (again rightfully) place a lot of scoring emphasis on how even the two beams are above the shovels. A head burdened with growing a large shovel, while the other side grows only a stunted prong, is going to tend to be less than perfectly matched in the upper beam area. But this is not necessarily so, because I've seen big single-shovel heads that scored out amazingly evenly. However, most of the time the double-shovel head will lose less points to asymmetry.

As for scoring of the shovels themselves, a bull with a single shovel and a long prong (rather than a second shovel) may often score about as high as a bull with double shovels. Let's compare two hypothetical caribou heads and assume that both have equal "first" shovels and that the prong on the single-shovel bull is as long as the "second" shovel on the double-shovel guy. Here's how they might well stack up in many cases:

Double-shovel Bull	Points	Single-shovel Bull	Points
1. Length of second shovel: 13 inches	*13*	1. Length of second shovel: 13 inches	13
2. Width: 4 inches	*4*	2. Width: ½ inch	½
3. Number of points on second shovel	*3*	3. Number of points on prong	*1*
Total points	*20*		*14½*

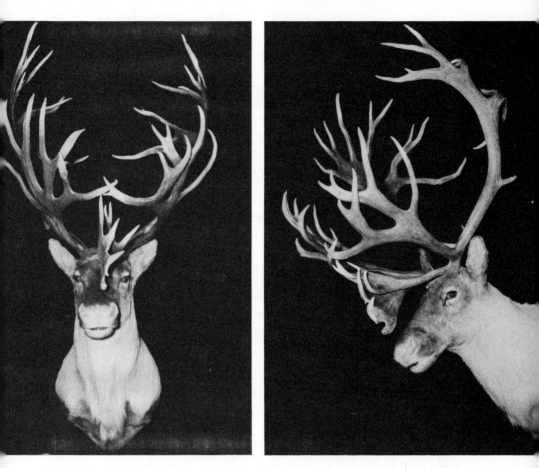

Shot in the Cassiars by Elgin Gates in 1953, this massive mountain caribou scored 417⁴/₈ points and still rated a tie for 15th place in the 1971 record book. Though this head has a narrow spread (30 inches) and short main beams (43 inches), it has heavy beams, two good shovels, numerous long top points, and magnificent bez formations. In anyone's view this is a great head, the forest of points instantly proclaiming, "Record!"

Thus, in this rather typical case, only a bonus of some 5½ points would be credited the double-shovel formation per se. Certainly those 5-plus points are important but not necessarily earth shattering. Of course if you assume that the second shovel were larger than the one I've described, that would make a difference. But, then again, if the "*first*" shovel were somewhat larger because little competing growth went into the prong, then perhaps the score points that would have come from a second shovel would have been largely or completely compensated for. Food for thought, anyway.

Thus, the ultimate scoring advantage of double shovels may be as much the *indirect one* of encouraging overall head symmetry as it is the *obvious one* of adding more points on its own. In any event, there's no doubt that double shovels improve a head, either in appearance or in scoring.

Since a big caribou bull will stand some 50 to 60 inches high at the shoulder (highest point on backline), any head is a good one if the main beam length, including curvature, appears to match the shoulder height. Most big bulls will be about 16 to 17 inches thick across the body up front, when viewed from the front. (Their body width varies around the belly, depending upon fat and when they last ate.) Viewed from the front, a rack that appears to stick out about 10 inches on each side of the bull's frontal body will probably carry a spread of about 36 inches and is starting to get interesting.

A big bull's head will be just about 13 to 14 inches long from antler base to nose tip. Use that as an indicator when trying to estimate the length of the brow shovels and the bez. However, remember that, because the antlers sweep back from their bases, both the bez and the shovels start farther back than the base of the antlers. And they also inevitably curve and/or flare upward as they come forward. Thus, if either of these formations appears to extend about 9 inches down the face of the bull, they are actually several inches longer.

It is vital to use a spotting scope if at all possible to properly size up all the many characteristics of a big bull caribou and to determine symmetry. A final word of caution: Not all big bulls carry the flowing white mane. So don't automatically discount an animal that appears large but doesn't have a prominent white mane. Almost all these manes are a mouse-grey until they start to turn white just after mid-August. Some turn color later than others, and this can fool you. Still other manes, for some reason, never achieve the really prominent whiteness. I've seen some very large, high-scoring bull caribou carrying rather nondescript grey necks in September.

Try to glass caribou carefully and dispassionately. Just as most moose look fairly small racked (to me anyway) because of their huge body size, almost all decent caribou bulls look *big* in the antlers. Another fooler is that a bull with bleached antlers newly out of the velvet can appear to be carrying a far larger rack than he is, especially if the morning sun is hitting him just right. Any palmation and shovel size will show up almost with a glare, and can even fool guides and seasoned caribou spotters. And due to palmation, this is also true with moose.

Caribou are grand trophies and exciting to watch. You never know what they'll do from moment to moment—because *they* don't either. And that keeps things lively!

The Noblest Stag: Elk

9

The Almighty must have felt good the day he created the American elk, or wapiti — the Shawnee Indian name, meaning "white rump." For he is indeed a grand game animal. Many veteran hunters argue that he is the best all-round trophy animal in North America. While this kind of statement is always open to debate, the partisans of the elk can present a strong case.

He's large and impressive, with big bulls weighing from 600 pounds to over 1,000 in some special cases. He is also a majestically beautiful animal with an attractive, intelligent looking face, a powerful but well shaped body and marvelous sweeping antlers. And all of these purely physical characteristics are tied together and enhanced by a carriage and bearing as regal as that of any animal on earth. The way that a big bull elk stands, carries his head, and moves is lordly and impressive. It is almost impossible for the bulls to look awkward or uninspiring. The cows are far smaller animals, and their general plug-horse spavined-back look is as unattractive as their lordly sire's look is attractive.

Furthermore the elk is highly intelligent and is gifted with keen senses. He does almost everything well. He has sharp eyes, keen ears and a good nose. He is wary, alert and decisive. Once he makes up his mind to decamp to safer territory, he usually does so at flank speed with no hesitancy or indecision. He has tremendous vitality. A mortally wounded bull elk will often carry on with amazing vigor. Elk are far harder to put down and keep down than big bull moose which may weigh more than twice as much. Elk are *game* in the very best sense of that word.

The North American elk is the largest round-antlered deer in the world. He was misnamed by the early settlers on our East

Coast because most of them had only heard of, not actually seen, the European elk which is the same animal as our moose. Among all the world's deer, only the moose is larger.

The American elk is closely related to the red deer of Europe and the Near East as well as the old world equivalents of the American elk found in eastern Asia, and known by many names. Though the red deer are considerably smaller than our elk and their antler conformation is somewhat different (with a tendency to develop a "cup" of tines near the tips), many taxonomists consider them the same species as our elk. Though I know of no instances in the wild where the two have intergraded, I do know of several game farms where elk and red deer have readily crossed. So this would tend to support the view that they are ultimately the same species. Though some of the more easterly and northerly Asiatic wapiti closely resemble our elk in size and appearance, as in the case of moose and caribou, none of the foreign races quite equal our animal in size or trophy-antler quality.

There are three recognized species of North American elk, one of which is subdivided into four races. The two lesser species are of no current interest to hunters, one being the extinct Merriams elk *(Cervus merriami)* which inhabited several isolated mountain ranges in Arizona and New Mexico and probably became extinct around 1900. The second is the dwarf or Tule elk *(Cervus nannodes)* which is far smaller than the other elk and has limited antler development. Perhaps 400 Tule elk exist under closely supervised conditions in California. Actually, there is a good chance that both of these species are the same animal as the "basic" elk *(Cervus canadensis),* but there is no proof of intergradation.

The Merriams elk, which was a paler animal than the rest, apparently was somewhat larger than any of the other races or species. Whether the antler development was commensurately larger, which is not necessarily so as we will see in a moment when considering the Afognak island elk, taxonomists have not been able to determine.

The animal that we all refer to when we discuss "elk" is divided into four acknowledged races. The "eastern" elk *(Cervus canadensis canadensis)* once inhabited southern Quebec and Ontario and almost all of the eastern U.S., except New England, and ranged as far south as Tennessee and northern Georgia. This animal has been extinct since the early settlement of America, and the few small groups of elk now living in this vast area are of the "Rocky Mountain" type, as are the current elk of Arizona and New Mexico.

These eastern elk were decimated with an appalling ruthlessness. A number of factors contributed to their eradication. Their range was quickly cut up by fences and dominated by domestic livestock. And since elk are large animals that provide very tasty eating (I far prefer prime elk meat to any venison), they were market-hunted with mindless efficiency by the early settlers, hide hunters and labor gangs of various sorts. Entire herds were also slaughtered for their two unique "tusks" or canine teeth which brought as much as $75 a pair from certain lodge members. That was a lot of money in the 1800s!

Most of the eastern elk herds were gone before 1800. They survived in the Great Lakes area until about 1830 and in midwestern prairie and hardwood areas until a bit beyond the middle of the century. They were extirpated from Iowa about 1867, from Nebraska and South Dakota in the 1870s and were mostly gone from North Dakota by that time, though a few hung on until the late 1890s. The last elk was killed in Minnesota in 1908, and the last one was seen there in 1917. (Though a few have since been reintroduced.) Sport and trophy hunting had absolutely nothing to do with this sad decline, the reasons being commercial and subsistence hunting and general land use incompatible with free-roaming herds of large animals such as elk.

Cervus canadensis manitobensis inhabits the Canadian provinces of Saskatchewan and Manitoba. Though the herds here are reasonably large (about 7,500 in each province), this race is somewhat darker colored and smaller antlered and not of special interest to the trophy hunter. About 800 animals are killed in each area on permit hunting. Though nonresidents have generally been barred from these hunts, this could be changed in the future.

Where to Hunt

This brings us down to the two races of elk of primary interest to the sport and trophy hunter. The Rocky Mountain elk (*nelsoni*) is somewhat lighter colored, lighter bodied and longer antlered than the Roosevelt or Olympic (*roosevelti*) elk which inhabits the western half of Washington and Oregon, northwestern California, extreme southwestern British Columbia and

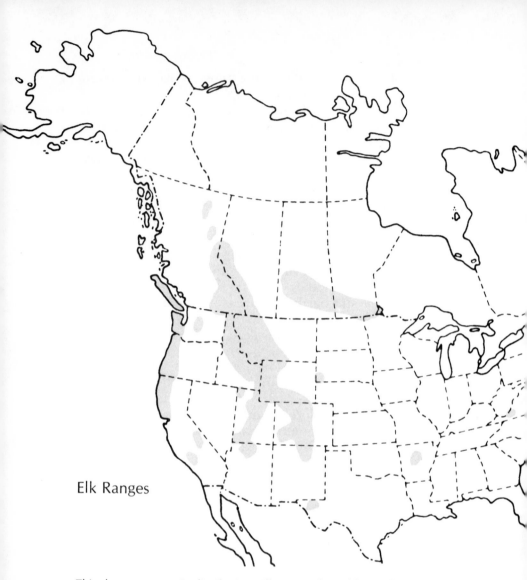

Elk Ranges

This shows taxonomic distribution. Elk are not huntable in all these areas.

Afognak Island off the coast of Alaska. Though the shorter antlers of the Olympic elk can be very heavy and some quite nice trophies are taken each year, the Rocky Mountain elk completely dominates the trophy lists. And this is the animal that most serious trophy hunters concentrate on. Incidentally, some Olympic elk were introduced to Afognak Island off the Alaskan coast. Here they have attained the all-time body weight records for any type of elk, with some animals weighing as much as 1,300 pounds. The hunting is hellishly rough here, and usually only about 50 to 100 animals are taken out of the 900 to 1,000 permits that are awarded — about 40 permits going to nonresidents. The herd varies from about 900 to 1,500 animals in this closed system situation. And, unfortunately, the antler growth has not increased above normal even though the enormous body weights have been attained.

The "big" elk states furnishing considerable nonresident trophy hunting for Rocky Mountain elk are Montana, Wyoming, Colorado and Idaho. Washington and Oregon also have large elk herds at about 60,000 and 95,000 animals respectively, but many of these animals are Olympic elk. The eastern portions of Washington and Oregon, where the Rocky Mountain elk do range, don't seem to produce their share of large trophies.

Colorado has a herd of approximately 95,000 animals and yields a 23 percent hunter success ratio for *all* elk, not just trophy bulls. This is rather high as elk figures go. Although the current world record head, taken in 1915, comes from Colorado and the 6th ranking head was also taken there as recently as 1967, I would not look to Colorado for the best chance at large elk. Though there is a fair share of Colorado heads in the book, this is a very heavily hunted state. By any reasonable relationship total number of elk harvested and total number of hunting hours spent, Colorado has not produced its share of record heads. If I were hunting Colorado, I would look to certain areas in the southeastern corner of the state.

Utah has a relatively nice elk herd of some 12,000 to 14,000 animals, but practically no nonresident elk hunting is allowed. Through the years this area has not produced its share of really large heads.

Arizona has produced a few nice heads for its smallish elk herd of 10,000 or so, but with only about 160 of the 7,000 permits awarded to nonresidents, there are not many opportunities for visiting elk hunters.

Wyoming has a large herd of about 70,000 elk. With some 19,000 animals taken out of the 56,000 licenses, the hunter success ratio is a whopping 40 percent. That's very large for a broad-based hunting population of such a wary animal.

I have not been able to secure any estimates on the size of the Montana elk herd, but it is large. About 85,000 to 90,000 elk licenses are awarded annually with about 12,000 animals harvested for a hunter success ratio of about 16 to 18 percent.

Idaho also has a large but unestimated herd, and about 9,000 animals are taken per year from the 75,000 to 77,000 elk licenses sold. This yields a hunter success ratio of about 12 percent.

If I were looking for the top chances at really large bull elk, some of the best choices would be:

- *Montana.* General southwestern corner near Yellowstone; Big Hole, Bitteroot and Madison ranges.
- *Idaho.* Montana border, in the most rugged and remote country possible.
- *Wyoming.* Northwestern corner near Yellowstone.

There are a few other attractive but limited opportunities for trophy elk. New Mexico has a smallish herd of about 11,000 and limits nonresident hunting to about 700 licenses per year. But the state produces some very nice bulls in the northwestern corner, up around Chama.

A real "sleeper" of an opportunity for big elk, one that's largely gone unnoticed even by most serious elk trophy seekers, lies in British Columbia—but not in the more southerly areas that one usually associates with elk in that giant province. Gradually, elk have been pushing their way northward in the eastern portions of the province. Some extremely large bulls are taken each year up in the general area of Mile 200 to Mile 400 off the Alcan Highway. Most of the hunters going on the expensive, guided, deep-wilderness, mixed-game hunts in these areas are primarily after sheep and grizzly, with moose and caribou following closely behind. The elk still are not thickly populated; the whole herd in British Columbia isn't all that large. But more and more "targets of opportunity" are occurring each year in this far-north area. I would imagine there are about as many big bull elk dying of old age here as anywhere on the continent.

Western Alberta which has provided many record-book elk heads over the years—and from a relatively modest herd of 18,000 to 20,000 animals—has not been so desirable for big trophy bulls in recent years. This is partly due to considerably increased resident hunting pressure in the prime elk areas in the rugged western part of the province. And, in part, it is due to an (enlightened) management policy, which is to somewhat reduce the elk herds in order to lessen the indirect competition with Alberta's precious and failing bighorn herds.

How to Get a Trophy

The first rule of *trophy* elk hunting should be engraved in stone, in letters over six feet high so it would be difficult to forget! *BE IN TOP PHYSICAL CONDITION!* Most elk hunting is a tough physical proposition, and trophy elk hunting for the big old fellows with outsized hatracks and high IQs is about the toughest hunting in North America. It has been my experience that trophy elk hunting is generally tougher than sheep hunting.

Big bulls usually frequent rougher country than sheep do. While it's true that a sheep can always outclimb an elk, sheep are usually found in easier country. And more often than not trophy elk are found at higher elevations than sheep.

Although just about all elk hunting is still based on an open number of licenses, most of the best trophy sheep hunting is more rigidly controlled. The controls are either direct, by limiting the number of permits as for desert sheep and most bighorn sheep, or indirect, based on the number of hunters that a controlled number of outfitters book for much of the deep wilderness hunting for thinhorn sheep. Probably the best trophy bighorn hunting left on the continent is the Sun River herd in Montana. Yet the trick here is to secure one of the forty or so permits awarded each year. For photographic purposes I have stalked to within 40 feet of nice rams in this country in late November only three days after the *limited* hunting season had ended. The mule deer were still up on tops of the peaks some 2,500 feet higher than most of the sheep and would spook at the slightest provocation. The elk were even itchier, and remained deeper inside the wilderness area, where they couldn't be reached on foot.

As with trophy hunting for whitetail, and increasingly so for mule deer, getting a trophy elk is difficult because the animals just don't live long enough. The demand for this highly prized trophy is such that game authorities quite understandably, are managing and harvesting for maximum quantity, not trophy quality. When a bull elk has made it through six or seven winters to become trophy-size, chances are that he has been hunted and harried very hard much of that time. He has learned that his only safety lies in frequenting the highest and roughest country he can find and in being the last to be driven down to lower elevations when the frozen fist of winter smashes the heights with full impact. He is every bit as wary as a hard-hunted ram. In addition, he sees almost as well as sheep and trusts his ears and nose far more. He's far tougher to put down and keep down. Almost any reasonable hit means a sheep brought to bag if the hunter has any tracking ability and perse-

This fine 6-pointer is near record-book class. Note the evenly matched corresponding tines and the "Y's" formed by the 5th and 6th points.

verance. Not so with a big bull elk pumping adrenaline.

Most elk hunting means horseback hunting. Not only to get "back in" where the big ones are but to scour the countryside once in prime territory. Elk are big, free-ranging animals that don't bed down predictably in relatively open country where they can be spotted and "worked on" as sheep do. A hunter usually must cover a lot of territory, most of it high and up-ended, to locate enough elk in order to have a fair chance at a big bull.

Probably the biggest single mistake that most nonresident elk hunters make is booking or trying to book a meat-elk hunt at meat-elk prices and then trying to take a trophy bull on a weak hope as thin as the outfitter's casual remark that "we saw two good bulls last year." (In how many man-days of hunting?) Trophy bull elk are becoming very hard to get. In this regard, some booking agents and hunting consultants are becoming more leery about booking trophy elk hunts except in the most clearly defined circumstances and with knowledgeable hunters. A good bull elk is far harder to take than a good equivalent size moose or caribou bull. And yet, probably because an elk is more of a "U.S. animal" and less foreign, hunters generally aren't willing to contribute as much money, time or energy for a big elk as they are for the other two. More and more outfitters are trying to sell the idea that a "trophy" elk is any bull with four or five points to the side — and not the classic 6-pointer. That's a matter of opinion, but I just can't go along with that idea.

Bugling, or calling elk in, during the September rut is still practiced with varying degrees of effectiveness in different areas. However, more and more the big fellows have learned

Though not in the record class, this is a respectable 6-point head with one abnormal point behind the left sword.

This is a marvelous 7-point (Imperial) head. Here the corresponding tines are evenly matched and all tines are located in the right places.

that being too loudmouthed leads to an early funeral. Big bulls bugle far less often than they did years ago in many gamefields, and are less likely to come to bugle. However, it's still worth trying as one method of locating them, even if it may not bring them in.

Commercial elk calls are inexpensive and are readily available in elk-country sporting goods stores. Many elk hunters also make their own calls, fashioning them from various materials: wood, rubber hose, metal or plastic tubing. The idea is to create a shrill whistling sound that trails off into a somewhat guttural terminus. The sound of an elk bugling or whistling is one of the glories of the outdoors, a strangely exotic and *wild* sound that's guaranteed to raise the hackles on the back of your neck. Experienced hands can usually tell something about how old a bull is by the timbre of his whistle, the older bulls usually having a less shrill, heavier-bodied bugle. Probably the single biggest mistake made in elk calling — as in calling for waterfowl, predators, or other big game — is overdoing it.

The call doesn't have to be particularly loud because elk hear phenomenally well. Nor does it have to be particularly frequent. Your target is either giddy enough with the rut to answer back, or else he is not. And repeated calling usually doesn't do anything but sober him up enough to run him off. The calling isn't too difficult and doesn't really have to resemble the animal's call to the degree that it must for waterfowl or turkey — though that always helps. Success with the ruse is determined more by the animal himself and how rut-crazed he is, and by your sparing use of the call, no matter how scrupulously accurate it is.

Elk can provide a lot of fine eating. Though devalued a bit by the rut, bull-elk meat can be reasonably edible — that is, except for the oldest and sourest of bulls which are taken at the very height of the rut and which may run over a lot of countryside before actually being killed. The trophy hunter should always consider how he is going to take the meat out. Horses make the whole chore pretty easy. But if you're hoofing it, you should be prepared to bone out the meat and have a heavy-duty pack frame handy so that you can begin ferrying it out.

As for most other hunters, the first larger-than-deer game that I ever shot was an elk. He was just a young eating-size bull sporting a pip-squeak-size set of spindly 4-point antlers. Though probably only a long two-year-old and certainly no trophy, he was just right for the pot. He was bringing up the rear of a band of some eight or ten cows and calves. As he came crashing out of the timber and began crossing the small open riverbed about 140 yards away, I laid a single 130-grain Nosler .270 bullet into his lungs. Caught completely unawares and not hyped-up with adrenaline, he whirled frantically away and piled up about 50 yards down the line.

As we dressed him out, I gaped and gawked as will any eastern whitetail hunter at his first close-up sight of elk. Though the animal weighed only about 350 to 400 pounds, the size and power that were to have been his were clearly written on that immature frame. I stood there in awe and contemplated the wonderful beast. That's a feeling that I have never quite lost, where elk are concerned.

My first big 6-point came on a bitter below-zero morning in the Alberta high country. A longish 300-yard-plus shot saved

Here the author poses with a big Alberta bull he took in the late season, after the bugling period. Earlier in the season, this bull would have been in much higher and deeper wilderness.

him for me just as he was crossing over a small ridge and was about to disappear. I don't believe I've ever had a bigger thrill than when I first approached that big bull. Magic moments like that are priceless. When they come, they insure that those hunts *never* end, for they are always there in the back of the mind to be pulled out and lovingly relived.

Fortunately, we had horses for the big elk. But I had to pack most of that first smaller bull out on my back. And, even though he was only a smallish meat bull, packing came as a rude awakening after having only skidded whitetail out of the woods. So, if you don't have horses on your elk hunt, be prepared with a sturdy pack frame. Just packing out the antlers, the cape, and perhaps the rest of the hide and a foot or two can be a very substantial chore. (The hide makes for a fine rug or buckskin, and the hoofs can be fashioned into such things as ashtrays, bookends, and gun racks.)

Guns for Elk

It has been my experience that there is at least as much difference between the superior vitality of elk as compared with
moose or caribou as there is between vitality of the latter two
animals when compared to that of whitetail, mule deer or
pronghorn. An elk is a tough guy to knock down, especially if
he's big and aroused. Also, there is a high chance that you will
have to make a long shot. The average elk is killed at longer
range than is the average moose, caribou, sheep or most other
big game. There are exceptions. When jumped on the hunter's side of a canyon, such as in some of the hellishly steep
Idaho elk country, many elk are shot within the 40- to 70-yard
range. However, even on these short-range shots, the elk is invariably aroused and is pumping adrenaline. Then he is just as
hard to knock down as an undisturbed animal out at 300 to 350
yards.

The minimum gun for the average elk hunter should be in
the .270-.280-.30/06 class. And, though the 130-grain bullet is
fine for the .270, I would much prefer the 180-grain bullet (not
150-grain pellets) in the .30/06. All bullets should be rather
heavily constructed, and so much the better if helped along by
reasonably warm handloads. One of the oldest and most inex-
tinguishable arguments in outdoor writing is whether the .270
is "adequate" for elk.

Some gun writers have sold many stories aimed at new gener-
ations of hunters by fighting and re-fighting that classic "re-
ligion and politics" type question. Given one set of circumstances, the .270 is perfectly adequate. Given another, the .270
often enables the big deer to escape. It all depends on many,
many variables, such as what range, how well hit, how aroused
the animal was, what load and bullet were used, how big the
animal was, whether a second or third shot was possible, how
good a tracker the hunter was, and any number of factors
including whether horses were available for speedy follow-up.
(I do *not* let elk run after being wounded, hoping they'll stop, lie
down, and stiffen up, as I do with moose. Elk usually will run
until they drop as if the hounds of Hell were pursuing them!)

I am certainly not anti .270 or .30/06. Both elk kills I just
described were made with the .270 and both with 130-grain
bullets rather than 150- or 160-grain pills. The small bull went
down and out with one shot. The big fellow was belted down
solidly with one shot, and as he whirled down the mountain in a
fantastic cascade of snow, I followed it up with a miss and

another hit that really wasn't necessary. So, the .270 when properly used, is certainly "adequate" for elk.

However—and here it comes, .270 fans—the .270 is and will always remain a somewhat *marginal* elk caliber, even with proper loads in the hands of a cool shot who doesn't abuse it. *If* the hunter can accurately handle one of the newer .284 or .308 magnums, I feel that the extra margin of power they offer is well worth having. In some instances it could make the difference between a successful hunt and, that worst situation of all, a lost major trophy—a wounded animal that is not only lost to that hunter but to all others as he dies in agony and is wasted.

The .338 and .35 Whelen are certainly decent elk calibers, though the .35 isn't the flattest shooting cartridge in the world. Actually, a good elk caliber will often fall into the .30- to .35-caliber group, which Americans have never particularly gone overboard for, much to the dismay of the manufacturers. I hope this doesn't categorize me as being of the "big-bore school" any more than it puts me in the "small-bore school." I never much liked any kind of school and don't feel that my convictions on guns fall into any single category.

What I am saying is that a big trophy elk is rapidly becoming one of the most difficult trophies of all to secure. If a fellow invests enough coin, he can practically be assured of bragging-size trophies from many of our species, including the two thinhorned sheep. Such is not the case with elk. So it's a double tragedy to get so close to collecting your big bull, and then lose him when perhaps just a bit of extra punch would have made the difference.

Estimating Trophy Heads

Due to tradition and to the fact that elk racks don't attain the regal sweep that we expect from a trophy until they have attained six points to a side, to me a trophy elk must be a 6-pointer, or more, or else he isn't a worthy trophy. True, there are some large 5-point heads that are attractive, and there are some 6-pointers that are so small that I wouldn't consider them to be of trophy class. Even some of the 7-point or 8-point heads aren't true trophies if they are on old bulls that have begun to decrease in vigor and antler size, and if the antlers have begun to freak in shape.

Some would argue that nice, even 5-point, or even 4-point, heads should now be considered "trophies." But as yet, I cannot agree with them. Since 6-point bulls probably comprise no

Elgin Gates here poses with a head he took in 1954 in Wyoming's Big Horn Mountains. It ranked 16th in the 1958 records and was still good enough to tie for 54th place in the 1971 book—an indication of the increasing difficulty of making the book. Though this head loses some points to the uneven number of tines (7 and 6), the massive and long main beams of 57⁶/₈ and 56⁴/₈ inches, the 51-inch inside spread, and the long tines make this a remarkable trophy.

more than 4 to 5 percent of an *un*-hunted herd and less of a hunted herd, you can see that the odds are against running into too many of these old-timers.

A classic 6-point head is easy to spot. It must have the "Y" at the end (5th and 6th points). Without the "Y" it's not a 6-point head or it's non-typical. Look for that "Y" first when sizing up a bull elk. If it's there, then try to estimate how long the "Y" prongs are. If they appear to be 6 inches and longer, the head is starting to get interesting, depending upon your specific goals and whether you have already taken any 6-point bulls.

On a really good 6-point bull, all of the points, except for the very long 4th or sword point, will appear to be almost the same size. This means that the 5th and 6th points (the "Y" again)

RECORDS OF NORTH AMERICAN BIG GAME COMMITTEE

Wapiti Minimum Score: 375

BOONE AND CROCKETT CLUB

RETURN TO:
N. A. B. G. Awards Program
1600 Rhode Island Ave. N. W.
Washington, D. C.   20036

WAPITI

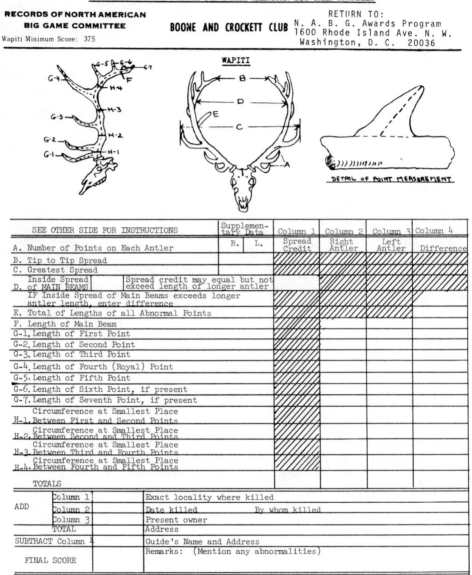

DETAIL OF POINT MEASUREMENT

SEE OTHER SIDE FOR INSTRUCTIONS	Supplementary Data R.	L.	Column 1 Spread Credit	Column 2 Right Antler	Column 3 Left Antler	Column 4 Difference
A. Number of Points on Each Antler			/////	/////		
B. Tip to Tip Spread			/////	/////	/////	/////
C. Greatest Spread			/////			
D. Inside Spread of MAIN BEAMS — Spread credit may equal but not exceed length of longer antler						
IF Inside Spread of Main Beams exceeds longer antler length, enter difference			/////	/////	/////	
E. Total of Lengths of all Abnormal Points			/////	/////		
F. Length of Main Beam			/////			
G-1. Length of First Point			/////			
G-2. Length of Second Point			/////			
G-3. Length of Third Point			/////			
G-4. Length of Fourth (Royal) Point			/////			
G-5. Length of Fifth Point			/////			
G-6. Length of Sixth Point, if present			/////			
G-7. Length of Seventh Point, if present			/////			
Circumference at Smallest Place H-1. Between First and Second Points			/////			
Circumference at Smallest Place H-2. Between Second and Third Points			/////			
Circumference at Smallest Place H-3. Between Third and Fourth Points			/////			
Circumference at Smallest Place H-4. Between Fourth and Fifth Points			/////			
TOTALS						

ADD	Column 1		Exact locality where killed	
	Column 2		Date killed	By whom killed
	Column 3		Present owner	
	TOTAL		Address	
SUBTRACT Column 4			Guide's Name and Address	
FINAL SCORE			Remarks: (Mention any abnormalities)	

I certify that I have measured the above trophy on _____ 19 _____

at (address) _____ City _____ State _____

and that these measurements and data are, to the best of my knowledge and belief, made in accordance with the instructions given.

Witness: _____ Signature: _____

Boone and Crockett Official Measurer

INSTRUCTIONS

All measurements must be made with a flexible steel tape to the nearest one-eighth of an inch. Wherever it is necessary to change direction of measurement, mark a control point and swing tape at this point. To simplify addition, please enter fractional figures in eighths.

Official measurements cannot be taken for at least sixty days after the animal was killed.

Please submit photographs of trophy front and sides.

Supplementary Data, measurements indicate conformation of the trophy, and none of the figures in Lines A, B and C are to be included in the score. Evaluation of conformation is a matter of personal preference.

A. Number of Points on Each Antler. To be counted a point, a projection must be at least one inch long AND its length must exceed the length of its base. All points are measured from tip of point to nearest edge of beam as illustrated. Beam tip is counted as a point but not measured as a point.

B. Tip to Tip Spread measured between tips of Main Beams.

C. Greatest Spread measured between perpendiculars at right angles to the center line of the skull at widest part whether across main beams or points.

D. Inside Spread of Main Beams measured at right angles to the center line of the skull at widest point between main beams. Enter this measurement again in "Spread Credit" column if it is less than or equal to the length of longer antler.

E. Total of Lengths of all Abnormal Points. Abnormal points are generally considered to be those nontypical in shape or location.

F. Length of Main Beam measured from lowest outside edge of burr over outer curve to the most distant point of what is, or appears to be, the main beam. The point of beginning is that point on the burr where the center line along the outer curve of the beam intersects the burr.

G-1-2-3-4-5-6-7. Length of Normal Points. Normal points project from main beam. They are measured from nearest edge of main beam over outer curve to tip. To determine nearest edge (top edge) of beam, lay the tape along the outer curve of the beam so that the top edge of the tape coincides with the top edge of the beam on both sides of the point. Draw line along top edge of tape. This line will be base line from which point is measured.

H-1-2-3-4. Circumferences - self explanatory.

* * * * * * * * * *

TROPHIES OBTAINED ONLY BY FAIR CHASE MAY BE ENTERED
IN ANY BOONE AND CROCKETT CLUB BIG GAME COMPETITION

To make use of the following methods shall be deemed UNFAIR CHASE and unsportsmanlike, and any trophy obtained by use of such means is disqualified from entry in any Boone and Crockett Club big game competition:

    I. Spotting or herding game from the air, followed by landing in its vicinity for pursuit;

    II. Herding or pursuing game with motor-powered vehicles;

    III. Use of electronic communications for attracting, locating or observing game, or guiding the hunter to such game.

* * * * * * * * * *

I certify that the trophy scored on this chart was not taken in UNFAIR CHASE as defined above by the Boone and Crockett Club.

I certify that it was not spotted or herded by guide or hunter from the air followed by landing in its vicinity for pursuit, nor herded or pursued on the ground by motor-powered vehicles.

I further certify that no electronic communications were used to attract, locate, observe, or guide the hunter to such game; and that it was taken in full compliance with the local game laws or regulations of the state, province or territory.

Date _____ Hunter _____

Copyright 1965 by Boone and Crockett Club
(Written request for privilege of complete reproduction is required.)

This chart is reproduced with permission of the Boone and Crockett Club, which, together with the National Rifle Association, co-sponsors the North American Big Game Awards Program.

151

should run 12 inches or longer. That's a good elk head. Depending upon final main beam length and spread, it will probably score at least near the record book minimum.

A big bull elk usually carries his head fairly well back, many believe out of habit developed in getting the sweeping antlers through the thick brush. From the side, the antlers should almost appear to sweep back to the bull's fanny, if the head is laid back a bit. A good elk head should run at least 4 feet in main beam length. However this is somewhat variable. My 6-pointer I mentioned earlier has nice heavy antlers, good even tines and about everything needed to put it well up in score except that I lost about 8 to 12 inches in main beam length that the head could easily have had, but didn't, between the swords and the beginning of the "Y." That's the place to check, if time allows, for final verification of main beam length. On that head the short distance between the swords and the "Y" meant a 345-point head, rather than a potential 370-point trophy. That's a wholly different class of head.

Usually the third point is the shortest of the first four points on an elk head. If, after careful scrutiny, you are pretty sure that both prongs of the "Y" equal or exceed the 3rd point in length, don't let the animal get away!

Body color is an indirect indicator. Frequently the big old bulls of the Rocky Mountain type develop yellowish body color. They are often called "buckskin bulls." And although the color doesn't automatically mean prime antlers, because the bull may be *too* old, it makes the bull readily visible from long distances. Thus you can tell quickly if a particular bunch of elk contains an old bull.

Actually, for your first trophy elk, you should probably be satisfied with almost any 6-pointer. There are occasional 6-point bulls that should not be shot because they're just too spindly and runty. Usually this occurs when a bull is growing his first 6-point rack too soon. Or the animal may have been ill during the antler growth period. But these are the exceptions. Any decent 6-point bull is a very respectable trophy, and the neophyte elk hunter would do well to take him and return another year to try for the big bull that scores well on up into the 300s.

Though the very top of the record book listings are dominated by animals wearing more than 6 points on one or both sides, these are very rare animals. The first "6x6" bull to appear down the list is tied for 14th place. Most big bulls are "6x6."

Often a bull carrying more than 6 points on one or both sides won't score as well as a big and even 6-point.

Probably less than half of the 7-point bulls carry their 7th (Imperial) point out at the end beyond the 6th (Royal) point where it should be, to be considered a normal point for scoring purposes. Many of them carry it as an extra brow tine, up where the sword forks off from the main beam, or it may be elsewhere. This can cost many points on the scoring since the logic of elk scoring takes into consideration evenness and conformation as well as size and number of points. So, if you see an "Imperial" head (7 points) or, rarer still, an 8-point or 9-point, look him over very carefully. You may have a fantastic trophy in your sights or a "fooler" that won't score nearly as well as an average adult 6-point.

The elk is one of the world's most magnificent trophies. And it's one of the hardest ones to secure, though *general* elk hunting is about the closest thing we have to an "everyman" sport beyond deer hunting. When hunting make sure you do your part. Carry enough gun, know how to use it, and be in top physical condition. Big bull elk don't die easy!

Prize of the Slopes: Wild Sheep

10

To many, the world's wild sheep rank at the very pinnacle of big game, and most especially at the pinnacle of hunting trophies. There are many reasons for this. Sheep live in high country that is challenging to the hunter — often demanding his best in both body and spirit. Sheep horns are magnificent physical trophies. By any ratio of horn length to body height or horn mass to body weight, no other animals in the world of either antlered or horned persuasions, carry such massive indicators of their maleness.

The world's wild sheep are distributed in two great arcs, one sweeping down from northeastern Siberia through Asia and the Near East to the islands of the Mediterranean and the other sweeping from northern Alaska down the spine of the Rocky Mountains and related ranges to northern Mexico. James L. Clark, the fine old taxidermist, sculptor, scientist and sheep hunter who was with the American Museum of Natural History in New York for many years, discovered and formulated this arc-distribution phenomenon and titled his landmark book on the subject *The Great Arc of the Wild Sheep*. Interestingly enough, when these "arcs" are marked onto a world map, they resemble a great, flaring set of sheep horns. Sheep dwell exclusively north of the equator and exist nowhere in the southern hemisphere, even though some of the world's greatest mountains are there.

The very largest sheep aren't North American. The fabled Marco Polo's sheep *(Ovis ammon poli)* inhabits a restricted area in the Russian Pamirs in one of the world's remotest corners, where Afghanistan, Pakistan, and Russia meet. One spectacular *poli* head measures 75 inches over the curl of each great horn. That's some 12½ feet for the combined horn length, or longer than any other set of horns from any species in the world! The *poli* is larger bodied than any American sheep. Big rams weigh-in at 350 pounds or more. Few Americans have taken this animal which many believe to be the premier trophy among all the world's wild game.

Clark himself and William Morden did so on their 1925 expedition for the American Museum of Natural History. Kermit Roosevelt and his brother Theodore, Jr., also did so a year later on their expedition for the Chicago Natural History Museum. No other American hunters took any until 1959 when Elgin Gates, of Needles, California, shot his. A very few, probably less than a dozen, have been shot since by trophy hunters.

Further to the north and east lies another great sheep which more and more hunters are coming to believe outstrips even the fantastic *poli* as being the grandest trophy of all. *Ovis ammon ammon* inhabits both the Greater and the Lesser Altai Mountains in outer Mongolia, with the largest heads coming from the Greater Altais. These are the largest sheep in the world, with big rams weighing from 400 pounds to possibly near 500. And, like the *poli,* they are "running" sheep rather than "climbing" sheep such as those found in North America. (Though the Asiatic *ammons* can certainly climb well and the American sheep can run, the Asian sheep are bigger bodied, longer-legged animals, inhabiting much higher rolling plateaus. They depend more on running for safety than the comparatively compact American animals.)

While the very largest *poli* rams have horns with basal circumferences of 16 inches, smaller than those of the largest bighorns and not much larger than the biggest Stones and Dalls, the mighty *ammon ammon's* frequently exceed 20 inches, with some running from 22 up to 24 inches!

The full significance of these base circumference measurements becomes clearer when you consider the *weight* of a set of the largest horns of each type sheep. And, although the factor of weight is nowhere considered in the Boone and Crockett scoring system (though there are those who think it should be in some instances), it is certainly a valid criterion to review when considering the overall trophy value of sheep horns since mass adds so much to the value of a long set. The long but fairly thin horns of a big *poli* ram will weigh approximately 25 pounds, while the shorter but heavier horns of a large American bighorn may run close to 40 pounds. But, the huge sweeping horns of the *ammon ammon* may weigh 50 pounds and even rival the *poli* in length.

In 1900 St. George Littledale took an *ammon ammon,* considered by many to be the greatest sheep head in the world, while hunting the Altais on the Siberian-Mongolian border. Littledale was a well known English hunter of the "classic" era. His great head measured 61½ inches in horn length with massive bases of 20½ inches in circumference. Clark himself thought that the head would probably never be equaled, much less surpassed. However, beginning in the early 1960s a handful of wealthy American hunters were allowed into the Mongolian sheep ranges. The result was that larger heads were taken. One of these fantastic heads was nearly half a foot longer than Clark's and had bases several inches larger.

However, our own North American sheep are very respectable members of the world-wide sheep community, ranging up near the top in desirability as trophies. Each horn of the great bighorn ram, killed by Simpson in British Columbia in 1920 and on display at the American Museum of Natural History in New York, exceeds four feet in length. Yet three bighorn heads in the record book still manage to outscore it! The magnificent Chadwick Stone ram killed in northern British Columbia in 1936 and the only known North American sheep to exceed 50 inches in horn length—which it does on both horns—is regarded by many as the finest trophy of any sort ever taken on this continent.

Though most taxonomists figure that there are a dozen or more separate races of sheep in North America, in a practical hunting sense there are two species, each of which divides into two subspecies. The Boone and Crockett system reflects this reality by allowing four categories for sheep—one for each of the separate subspecies. The two species are *Ovis canadensis* (the bighorns, which are subdivided as bighorn sheep and desert bighorn sheep) and *Ovis dalli* (the thinhorns, which are subdivided as Dall sheep and Stone sheep). A review of all four categories or subspecies is necessary for a proper perspective on North American sheep and sheep hunting.

The Bighorn Sheep (excluding the desert bighorn)

Though it is a matter of personal taste, many dedicated sheep hunters feel that the bighorns are slightly more desirable trophies than the thinhorns. Among this group, hunters are about equally divided in considering either the bighorn or the desert bighorn the more desirable, though the latter is even

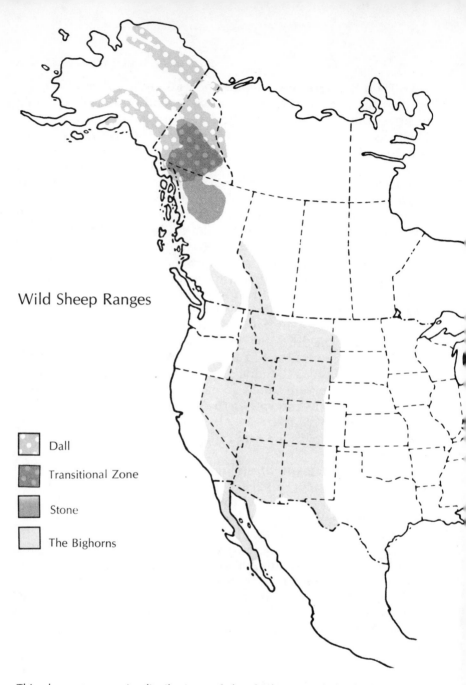

Wild Sheep Ranges

- Dall
- Transitional Zone
- Stone
- The Bighorns

This shows taxonomic distributions of the thinhorns and the bighorns. The thinhorns, Dalls and Stones, often intergrade in transitional zones. Their mixed-strain offspring are called Fannins. In trophy scoring, only pure white sheep are considered Dalls. Fannins are entered in the Stone category. The determination of "bighorn" and "desert bighorn" status is based primarily on comparison of horns with head and body size. In their deliberations, official scorers examine the horns and also consider photos, location of kill site, and subjective criteria.

scarcer. It is a commonly accepted theory that all North American sheep came from Asia over the periodically exposed land bridge that crosses the Bering Sea from Russia to Alaska. In theory, this bridge resulted when ocean levels dropped some 200 to 300 feet because the great Ice Age ice caps captured so much of the water. The animals probably came in two waves, with the bighorns arriving first — thus having had more time to work their way south — and the thinhorns coming later.

The bighorn is the basic "type" species of this group. The desert bighorn is something of a specialized and smaller offshoot. Bighorns were the earliest known of our sheep, sighted by Coronado in 1540. However, they were not discovered in the Canadian Rockies, where they seem to reach their maximum growth and horn size, until 1800. A large bighorn ram can weigh as much as 300 pounds, even slightly more, and carry as much as 12 percent of that weight on his head the year round!

Few animals have suffered so much as the bighorn sheep since the coming of the white man, though sport hunting and trophy hunting have not been the cause. Prior to disturbance by white men, bighorn were numerous in most western mountain ranges and in the "badlands" adjacent to many western rivers. Their range was considerably broader than it is today, coming east as far as the western Dakotas and extreme northwestern Nebraska and south as far as the mountains of trans-Pecos Texas. Many experts accept Ernest Thompson Seton's 1929 estimate of 1½- to 2-million sheep prior to the white man (for the whole bighorn species in all its subspecies, races and types).

The rapid decline of the bighorn sheep in the last half of the 19th century, although largely unheralded, is in its own way as dramatic as that of the bison. That decline continued into the 20th century and probably still continues today, though at a reduced rate. The causes for this catastrophe are complex and are still not fully understood. But some of them are competition from livestock, restriction of winter range due to various reasons (farming, highways, damming), a disease called scabies and excessive market hunting (this years ago and much less significant than the preceding listed problems).

In roughly the same fashion that Eskimos tended to catch TB and other "civilized" diseases from the white man and then die off in large numbers, wild sheep always died off when large numbers of domestic sheep were introduced onto their mountain ranges. Many of the western wild sheep herds were main-

Desert bighorns are lighter colored than the bighorns, and the two animals show marked differences in horn-to-body proportions. Note that the bighorn (below) is heavily built. But the desert bighorn is much slighter, and his massive horns appear to be almost too generous for the rest of him.

tained in reasonably good numbers until about the 1880s when large numbers of sheep and cattle began competing with them. In addition to catching diseases from the domesticated sheep, there is mounting evidence that bighorns are particularly susceptible to the early stages of range deterioration. Thus they have suffered severely from the common overgrazing of ranges by livestock. On a continent-wide basis, both types of bighorns can only be regarded as mere remnants of their former numbers. However, there is hope that hunting may improve as we learn more about the animal and his management and as we also decide to put sheep on a *priority-management* basis. Bighorns are still found in huntable numbers in the following areas:

Alberta. The Alberta eastern slope of the Rockies comprises an area of roughly 50x450 miles with about half of that lying within Canadian provincial parks. There are probably about 5,000 sheep outside these park boundaries in huntable ranges. Nonresident trophy hunting is regulated by permit with about 200 permits a year issued and some 100 sheep harvested on this basis. Additionally there is "nontrophy" sheep hunting by residents.

British Columbia. British Columbia has a bighorn herd estimated at about 3,000. At this writing, it appears a limited permit program will be instituted in the near future.

Idaho. As is the case in most of the other western states with bighorn, Idaho's once magnificent sheep herd experienced three severe die-offs between 1870 and 1910 (mostly from scabies). The herd now maintains a reasonably stable level at about 2,500 animals. Hunting is by permit only, with some 10 percent of the permits going to nonresidents. About 70 or 75 sheep are taken each year.

Montana. Montana features two very high, rugged areas immediately north of Yellowstone Park (areas #301 and #501) which are the only places left in the U.S. where bighorns can be hunted on an unlimited, nonpermit basis. There's a reason. The hunting is high—much of it over 10,000 feet—and hellishly steep and rough. Thus, most hunters simply can't cut it. The sheep aren't especially wild by bighorn standards, and some huge trophy rams probably die of old age every year. The problem is finding the sheep and then getting to them. Much of the camping would be in dry camps at very high altitude because you have to stay up with the sheep to have any decent chance of scoring. This is only for the dedicated sheep hunter!

The rest of Montana's respectable sheep herd is hunted on permits. If the sportsman can secure one of the 30 to 40 permits awarded for the Sun River area each year, that sheep herd (about 800 animals) furnishes the best bighorn hunting left on the continent.

Wyoming. There's a herd of some 2,600 sheep in Wyoming and all are on a permit-only basis, with a rather generous 25 percent of these permits allowed for nonresident hunters. Statewide, about 100 sheep are taken each year, and the best areas are around Dinwoody and Frank's Peak. As a general rule the sheep become a bit smaller as we work south into Wyoming and Colorado.

Colorado. There's a nice herd of about 3,700 to 4,000 bighorn here, but the hunting is limited to residents and very tightly restricted to small numbers of permits.

Other States. There are also small bighorn herds in South Dakota, Washington, Oregon and New Mexico which furnish some extremely limited resident-only hunting by permit.

Though census estimates for any wild, free ranging species are extremely chancy at best, especially for species living in difficult mountain terrain, there's a good possibility that there are only about 20,000 bighorn sheep on the continent. Maybe less.

The Desert Bighorn

The various races of this subspecies of bighorn have dwarfed to a degree because of the harsh and sterile desert environments that they inhabit. A big desert ram runs considerably smaller than the "basic" bighorn races and even at about 160 to 175 pounds or so, he's a bit smaller than a big Dall or Stone ram.

He's a good bit lighter in body weight and neck size than the much larger bodied bighorns. And though his horns are almost always shorter and more heavily broomed, they are almost as large at the bases as those of the larger bighorns. Relative to body size, a nice desert sheep carries far larger horns. Thus, real trophy rams have an unusual, heavy-horned/skinny-necked look that is reminiscent of pictures of the largest

Siberian Ibex, in which it appears impossible that the animal could carry around such enormous horns the year round.

I doubt that there have ever been large populations of desert sheep—this due to the limited ranges and thin densities that those ranges would afford even under the best of circumstances. Even in the good old days, hunting for desert sheep was always a quite limited sport, available only to a very few wealthy hunters and/or devotees who lived in the nearby thinly populated areas.

Shortly after World War II an outdoor writer and trophy hunter named Grancel Fitz coined the term "grand slam" to refer to the taking of all four of the North American mountain sheep. Though a perfectly legitimate concept at the first, over the years it became something of a status symbol among the wealthy. Some of these men only "collected" sheep in much the same way they collected art and weren't hunters by any reasonable standard. And the "grand slam" concept probably served to encourage some really scandalous practices.

As the least common and most difficult to secure leg of the "slam," the desert sheep suffered more from unethical and illegal practices than any other sheep. Though I certainly have no brief against any hunter setting for himself the task of collecting all four American sheep in a sporting manner, over the long term the high degree of institutionalization and publicity given to the "grand slam" label itself probably has not served sheep or sheep hunters well.

Legal desert sheep hunting on any reasonable basis has just about become a thing of the past. Arizona (fortunately!) has a herd of some 2,700 animals that continues at a rather stable level. About 70 highly prized permits are awarded each year, and 10 percent of them go to nonresidents. About 35 to 40 sheep are taken annually. Nevada has something less than 2,000 sheep. But the population has generally shown a downward trend even though only 15 to 20 sheep are harvested each year, with only two permits going to nonresidents. Hunting of the herds may be discontinued at any time.

The grand sport of trophy hunting has not caused the basic decline of the desert sheep though the popular press sometimes tries to give hunters the blame. California is a good example of this. All desert sheep hunting has been banned there for over a century by state charter, and yet the once healthy herd is down to some 2,000 and continues to decline annually.

The reasons for population decreases are manifold. Highway and irrigation projects, as well as other developments, disturb the sheep. Also sheep succumb to competition from the more aggressive species like mustang horses and feral burros which are, in turn, totally protected due to misplaced sentiment on the part of certain individuals and organizations.

Baja California allows some limited legal desert sheep hunting each year, with about 30 or so animals taken. A number of other "quasi-legal" animals are also taken. For it's one of the world's worst kept secrets that enough coin brought into conjunction with certain palms in Mexican officialdom gives hunters who simply cannot live without a "slam" the "right" to shoot a sheep. Legal desert sheep hunting ceased in Sonora some years ago and most of the American hunters who have taken desert sheep there over the years have done so on a questionable basis. There are a few transplanted desert sheep in Utah and west Texas and, though it is doubtful that any meaningful sport hunting may result there, it is hoped that reasonably healthy herds will develop.

I have never killed a desert sheep. And as long as the situation remains roughly what it has been throughout the postwar era, I doubt that I shall have much of a yen to. However, that is strictly a personal judgment, and there is certainly nothing wrong with the sportsman pursuing the desert sheep by legal and ethical means as long as the hunting regulations are set within the bounds of good game-management practices. As with most other species, the sport and trophy hunter, with his dollars and his political clout, remains the desert sheep's best friend and ally. Simple protectionism is certainly *not* an adequate answer to the animal's complex problems.

The Dall Sheep

By and large the thinhorns, since they live to the north, far from human population centers, have fared far better than the bighorns. Much good hunting remains for the Dall sheep, and there is reasonably good hunting for the Stone sheep.

A big Dall ram will weigh roughly 190 to 200 pounds. With his white coat and amber horns, he's a handsome fellow.

Alaska. The state has about 30,000 Dalls. With some local exceptions, the herds are holding up well, though the really large heads have become much rarer. About 1,000 to 1,200 sheep are shot annually by resident and nonresident sport hunters for a 40 to 45 percent hunter success ratio out of the 2,100 to 2,500 sheep licenses sold annually. But this doesn't take into account unrecorded and unrestricted native kills.

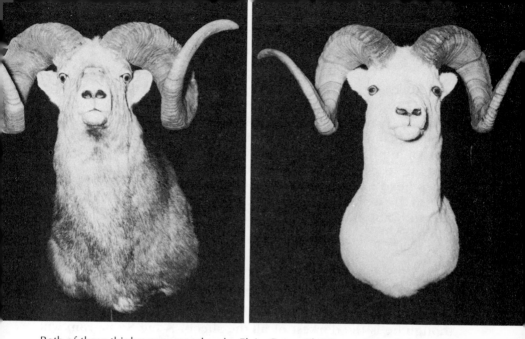

Both of these thinhorns were taken by Elgin Gates. The Stone sheep (left) scored 176⅛ points and ranked 70th in the 1971 records. The Dall scored 177⅝ and ranked 38th. Key factors in scoring are length of outside curves and horn mass. Long, flaring, unbroomed (unbroken) tips result in optimum scores for outside curve. But since tip-to-tip spread does not directly affect the score, massive horns that are broomed back may still score high. It would be possible to hunt a lifetime and never see, let alone take, a sheep like either of these two. A ram could well be 13 or 14 years years old and die of old age without carrying horns three-fourths the size of these. In addition to age, the main factors affecting horn development are nutrient and mineral content of forage, favorable growing seasons, and—possibly most important—quality genetic stocks.

Alaska's largest Dall populations are found in the giant Alaska and Brooks ranges, but the largest heads come from Alaska's steeper and harder-to-hunt Chugach and Wrangell ranges of the southeastern (not panhandle) region.

The Yukon. My diligent research has not revealed any estimate of the herd size in this giant territory. But the herd is large and healthy. About 250 to 300 are taken each year by trophy hunters. The harvesting is assuredly at a far lower ratio to herd size than Alaska's. Best bets for big rams are the areas around giant Kluane Lake in the southwestern part of the territory and in the Pelly Mountains farther to the east. As less sheep hunting is available in northern British Columbia, the pressure on the Yukon will inevitably mount. But there should be good sheep hunting in the Yukon for many years to come.

The Northwest Territories. The 150 or so nonresident sportsmen making the trek to this remote gamefield each year take about 130 sheep. Sport hunting wasn't opened to nonresidents here until the mid 1960s, and game populations are good. This hunting is similar to Alaskan sheep hunting in that most of it is by fly-in and then by foot rather than by horseback, as is the case in the Yukon and British Columbia. The average sheep head here is probably somewhat smaller than those farther to the west in Alaska and the Yukon, though this cannot be said with absolute certainty until there has been more harvesting.

The Stone Sheep

The Stone is a thinhorn, a subspecies of the snow-white Dall, though he is the darkest of all the sheep. A big Stone ram will weigh some 20 pounds more than a comparable Dall. With his dark blackish body sharply accented by the white underparts and the white nose patch, he is an extremely handsome fellow and a worthy foil to his all-white cousin to the north.

Northern British Columbia furnishes the only meaningful hunting for Stone sheep though a few dark sheep are found in certain southern Yukon pockets, especially in the Pelly Mountains. There are probably about 10,000 Stone sheep in British Columbia and the legal trophy-sport hunting harvest runs around 550 to 600 animals per year. The herds are in a reasonably healthy state, though there are some localized over-harvesting problems.

The Stone and Dall sheep, being of the same species, will interbreed regularly. As you would imagine, this produces a somewhat "dusky" or mottled grayish sheep that shows color characteristics of both parents. But the degree of darkness and whiteness can vary considerably, with some animals looking more "Dallish" than others, while some others lean toward the Stone look. For some years after the turn of the century, sightings of this animal excited both hunters and taxonomists into believing that this was possibly a different subspecies rather than merely an intergrade between Dall and Stone. For a time some taxonomists even granted the animal subspecific designation (*Ovis canadensis fannini*).

However, it is now generally accepted that the so-called "Fannin" sheep is merely an intergrade, and he is considered to be a true Stone sheep (*Ovis dalli stonei*). These animals are encountered occasionally in both the extreme northern reaches of

British Columbia, where a few white sheep are also seen, and the southernmost areas of the Yukon, where a few black sheep are seen. Their horn growth doesn't appear to vary from that on Stones, being roughly the same size and conformation. And their coloration makes them an interesting and slightly off-beat trophy. However, the sportsman after his first thinhorn sheep would probably do well to concentrate on first taking the more typically colored Stone and Dall before possibly considering one of the Fannins. Though Dall and Stone sheep are of the same species, they must have come over from Asia in two separate waves. Or else they must have been separated from each other for a very long time in order to evolve two such markedly different colorations. It appears that during our recorded history the Stones have tended to drift north a bit more. And the Dalls have worked south so that these Fannins, or intergrades, have become somewhat more common.

The best areas in British Columbia for big Stone sheep are in the general Cassiar Mountain area including the headwaters of the Kechika and Turnagain rivers, the Eagles Nest Range south of Coldfish Lake, the head of the Cattaga River.

How to Estimate Sheep Heads

The four subspecies of sheep vary a bit in horn size and conformation. The bighorns usually have more tightly curled horns. The thinhorns tend more toward the outward flaring or argali type of head. But estimating them all is done in a similar fashion.

Elgin Gates has an unrivaled collection of *large* game heads from almost every major game species in the world, including all the major sheep. Yet he considers himself first and foremost to be a sheep hunter. Here's what he wrote me about estimating sheep horns:

> Like many other trophy animals, a really big sheep head needs no study. At first glance, even from a long distance, the horns are so massive as to make the ram look undersized. And the real trophy horns, especially on bighorns and desert rams, are almost always broomed way back. Usually, the first year's growth and part of the second are worn off. If the horns curve down level with, or slightly below, his jaw line and then flare upward so that the heavy blunted tips reach to eye level, here is a trophy well worth collecting. If the heavily broomed tips come up to the bridge of the nose or above, the ram will likely make the record book and is well worth a long, hard hunt.

RECORDS OF NORTH AMERICAN BIG GAME COMMITTEE

BOONE AND CROCKETT CLUB

RETURN TO:
N. A. B. G. Awards Program
1600 Rhode Island Ave. N. W.
Washington, D. C. 20036

Minimum Score: Sheep
Bighorn   — 180
Desert   — 168
Stone   — 170
White or Dall — 170

<u>SHEEP</u>

<u>KIND OF SHEEP</u> _____

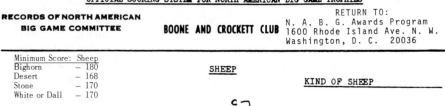

SEE OTHER SIDE FOR INSTRUCTIONS	Supplementary Data	Column 1	Column 2	Column 3
A. Greatest Spread (Is often Tip to Tip Spread)		Right Horn	Left Horn	
(If Greatest Spread, B. Tip to Tip Spread (Enter again here)				Difference
C. Length of Horn				/////////
D-1. Circumference of Base				
D-2. Circumference at First Quarter				
D-3. Circumference at Second Quarter				
D-4. Circumference at Third Quarter				
TOTALS				

ADD	Column 1		Exact locality where killed
	Column 2		Date killed By whom killed
	TOTAL		Present owner
SUBTRACT Column 3			Address
FINAL SCORE			Guide's Name and Address
			Remarks: (Mention any abnormalities)

I certify that I have measured the above trophy on _____ 19____
at (address) _____ City _____ State _____
and that these measurements and data are, to the best of my knowledge and belief, made in
accordance with the instructions given.

Witness: _____   Signature: _____

Boone and Crockett Official Measurer

168

All measurements must be made with a flexible steel tape to the nearest one-eighth
of an inch. Wherever it is necessary to change direction of measurement, mark a control
point and swing tape at this point. To simplify addition, please enter fractional
figures in eighths.

Official measurements cannot be taken for at least sixty days after the animal was killed.
Please submit photographs of trophy front and sides.

Supplementary Data measurements indicate conformation of the trophy.
None of the figures in Lines A and B are to be included in the score. Evaluation of
conformation is a matter of personal preference.

A. Greatest Spread measured between perpendiculars at right angles to the center line
of the skull.

B. Tip to Tip Spread measured from outer edge of tips of horns.

C. Length of Horn measured from lowest point in front on outer curve to a point in line
with tip. DO NOT press tape into depressions. The low point of the outer curve of the
horn is considered to be the low point of the frontal portion of the horn, situated above
and slightly medial to the eye socket, (not on the outside edge of the horn.)

D-1 Circumference of Base measured at right angles to axis of horn. DO NOT follow
irregular edge of horn.

D-2-3-4. Divide measurement C of LONGER horn by four, mark BOTH horns at these quarters
even though other horn is shorter, and measure circumferences at these marks.

*   *   *   *   *   *   *   *   *   *   *   *   *   *

TROPHIES OBTAINED ONLY BY FAIR CHASE MAY BE ENTERED
IN ANY BOONE AND CROCKETT CLUB BIG GAME COMPETITION

To make use of the following methods shall be deemed UNFAIR CHASE and unsportsmanlike, and any trophy
obtained by use of such means is disqualified from entry in any Boone and Crockett Club big game competition:

    I. Spotting or herding game from the air, followed by landing in its vicinity for pursuit;

    II. Herding or pursuing game with motor-powered vehicles;

    III. Use of electronic communications for attracting, locating or observing game, or guiding the
    hunter to such game.

           * * * * * * * * * *

I certify that the trophy scored on this chart was not taken in UNFAIR CHASE as defined above by the Boone
and Crockett Club.

I certify that it was not spotted or herded by guide or hunter from the air followed by landing in its vicinity for
pursuit, nor herded or pursued on the ground by motor-powered vehicles.

I further certify that no electronic communications were used to attract, locate, observe, or guide the hunter to
such game; and that it was taken in full compliance with the local game laws or regulations of the state,
province or territory.

Date _____ Hunter _____

This chart is reproduced with permission of the Boone and Crockett Club, which,
together with the National Rifle Association, co-sponsors the North American Big
Game Awards Program.

Beware if the ram carries rather thin horns, especially if the points are perfect and curve up to eye level or even above. This will be a young animal, hardly worth shooting. Many are the disappointed hunters who have shot such a ram and then found the horns to be less than 35 inches, and the base circumference less than 13 inches.

Dall and Stone rams will sometimes retain their horn tips. A real trophy head with perfect tips curling up high above the nose to the level of the top of the horns, or flaring out in the classic Argali configuration, is a sight to behold. The famous world record Chadwick Stone sheep head is an example of the latter. The tips are starting their second downward curve. Again, there is never a vestige of doubt when a head of this caliber is seen at any distance.

The same basic rule-of-thumb applies to Dall and Stone heads as to bighorn and desert sheep. If the horns are light, with a shallow curve that does not reach the lower jaw line, and with thin tips that end at eye level or even a bit above, it will likely be a young ram of six or seven years, not worth taking by the real trophy hunter.

This Dall is about the average size now being taken in Alaska and the Yukon. Horn curves run slightly over 35 inches. Though far from record class, a sheep like this, taken in fair chase, is a worthy trophy.

Gates has looked over more than his share of sheep and has shot some of the finest heads ever taken. His advice on how to size up sheep heads is certainly worth listening to.

However, many of his heads were taken some years ago when the sheep hunting, especially for the two bighorns, was considerably better. Among pragmatic sportsmen of more moderate means, another school of thought has surfaced regarding what constitutes a "trophy" bighorn or desert sheep head. This approach holds that *any* legal bighorn or desert sheep, if it is the sportsman's first, is a fine trophy and should be taken. Then the sportsman can try to return and hunt far more selectively for the larger head, which he may never see. With the expense of hunting the two bighorns being what it is today and the chances for big rams being what they are, the evolution of this approach was inevitable. Each sportsman must decide for himself exactly what constitutes a "trophy" sheep, especially among the two bighorns.

I will add one observation, and here I'm not referring to Gates. It appears a bit smug and self-serving to me for some sheep hunters who collected their heads 20 to 30 years ago to tell today's hunter, who is certainly every bit as sportingly inclined and quality conscious, that he should not even *consider* shooting a bighorn ram of less than 38 inches. Sheep hunting has changed so much in the interim.

How to Hunt Them

The classic formula for sheep hunting is this:

1. Glass large expanses of territory in order to spot the quarry before he can spot you with those phenomenal eyes that are the equivalent of 8x or 9x binoculars.

2. Having located the sheep, plot out a stalk that hides you entirely from the herd's view and allows you to climb above them to shoot. (Sheep, though among the wariest of animals when hunted, seldom look up.)

3. Before taking the final shot, glass the one trophy animal steadily one last time to be sure that he is both legal and of adequate trophy size to meet your desires.

Sheep are not the most intelligent big-game animals in North America. Of the mountain game, I would rate the elk far above them in that respect. But, although they quickly tame down to be the most trusting and confiding of animals in parks and sanctuaries, when they are hunted, no animal is warier (which is

This ancient Dall is the same one shown in the opening photo of this chapter. He is the largest live sheep the author has seen. Photographed by Jerry Manley in the upper Alaska Range, this ram was so old that he probably failed to survive the next winter. Advanced age is evidenced in the development of the horns and in the old look of the body. Note how the body sags and has lost muscle tone. The muscles and flesh on the hind legs are flaccid. The eyes appear dark and rheumy.

different from intelligence). In fact, when hunted over a period of time, sheep do become somewhat more inclined to look up as well as down, though it's still the best bet to climb above them.

Sheep hunting, unlike most other trophy hunting, is not necessarily an early-morning occupation. Sheep feed early and usually bed down about mid-morning. This is the best time to spot them and stalk them.

Often the sheep stalk involves a long climb up the backside of the mountain, the sheep hidden from the hunters perhaps several hours at a time. Far better to wait until the sheep bed down so that there is a better chance they will still be there when you emerge above them several hours later with jellied legs and burning lungs.

Sportsmen new to sheep hunting often have the wrong idea as to where to find the sheep. Sheep do not inhabit the steepest or highest parts of the mountain. They much prefer the gently rolling pastures found on the rounded shoulders and knolls. Sheep are not often found on or in cliffs, though they do like to be near a bit of broken, "cliffy" country so that they can flee

there if danger threatens. I have found many sheep in the flattest, "easiest" country imaginable, once the basic climb up to
their general altitude was made. And, at times, they have been
surprisingly far from the smallest postage-stamp-size bits of
bluff or cliff.

However, a sheep really doesn't need much "rough" for him
to find safety in it. He can flee to the smallest of areas and run
wolves or other potential predators ragged by bouncing around
the same little half acre of rocks at speeds that they cannot
match. Many sheep, especially the old solitary trophy rams, are
found in hidden basins with a sheer wall rising at the back and a
small stream or lake at the bottom, surrounded on the "floor"
and sides by succulent green grass.

The old ram can find everything he wants here: food, water,
and a safe place to bed down. Once you locate a ram in one of
these basins, if he isn't disturbed, he may still be there weeks
later. Most hunters tend to look too high up for sheep and in
too rough country.

This massive bighorn was taken by Elgin Gates in the 1950s. Scoring 185⁴/₈
points, it ranked 132d in the 1971 records.

Like their domestic cousins, mountain sheep are intensive feeders, nipping the grass well down. You can often look at a hillside from a distance and tell whether deer or sheep have been feeding on it. Sheep will take the grass all the way down to the roots. As fall comes in, sheep often move to the north face of the mountain because their winter coats are growing in, forcing the move to cooler and shadier slopes. So if the north face fits the other general sheep requirements, it is always the face to check during hunting season.

Also, due to less sun, the north face still has moisture in the grass at the inch nearest the ground. Thus, from a distance these grassy hillsides will often appear a bit greener than the more sun-dried grasses on the south face. Sheep much prefer this more succulent grass.

Another mistake many sportsmen make is in not looking often enough for sheep down in the trees. Sheep will often stay in the same copse for weeks, especially on the north face of the mountain. Grass is there. The timber offers protection from the wind. So if water is nearby, why move?

If there is a suitable rough nearby to flee to, many sheep live in and around these timber pockets and hardly ever see the great open basins that are always pictured as the classic sheep grounds.

Beginning sheep hunters often look for their sheep in country that is too high, too steep and too rough. Goat country. Sheep don't frequent these grounds, by far preferring the greener, more succulent grasses to the coarser, drier vegetation that the goat seeks at these heights. Actually, in good mixed-game country, more times than not the hunter will see elk or caribou (or even moose, occasionally) feeding above the sheep and in rougher ground than the sheep are working. If threatened though, the sheep will immediately head for the cliffs to seek vertical safety, while the larger animals will take off on a long distance run, relying on their speed and endurance to carry them to safety.

Guns for Sheep

The sheep, though approximately the same size as the goat, have far less vitality. I believe that this is primarily due to the difference in temperaments. The sheep is a considerably more high-strung animal. And thus apparently his nervous system is far more susceptible to the shock effects that modern, high-

This is a typical out-camp, which is midway in luxury between the hard-roofed base camp and the primitive spike camp. When after the largest trophies, you greatly improve your chances by backpacking with your guide to the heights and hunting out of a spike camp.

velocity centerfire rifles primarily depend on for their killing power.

For sheep only, guns of the .243, 6mm, .257 class are fine though the .25/06 or the .240 or the .257 Weatherby would give a bit more killing power out at 300-yards and beyond. Actually, most sheep should be shot at rather close range if the hunter has done his part in locating them before being spotted and then climbing above or up to the unalarmed game. Most shots at sheep seem to fall into one of two vastly different categories: either within 150 yards at bedded or almost still animals or well out beyond 300 yards at rapidly moving animals. The smaller guns will do fine for the first type of shot and most of the long, running shots shouldn't even be taken. All too often a hunter may feel that the outsized cannon in his hands that, *on paper,* gives him a tremendous long-distance capability, also gives him a license to take some ungodly long shots at sheep, and other animals.

There is nothing wrong with long shots under the proper conditions. A cool head who knows his gun and its trajectory

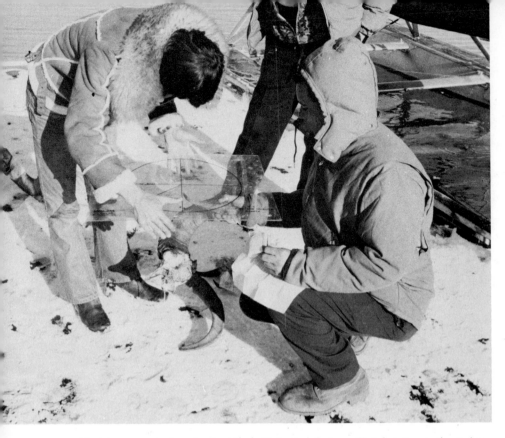

Here horns are being checked for sufficient curl at an official station in the Yukon. The markings on the plexiglass show whether the curl meets requirements. Such requirements vary among the states and provinces.

and is a fair hand at estimating range is certainly entitled to take the long shot. This is especially valid if the animals are still or almost so and if there is little or no chance of hitting other animals by mistake. But, the fantastically long shot, made on a "flock-shooting" basis at running animals at uncertain ranges has been responsible for the waste of a tremendous number of sheep and pronghorn over the years.

If the hunter is on a mixed-game hunt with moose and grizzly on the agenda, then a gun with a bigger barrel hole is called for. A .270 or .30/06 or perhaps one of the newer .284 or .308 magnums with reasonably heavily constructed bullets would be more in order. Any mountain-hunting rifle should be flat-shooting. And whatever caliber, in order to provide the necessary flexibility, it should generally close to a 300-yard point-blank range; that is, with the bullet rising no more than 3 to 3½ inches at mid-range and sinking no more than that after recrossing the line of sight.

Optics

Good optics are vital in sheep hunting. So top-quality binoculars of 8x to 10x and a good spotting scope are necessary. The spotting scope should either be of the variable type or of fixed power. If it is of fixed power, the hunter should carry several interchangeable eyepieces of approximately 20x, 30x and 45x. A good riflescope is also necessary, and though I prefer the fixed-power spotting scopes over the zooms for the very finest resolution of horn sizes at long distances, I usually mount my rifles with variable-power riflescopes of 2x-7x or 3x-9x, rather than using the fixed-power 4x or 6x models.

Sheep hunting is far more than the securing of a big set of horns. It's a contradictory sport, consisting of long, contemplative hours of scouting and glassing interspersed with bursts of excitement while the actual stalk is made.

When your sheep is down and your pictures are snapped, you would do well to pause a moment before field-dressing and caping the animal. Take a moment to savor the thrill, the excitement, the feeling of accomplishment, and—yes—to note strange overtones of muted sadness that come to every thinking hunter when his prized and fairly-taken quarry is finally downed. You have just taken one of the finest game animals in the world. And you are a fortunate man to have done so.

Dazzling Cragmaster: Mountain Goa

11

Mountain goat are, perhaps, our most underrated trophy game. That's unfortunate because in many ways they are unique animals, and a mountain-goat stalk is often one of the most exciting of experiences. The goat does not receive his just dues for several reasons, but chief among them is the fact that he is inevitably compared to his more glamorous high-country neighbors, the mountain sheep. Though sheep are magnificent animals — as anyone who has hunted, observed and photographed them can attest — their popularity is due in part to the fact that they have had a better press throughout the years than the more phlegmatic, slab-sided goat.

Goats generally run larger than the two thinhorn sheep and the desert bighorns, and they equal or exceed the size of really large Rocky Mountain bighorns. A mature, robust billy can weigh as much as 275 to 325 pounds, depending upon the amount of food available and the time of year. In his charming *Camp-fires in the Canadian Rockies,* which recounts an extended 1905 hunting trip and scientific expedition to the Fernie area of southeastern British Columbia, William T. Hornaday indicates that the largest of several goats killed weighed 276 pounds. (The limit was *five* per person in those halcyon days!) Since Hornaday was director of the New York Zoological Park and a scientist of some note, care was taken in the weighing process. So we can expect that the weight was reasonably accurate by field standards.

Although several authorities indicate that goats have been taken with verified weights of 500 pounds, I have never shot, observed or heard first-hand of a billy that I thought would exceed 325 pounds. There is no doubt that the elegant, little, black dagger horns of the goat don't have either the mass or the glamor of the huge, curling wild sheep horns. However, the goat is a striking trophy with his ebony horns (once they have been cleaned) and debonair black hoofs, set off by the contrasting white or yellow-white coat.

Incidentally, it is typical for the older billies in the trophy class to have a fair amount of cream or yellow in their coat. If your trophy comes back from the taxidermist with some yellow in it, it wasn't accidentally "stained." Or if the fee indicates a small added charge for bleaching out some yellow, the taxidermist probably isn't just trying to gouge a little out of *your* hide!

When you take your trophy goat, skin out the whole animal. After caping out the head and front half of the animal for a shoulder mount, skin the back half, which makes for a small but beautiful, fleecy white rug. Edged in black-and-gold or blue-and-white felt, it makes a striking addition to any trophy or powder room. You can even use the whole hide to make a head-on rug, similar to a bear rug but with the mouth closed. Hoofs can be on or off, depending on your taste.

The goat is basically a northern or Canadian animal, though we have healthy, but small, populations in certain areas of the northwestern contiguous states. Though most taxonomists recognize four races of goat, the Boone and Crockett Club has wisely limited goat to a single category in the trophy book, this due to the similarity of these animals in general size and appearance.

Unlike the elk, moose, caribou and certain other species, the mountain goat is strictly a North American animal. His nearest relatives are certain other goat-like animals such as the Tahrs (northern India, New Zealand); the Serows or forest goats (northeast Asia and Japan); the Chamois (southern Europe); and the Takin (southern China).

For many years it has been the practice to refer to the mountain goat (and the others just mentioned) as "goat-antelopes." The exact weighting that the "antelope" portion receives at any given time varies, depending upon the authority cited and the era. Alas, taxonomy is not an absolute science, and fashions in taxonomic thought ebb and flow just as surely as they do in women's hemlines and hairstyles.

Though the mountain goat does have certain distinguishing characteristics that prevent his inclusion in the subfamily *Caprinae*, that is, of long horned or "true" goats, to my mind some of the "antelope" talk borders a bit on the brink of a precious distinction—especially in a hunting sense. To allow that the mountain goat (and the other "short-horned goats" mentioned) are not "goats" just because they are placed in the subfamily *Rupicaprinae* is somewhat similar to saying that whitetail and mule deer are not "deer" because they don't fall into the *Cervidae* group with elk, moose, and caribou. The mountain goat looks more like a goat than anything else, acts more like one, and is hunted more like one. So that's what we'll consider him for the balance of this book.

The mountain goat's white pelage is distinctive and attractive. Only two other large animals in the world wear white the year round. Interestingly enough, both of these animals are also found in North America; they are the Dall sheep and the polar bear.

With the exception of the coat of the musk ox, the goat's coat is finer, softer, and probably warmer, than that of any other hoofed animal on the continent. There are actually two coats. A fine undercoat, almost as soft as down, provides enormous warmth and yarn that can be fashioned into garments that are among the world's softest. This undercoat is covered by a coarser, straighter outer coat which, beginning in September, grows longer in order to provide more warmth and extra protection from the snow and rain.

The outer coat's long guard hairs provide the goat's characteristic beard and leggings, which as much as the horns themselves are the true glory of a big old cragmaster billy. Although the goat's beard and knee breeches don't reach their full length until November, they are usually of good attractive length by early September. Thus, depending upon the particular year and the exact locale, it's usually wise to wait until September to take your trophy, the later in September the better. However, don't wait in the harsh heights until the onset of winter, which suddenly seals the goats off from hunting. Sheep generally drop to the lower, more protected areas when the weather on top becomes too brutal. But goats, true top-of-the-world dwellers that they are, cling to their beloved heights no matter what. They merely search for lees to bed in. And they feed in windswept areas where the scanty grasses and plants they require are either uncovered or close to the surface of the snow.

Goats are rather stocky, slab-sided animals standing some 36 to 40 inches at the shoulder, though Hornaday and others have measured animals up to 42 inches. Their deep, slab-sided conformation makes for good cliff hugging and ledge walking, and their powerful legs enable them to lever themselves slowly up and down almost sheer cliffs — much as a man climbs with his hands and feet. Though goats don't possess the dazzling cliff-

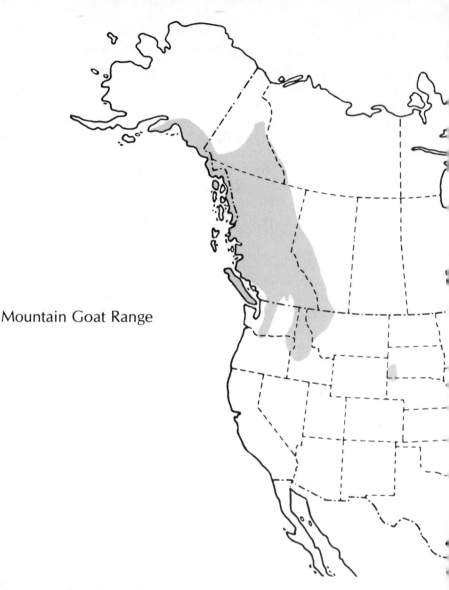

Mountain Goat Range

Goat are not huntable in all portions of the range.

manship of sheep, they have a sure-footedness that lets them clamber around ledges that sheep would fall from.

Even the goat's disposition is well suited for the life he leads. He is a rather slow, deliberate chap who takes his time to think things through rather than being fidgety and flighty like the sheep. While sheep are basically running animals, who run reasonably well on hillsides and run when climbing the rough

182

cliffs that they flee to, goats are walkers and slow climbers. They have to be. Nothing in this world, not even markhor or ibex, can *run* up and down the cliffs that the goat prefers.

When a goat spots potential danger he usually moves off at a rather deliberate pace that some observers characterize as slow or leisurely. I prefer to charge this off to the fact that the goat must choose his escape route with some care. His objective is to hide from sight as soon as possible, yet he cannot allow himself to be "rimrocked" or trapped into a cul-de-sac. (Yes, that happens to goats, too.) Choosing the route and then negotiating it surely takes a bit of doing, and this is not a process calling for undue haste.

The goat has a characteristic shoulder hump something like that of a bison, and he even roughly resembles a bison in outline. (The awe-struck mountain men first encountering goats in the far West during the early 19th century called them "white buffaler," because of this resemblance.) The goat carries his head low, and although he can raise it above the line of his neck and shoulders in order to look up, he seldom has need to. The vast majority of a goat's life is spent looking down at the world and its other inhabitants.

The goat's horns are round, black, smooth for their last half or so, and are literally as sharp as daggers. While sheep grow their magnificent horns expressly for the rams to fight with and thus assert dominance, goats seldom ever fight seriously with their smaller but far more lethal horns. They would simply kill each other off too frequently in any extended combat.

Though these small but deadly horns are rather brittle, it's amazing how often they survive unbroken when the goat takes a wild, cartwheeling fall down the mountainside after being shot. This kind of fall occurs rather frequently in goat hunting. So, before shooting a goat, the hunter should always check to determine if he can recover the animal after the fall or if, by waiting and letting the animal move a bit, recovery after the kill will be easier. I, and most other goat hunters I know, have had to pass up shots at more than one good trophy billy because he would simply not have been recoverable after falling. Thus, to shoot him would have been a waste. Alas, the only billy I have ever had in my sights which I'm sure had horns more than 10-inches in length was one of these animals.

Actually, more often than not, the major damage sustained by a goat during a sliding, skidding tumble down the mountainside is to the hide, especially around the face and neck, rather than to the horns. Some goat trophies are so skinned and abraded that, even with all the taxidermist's considerable skills (at substantial extra repair costs), the trophy mount simply cannot be completely restored.

Also, when sizing up a potential shot at a goat above, the hunter should remember that the goat just may tumble right over him on the way down and knock him off the mountainside. This almost happened to me once.

Early one glorious September morning in the Cassiars of northern British Columbia, we had glassed two big caribou bulls pretty high up on one face of a mountain and a nice goat on another face of the same peak. The goat was even higher up and in far rougher terrain. Since it was early and I was rested and in good condition for the two climbs, I elected to try for both animals. By 11 o'clock I had the big, near record, Osborn bull down, field-dressed and rough-caped. Next came the goat.

We had to drop back down the mountain losing more than half of our precious altitude to snake around and over a torturous dragon's back in order to get to the infinitely rougher face where the goat was calmly surveying the world. Actually there was some doubt that we could even make the climb and get within range because the going was very bad—well into the "hand-over-hand" stage that goat hunting often confronts the hunter with.

However, an enormous billy had been spotted on this peak several weeks earlier. And the goat we were after, alone and almost at the very crown of this abominable pile of rocks certainly was doing things the way a really big billy should. So, with a few misgivings we set out. The going became rougher and rougher, almost forcing us to turn back twice, but each time we found alternate routes and continued on.

Finally we pulled within 350 yards of baggy pants and it appeared we could go no farther. He had spotted us but was not unduly alarmed. And, from the looks of that mountain, I could understand why. I had had to leave the spotting scope behind. Yet, through the 8x binoculars, he did not seem as big as the 11-inch-class monster that had been spotted here earlier. However, goats are very deceptive to estimate. In any case, it was plain he was a nice animal. I bellied into a contorted prone-standing shot (on that slope they were one and the same!), scrabbling out as much purchase as I could by digging my feet in. The guide held grimly onto my belt to try to anchor me to the mountain lest the recoil from the shot send me down a lot quicker than it took to come up.

After the shot, the goat displayed the legendary vitality of his race. He merely flinched and humped up as a red patch suddenly bloomed behind his shoulder but well into the critical heart-lung area. Quickly I jacked in another shell, but the goat had wheeled behind a rock outcropping and gave us only scattered glimpses of himself as he picked his way across the slope to a chimney leading to the very apex of the mountain. All I got was a single additional shot at him when he passed momentarily into view, and that was a clean miss — gray rock dust geysering into the air about a foot behind him.

The goat then disappeared into the chimney, completely hidden from view by the front edge. I was sick at heart. I was sure the animal was mortally hit and, to date I have been fortunate enough never to lose a trophy that I have wounded. I have certainly missed my share of shots but, through a combination of luck and stubborness, have not lost a wounded animal. We talked it over and decided to try to go on. I couldn't believe that even a big goat, anchored as solidly with a big magnum cartridge, could make it all the way up that nearly vertical chimney to the top and get away. And I couldn't abide the thought of a fine trophy, fought for so hard, dying and going to waste when it was almost within grasp.

Somehow we made it to the base of the chimney, but the goat wasn't in sight. Then we started up the edge of the chimney, staying as much as possible out of the treacherous loose rock and scree that could whisk us right off the steep incline. I led the way so I could shoot without hesitation. Suddenly, almost at the top of the chimney and about 100 feet directly above us, the goat hoisted himself to his feet and lumbered toward the top. There was no time, in three steps he would be over. So it was now or never — more like jump-shooting a cottontail than making the classically-deliberate long-range mountain shot.

I shot, the goat faltered, stumbled and then — almost in slow motion — sailed out into space and hit the loose scree 10 feet below where he had been standing, madly sliding and tumbling our way. We flattened ourselves against the wall of the chimney, fortunately finding a little shelter in a crack there as the goat flew by close enough to touch. His mad, 200-foot slide stopped only against the final rock between him and a 500-foot vertical drop. We shook and puffed, both scared to death and glad to still be alive. My knees wouldn't work right and I had to pause for several minutes to recover enough in order to safely pick my way down to the goat. It wasn't the monster we had hoped for, but it was a nice trophy. And I was proud of the climb and stalk that took him. But, today, each time I look at that head on the wall, I recall that that goat brought us within 18 inches of eternity. If he had hit me, there is no possible way I could have survived the fall that would have followed. So, let this be a word to the wise regarding shooting at goat directly above!

Where to Get a Trophy

Alaska. Although British Columbia has dominated goat hunting historically, Alaska is the real sleeper. There are an estimated 20,000 goat in Alaska, all near the coast and most in the state's southeastern panhandle. Better yet, probably the biggest goat in the world live in this coastal range—both on the western, or Alaska side, and on the eastern, or British Columbia side.

And yet goat hunting is very neglected in this region. And Alaskan goat hunting is almost unknown to most nonresident trophy hunters. The annual harvest runs only 500 to 600 animals. Most of these are taken by residents who live in the general area. How can this be? There are several reasons. For one thing, Alaska is so much better known for its other major trophies (sheep, grizzly, moose, caribou, black bear) that goats receive little or no publicity. Also, most of the goat hunting is a bit off the beaten track from the classic Alaskan hunting grounds in the Brooks and the Alaska ranges and in the Wrangell and the Talkeetna mountains.

Though more and more hunters are coming to the coastal panhandle for brown bear, few bother to climb the nearby but ferociously rugged coastal mountains in search of goat. And, as yet, there are few professional Alaskan guides or outfitters actively promoting goat hunting. I believe this will change in the coming years. The hunting is simply too good to warrant its continued neglect.

In fact, the Alaskan goat population is so healthy and underharvested that, as this is written, the limit is still *two* goat per hunter. For a dedicated trophy hunter with his heart set on a big goat, I can think of no better opportunity than the Alaskan coastal range. Some goat-only hunts can be made for very reasonable costs in this area, and chances for a big head are high.

Be warned though. This is rugged hunting, even by goat climbing standards. Be in good physical condition with no excess weight. Quit or cut down on the smoking and train hard for the hunt, especially if you live in a lowland area. Be sure you

The big solitary billies favor the steepest terrain. Fair chase for the old mountain bills can be the most challenging of hunting.

have the right gear: heavy-duty mountain boots for rough, hard, rock work; light but tough raingear; down clothing; wide-brimmed hat and flat-shooting rifle that you can hit with, out to 300 yards.

British Columbia. This area has dominated the goat-hunting scene for years, and there are still healthy populations of trophy animals in the northern part of this giant province. The classic goat grounds farther to the south such as in the magnificent Kootenays have been combed pretty hard though, and general real estate development has not helped the goat populations.

The annual harvest in British Columbia is in the 1,200 to 1,500 range, or about two to three times that of Alaska. Hunter success ratios are still rather high for this type of hunting, around 32 to 35 percent. However, the comparable Alaskan figure of 50 to 60 percent is even better!

B.C.'s two prime big-goat areas are the eastern side of the coastal range in the far northwestern part of the province and the Cassiar Mountains in the near northwest. There is little or no trophy hunting for goat on the eastern side of the coastal range now because the several outfitters who have exclusive hunting rights there either concentrate on the big salmon-eating grizzly around the Taku River or on general mixed-game hunts which stress sheep and antlered game far more than goat.

The other area, the Cassiar Mountains, also features many large goat. They are harvested a bit more here as part of the general mixed-game hunts conducted in the area, but populations of trophy-size animals remain high.

I know of no goat-only hunts available in either of these two areas, though combination goat-caribou-moose hunts (without the two more expensive sheep and grizzly) are available farther south.

Yukon Territory. The goat are limited in number here, and the hunting is sparse. There are some goat in pockets of the southernmost portions of the territory, but this is not the place for the serious goat hunter, as most are picked up only as "bonus" trophies, incidental to the other hunting.

Alberta. Though there has been good goat hunting here in past years and a few Alberta heads rank high in the record book, the season is currently closed on them, and I don't expect it to reopen.

Northwest Territories. This offers a similar goat-hunting situation to that of the Yukon. There are scattered pockets that contain goat but only 10 to 15 a year are taken by visiting hunters, for a very low hunter success ratio of around 10 percent. Goat are just an incidental "target of opportunity" here rather than being a mainstay.

Montana. Montana has a healthy goat herd. The harvest runs around 300 per year on a permit-by-drawing system. Hunter success ratios (of those fortunate enough to draw a permit) run high, around 40 to 45 percent. Nonresidents generally receive around 25 to 30 percent of the 800 to 1,000 permits awarded.

Washington. Washington also has good goat hunting, with figures roughly similar to those in Montana. About 250 to 300 goat are taken each year out of the 900 or so permits. Competition for the prized permits is high, since some 6,500 to 7,500 hunters apply annually.

Idaho. Goat hunting is more limited here than in neighboring Washington and Montana. About 300 permits are allowed each year, with 10 percent going to nonresidents. Around 130 goat are usually taken for a 40 to 45 percent hunter success ratio. There are usually some 1,600 to 2,000 permit applicants.

Wyoming and South Dakota. These states allow some extremely limited goat hunting, usually restricted to residents only.

How to Hunt

Goat often inhabit the same general regions as moose, elk, caribou, grizzly and sheep. I have seen goat on the same mountain with each of these other species. But "goat country" differs from the living environs of the others. Since the mountain goat is the preeminent mountaineer among North American large game animals, he inhabits the roughest, steepest and highest terrain of all.

Though sheep prefer nicely rounded grassy slopes and pastures with a bit of cliffy rough nearby to flee to in case of trouble, the goat lives full time in even rougher terrain than that which a sheep will use only for an escape route. Goats see well, though some hunters in years gone by felt they didn't. I believe this was because the goat didn't immediately "register" alarm or fright upon seeing hunters. So the hunters felt that the goat's eyes must be less than extraordinary. The fact that the animals don't react quickly (like most sheep) is, of course, more due to their deliberate temperament than to myopia.

Goats have almost no natural enemies except man and eagles, which may occasionally carry off a very small kid. The grizzly, wolf, and cougar know all too well that the goat is not for them. (Though I do believe that wolves take more sheep than was once believed.)

Goats simply aren't used to being afraid. The only "enemies" they live with consistently are the harsh and uncompromising weather and the treacherous footing. When pushed, goats *can* run rather well. I shot one goat at a full run in the Kootenays and was amazed at the rapid pace he was making up a steep

Still in summer pelage, this billy would be of twice the trophy value later in the year because long beard and leggings rate at least half of his glory.

slope which offered some very bad going.

The place to look for goats is generally the roughest faces of the roughest mountains, up near the top. Incidentally, goats don't necessarily live on top of the highest peaks, just the roughest.

The standard axiom when hunting sheep, grizzly and most high-country game is to get above the quarry. This is not so valid in goat hunting. For one thing, it often simply isn't possible. For another, I have done it often enough to know that the terrain may be so steep and rough that the goat will frequently be hidden from view by intervening spurs and outcroppings that you couldn't spot when doping out the stalk from below. And oftentimes once you do get above the goat, you will not be able to shift around very much in order to get him back in sight.

Again, goat usually don't alarm as quickly as the more skittish sheep. And when they move off, it is frequently at a slower, more deliberate pace, allowing the hunter time to shoot.

If it is feasible, I will climb above goats and drop down on them. But, if it is overly difficult to attain a vantage from above, I have few misgivings about climbing up to them or — better yet — climbing up to their general elevation and then sidehilling around the mountain and approaching them "on the level."

This latter technique is the one that I have used most frequently and with the most success in approaching to within shooting range (or, closer yet, photographic range). Bear in mind that the real trophy billy is the one that will usually be all alone on top of the very roughest peak in the whole area. This makes getting above him even more chancy than stalking just any goat.

The more one hunts and photographs and watches wild animals — and birds, for that matter — the more one learns that "always" is a word that does not apply. Game animals do not read well. So they don't know that they are "always" supposed to behave in established ways. Thus, though goats are *almost* always well above timberline on the roughest cliffs, I have seen them down in timber a couple of times. Both times they calmly sauntered out of the spruce trees and into the open as casually as a commuter early for the 7:34. They moved off at a leisurely pace. I do not know what they were doing down that low. They did not appear to be feeding or trying to bed down.

Also, though I have never seen them down in the valley floor myself, I have spoken to more than one dependable eyewitness who has. Sam Sands, the Rocky Mountain House, Alberta, outfitter, took the largest billy he ever guided a hunter to up in the White Goat Wilderness Area of west-central Alberta — right out in the middle of a broad valley, flat as a ball field. Old baggy pants wasn't within a mile of a mountain, and though he was probably crossing from one peak to another, he did not seem to be heading directly toward any particular mountain. The hunter dismounted and calmly powdered the huge near-11-inch goat just as if he were shooting pronghorn antelope on a Wyoming flat. And this was a big outsized trophy billy, not some hare-brained juvenile! So, if the goats aren't where they should be, don't be afraid to look where they shouldn't be.

Estimating Trophy Quality

The hunter is faced with a unique problem in sizing up goat heads — a problem that exists with no other major horned or antlered North American game species. He must distinguish between the nannies and the billies. From a long distance, this can be difficult.

In many areas it is illegal to shoot nannies. Even where nannies are legal, most hunters prefer to take the heavier-horned billies. Nannies often do grow quite long horns. In fact, the

A billy's ears generally run about 4 inches. So this billy's horns would be about 8 to 9 inches. Another feature for comparison is the distance from the corner of the eye to the nose, about 8 to 8½ inches.

longest horns listed in the 1971 Boone and Crockett book belonged to a nanny killed many years ago in the Cassiars.

This old girl must have been an ancient matriarch indeed, as she carried horns that swept back 12⅛ inches and 12⁴⁄₈ inches! For many years when goat horns were evaluated as trophies solely on length, this head was considered to be the world's record. Now that horn mass (circumference at base and at each quarter of the horn's length) is also considered, this head has dropped well down to tie for 148th place in the listings. The current world record is an almost equally sweeping billy head with two horns of 12-inch length but scoring a full 6⅖ points more than the old girl because of the mass. (By goat-scoring standards, the 6⅖ is a big difference.) I am convinced that there will be more than one 13-inch billy roaming the high places of coastal Alaska or northern British Columbia as you read this.

So, in addition to estimating how long a goat's horns are, the hunter also needs to determine whether it's a billy or a nanny in order to take the heaviest horns. There are several ways to do this, depending upon the time of year, and the range and angle at which the hunter is viewing the animal. If you see any young goats with an adult, chances are you're viewing only nannies and kids. Rarely do you find trophy billies with nannies or young except during the breeding season in November and December. Usually males are solitary or near solitary animals in the late summer and fall-to-early-winter hunting seasons.

However, this is not an infallible rule. So other indicators are also handy. If viewing an animal from fairly close range early in the year when the hair is still short, you can often confirm the sex by looking at the genitals. Also, the older and larger billies, like big old "buckskin" bull elk, tend to have more cream or yellow in their coat than nannies or younger billies.

The horns themselves should be sized up critically. When viewed from the side, nanny horns, though often quite long, are shaped differently than those of a billy. A nanny has long, spindly horns that hook back and down far more sharply at the ends. Billy horns are heavier and "lay back" gradually all along their length rather than rising sharply toward the vertical and then hooking back more sharply near the end as nanny horns do.

From the front, the goat's ears are the most reliable reference as you estimate trophy quality of the horns. Thus, like pronghorn and (to a lesser degree) deer, the goat is an "ear-rated" rather than a "body-rated" trophy, as are moose, elk and caribou. The spread on goat horns is a highly variable thing and it thus can be a deceiving reference. Anyway, the spread does not contribute to the score. It is merely recorded as "supplementary data."

Normally when a goat is not disturbed his ears stick straight out or even droop a bit, rather than sticking up. Though the ears are actually longer, they will appear to be about 4 inches long in their normal relaxed position because the goat's long hair will cover them partially. Any horns that are noticeably more than twice as long as the goat's ears bear some closer appraisal.

The horns of about 75 percent of all adult goats probably run 8 to 9 inches in length. Those running over 9 inches are a re-

RECORDS OF NORTH AMERICAN
BIG GAME COMMITTEE
Goat Minimum Score: 50

BOONE AND CROCKETT CLUB

RETURN TO:
N. A. B. G. Awards Program
1600 Rhode Island Ave. N. W.
Washington, D. C. 20036

ROCKY MOUNTAIN GOAT

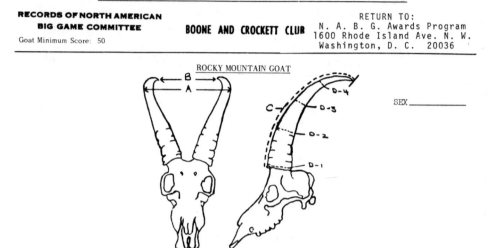

SEX_____

SEE OTHER SIDE FOR INSTRUCTIONS	Supplementary Data	Column 1	Column 2	Column 3
		Right Horn	Left Horn	Difference
A. Greatest Spread				
B. Tip to Tip Spread				
C. Length of Horn				
D-1. Circumference of Base				
D-2. Circumference at First Quarter				
D-3. Circumference at Second Quarter				
D-4. Circumference at Third Quarter				
TOTALS				

ADD	Column 1		Exact locality where killed	
	Column 2		Date killed By whom killed	
	TOTAL		Present owner	
SUBTRACT Column 3			Address	
			Guide's Name and Address	
FINAL SCORE			Remarks: (Mention any abnormalities)	

I certify that I have measured the above trophy on   19
at (address)   City   State
and that these measurements and data are, to the best of my knowledge and belief, made in
accordance with the instructions given.

Witness:_____ Signature:_____

Boone & Crockett Official Measurer

INSTRUCTIONS

All measurements must be made with a flexible steel tape to the nearest one-eighth of an inch. Wherever it is necessary to change direction of measurement, mark a control point and swing tape at this point. To simplify addition, please enter fractional figures in eighths.

Official measurements cannot be taken for at least sixty days after the animal was killed.

Please submit photographs of trophy front and sides.

Supplementary Data measurements indicate conformation of the trophy. None of the figures in Lines A and B are to be included in the score. Evaluation of conformation is a matter of personal preference.

A. Greatest Spread measured between perpendiculars at right angles to the center line of the skull.

B. Tip to Tip Spread measured between tips of horns.

C. Length of Horn measured from lowest point in front over outer curve to a point in line with tip.

D-1 Circumference of Base measured at right angles to axis of horn. DO NOT follow irregular edge of horn.

D-2-3-4. Divide measurement C of LONGER horn by four, mark BOTH horns at these quarters even though other horn is shorter, and measure circumferences at these marks.

* * * * * * * * * * * *

TROPHIES OBTAINED ONLY BY FAIR CHASE MAY BE ENTERED
IN ANY BOONE AND CROCKETT CLUB BIG GAME COMPETITION

To make use of the following methods shall be deemed UNFAIR CHASE and unsportsmanlike, and any trophy obtained by use of such means is disqualified from entry in any Boone and Crockett Club big game competition:

     I. Spotting or herding game from the air, followed by landing in its vicinity for pursuit;

    II. Herding or pursuing game with motor-powered vehicles;

    III. Use of electronic communications for attracting, locating or observing game, or guiding the hunter to such game.

* * * * * * * * * *

I certify that the trophy scored on this chart was not taken in UNFAIR CHASE as defined above by the Boone and Crockett Club.

I certify that it was not spotted or herded by guide or hunter from the air followed by landing in its vicinity for pursuit, nor herded or pursued on the ground by motor-powered vehicles.

I further certify that no electronic communications were used to attract, locate, observe, or guide the hunter to such game; and that it was taken in full compliance with the local game laws or regulations of the state, province or territory.

Date_____ Signature of Hunter _____

This chart is reproduced with permission of the Boone and Crockett Club, which, together with the National Rifle Association, co-sponsors the North American Big Game Awards Program.

spectable trophy but nothing outstanding. If they run over 10 inches, things start to get interesting, especially if the horns are heavy. Eleven inches and more puts the horns way up in the book and may well indicate the trophy of a lifetime.

From the front or inside corner of his eye to the tip of his nose, a nice billy will average about 8 inches. A really big one will go 9 inches, while a nanny will average about 6½ inches, with anything over 7 inches being a very large female. Thus, any billy goat whose horn appears substantially longer than the distance from eye corner to tip of nose is a good goat.

Beware of the occasional freakish "miniature" goat. These goats, like miniature sheep, are undersized animals which are

Many a hunter has taken an undistinguished nanny he mistook for a good billy. Though a nanny's horns are often longer than those of a comparable billy, they lack the mass. This billy (left) and nanny belong to George Parker.

perfectly proportioned. Thus, estimating by comparing the horns with other body parts will fool even the most seasoned hunter.

Fortunately, these miniatures are uncommon. One way to guard against being fooled by them is to check the size of the tracks when stalking. A big foot means a big animal, and you can somewhat more safely assume with horned animals — (rather than antlered game) — that a big track means a big set of horns. At the least, the track can help you distinguish more readily between the sexes. The length of a nanny front track will be around 2 inches, possibly slightly more for a very large animal. Any track running over 2½ and up to 3 inches and better is a billy. (Be careful not to let splaying in mud or soft ground mislead you as to true track size.)

When you do see several goats together and one stands out as being far larger than the rest, it's either a nanny with a bunch of kids or a big billy breaking the solitary "rule." Since goats have only single or twin kids, if several smaller animals are present and no other large animals feed or move into sight after a time, chances are you're not glassing a nanny and kids, but a big billy and smaller animals. Just as most men are about 5 foot, 10 inches in height, most adult goats are average size. If one goat stands out as being *huge*, like a 6-foot 8-inch basketball player would among normal-size men, chances are you're looking at a real trophy billy.

Guns for Goat

Goat are usually characterized as being hardy, armor-plated citizens that take a good bit of killing. That has been my experience, also. I've never killed a goat outright with a single shot, though one of my goats would have died shortly without the second shot. If a goat is aware of your presence and is aroused enough to be pumping some adrenaline, he can absorb a lot of punishment — especially if the first shot isn't good. In that case he seems to swallow up additional shots as if you were pelting him with birdshot.

But goats are mortal. If well hit with a reasonably well constructed bullet, they will go down and die. But they do at times exhibit amazing vitality for an animal often weighing closer to 200 pounds than 300. Part of this is due to the shock-absorbing qualities of their thick, double layer coat, but most of it is due to their stolid, phlegmatic temperament. Like the African cape buffalo, the mountain goat just doesn't seem to have a nervous system subject to shock.

My brother John killed his first goat with the then-new Remington 7mm Magnum and heavily constructed Nosler bullets, pushed along by a hot handload. He hit the animal four times at between 250 and 300 yards as it slowly walked off. He actually thought he was missing because the goat showed no effect. Finally, after the fourth shot the big goat sat down, then lay down and finally passed on to his reward.

When John clambered up to the supine goat, he found that all four shots could have been covered by a saucer and that the heart and lungs were literally a sieve when he opened the animal up. And yet the animal had moved over 50 yards and had taken some five minutes or better to die. That's a long time and a long way when such enormous shocks are being absorbed.

While I would cheerfully go sheep hunting with a .243 or .257 — providing I weren't also after grizzly or moose — I would prefer not to use those guns for goat. Under the right circumstances they could certainly be effective, but I would normally not like to use anything lighter than a .270 with well constructed 130-grain bullets or a .30/06 with similarly made 150- or 180-grain pellets. For the possible long-range shot, which happens more often in goat hunting than in sheep hunting, a .284- or .308-type magnum would be a bit better, *if* the hunter can handle it accurately.

Since goat are probably shot at longer ranges on average than any other game except pronghorn (or wolf), I would prefer a caliber which would give a better than 300-yard, point-blank range, with the mid-range trajectory rising no more than 3 to 3½ inches. Long shots are not always necessary, but it's wise to be prepared for them.

A sharp-pointed, somewhat heavily constructed bullet is a good bet for goat hunting. True, it may have to open up at 300 yards but, it may also have to penetrate a lot of tough hide, hair and meat at much shorter ranges. The ideal whitetail load may cost you a goat under some circumstances. So I usually opt for bullets of the Core-Lokt or Nosler persuasion, though many other good makes are also available.

It's been said that "when you see one goat, you've seen 'em all." And it's true that there is probably less variety in the size and conformation of goat heads than in that of any other major North American species. But, it's not true that "when you *hunt* one goat, you've hunted 'em all!" Due to the rugged terrain and harsh climatic conditions that goats prefer, to me, there is no other type of hunting that can produce as many thrills or as much variety. And many of us feel that the hunting is just as important as the head itself.

With this outlook, goat hunting ranks up with the best sport provided by other species. A mountain goat gets you up into high, beautiful country. And, as with the sheep, the stalks for him are often long and exciting. Though the quality of sheep hunting in general is gradually declining and the long-term trend appears to be negative, prospects for goat and goat hunting continue to be bright in most areas. That's a big plus for the ever-growing numbers of hunters who like to hunt up on the "roof of the world."

The Big Bruins:
Black, Brown, Grizzly

12

The presence of bears adds spice to the occasion, whether it's hunting them, photographing them or just observing them in the wild. In terms of general trophy esteem they compare to the other hornless game — the cats and canids — in about the same way that sheep do to goat. And, just as North America is abundantly blessed with several races of sheep, all of them among the best of their kind in the world, so it is with the bears. Though North America does not have cats to rival those of Africa or Asia, nor goats that compare with those of Eurasia, no area in the world approaches it in richness when the subject is bears.

Taxonomically, North America has three bears, the black bear, the grizzly/brown bear, and the polar bear. In practical trophy hunting terms we also have three bears but, as is often the case, the hunting categories do not align exactly with the scientific ones.

The great ice bear is no longer hunted for sport in this country. Limited sport hunting is allowed in Canada only as a special-permit Eskimo activity. And off the Scandinavian coast, general sport hunting has periodically been available in recent years. But since it is now illegal to import polar bear trophies and hides into the U.S., for all practical purposes, polar bear hunting is now closed to U.S. sportsmen.

In some ways, that may be quite unfortunate. The great white bear of the far north is one of the most interesting animals on earth. He rivals — probably even outstrips — the largest grizzly/brown bears in size. And no animal in the world makes a more regal trophy. There is growing evidence that worldwide polar bear populations could well stand a limited, highly monitored sport-hunting harvest. If permits were highly expensive,

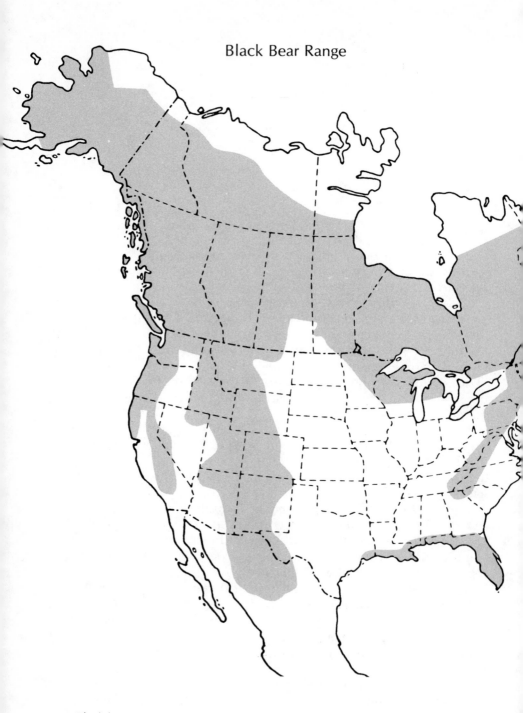

Black Bear Range

Black bears are protected in many of the areas in the range.

the income from this hunting could be used to finance further research on polar bear. And the data collected from carcasses and the questionnaires filled out by the hunters would be of scientific value. The sport might also provide some employment for a few otherwise largely unemployable natives.

Also, it has been proven that sport hunters are inevitably an animal's strongest and most effective "constituency." Complete preservation status, although necessary with some species, always tends over a period to somewhat erode this constituency. Even the most limited hunting, with the vast majority of us knowing full well that we will probably never participate, tends to strengthen and reenforce an animal's backing from the hunting fraternity. However, due to the polar bear's status as this is written, the animal does not warrant more detailed coverage in this book.

This leaves the black bear and the grizzly/brown bear. Although the polar bear and grizzly also reside in Asia, the black bear which undoubtedly immigrated to North America from Asia about 500,000 years ago is now an "All American," with no black bears residing anywhere else in the world.

The bears have always been something of a taxonomic nightmare. Fashions in ursine taxonomic thought change. "Practical" scientists tend to divide the two species into a few races. But the "specific" technicians apply 70, 80, or more different species or subspecies designations to the grizzly alone. All this at times approaches a mild sort of lunacy and is of no relevance to the sportsman.

For the purposes of this book, we can readily assume, as the Boone and Crockett Club does, that all black bears fall under one species and that, for record keeping purposes, they are grouped together. There are some interesting varieties in the black bear clan. The relatively rare "blue" glacier bear of southeastern Alaska, is an attractive and unusual trophy. But he does not reach a particularly large trophy size, nor is he accorded separate trophy classification. The extremely rare white (not an albino), or kermode strain, of the black bear found off the coast of British Columbia is strictly protected, and no sport hunting is allowed.

The so-called cinnamon or brown bear, though stoutly defended as a "different" bear by many backwoods taxonomists, is actually a black bear—no more, no less. I have been regaled more than once by some highly imaginative and fanciful comments on the cinnamon bear's reputed differences in skull proportion and behavior from those of the black bear. When I

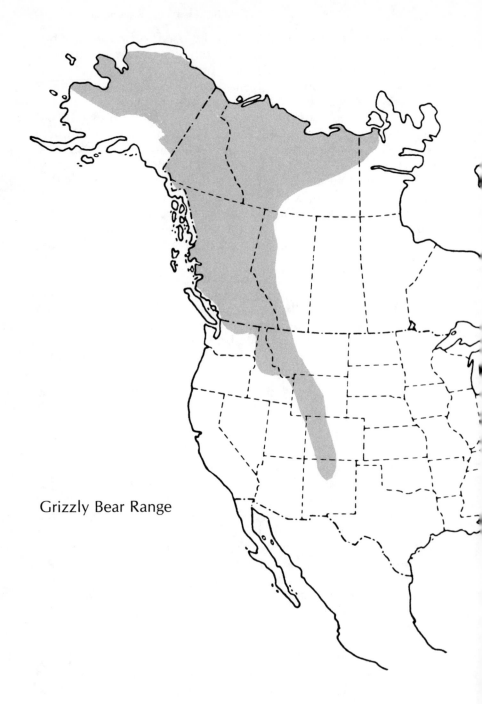

Grizzly Bear Range

For scoring by the Boone and Crockett system, this is the complete range of the grizzly. But bears termed "browns" by hunters along Alaska's southern coast are considered grizzlies by most taxonomists.

204

have challenged this mistaken distinction by questioning how the same sow might have one cub each of the cinnamon and black types, the replies I've received have been mind boggling. In these instances, untrained observers are taking that weakest and most undependable of all taxonomic characteristics, general body coloration, and pyramiding upon it an often fascinating but highly fanciful set of other "characteristics" to "prove" that the two animals are completely different species.

The brown phase of the black bear tends to show up most often in the Rocky Mountain West. It is also seen in Alaska. It is practically never observed in the East. Though Washington state is a bear mecca, the brown phase is less common there than it is in western Montana or Wyoming. Some of the lighter examples of these "brown" bear are almost blond and make a truly beautiful rug mount if taken unrubbed and in good pelage.

The "real" brown bear, also called the Alaskan brown or the Kodiak bear, is now generally accepted to be the same animal *(Ursus arctos)* as the bear popularly called the grizzly. These two bears are the same except that the brown is a coastal dwelling grizzly that lives roughly within 75 miles of Alaska's southern coast and attains a larger size due to a longer growing season and a richer protein diet, based partially on salmon.

Classification of these bears — classification that is as fair as possible to most sportsmen and is practical in application — has been a particularly vexing problem for the Boone and Crockett Club. But over many years, the Club has developed a reasonable compromise system. It separates the brown bear and the grizzly for sporting purposes, though scientifically they are one species. Here the distinction is based solely on geographic locations in which the bears are taken. Thus, for the purposes in this book, the term "brown" bear will mean the big coastal grizzly, and "grizzly" bear will mean the inland grizzly.

Comparative Sizes

Though bears are well known to most people, there are few animals about which so much misinformation and so many myths have been circulated. Most people invariably tend to believe the bears are far larger than they are. Even when these people see large zoo or garbage-fattened park bear, they are often disappointed by the small size relative to their conceptions. Of course, in the wild the animals are smaller than these artificially fattened bears.

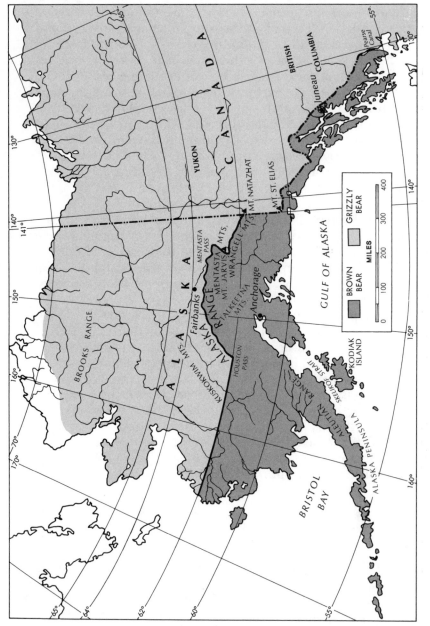

This shows the demarcation between the ranges of the browns and the grizzlies for Boone and Crockett records purposes. In the middle portion, the line is determined by the divides of the Mentasta Mountains, the Wrangell Mountains, and the Alaska Range.

This close-up of a big Alaska brown bear shows the two structural features that distinguish browns and grizzlies from their black bear cousins: the dished or straighter facial profile and the pronounced shoulder hump.

The average black-bear adult boar weighs about 175 to 200 pounds. Even 200-pound animals are unusually large. There are probably about as many 200-pound black bears, relatively, as there are 200-pound men. True, there have been recorded instances of black bears weighing over 600, even over 700 pounds liveweight. But, there also have been verified instances of men weighing over 800, even over 900 pounds. Frequency is probably about equal in both cases. Bears do vary tremendously in weight throughout the year, tending to gain large amounts of weight prior to denning up for the winter. So, the actual size of a particular black bear will depend on a variety of factors: his age, his general health, the amount and type of food available, time of year, and others.

Due to the grizzly's often lurid reputation, his size is usually exaggerated even further out of proportion than that of the black. The "average" adult grizzly bear would weigh about 350 to 400 pounds. The average adult females of both kinds of bears run considerably smaller, weighing about one-half to two-thirds as much as the males. Again, there are large grizzlies taken in the prime of life, season and habitat which weigh considerably more. However, there are very few grizzlies that ever scale more than 700 pounds liveweight without either being close enough to the sea to get "brown bear exposure" or else having access to a garbage dump or some other artificial food supply. (Remember if these "grizzlies" are killed within the southern coastal area mapped out by the Boone and Crockett Club, they are considered "browns" for scoring purposes.)

The legendary size of the Alaskan brown bears is another matter entirely. Much depends upon where they live. Historically, the largest brown bears have always come from Kodiak Island or the nearby Alaska Peninsula. The bears farther south and east, off the southeastern Alaska panhandle, are certainly large and impressive specimens, but have not at optimum approached the Kodiak and Alaskan Peninsula bears in size. (Interestingly enough, there is a fair amount of evidence that two now extinct bears possibly exceeded the brown bear's size. These were the "golden bear" of California—which was also a coastal-dwelling, salmon-eating, brown-bear type—and the giant buffalo-eating plains grizzly.)

A prime, adult, brown-bear boar from southeastern Alaska can easily weigh 800 to 1,000 pounds liveweight, and may weigh considerably more at his largest. A similar bear up on the Peninsula or on Kodiak Island could weigh 1,000 to 1,300 pounds, with some behemoths tipping the beam at 1,600 pounds. Though I have never been able to fully verify this, other browns are rumored to scale a full 1,800 pounds and more. Whatever their very largest size, these are truly enormous animals. True monarchs of the wild, rivaled only by their near cousins in Siberia, they are a precious legacy from a wilder, more pristine past that we sportsmen must help to save for our children.

Trophy Considerations

Since bears, like cats, canids, swine and certain other types of trophy animals carry no antlers or horns to use as a basis for scoring, many scoring approaches have been considered, tried, and ultimately rejected in favor of using the skull. True, the skull is an incomplete and less than ideal basis of trophy scoring. There are "big-headed" small bears and "small-headed" big bears, for which the use of the skull may not be a completely accurate way of assessing trophy worth. But all other possible bases are even more suspect.

Certainly the condition of the pelage is a key factor in evaluating the overall impressiveness of any bear trophy. Considerations include length of hair, color or colors of hair, condition of pelt with glossy hair and presence of rubbed spots, etc. But no one has ever been able to devise a uniform scale, with quantitative values, that the experts could agree upon for evaluation purposes. And it seems hardly likely that anyone will ever succeed in doing so. Even if a system were developed, it would doubtless be rather impractical for people all over the continent to apply and use. There are just too many subjective factors involved.

The size of a bear could be considered several ways. The overall length and width of the hide would be one. This is called the "square" and is determined by adding length from nose-to-tail to width across the front paws and dividing the total by two. But hides are undependable materials that may be stretched and worked larger, and they are subject to many differing tanning methods which may affect their ultimate size. Incidentally, a bear will usually run just about a foot wider across the front paws than in length. Small bears often have a bit less difference. And very large bruins sometimes measure more than 18 inches wider than long. In other words, on average, a bear that squared out at 8 feet would usually be about 7 feet in nose-to-tail length and about 9 feet across the front paws. This, of course, means that you couldn't hang an average grizzly or brown rug sideways in a room with only an 8-foot ceiling.

Weight is another factor that could be considered in scoring. But, a structurally smaller bear shot at his maximum weight before denning up in the fall could actually weigh more than a larger bear that has just come out of hibernation in the spring. Would this kind of inequity be fair? Also, weight is difficult to measure accurately under field conditions, especially when very large bears are involved. Also, weight score would be subject to cheating: adding lead weights to the carcass, adding water, and so on.

Literally everything, even length of claws, has been considered as possible factors for scoring. Inevitably, we return to the skull as the best of a bad lot of possibilities. The bear skulls are officially measured to the nearest sixteenth of an inch in both length and width, after at least 60 days of drying. (This 60-day waiting period applies to all trophies to be officially scored by

RECORDS OF NORTH AMERICAN
BIG GAME COMMITTEE

BOONE AND CROCKETT CLUB

RETURN TO:
N. A. B. G. Awards Program
1600 Rhode Island Ave. N. W.
Washington, D. C.   20036

Minimum Score:	Bear
Alaskan Brown	— 28
Black	— 21
Grizzly	— 24
Polar	— 27

BEAR

KIND OF BEAR
_____

SEX _____

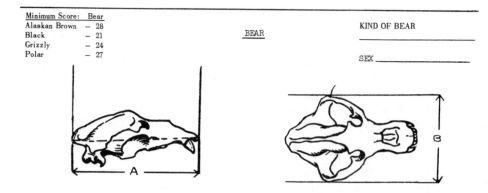

SEE OTHER SIDE FOR INSTRUCTIONS	Measurements
A. Greatest Length Without Lower Jaw	
B. Greatest Width	
TOTAL and FINAL SCORE	

Exact locality where killed
Date killed _____   By whom killed _____
Present owner
Address
Guide's Name and Address
Remarks: (Mention any abnormalities)

I certify that I have measured the above trophy on   19
at (address)   City   State
and that these measurements and data are, to the best of my knowledge and belief, made in
accordance with the instructions given.

Witness: _____   Signature: _____
                                                   Boone and Crockett Official Measurer

210

INSTRUCTIONS

These measurements are best taken with calipers to the nearest one-sixteenth of an inch.

Official measurements cannot be taken for at least sixty days after the animal was killed.

Please submit photographs of skull front and sides.

A. Greatest Length measured between perpendiculars to the long axis of the skull WITHOUT the lower jaw and EXCLUDING malformations.

B. Greatest Width measured between perpendiculars at right angles to the long axis.

All adhering flesh, membrane and cartilage must be completely removed before official measurements are taken.

*   *   *   *   *   *   *   *   *   *   *   *   *   *

TROPHIES OBTAINED ONLY BY FAIR CHASE MAY BE ENTERED
IN ANY BOONE AND CROCKETT CLUB BIG GAME COMPETITION

To make use of the following methods shall be deemed UNFAIR CHASE and unsportsmanlike, and any trophy obtained by use of such means is disqualified from entry in any Boone and Crockett Club big game competition:

    I. Spotting or herding game from the air, followed by landing in its vicinity for pursuit;

    II. Herding or pursuing game with motor-powered vehicles;

    III. Use of electronic communications for attracting, locating or observing game, or guiding the hunter to such game.

* * * * * * * * * *

I certify that the trophy scored on this chart was not taken in UNFAIR CHASE as defined above by the Boone and Crockett Club.

I certify that it was not spotted or herded by guide or hunter from the air followed by landing in its vicinity for pursuit, nor herded or pursued on the ground by motor-powered vehicles.

I further certify that no electronic communications were used to attract, locate, observe, or guide the hunter to such game; and that it was taken in full compliance with the local game laws or regulations of the state, province or territory.

Date _____ Hunter _____

This chart is reproduced with permission of the Boone and Crockett Club, which, together with the National Rifle Association, co-sponsors the North American Big Game Awards Program.

Boone and Crockett standards.) Since many, but not all, bears are "undershot," with the lower jaw protruding beyond the upper, only the upper-jaw portion of the skull is measured. This insures scoring uniformity and guards against credit for a freak lower jaw.

The disadvantages of a skull-oriented system are legion. It may not reflect the true overall size of the trophy (or quality) in some cases. Skull size is extremely difficult to estimate when glassing a live animal. And it is highly variable, even among like-size animals. But, it is the best that we have to use in the case of bears and cats.

Evaluating Trophies in the Field

Here we get into a whole new set of factors from those involved in the estimating of horned or antlered trophies. When estimating sheep, deer, elk or other antlered game, we can at least work *directly* and estimate the size of the actual trophy — the horns or antlers. Not so with the bears. No one can truly and accurately make *direct* estimates of the live animal's skull size while the skull is fully encased in hide and meat that may be well over an inch thick. If someone tells you he can make such an estimate, you are being had.

Rather, estimating bear trophies is done by using a lot of assumptions and interpretations based on indirect comparisons. And it's hoped that they prove out, which they usually, but not always, do. First, let's talk about the assumptions. We assume generally that a big-footed bear is *usually* a large and large-headed bear, because this is usually true. Secondly, we assume that an older bear is usually a larger and larger-headed bear. Thirdly, we assume that a really large bear will look "small-headed" because of his enormous bulk, while younger or smaller bears will look "large-headed" because of their smaller body size. These assumptions *usually* hold true, but the occasional bear can break them wide open.

A tape measure is a handy tool for any hunter to carry. For a trophy hunter, it's a necessity. You should measure bear tracks when trying to determine if a bear is worth "working on." The front track, which will appear squarer and less man-like than the rear print, is the one to work with. Measure the width of the front track. Take into account any slipping in mud or soft ground that may splay the track and thus make the track appear larger than the foot, itself, is.

The skull of this grizzly probably would not be record-book size because the head appears larger in relation to the body than would be normal for big grizzlies.

The above two photos show the marked differences in facial and shoulder profiles of the grizzly (top) and the black. In the Rockies especially, blacks may be brown, cinnamon or even blond in color.

The old but accurate rule on measuring bear tracks is to convert the inches, width of the front track to feet, and then add 1 foot to get the square of the hide. In other words, a grizzly that squares out at 7 feet, about average, will measure 6 inches across an unsplayed front track. A brown bear that squares out at 10 feet will measure about 9 inches across the front foot.

Any black bear that might square out at 5½ to 6 feet is starting to get interesting. Over 6 feet, and he's probably a very good bear. Thus, if his track measures over 5 inches across the front palm, the bear is worth taking a closer look at. Any grizzly over 6 inches across the front track (7-foot square) is worth looking at. Any brown bear over 7 inches across the front foot (8-foot square) is worth looking at, especially in southeastern Alaska where they run smaller. These bear won't make the book, but they certainly make fine trophies. Any bear with a front track over 8 inches wide (9-foot square) is an exceptional bear these days. And depending upon his exact proportions, he may possibly be getting up toward the record-book minimums in skull size.

As a brown bear reaches 9½ feet in squared hide, he becomes a trophy of a lifetime. At 10 feet, he's certainly a likely entrant in the record book.

Admittedly, this track method of estimating takes into account *two* indirect or inferred factors. First, we infer the bear's hide square from the size of the track, but this is generally rather accurate. Secondly, we infer that the larger a bear's hide squares, the bigger his head. This is also normally true, but not always in predictable proportions. However, using tracks can save wasted time and missed opportunities, and it is one of several techniques the bear hunter should have in his arsenal.

We also assume that older bears are larger. Skulls, like horns, don't shrink. So the skull should continue to grow as the animal gets larger and older. How do you tell an older bear? Well, here again we're in the inferring business. All bears are plantigrade —meaning, like man, they walk with sole and heel on the ground. Young and middle-age bears walk with a rolling, squishy gait. But an older bear often walks with mincing steps as though his feet hurt or are tender, which is probably the case. An older grizzly or brown bear is usually darker in color, many appearing almost black. But this may vary. Because there are many blonds, an older blond would be a darker blond. Also, often a bear's hide is somewhat bleached in appearance when he first comes out of his den in the spring, but it soon "weathers up."

A big, old bear will walk with a ponderous, rolling stride. Though it's hard to explain, he just *looks* old. When he's a really big fellow, his head will look rather small against that massive, blocky body. Ironically, though you are searching for a large-skulled animal and this one looks little-headed, this is the very animal that you want to look over more closely and probably take. The bear that looks big-headed is probably a juvenile or a young adult that has not fully filled out and fleshed out, much as with men in later years. Thus these younger bears don't have the fully developed ponderous body. Remember it's those key later years that result in the slight, but all-important, added skull growth.

Incidentally, though the condition of the pelt isn't an outright scoring factor, it certainly is important to most of us in determining the overall *quality* of the trophy. Be sure to carefully glass any bear you are thinking of taking in order to check for unwanted rubs on the pelt. Bears first begin to lose their hair around the eyes and on their toes. So if you're close enough to glass these two small areas, they can give you some clue as to whether the animal has started to lose hair on other portions of his body that aren't visible to you. This is very important. More than one sportsman has been bitterly disappointed to find his large trophy carried badly rubbed spots that weren't visible before the shooting.

How and Where to Hunt

Bears were originally carnivorous animals. But through the eons they have evolved into being the most omnivorous animals in the world, aside from man, that is. Bears will eat just about anything. They regard fresh meat as a delicacy and value rancid meat even more highly. The major part of most bear diets is vegetable, however. It's amazing to see a huge brown bear grazing on grasses and sedges as contentedly as any barnyard cow.

The bear's principal sense and first line of defense is his nose, which is among the keenest of all animals. The polar bear is the most carnivorous of the bears and, probably due to that, has the keenest sense of smell. There are recorded instances of the great white killers being drawn to beached and rancid whales from distances of twenty miles and more! However, all bears smell well. So proper allowance for the wind direction is especially critical when stalking any bear.

All bear hear well, with the black bear probably having the

keenest auditory sense. The black's ears are the largest, and this feature undoubtedly reflects the animal's predominantly furtive, heavy-cover existence, especially in the deciduous forests in the East. Even before the white man's time, the grizzly never ranged east of the Mississippi. He has always been more of an open country animal than the black, and thus has relied somewhat less on his hearing.

None of the bear are very keen-sighted, as animal vision goes. This is reflected in the fact that, relative to their overall body size, their pig-like eyes are very small. However, there is much disagreement, even among men of considerable experience as to just *how* bad the bear's vision really is. Most do not dispute that it is quite second-rate when trying to resolve stationary objects. I have moved to within 50 yards of bears, apparently without being spotted, by moving only when their head was down and facing away from me. I have had them stare straight at me — actually *through* me — when I was motionless. And after looking for a moment and apparently deciding there was nothing of interest there, they completely disregarded me. Where most of the disagreement comes in is on determining how well bear can see moving objects. The first grizzly I ever shot spotted me when I was a bit over 150 yards out, even though I was moving rather slowly and through cover that was almost shoulder high in most spots. I know he didn't wind or hear me. So it must have been solely his vision that warned him. However, he probably couldn't see me well enough to decide much about me or what I was up to, because he acted confused and stuck around for several moments too long. That's why he's now hanging on the wall in my living room.

Bear are intelligent and highly adaptable animals. The eastern black bear has learned how to exist very well in close confines with man. Every year some of these animals are killed in the most crowded section of that beehive that is the Eastern Seaboard, within 50 miles of downtown Manhattan.

These blacks have survived and prospered by becoming completely nocturnal and by learning to avoid man and even his easy food around most garbage dumps and refuse areas. Even the mighty grizzly has learned that man is to be feared and avoided. To my knowledge there is no wilderness left on this continent where the grizzly has not learned that man can strike him with sledgehammer blows and do it over long distances. Only the polar bear is still, in some cases, oblivious to man and the danger he presents. (This serves to make the ice bear the most dangerous of the bruin clan to man.)

The vast majority of black bears are taken as secondary, or "bonus," trophies—while the hunter is primarily after other game. There are few places where bears are "dependable" enough to truly warrant selective trophy hunting. (But, then, if you have already shot one or more blacks, you might be willing to pass up medium-size bears while looking for the big one.)

Washington state is a veritable black bear heaven, with some 30,000 of them. Here bear can be reliably hunted with hounds so that the sportsman can be unusually selective. Oregon has about 20,000 of them. California and Alaska have about 30,000 and 45,000 respectively. However, the latter two states are far larger areas; so the bear density is undoubtedly greater in Washington and Oregon.

Other states such as Maine, Michigan, Wisconsin, Wyoming, Montana and North Carolina have good populations, but the densities are generally not sufficient enough to justify anything like the sort of selectivity possible in the four big black-bear states in the West. This is especially significant when you consider the high hunting pressure in some of the eastern states.

Certain coastal areas of Alaska offer excellent possibilities for *large* black bears since these bears feed and fatten on the salmon just as their outsized brown-bear cousins do. However, black and brown bears do not overlap in all areas. But when they do, the black bear densities are often low. This is because the brown bear, if he can, will catch, kill and eat the smaller black. The reverse happens occasionally when large black bear can catch cubs or juvenile brown bears. However, though the black bear densities may not be heavy in these salmon-run coastal areas, the black bears here are often large.

Frankly, many a large trophy-size black bear is taken by locating an area, say, in western Canada where many locals still regard blacks merely as vermin rather than as fine game animals. There the bear aren't harried about much, and they do come in to feed on city dumps. The "sport" hunter then posts himself at the garbage area and proceeds to check out all incoming bears. Many of these bear are rather blasé about the presence of humans. Then the "sport" takes his big garbage-fattened "trophy." This is not a sporting or interesting way of taking a bear, and I would not shoot one on this basis. Others have, though, and have taken quite large bear by doing it.

Many bear are shot off the remains of other kills. Both blacks and grizzlies can usually be baited-in, where legal. This method of hunting is usually practiced in the spring, though it works in both spring and fall. Generally the guide or outfitter will lead out an old crowbait horse or two and shoot them, putting them down in several strategic bear areas. Other hunters use plastic bags to "cook" (sour) a good mess of rancid fish and then scatter these around to draw the bear in.

In other cases when an elk, moose or caribou is laid down, often a bear will come to the viscera and other inedible remains left by the hunters. Probably the vast majority of deep wilderness grizzlies (as well as wolves and wolverines) have been taken in this fashion over the years.

Any adult mountain grizzly in good pelage is a fine trophy for the sportsman who has never taken one. After his first grizzly, the sportsman can then limit his grizzly hunting to a trophy that would square well over 7 feet. Or as more and more hunters are doing, he could restrict himself to killing only a single grizzly in his lifetime.

British Columbia has a reasonably large population of grizzly, probably somewhere between 5,000 and 10,000 animals, including both coastal and inland bears. The very largest are found on the Taku River in northwestern B.C., where they thrive and fatten on the salmon. The Yukon also has goodly numbers of bear, though they often aren't quite as large as their counterparts farther to the south in B.C. However, some very large bear are taken each year in the Yukon, where hunting pressure on them in this very sparsely settled territory is lighter than to the south. The western end of the Northwest Territories has reasonably good populations of the small tundra grizzly.

Alaska has more grizzlies and browns than any other area — something between 15,000 and 20,000. The brown bears inhabit a large crescent of the southern and southeastern coast line. The very largest come from the northern and western terminus, Kodiak Island and the Alaska Peninsula. However, there are probably more bear in southeastern Alaska now than in these two more heavily hunted areas to the west. Though the largest bear to the west in Alaska are larger than the largest bear in southeastern Alaska, your chances of taking a nice 8- to 8½-foot square bear are as good or better in southeastern Alaska. The hunting is also somewhat cheaper here. Boat hunts are available for older hunters and hunters who are out of condition.

A 10-day hunt is the minimum you should allow for these coastal brown bear. But since the coastal weather is some of the

The Alaska brown bear probably evolved as a larger bear than the inland grizzly because of the longer growing season along the coast and the easy availability of protein-rich salmon.

wettest and most fickle anywhere in the world, 14 or 15 days is far better. Brown-bear hunting is rough, rougher than most people tend to expect. The bears live in thick, rough country. And it is seldom that the *big* fellows can be taken "easily" down on the beaches or along open shoreline conveniently near the boat or the hunting camp.

I believe that the very largest brown bears are probably now on the rougher, southern (or eastern) side of the Alaska Peninsula rather than on Kodiak. But there are still some very large bears in both areas. Both areas are fearsomely rough to hunt thoroughly. This is especially so on the south side of the Peninsula. You should be in good condition and be ready to walk and climb a lot through very dense cover.

Further inland, the large grizzlies tend to be in the southern and eastern parts of the state, though a good bear can be taken almost anywhere. There are still relatively good populations in the Brooks and Alaska ranges and in the Talkeetnas immediately north of Anchorage.

Outside Alaska, mountain or inland grizzly hunting is about finished in the U.S. Among them, Montana, Idaho and Wyoming probably still have about 500 grizzlies. Most of these animals live in parks, though there is some limited sport hunting. Montana usually harvests about 10 to 15 per year, mostly outside Yellowstone or up in the Bob Marshall Wilderness Area. Wyoming's kill runs about 2 to 8 annually.

Alberta, once fine ground for the big bear, has only about 500 to 1,000 of them, and hunting is restricted to the spring season only. During this time about 15 or 18 are taken by visiting sport hunters.

When to Hunt

Bears are interesting in that they are among the few trophies that may still be taken in either spring or fall. Each season has its advantages and disadvantages. If you take a bear in prime coat within the first two to three weeks after he's come out of the den, you'll have him in the best pelage of the year. The prime fall coat doesn't approach the best spring hair in length, glossiness or thickness. However, after the bears have been out for a short time, they start rubbing. Be sure that you don't shoot one with a bad coat. Then too, bears also may rub their coat in the den. So check each potential trophy carefully in the spring, even if you catch him literally coming out of his den.

In the fall most bears do not start coming into good coat until September, even in the far north. Even though August grizzly are legal in some areas, check carefully before shooting. Unless you check you may make an expensive and regrettable mistake. Incidentally, no bear, even in best coat, has a perfectly even, luxuriant coat. This is an animal skin, subject to the irregularities of its kind. It's not a man-made rug.

Bear, like all furred animals, normally have thin, or "short," spots on their coat. These spots always occur on the undersides, especially under the legs. This is true even in the midst of winter when the coat is at its longest. You can very easily check this out by rolling your own dog or cat over. You'll notice the thinner spots that I am referring to, even in deepest winter.

The choice between a spring and a fall bear hunt is a significant one. In spring, most guided or outfitted hunts cost about the same as their fall counterparts even though the variety of game available is often more limited. This is because the outfitter's expenses for supplies, stock and staff are about the same in either season. In the spring about the only other trophies that might be taken are wolf or wolverine in some areas. But these are always marginal "bonus" trophies taken on an "as they come" basis at best. On some spring grizzly hunts, a black bear is also a possibility. Or after you secure the main trophy, you may want to squeeze in some spring fishing or try varmint hunting for alpine marmots and ravens.

Perhaps due to its easier, salmon-fed existence, the brown bear is not generally reputed to be as short-tempered as the grizzly. But this is not a rigid rule. Brown bears of Admiralty Island and some of the southeastern islands are considered more crotchety than larger browns on Kodiak Island and the Alaska Peninsula.

On the plus side of spring hunting, chances of spotting and taking a bear are usually better than on a fall hunt—especially for grizzly. All the bears have just come out of their dens and can often be spotted searching for food on the bare high alpine slopes. They'll be looking for winter kills or victims of avalanches. They dig out marmots or find certain vegetation to help uncork their stomach and get their digestive juices flowing again after the long winter fast. The bear are usually moving around a lot and are easy to spot. The weather is often balmy and pleasing, yet still with just a small bite of winter. When a trophy is taken, chances are the pelt will be at its very best. And, finally, a spring bear hunt is one of the basic hunting rituals, and every sportsman should try to make at least one such trip.

There are things to be said for the fall trip though. The antlered and horned game is also available, along with the bear, often for little or no extra cost. Plus, many hunters just feel a hunting trip should occur in the fall; they feel strange hunting in the spring. In fall the days get steadily shorter, rather than longer. The weather becomes more blustery, rather than salubrious. Depending on exactly where and when the hunt is made, the fall colors may be unrivalled for photographing and enjoying the scenery. Among all trophy hunters, only the bear hunter has this interesting spring-or-fall option.

Trophy Mounting

Bears make handsome additions to any trophy room. The traditional mount is the rug with the mouth-open and the feet-and-claws-on, although life-size mounts and head mounts can also be effective.

However, the life-size mounts are very expensive and take up a lot of space even in a large room. Bear head mounts are usually resorted to only when the hide is so badly rubbed that it isn't any good for mounting. The rug mount is very attractive, whether hung on a wall or displayed on the floor. However, if placed on the floor, be sure to put it well out of the traffic pattern. No animal-hair "rug" is truly a rug for walking on. The hair will break, dirty-up and begin to fall out all too quickly. Also, a rug displayed on the floor will soak up a lot more dust and dirt. Better that it lie on a second rug (which will absorb some of the atmospheric dust) and that it be in a room where the windows or doors do not open to the outside. All things considered, the rug is probably better off hung on a wall.

The bear's actual skull should never be left in the head portion of the rug mount. All real teeth are subject to shrinkage and cracking. So it's far better to use one of the realistic and permanent head forms with plastic teeth. Also, this enables you to save the actual skull itself, which should be thoroughly boiled out and cleaned. (Soak the skull in sal soda, which you can buy inexpensively from many large grocery stores, to remove all meat. Then dry it thoroughly. Sprinkle the dried skull with borax — Boraxo will do — to kill any remaining bugs or mites. And, if you like, bleach the skull whiter with some peroxide.) All teeth will shrink and may begin to fall out. Test them by tugging on them, and pull as many out as possible. Then glue them back in permanently so that they don't fall out and become lost.

This skull becomes an attractive and interesting bonus trophy in its own right. It can be displayed on a table or mantelpiece, or it can be attached to a plaque and hung on the wall. I have used a felt-tip marker to neatly letter across the top of several of mine such pertinent data as date and place killed, caliber and bullet used, and range.

Personally, I don't like the rabidly "snarling" bear mount whether it be rug or life-size. The teeth on bear trophies are certainly interesting and attractive and should be displayed. However, the exaggerated wrinkles on the snout and the leering countenance that some taxidermists impart to make the bear "ferocious" only look ridiculous to me and detract from an otherwise attractive trophy.

Are Bears Ferocious?

This is a common question. But it's something akin to asking, "Are blondes passionate?" (And it's about as safe to answer!) Anyone who has been around wild animals comes to respect them very quickly. Compared to puny humans, they are enormously strong critters. I have helped catch and wrestle to the ground a 125-pound whitetail deer in order to transfer it from one enclosure to another. I was astonished at the strength and power of this relatively small animal. And this from a pen-reared "wild" animal!

All bears are enormously strong. When you skin one out, you'll quickly note the bulging muscles and ropy sinews amply attesting to the power. This is true even on a medium-size black bear, much more so on a large grizzly or brown bear. To see a grizzly casually plowing up huge chunks of earth, easily removing large rocks and roots while trying to dig marmots, is to know instantly that this is a powerful fellow indeed.

Of all bears, the black bear generally has the shiest and most furtive of temperaments. Yet he has the physical equipment to commit mayhem with the greatest of ease. And in his ranks is the most dangerous animal in North America: the garbage-fed, park bear which has lost all fear of, and thus respect for, man.

Toby Tobias, a friend and hunting compadre of mine, has raised three black bears in his house. They are lovable and fun to play with. But, even at a trifling weight of 12 or 15 pounds, they are very difficult to manhandle. Wrestling around with a 50-pound cub is a chastening experience.

One of the more heinous backwoods practices of years gone by was to capture a black bear cub and keep him chained out back. The locals would then, for amusement and gambling, match up the cub with all the outsized local curs, some of them having ample dollops of wild wolf in their family trees. A 40-pound cub can handily unzip a hulking cur outweighing him three-to-one—this more times than not. And the bear backers always gave, never took, odds in the betting.

Now, having emphasized how *potentially* dangerous *all* bears are, it is time to make the point that most stories about bear-man incidents are greatly exaggerated. Practically all bear, even the grizzly of the far north, have learned to fear and flee from man. Bears know all too well that man is different and not to be challenged.

The bear-man incidents come about through a variety of readily understandable circumstances and not because bears are generally and normally "ferocious." You may run into an ornery bear that is suffering from an abscessed tooth and has a king-size toothache. Or he may be suffering from an old wound or sore that is making him ill tempered. Then, of course, there is always the possibility that you may come between a sow and her cub; though she may run off and leave him. None of these situations means the bear will automatically "charge" you (as the weathered phrase has it), but any of these situations can affect the bear such that if you insist upon pushing him and aggravating him by approaching, he may decide to do something about it. That "something" is usually a mock huffing-and-puffing or a short charge, but it certainly can be something more serious.

In grizzly and brown bear country it's always a good plan to keep your rifle handy—such as when walking through heavy underbrush in which it is difficult to see around you or very far ahead. And this precaution is especially important when you are on a bear trail.

In these circumstances you could round a bend and suddenly be upon a bear—to your mutual surprise. Grizzly, even more than most four-legged citizens, don't like to feel that they are being cornered, or "braced." This is something they never tolerate from other animals, and they don't take well to it from man. If you inadvertently startle and push a bear like this, he may leave some bear prints up your back, just trying to get out of there and, in the process, opting for the wrong direction. Whether he "meant" to charge or not may be beside the point at that juncture.

Another way folks get into trouble in bear country is to camp with bear-goodies like bacon in the tent with them. If the bear is hungry enough, he just may try some nocturnal grand larceny that can put some wear and tear on both the camp and the campers. Better to hang the goodies in a tree outside rather than sleep with them under your pillow.

No, bear are not inherently ferocious—not even the mighty grizzly in this man-dominated era. They are just powerful animals who are, especially in the case of grizzlies and brownies, rugged individualists. They should be treated with respect and approached with caution. No more, no less.

Guns for Bears

Black bears are not especially tenacious of life. A well delivered hit with a .257-class rifle will usually dispatch one quite handily. However, I would prefer a .270- to .30/06-class gun for the longer or more difficult shots.

I prefer the more potent medicine not because of any danger from the animal but because it could reduce the chances of losing him. Bears are very difficult to hit while running. For me they present the most difficult of running shots of all big game. This is so, not because of their speed, but because of that rolling, squishy, "slinky-spring" gait of theirs. And since it's difficult to place the running shot well, a bit of extra power may help bring the animal down.

Grizzly and brown bears are something else entirely. Both animals have tremendous vitality and are well armored by thick hides. In the fall, a heavy belt of fat envelops much of their body. If they are pumping adrenaline before being hit or if the first hit is placed badly so that they are aroused when hit with follow-up shots, they can be very difficult to lay down. The .270 and the .30/06 with heavy loads and well constructed bullets are adequate for grizzly. They have killed legions of them. For myself, I prefer a bit more power, especially if there is heavy cover and the bear may have to be knocked down outright to insure that he doesn't get away.

A 7mm Magnum or one of the medium to heavy .300 magnums makes good sense here. If you can handle a .338 or similar gun with assurance, that's fine, too. I have never had any trouble killing grizzly with a 7mm Magnum, but I do know of several instances in which aroused but not overlarge grizzlies and brown bears soaked up several 175-grain 7mm Magnum bullets before calling it a day. And the hits were decent, not shots in the foot or the rear end, which would just aggravate the beast.

The bear is the one North American animal that should be shoulder shot rather than lung shot if at all possible — and this means in the *front* shoulder. A grizzly or brown can still cover a lot of ground and do it with amazing speed with his hindquarters broken. But if his front shoulders are smashed, he will be anchored. No brown or grizzly should be shot when he is directly above the hunter. It's all too easy for him to — bearlike — tuck those legs in and roll, like a giant ball, right down on the hunter, even if his shoulders *are* broken.

I would recommend a gun larger than the 7mm Magnum-class for brown bear. These animals are most often shot in heavy cover where they have to be *stopped* — dropped on the spot if at all possible. I know of too many cases in which the 7mm class of cartridge has just not measured up in day-to-day brown bear hunting situations. Yet the 7mm is the one I swear by and use more than any other for all-around hunting.

There are as many opinions as there are hunters regarding what makes a good grizzly or brown bear gun. I am well aware that several of the most experienced brown-bear guides and hunters — past and present — have always used and sworn by the grand old .30/06.

However, I would still recommend much stronger medicine. The .338 is good, as is the fine old .375. The old .35 Whelen can be used effectively as can a host of "mid-.30s" developing around 3,500 pounds of energy at the muzzle. There is good reason for the standard rule on most brown bear hunts that the paying "sport" gets the first shot but that the guide can then, at his option, begin shooting immediately. Both men are to keep shooting until the bear is both down and still. The guide almost always elects to exercise that option, and shoots early and fast.

The bears are fascinating animals from a natural history standpoint, and they make marvelous hunting trophies. This is especially true of grizzlies and big browns. Our wilderness and our hunting experiences are richer just because the bears are there. They should be treated with respect, hunted fairly in a sporting fashion, and killed cleanly. (Brown bear hunting has probably had more abuses connected with it than with any other North American hunting, except possibly sheep hunting.) Without bears our hunting scene just wouldn't be the same.

How to Set Up a Trophy Hunt

13

The very first thing, obvious as it may sound, is to decide firmly what your objective is both as to species and size of trophy. More good hunts are ruined at this stage than at any other by fuzzy thinking. It's all too easy to slide into going on a particular hunt because there's a chance at "several" species that you may be interested in. All of us can easily become intrigued with the "one-of-each" syndrome or "more-for-our-money" thinking. When we add an outside chance for this or that additional species, often we are also decreasing our chances for the primary game or for a *large* head of the primary game.

More often than not, good sheep range is not good moose ground. Or the best chance for grizzly doesn't lie in an area that abounds in goat or caribou. Sometimes an area is exceptionally good for several species, but don't count on it. Also, if several species are available, the area probably won't be the best for a *big* head of your primary species. So, once you've decided on your primary species, the next step is to decide how large a head you want.

Adjectives are no good here. What's a "nice" head to one fellow may be "outstanding" to another but only "fair" to yet another. Here's where you should come up with some numbers or at least a range of numbers. Decide if the minimum goat you'll settle for must run 9 inches in horn length and whether you want to work hard for a goat 10 inches or over, knowing you might have to settle for a shot at a 9-inch billy as a last resort near the end of the hunt. Do you want a barren ground caribou that you figure scores a minimum of 375? Or do you want to work hard for a 400-point records qualifier initially? Or, will you settle for a moose head with a spread of less than 60 inches? Whatever the animal, whatever your general situation, think this through carefully. All hunts begin in your head, and everything else proceeds from your decisions on the questions What? and How Big?

Remember that the larger the head you are trying for, usually the more demanding your task. Greater size practically always devolves to more time in the field and more money laid out both per day and for the extended length of the hunt. Usually the area that offers the biggest heads will be one that is not particularly good for other species and may not even be the best general area for the primary species. And it may mean an "all or nothing" situation in which your increased chances for a really big trophy leave you less chance for a small-to-medium head.

Once you have established your basic objectives, it's a good idea to write them down. If you do an aggressive, energetic job of checking into the myriad possibilities, sometimes so many intriguing opportunities present themselves that your original target can become a bit blurred and even get lost in the process.

Now you have to decide where, when and how. Although you probably have formed some tentative ideas on these factors, most of your "homework" will be tied up with resolving them and making them mesh with your time and money availabilities. Here again, *before* you get into checking all the details, sit down and decide how much money and how much time. Most of us are pretty conscientious about nailing down the latter but not the former.

I always list two figures: the most money that I *should* spend and the most that I can possibly scrape together. Alas, in my weak-willed case, I can usually scrape together more than I *should*. But, at least with these two figures at hand, I can chart my course without getting unduly sidetracked either by those possibilities that are patently beyond my means or by those others that just sound too good to be true for the quality of hunt and trophy that I may have in mind. Like most hunters I'm a practical type who didn't inherit a pile of chips from his dear old Aunt Sadie, so I'm always aware of the value of a buck. However, my ears perk up and the warning lights start flashing when I hear the siren's song of the something-for-nothing operator who's just promising too much for the amount of money he's asking. I suggest you also approach these miracle boys carefully. Remember, important though the money is, it's not everything. You're also tying up that precious annual vacation that won't roll around for another full year. And a hunt that doesn't net you the game you wanted and isn't enjoyable is too expensive at any price. A successful hunt that gets you the game and provides a lifetime of memories is a value at any price.

Now we run into the basic options. If you're going on a do-it-yourself hunt you must do all the checking yourself. If you're looking to make a guided hunt, you can get help from others.

The Do-It-Yourself Hunt

The best way to start here is with a buddy or two that you have hunted with before, provided you know you can get along in a hunting camp. This way there are several of you to split the chores and costs of checking information out and to deliberate and decide what to do based on the research. And there are several of you to split travel expenses if you drive and camp expenses for any gear that you may need to buy.

Now to begin the data gathering, make a list of the possible states or provinces where you might make the hunt. Write to game authorities for their basic "package" of information on license costs, season dates, maps, permit costs, availabilities of certain species, and general hunting regulations.

In addition to the general or basic information, I also request specific information on the species that's my primary objective. I usually ask for any harvest data that will show me which game management areas or hunting areas had the largest harvests of those animals and which areas had the most big heads come through. I try to get any other information such as how many hunters may have hunted those areas. I also ask, if applicable, how many permits will be available in the coming year and how many people usually apply.

Most fish and game departments try to be very helpful, but they may not be able to furnish you with all the information I've mentioned—at least not at this stage. However, it's a good idea to go ahead and commit these questions to paper. You may get more info than you counted on and the discipline of defining your questions clearly at this stage will come in handy later. (Addresses of all state and provincial game departments are listed at the back of this book.)

When you receive a reply, study all the information thoroughly. If your original letter was polite and realistic enough you may receive a cover letter answering some of your special questions as well as the general printed "kit" information. The person's name on this letter is your next lead.

Often at this stage it's a good idea to phone this person. Make up a list of questions in advance to minimize the expense. Usually the fellows working for the state game and fish departments will "give" a little more handily over the phone than on paper. It's more convenient for them, and also it's off the record. Since these agencies are publicly financed, employees have to be rather cautious about recommending particular areas or outfitters and guides.

When you call, try to zero in on one or two specific hunting areas that look attractive. In addition to asking general questions about the hunting outlook for those areas in the coming fall, you should also try to get the names of the particular wildlife biologists, wildlife technicians or other people the Department has covering those areas. These are the people who can really give you the inside dope. Also, try to get the names of local ranchers, personal acquaintances, or other people who may have more first-hand knowledge of the areas.

When you have these names you can really start getting detailed in your questions. However, remember that some of these people aren't obligated to disseminate information. You will be asking them for a favor — not a job they are paid for.

So make your inquiries for the information as convenient as possible for these people to answer. A telephone call is best but, a courteous letter will do. It's wise to enclose a stamped self-addressed return envelope. I usually include a fill-in-the-blank or multiple-choice questionnaire to make it still more convenient for them, and I limit the number of questions to those basic, important ones so that the person doesn't feel overloaded.

If you have difficulty locating sources outside the game department, there are other avenues open. I have written and/or called local chambers of commerce for information or leads to other sources of info. Ditto for sporting goods stores and motels catering to hunters in that area. Remember the obvious: These folks make a living off the hunting in the area, so they may be inclined to "accentuate the positive" a bit. However, you can often get good information from them. More than once I have ended up hunting with someone I met this way — which is almost like having a guide along when you get there!

The Guided or Outfitted Hunt

You can use all of the options I just discussed for a do-it-yourself hunt when setting up a guided hunt. And it's not a bad idea to gather info this way even though you also have other, more convenient methods available. This gives you a good chance to double-check your other information and to better educate yourself in general. And if, like me, you just enjoy puttering around during the late winter dog days setting up the next year's big hunt, it's also fun!

However, this is also the time to contact the various outfitters and select one. You can do this directly or through a third party: a hunting consultant or booking agent specializing in this type of planning. Get a list of the outfitters available from the fish and game department and/or the appropriate guides and outfitters association, also listed in the back of this book.

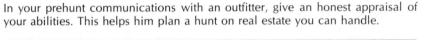

In your prehunt communications with an outfitter, give an honest appraisal of your abilities. This helps him plan a hunt on real estate you can handle.

When you contact the outfitter, tell him clearly and precisely what you're after. Tell him your age and general physical condition (be honest!) and what gun(s) you'll be shooting. Indicate to him your past experience—what you have hunted to date and where. Don't be shy about telling him this is only your first or second "big" hunt. The idea here isn't to impress the outfitter—though all too many hunters seem to think so—but to tell him briefly and honestly what you want to accomplish and what resources you have, such as experience, shooting ability, physical condition and time available. Good outfitters don't "mind" taking greenhorns out on their first or second hunt. Many even prefer it. The newer hunter often gets a bigger thrill out of the whole affair than the seasoned hand, and that's gratifying to those putting on the hunt. And the newer hunter usually does what the outfitter or guide asks him to do rather than trying to run the whole show himself and botching things.

Everyone has to start sometime, and there's nothing wrong with being a beginner. Outfitters do sob gently under their breath and reach for a snort of the snakebite medicine when a hunter lies outright to them. And this happens all too often. The stories are legion. Some make you want to laugh and others are just pathetic. Often the very same hunter who insists on the highest standard of "honesty" from the outfitter will send a picture of himself to the outfitter that was made twenty years or twenty pounds ago. Some will lie about their experience level, shooting ability or—most often—general physical condition. Perhaps "lie" is a bit harsh in many instances. There's also a definition problem here. What may be "fair" or even "good" condition to the sedentary hunter in middle age who lives at an elevation of less than 1,000 feet is downright terrible to the outfitter who lives a physical existence and hunts at better than 5,000 feet—often using guides in their 20s to shepherd his hunters around.

Honesty really is the best policy. It will help the outfitter give you a successful hunt by assigning the right guide to you, suggesting when and how long to hunt, and putting you in the right camp or specific area within his general area. The savvy outfitter usually has certain places reserved for the older, out-of-condition hunter or the hunter with a health problem. There's no shame in that. The only stupid thing is to pay a lot of money for a guided hunt and then have it go completely sour due to your own misrepresentations.

If you want to concentrate on a 60-inch moose or 36-inch sheep, or whatever more than anything—to the exclusion of all others—tell the outfitter. Then you'll work on any other secondary possibilities after success with your main objective. This also helps the outfitter tell you when to come, and it helps him to assign you to the right part of his area and to the right type of hunt.

It's also a good idea to tell him your general outlook on the hunt. If achieving that trophy goal is all-important and you are willing to work long and hard to do it, tell him so. But don't say that unless you mean it. Conversely, if you are more interested in the total experience and not quite so stringently dedicated to spike-camping out on a bread-jam-and-beans diet and in a small tent, let him know that.

Every outfitter in the business for several years has had at least one client earnestly assure him he's ready to go-go-go when he gets there, and then had the fellow show up with a case of booze or an extra twenty pounds of weight. After several of these instances most outfitters become a mite suspicious of the hunters who write about their Olympic-like physical assets and their monklike dedication to a "serious hunt." If you smoke, you might as well let the outfitter know ahead of time. It's one of the first things he'll be looking out for when you shake hands with him.

When contacting the outfitter, it is generally best to keep your first letter and request for information fairly crisp and brief. Sure, he's in business to give you information about his hunts and you're not asking him for a favor when you ask for information. On the other hand, from his point of view about 98 percent of the people who write him do not end up booking hunts. Some decide not to go, some book with other outfitters and all too many are just browsing.

If your first letter is just too involved, it may delay your getting any sort of answer and it may actually decrease the amount of information you get, in addition to the basic printed folder. Here the outfitter may feel you're not a good prospect. Outfitters don't run clerical offices with staffs to handle questions, write letters, and research special requests for information. He must assign his time as well as possible and that means priorities, which often results in an uneven handling of responses. So, on the first note keep it to the point: Ask for names of recent hunters you may use as references as well as the basic price list and hunting information. Also tell the outfitter what you're specifically interested in.

In your second letter you can go into more detail. This can be followed up by a phone call and then a third letter. By now you've probably convinced the guy you're a serious prospect, and he'll do his best to furnish you with all the answers you requested.

Throughout this 3- or 4-step information-gathering campaign, there are several primary matters that you should cover. Ask for references, of course, making sure that most of them are from the last year or two. Someone could well have had a good hunt three or four years earlier, but the situation could have changed totally since then. (When you do check these references, be sure to ask for the names of other people who hunted with the same outfitter. That way you are sure to get a good cross-section of the hunters and not just the few that the outfitter wants you to talk to.)

Find out from the outfitter how many heads were taken of the particular species that you are most interested in. If you want to shoot a Dall sheep, find out how many sheep hunters the man had and how many rams were taken. Then find out not only what the two or three largest were but also what the average size was. Also, find out what his results on sheep were for the last couple of years, and ask about the outlook for the next season. Find out if the area experienced a particularly severe winter kill or if any other factors will significantly affect the hunting, one way or the other, for the next season.

Using a Booking Agent or Hunting Consultant

Since the early 1960s there has been a substantial increase in the number of "middlemen" who are variously called hunting consultants or booking agents. These fellows operate somewhat like a general travel agent, but they specialize in outdoor trips — often booking fishing, photographic, climbing and family outings as well as serious hunting trips.

Most of these operations sprang up as adjuncts of the larger taxidermy houses. This was a natural evolution because the taxidermists knew where the major trophies were coming from each year and were constantly being asked where to go by their clients. Also, many of these taxidermists were avid and knowledgeable hunters themselves, which is why they went into taxidermy to begin with. So it was a short step from informal advice to more formal booking procedures. A large portion of these hunting consultants are still attached to the taxidermies; others have left taxidermy and set up their own independent booking agencies, concentrating only on hunt planning and booking.

These fellows operate by charging the outfitter 10 to 15 percent of the total hunt cost. Thus, unless the outfitter is charging one price for hunts he books himself and another for those booked through an agent, the consultant's fee is actually "free," costing the hunter nothing. Again this is much the same way a general travel agent works. Incidentally, I don't feel that it is ethical for the outfitter to charge two different fees. If the outfitter doesn't want to avail himself of the services and business resulting from the hunting consultant's labors, fine. But if he does, he should pay for it and not just load it right back onto the costs of the hunter. However, that's a personal opinion and I'm sure some outfitters might disagree.

A good hunting consultant can play a very constructive role for both the outfitter and the hunter. At their best, these consultants are jewels beyond compare who are well worth their commissions. A bad one can cause confusion, problems and even lawsuits.

Because some types of big-game hunts have become larger and larger enterprises, requiring substantial capital outlays for planes, equipment and staff, the old-time rough-and-ready outfitter has somewhat given way to today's professional entrepreneur. Today's outfitter must often spend much time and attention buying, maintaining and trading equipment, as well as hiring, firing and — at times — training his staff. Also, to better amortize his substantial investment, he works harder at running a year-round business that may include fishing in spring and summer, spring bear hunts, winter outdoor excursions and photo trips, and other activities in addition to his bread-and-butter fall-and-early-winter hunting. All this often leaves him less time to spend dealing with potential clients and furnishing them with information.

There have been changes on the hunter's side, too. Before World War II and into the early 50s, most hunters were wealthy older men who had taken some years to accumulate the money necessary to make these expensive trophy hunts. And along the way they had also usually accumulated a fair amount of hunting experience. The great increase in both general living standards and easily available credit, as well as the advent of rapid mass transportation, has changed all that. Today's hunter making the trek west or north for a major trophy hunt is younger than his counterpart of a generation ago, and he may well have less practical field experience simply because of his age. (However, let me stress here that I do think today's American trophy hunters are by and large the most knowledgeable and skilled large group of hunters that have ever been afield in this or any other country.)

The competent, professional hunting consultant can play a vital communications role between the busy outfitter and the hunter desiring considerable volumes of information. He has the time to do this and he should have the knowledge. For after all, it's what he's paid for.

When selecting your booking agent or hunting consultant, find out how much he is in the field himself. For best results your man should not be desk bound. Even though he deals with many outfitters in different areas and therefore should be able to tailor your hunt to fit your goals and resources, there is nothing like practical field exposure to insure that his opinions and information are correct and up to the minute. Things can change rapidly in only a season or two. What was a good area only a year or two ago can now be far less attractive because of overharvesting, a couple of bad winters, a population explosion of wolves and other predators, or mineral or hydroelectric development. The man who was an excellent outfitter two years back may be having family or financial problems that are now affecting how he runs his business. He may be neglecting the replacement of saddlery, tentage, and other gear. Or he may be having major staff problems, which are always an outfitter's chief difficulty anyway. There is nothing like a *current, first-hand* look by the consultant to verify the up-to-the-minute ground situation. This is one of the things you pay for — and should receive — with that commission.

When working with a consultant, it's a good idea to check him out if you've never booked a hunt with him before. This can be done a number of ways. Ask him about his own field and hunting experience and ask him which areas he represents. That is, if he works with no outfitters in British Columbia, then you can't expect a purely objective assessment as to whether a B.C. trip or an Alaska trip best fulfills your objectives. Ask him for the names of some clients he's booked before. These clients should be familiar with different outfitters and areas as well as the type of trophy and hunt that you're interested in. Then contact these clients, getting their opinion of the outfitter and area, and also inquiring if the hunt was satisfactory and as represented by the consultant. Ask if the consultant was helpful and knowledgeable in securing any needed airline tickets, information on any special licenses or export permits, or other bureaucratic spaghetti that may have been required.

Check out the hunting consultant thoroughly, and then, if he checks out, trust him and his judgment. Note: Neither the consultant nor the outfitter is "guaranteeing" you the game! You are buying a hunt, not the game. If the hunt is a disappointment, you must decide if it was due to factors beyond the outfitter's control or to factors that you could not reasonably have expected the consultant to know about. As long as sport hunting *is* sporting, there will be the occasional bad trip and empty game bag.

That's what keeps the pastime endlessly interesting and challenging. When you plunk your hard-earned money down, you are buying a hunt. All that either the consultant or outfitter should be expected to provide is what they represented they would. Good gear and horses, a generally good game area, competent guides, a sporting hunt—all these should be expected. A trophy bull elk at meat-elk prices or a two-week bag on a five-day hunt shouldn't be expected.

Another thing to remember is that ultimately the responsibility for having a good hunt rests on you more than on anyone else. Sure, the outfitter and the consultant agent have their responsibilities and you should expect them to fulfill them. But if you can't walk and climb; if you can't shoot; if you didn't bother to do some homework yourself; if you naively accepted all sorts of outrageous claims and implied "guarantees" (from either the outfitter or the consultant) at ridiculously low prices; if you made yourself and everyone else the victim of foggy thinking on your part as to your priorities on the hunt in both quantity and quality of game—then you know whom you ultimately must turn to when assessing "blame" for a ruined hunt.

Picking the Right Gun and Scope

14

Opinions give life its spice and verve, and without them the world would be a strictly ho-hum place. If we all felt the same way about things, there would be no bookies, Parisienne dressmakers would get by just fine with nothing more than flour sacking and cotton thread, and there would be no balloting for beauty crowns and show business awards.

Besides trophy-hunting gun nuts, I know of no consumer group that can field so many people who are equally knowledgeable and proficient at their hobby, yet possess such widely diverging views. Guns, scopes, loads and similar paraphernalia bring out the individualist.

A practical, down-to-earth trophy hunter really "needs" only about two rifles—and usually has at least thrice that many. Thank goodness. This penchant for searching out the new and the different has fueled a product development revolution in firearms and related items since 1950 with the result that today's hunter has a far wider choice of weaponry to fulfill his needs and is better equipped than at any time in history. But still the unending search goes on, and the experts continue to voice differing opinions. After all, you "need" only one or two guns in the same sense that a woman "needs" only one or two dresses to maintain the conventions of modesty and comfort.

Types of Actions

American centerfire hunting rifles roughly break down into four types: 1) bolt action, 2) lever action, 3) slide or pump action, and 4) autoloader or "automatic." All four have their advantages and disadvantages — their hot-eyed fans and their detractors.

Lever Action. The lever action has a charm and charisma that is peculiarly American, and it is rapid firing in the trained hand. It is also slab-sided and rides well in a saddle scabbard. Most models are compact and well balanced for carrying in the hand. Newer models in this category carry far stronger actions than in the past, and some pretty potent cartridges are now available for lever action guns.

There are even some lever action models with the accuracy-improving rigidity of a one-piece stock. Generally speaking, the hunter now has an extremely wide choice of cartridges, barrel lengths and gun weights and subtypes of lever actions. Long gone are the days when the lever-gun hunter was almost completely limited to the short, light carbine type of weapon that fired low-power loads of the "thutty-thutty" (that is .30-30), .32 Special and .35 Remington class.

Slide Action and Autoloading. The slide action and autoloading guns have also come of age since 1950, with several brands and models made for a wide choice of cartridges and bullet weights. Many hunters who do a lot of shotgunning and are used to shooting the pump or autoloading scatterguns feel more at home with a similar type centerfire rifle in hand. These guns are also compact. And since there is no bolt protruding off to one side, they are balanced and even-sided. Firepower is their chief advantage. With either type the hunter can lay out quite a stream of lead at a fast-departing trophy about to disappear over a hill. This firepower can sometimes make the difference between success and failure. The pump-actioned gun is extremely fast in this respect, and a trained hunter can fire it faster than he can an autoloader. The autoloader, on the other hand, also has the secondary advantage of absorbing varying amounts of the recoil with its blowback action; this depends on its design and specifications and can be something of a help with some of the heftier cartridges.

Bolt Action. You guessed it. I saved the bolt-action gun until last because, quite frankly, I prefer it in almost every respect to the other three. And that's certainly not to take anything away from the others. All three have been improved to levels of durability, reliability and accuracy that at one time many felt were almost impossible to attain in mass-produced guns of these types. But the bolt gun has always been my favorite.

My reasons for this lopsided preference are legion — ranging from the rational to the emotional. On the emotional side, bolt guns just signify the American sport and trophy hunting that began just after the turn of the century. This symbolism rivals that of the drilling in the hands of the German hunter, the double rifle used by the British sport hunter in India and Africa, or the side-by-side scattergun in the hands of the well-bred continental or British bird shooter. Ever since novelist Stewart Edward White and a few other pioneers had their early Springfields customized before the first big war, Americans have taken bolt-action guns to their hearts with a fervor rivaling that of their earlier preference for lever-action centerfire guns during the late 19th century. I am well aware that no centerfire gun in history has even come close to matching the sales of the Winchester 94 lever action, which was and is a nice little package for the money. But these millions of guns have often been bought and used as "working guns" to control pests, dispatch sick or hurt stock, and occasionally pot camp meat.

Though trophy hunters may have several guns of the other three types in their rack, the vast majority rely on bolt guns as their workhorses for the toughest and most demanding jobs. Bolt-action guns are inherently the strongest, meaning that they can absorb the pressure of today's hot, high-density factory loads and — *most especially* — hot, special-purpose handloads. And they afford the shooter the largest margin of safety. Bolt guns have tremendous camming power. And if the brass cartridge — the weakest link in the shooting chain — gives way in the field, there is more chance of clearing the jammed bolt gun. Also, bolt guns are far more resistant to jamming from the gunk and residue which, to a degree, is somewhat unavoidable in heavy-duty, deep wilderness use. Ditto on temperature problems. Some outfitters who run a lot of late-season hunts in cold far north areas literally will not let a hunter go out with a nonbolt gun. They've lost too many trophies due to critical jamming in below-zero weather, even with "winterized" guns carrying the more complicated actions. It takes only a moment to field-strip and clean a bolt gun. And that enormous camming power can be a lifesaver, or trophy saver, at the right time.

Generally, bolt guns are inherently more accurate weapons due to their one-piece stocks and basic designs. And bolt guns are surprisingly fast to fire, if you practice. Trophy hunters tend to be *riflemen*, as opposed to rifle users. Ultra-fast fire-

It's wise to recheck your rifle immediately before the hunt. A jar or bump in transit can knock a scope out of register. Moisture and altitude changes can also affect point of impact by swelling or shrinking the stock. And this "shooting-in" gives the guide a better idea of your shooting ability.

power is not quite so important to the highly trained hunter and rifleman who takes pride in his ability to locate and stalk game for a standing shot and in his ability to hit game with the first or second shot. Though there are some instances in which rapid shooting is a necessity; generally it's not considered the best of form to spray the landscape with lead and hope that the trophy runs into one of the bullets. The extra accuracy and durability of the bolt gun more than offsets its somewhat slower rate of fire in the eyes of a majority of gun-oriented hunters.

The Right Cartridge for You

Time was when the major ammunition manufacturers lived in the "Give 'em any color as long as it's black" age. Then, starting in the late 1950s and spurred on both by the success of people like Roy Weatherby and the obviously increasing sophistication of American big-game hunters, the big companies entered the go-go era of cartridge proliferation. Though handloading still affords you the flexibility to work up special loads that make your gun purr better than any factory fodder or special-purpose loads, such as low-velocity small-game loads or special bullet weights, there is no basic North American Hunting situation that is not now reasonably well served by one or more factory rounds.

The arguments about what constitutes the "best" or most "all-around" cartridge for North American hunting are endless — and endlessly fascinating. Probably the .270 and the .30/06 still come about as close as any, with the marvelous 7mm Remington Magnum perhaps edging them out in a few respects. At the cash register where it counts, Americans have always opted for cartridges in the .24 to .30 caliber range. In the smokeless powder era anyway, no cartridge larger than .308 has done too well in this country. That's a shame because there has been a spate of good ones, both off the shelf and wildcats.

The little .358 Winchester is an easy-to-live-with load that has the bullet weight and diameter to be a close-to-medium-range elk convincer of the first magnitude. Teamed up with a pre-1964 Model 99 Savage, the .358 makes a superlative second gun or woman's gun on an elk or moose hunt. And there's certainly nothing wrong with using it on woods-wise whitetail, though all that power isn't quite necessary. The .350 Remington Magnum is another sad tale. This hot little shortie was perhaps one of the most ballistically balanced "mediums" ever brought out in this country. Reasonably flat shooting and packing a lot of punch, it could serve in a pinch for any hunting we have to offer. The general lack of enthusiasm for .35s in this country, plus the short and not overly lovely carbine that Remington introduced the .350 with, served to kill any real potential that the fine little round may have had.

There are other good performers among the big bores, too. The .348 is a fine old cartridge for the right sort of short-to-medium-range, heavy-duty situations, as is the old .33 Winchester in the model 1886 Winchester lever gun. The .35 Whelen, which is simply the .30/06 necked up, has proven itself a competent performer many times over through the years. Of course, the .375, the .338 and the .458 all do what they are supposed to do eminently well. With polar bear off the North American hunting list, about the only hunting on this side of the water really calling for possible use of these latter three rounds is close-range brown bear shooting in the heavy cover of southeastern Alaska or up on the famed slopes of Kodiak Island or the Alaska Peninsula. The .375 H&H Magnum is one of the queens of the worldwide rifleman's battery. And I tend to have a feeling that every serious rifleman ought to have *one* at some time or another, for nostalgic reasons at least. That kind of thinking keeps the Winchester and Remington coffers full and mine empty, but I freely confess to this kind of weakness.

The .24-to-.30 Caliber Cartridges. However, the real "action" occurs in the .24-to-.30 caliber group of cartridges — of course, leaving out varmint rounds for our purposes here. Since I have covered rifle choices for each species of game in the chapters relating to those animals, I will merely present an overview. But I could dwell lovingly on this subject here for all too long! This "action" group could be broken down into three subgroups.

SUBGROUP I. This includes the .250/3000, .243, 6mm Remington, .257 Roberts class of cartridge and features bullets in the 80- to 120-grain category and muzzle energies running around 1800 to 2300 foot pounds. (Theoretically, this is the amount of kinetic energy needed to raise 1800 to 2300 pounds 1 foot in the air or raise a 1-pound weight 1800 to 2300 feet into the air.) These cartridges are all flat-shooting shells with light recoil and low muzzle blast, and they are very comfortable to shoot. Guns for these cartridges do especially well for youngsters or ladies. And with proper bullet placement, they will readily account for all game up to and including caribou. With this class of animal (whitetail, mule deer, the sheep, black bear, goat and caribou) they perform well — the goat being the severest test. They are fine options as lightweight mountain rifles. Usually when you see a man afield with one of these guns, he knows his way around a rifle.

SUBGROUP II. The "medium-mediums" are the classic .270, .30/06, .280 Remington, .284 Winchester series of shells. There is a gray area here with some people preferring to assign the fine old 7x57 Mauser load to this group, which it most resembles in bullet-weight availability. Other people consider the 7x57 to be more of a peer of the .257 Roberts subgroup group, which it most resembles in muzzle energy figures. On the other "edge" of this group are the .264 Winchester, the .257 Weatherby and similar cartridges which are a bit lighter than the big .284 and .308 Magnums, but due to their extreme velocities, they carry stronger energy figures than the .270 to .30/06 clan.

Suffice to say that this group of cartridges carry bullets running from 100 grains to 220 grains but that their most common and effective loads generally feature 130- to 180-grain pills and turn up 2,500 to 3,000 foot pounds of energy at the muzzle. These guns are quite capable of killing anything in North America and most game in the world; in the hands of capable riflemen they have done that for many years. However, they are a bit light for brown bear, elk and moose (and even goat) in some situations. Nor are they the very best of grizzly medicine. The handloader can expand their flexibility enormously by using more heavily constructed bullets than those available off the shelf or, when chamber and gun allow, by speeding up the velocity just enough to make that all important difference.

SUBGROUP III. The next group of cartridges have really come into their own since the mid 1950s. These include the 7mm magnums through the .30 caliber magnums. Such cartridges as the peerless 7mm Remington Magnum, the 7mm Mashburn, the .308 Winchester Magnum, the .308 Norma, the .300 Weatherby and a host of others all offer a bit more power, and shooting unpleasantness, than the .270 to .30/06 class of shell. These guns will handle anything in North America, with the only marginal situation being that of shooting large brown bear in heavy cover. They are powerful and flat shooting. In the hands of a hunter who can shoot well enough to realize their potential, they expand his *practical* killing range about 50 to 75 yards over the less powerful loads.

However, ballistic tables reporting low drop and high energy and velocity figures never killed any game. It must be said that these fine cartridges can also beguile the hunter into trying shots that he shouldn't and thereby wounding and losing game. For the average hunter, 275 to 300 yards is a long shot and 350 is about the longest that should be attempted with these guns under many circumstances. If the man is a cool shot with time to assume a solid rest on stationary or almost stationary animals *with little cross-wind* (which is probably the most overlooked factor causing misses in the field), then of course longer shots are possible.

I have used the 7mm Remington Magnum to kill more head of game than any other cartridge. It has never let me down on anything including elk, moose and grizzly. The .270 was and is a particular favorite of mine and it is often afield with me, usually as a back-up to the big 7.

Rifle Specifications

I prefer a 22-inch barrel on most nonmagnum rifles; though in a few cases when I have been shaving ounces to come up with a light mountain gun, I have dropped this to 20.5 inches or 21 inches. I prefer 24 inches on magnums and will not have a 26-

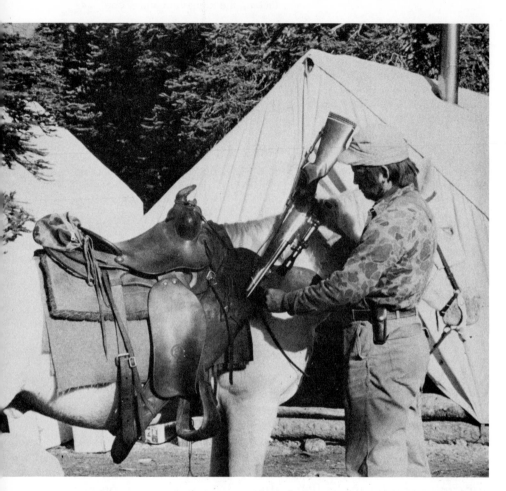

It's always smart to examine your rifle and scope each morning. The author once missed a chance at a big wolf because blood from a caribou shot the day before had smeared the scope's objective lens when the rifle was laid against the trophy for photographs.

inch barrel on a big-game rifle. All my rifles are equipped with slings, more for carrying than for shooting, though you can lock yourself tightly into a nice rest if you have time afield by properly lacing the sling around your "off" arm. I prefer the 1-inch Whelen sling to both the military sling and the simple carrying straps and fancy "California" straps that pop up from time to time.

Gun weights are tricky things. Generally, the heavier the

gun, the better it "hangs" on the target. But the heavier gun is more difficult to carry afield on arduous hunts and at high altitudes. Though there is a lot of talk about rifles under 8 pounds, the hunter will almost always end up with a gun around 9 pounds, possibly an ounce or two heavier with one of the 24-inch barreled magnums from the factory, topped off by one of the preferred 2x7 or 3x9 variable scopes and a sling with detachable swivels. Figure about a half-pound less—say, 8¼ to 8½ pounds for the equivalent gun in the .270 to .30/06 class. The smaller, lighter, .257-type rifle can be brought in right around 8 pounds, depending upon scope and mount, but to break the 8-pound mark generally requires some relatively expensive customizing and semi-customizing that reduces barrel contours and skeletonizes certain parts.

The Scope and Mount for You

Lightweight scopes of aluminum, Duraluminum, and similar light metals and alloys have almost replaced the heavier and somewhat stronger steel tubes of yesteryear in quality 1-inch tube hunting scopes. As the heavier and longer variable-power scopes have come into their heyday, this trend has accelerated. In the early years of variable-power scopes, light-metal scopes were considerably more sensitive and delicate than their fixed-power cousins. Not so today.

The modern vari-power hunting scope of today is bright, tough and able to take anything in the field, with reasonable care assumed. My .375 Magnum has comfortably worn a 1.5x4.5x variable with never a whimper from either field handling or the sizable recoil of the gun itself. I have evolved into using the vari-powers almost to the exclusion of fixed-power scopes for big-game hunting, though there is certainly nothing wrong with fixed-powers, which do afford lighter weight when you're trying to eliminate ounces.

I prefer the 2x7 variable for nonmagnum use but opt for the big 3x9 for the flat-shooting calibers like the 7mm Remington Magnum. I have only had one of these variables fog on me and that was years ago in their early days. The "widefield" versions of these variables now offered by many leading makers are a good idea, considerably expanding the hunter's field of view. This can be important when racking the scope out to the high powers. Widefields do add more to the price tag, though.

There are all sorts of scope mounts ranging from the standard top mount and side mount through the various flip-overs and quick-detachables of one sort or another. Also, there is a periodic re-emergence of the high-mounted scope that allows the use of iron sights underneath. This old, and to my mind, generally discredited approach is periodically "rediscovered," like trading stamps. I don't like it because it raises the scope higher off the barrel, thus making for a bulkier total package, and it makes for somewhat weaker mounting. The main thing I have against a high-mounted scope is that it usually pulls your cheek up off the comb of the stock. Thus it reduces accuracy. The low-mounted scope, which anchors the cheek solidly into the stock, promotes accuracy. Raising the stock enough for a high-mounted scope so that the cheek rests on the stock results in less attractive stock lines and more stock weight. And if you ever have to use the iron sights, the raised stock makes it difficult for you to squash your eye down low enough.

There are times when the high-mounted scope could come in handy. On a mountainside in the Cassiars of northern B.C., I had a chance at a gorgeous big black wolf that must have weighed close to 150 pounds. He stood broadside to me hardly 60 yards away, but I lost him because the sun glare entering directly into the front of the scope was overwhelming. A through-the-mount sighting, or a quick-detachable mount which I use on some guns, would have meant a dead wolf rather than a greatly disappointed outdoor writer. However, I just don't like many quick-detachable or flip-over mounts, though there is nothing at all wrong with the better grades of the conventional ones.

After much experimentation I have standardized on the tapered crosshair or "duplex" crosshair reticle on all my scopes. This reticle provides the best of both worlds with its heavy outer arms offering the advantages of post type reticles and its smaller, finer central crosshair offering fine-sighting capability.

Perhaps I'm just too much of a traditionalist, but I don't much go for the various and overly complex range-estimating reticles. Some of these things would make a nazi U-boat captain shudder — and undoubtedly miss his target. They are confusing to use quickly on jump shots or running animals, and under "hyper" field conditions most hunters find that the calculations and factors to remember for differing-size animals are much more difficult than straightforward range estimating. The dot-reticle was the only type range estimating device that I ever halfway liked, and this was due primarily to its simplicity. Here again it was necessary to remember all those body depths for differing species. The various calculations always left me more doubtful than when I started.

One final small, but important, gun-related item is the ammunition pouch. I prefer the belt type which allows me to carry 10 or 12 rounds under my coat and out of the weather in an unobtrusive, non-clinking fashion. I don't like the 20-cartridge types with the larger shells because that gets so bulky and weighty that I feel as though I may start listing to starboard. Ammunition should never be carried in the pants pockets, where it rattles, binds the hunter, and gets gunked up. I do usually carry a single round in each shirt breast pocket as a reserve.

Things that Increase Enjoyment

15

There are many items that the well equipped trophy hunter should have and use if he is to be successful. This includes gear such as sleeping bags, clothing, and protective cases; equipment such as guns, scopes, and knives; and miscellaneous small items such as shell holders, slings, compasses, whetstones, and sunglasses.

Since these are "basics" that you will already own, I'm going to bypass them here and dwell on some items that are unusual and also on some conventional items I have found to be of benefit in unusual situations. Some of these tread rather close to the outright "gimmick" designation but, when you need it, the right "gimmick" is worth its weight in efficiency or added enjoyment.

However, if you are searching for one of the more basic items to replace the one you have been using, please refer to the list of best quality mail order houses included in the back of this book. I have dealt with all of these reputable companies personally, and they are all staffed with knowledgeable folks who can help you to select the best merchandise for your needs and then see to it that you receive it at a fair price.

It's probably best to order catalogs first. Then you know which companies offer what you want. You can also write or phone these companies for advice on major purchases. The give-and-take possible in a phone call is well worth the extra cost involved if you are purchasing an important item. You can minimize your telephone expense by direct dialing (often after hours with the major mail order houses), by outlining your questions in advance, and by watching the time.

Special Items

The average trophy hunt is usually in rougher country than the average meat hunt. In some of these situations, special items really can come into their own, though their utility on a particular hunt will vary somewhat depending upon the situation and how critical weight is. Extended backpacking can make a man count ounces with religious fervor!

Here are items I recommend, in no particular order.

Rope. I always carry a short rope with me. Depending on the situation, I may have anything from a 25- to 30-foot length of lightweight synthetic rope on up to a 50- to 75-foot length of heavier hemp. If I'm backpacking I'll usually opt for the short length of the lighter synthetic. These ropes are far stronger (for equivalent diameter and weight) than the strongest manila hemp, and they don't stretch as much when wet. Disadvantages are that they will usually burn rather easily and they do not "bind" on themselves well.

More than once a short length of artificial rope has helped me pick my way down off the rough backside of a mountain. Rope is also quite handy for tying into position and field butchering large animals like moose and elk. Twenty-five feet of quarter-inch rope is very little weight or bulk to add to a pack, and it can sure come in handy!

The longer lengths of good-quality manila hemp can be put to good use back in camp, rigging lean-to's, meat racks, gin poles or just helping to secure the tent. The heavier hemp binds onto itself much better without constantly slipping under tension and thus is much better for these "permanent" type jobs. But you'll have to check it when it begins to stretch during a prolonged rainfall or snow storm.

Incidentally, if you're using a length of either nylon or hemp to help pick your way down off a mountain, especially in fast-receding light, tie knots in the rope about every 30 inches to keep it from inadvertently slipping through your tired hands. This knotting also tells when you've reached the "end of your rope," literally and figuratively. I almost backhanded myself right off a rope one time because I was tired and in a hurry. This could have led to a 500-foot fall.

Heavy-duty Monofilament Fishing Line. A short 50- to 100-yard length of this heavy-duty nylon line takes up practically no room in your pack and weighs less than a single rifle shell. It can handily be used to cinch antlers or meat to a packframe, tie down flapping boot soles until you can reach camp, or perform a number of other light-to-medium chores if you don't have rope along. In some cases the mono will work better than the rope. And for a 4-bit investment that weighs next to nothing, you can't beat it for usefulness.

Tape Measure. Though I have mentioned the use of this little device throughout the book, it is *so* important that I would be remiss if I didn't cover it here. It should be a lightweight, retractable, quarter-inch metal tape, as required by the Boone and Crockett Club for their later official measurement. This tape doesn't have to be long. A 6- or 8-footer will do fine. There are so many uses for this little gem that it's impossible to list them all, but the most important is the rough field measurement of antlers or horns, or of length of bear hide and skull. This tells the curious hunter if he has a chance of "making the book" as well as how accurately he estimated the trophy when he decided to take it. Also, if he's shipping direct from the field to the taxidermist, he can jot down the specific measurements for his peace of mind when he later wants to verify whether he got the same head or rug back from the taxidermist. (You can expect horns and antlers to have shrunk 5 to 10 percent. And through proper processing, the taxidermist ought to be able to hold rug shrinkage to about 15 percent.)

A tape measure can also be used to measure tracks in order to get a better idea of an animal's size, and to measure the span between tracks for the same purpose. In fact, if you're an inquisitive sort and want to learn more about the outdoors, you'll be simply astounded at how many things there are around to be measured, from the body lengths and shoulder heights of downed animals to the height of browse lines on trees. I always carry several of these inexpensive little gadgets because I find that, between my losing them and guides and other hunters permanently "borrowing" them, I can use more than one.

Folding Drinking Cup. This is one of those inexpensive, lightweight amenities that can make life far easier at times. Though I have nothing against cupping my hands and drinking from them, there are times — such as immediately after field dressing an animal — when it's difficult to get them completely clean and "drinkable." Also, often the area around the small mountain stream you are drinking from is damp or snowy and, if you have to stretch out full length to drink prone, you're going to get wet. Plus, if you're pretty hot and that good mountain water is typically chilled, drinking directly from the stream is a slower and less convenient process than using a small cup.

Reading Material. Sound odd? I always carry something to read, even on the most spartan backpacking jaunts. A day of rain can drag by with wearisome slowness. So it's good to be able to "tune out" the storm with a little light reading matter. On longer hunts where weight isn't critical, I always carry several paperback books and leave them in camp when I finish the hunt. Often it's a good idea to mix up your selection of titles a bit, carrying those light mysteries and adventure stories that you would assume to make good hunting camp fare and then maybe one "serious" title. You never can tell what you'll feel like reading afield, and sometimes I have the urge to read something fairly heavy.

First Aid Kit. This is a basic, so I won't dwell on it except to say that you should *always* carry a kit of your own, even on the fanciest and best-equipped of guided and outfitted hunts. Surprisingly, most of the things written on this subject stress bandages and medications for cuts, bruises, sore muscles and the like. But the two most common and (don't laugh) most debilitating problems the majority of hunters run into on strenuous deep wilderness hunts are diarrhea and constipation. To handle both eventualities, you should carry some dependable medications that you know from experience will work for you. The heavy physical stress you are under, generally at higher altitudes than you may be used to, teamed with a change in both diet and cooking style that usually includes much more "red meat," all serve to put your plumbing under severe strain. Be ready! It's not funny when it happens to *you*.

Watch Cap and Dickey. These are my two secret weapons. A wool or orlon watch cap or ski mask and a slipover turtleneck dickey, together, cost only about what a box of ammo sets you back and can easily be stuffed into your jacket pockets on cold-weather hunts. The cap or ski mask can be a godsend on cold, windy days that can give you the severest of all pains—an earache. The little dickey, almost never seen afield, is almost the equivalent of putting on another wool shirt, though it weighs far less. Its secret is that it helps to seal off the "blow hole" around your neck and insulate you from the cold damp outside chill. The more you can keep this chill from penetrating your body, the more comfortable you'll be and the less energy you'll use up trying to stay warm. The little dickey works miracles here.

Tape Recorder. I often take one of the new solid-state cassette tape recorders with me. These little marvels can take a lot of punishment and they are amazingly light and compact, hardly larger than a big paperback book. Also, I carry a number of the 120-minute cassettes with me. This enables me to record the other hunters names and addresses, hunting tips or interesting comments that I run onto, or just general cook-tent palaver.

I have even carried the little recorder afield frequently and recorded actual stalks and kills, as they took place. These little machines are wonderful at bringing the whole hunt back to you years later, just as it happened. Often, I probably would not take the time to write down some names or addresses or tips that I should. Merely pressing a button and recording the item in question makes it all so easy and routine. And of course some of the unforgettable characters that I have broken bread with and hunted with around the world would eventually begin to dim and fade in my memory without the tapes of spike-camp bull sessions or high-country lunch-time chats to snap them sharply back into focus.

Movie Camera. Photographs must rank right up at the top in any listing of things that help you to relive and enjoy a hunt years later. Since chapters 25 through 27 are devoted to taking better still photos, and enjoying it more, I won't go into still photography here. However, in addition to the still photos which I take professionally the year-round, I also shoot a Super 8mm movie camera, strictly for my own and my family's enjoyment. There are some do's and don'ts on amateur movie making that I've discovered over the years that result in better pictures.

The single most important thing that you should remember about making moving pictures is that first word. They should be *moving.* Far too many people shoot "posed" movies of a static situation, such as a fellow just standing there with his trophy. What they end up with is an extended photograph, not a "movie."

The place where the movie camera shines is around camp. Show people doing things: saddling horses, cooking, chopping wood, lounging around, putting up camp, packing a horse, cutting off a shirttail after someone's missed his buck. This is important in the making of good still photos also, but with movies it is absolutely essential. The movie pan shot showing a 180- to 360-degree view of blank unmoving scenery, however spectacular, is pretty ho-hum — especially to those who weren't there.

Try to break this kind of shot up with some sort of limited activity in the foreground or midground of the picture. Show horses and riders coming back into camp or zoom in on the camp itself briefly as you pan by. You may have to stage this.

About those zoom lenses. Most people overuse them greatly, zooming back and forth madly and giving their audiences vertigo when the film is shown. Use that zoom sparingly, slowly, so that it doesn't disorient the viewer, and use it to a purpose. If you want to get any sort of decent wildlife pictures, a 5-to-1 zoom is far better than a 3-to-1. I use a camera with a 5-to-1 and carry a tele-extender made for it that gets it up to 6-power on the telephoto end. (Note: Most 5-to-1 zooms are only around 4x telephoto, since part of the zoom range goes to wide-angle viewing. Thus, most 3-to-1 zooms do not even give you a 3x telephoto.)

If you're careful and use a rest and steady your breathing, you can usually hand-hold or semi hand-hold a 5-to-1 zoom fairly well. To go much beyond that on wildlife often requires a tripod for really good results. Although at heart I'm a still photographer, I must admit that movies bring a unique dimension of drama and excitement to a pair of bull elk fighting, a herd of caribou bouncing by on that peculiar spongy gait of theirs or the elegant grace of a whitetail bounding away with that alarm flag hoisted high.

There has been an enormous explosion of interest among serious amateurs in Super-8-format movie making in recent years. Nowadays there are cameras available with all sorts of features ranging from highly variable frame speeds and lap dissolves on into extremely esoteric considerations. These enable the "serious" and creative Super 8 movie maker to come up with highly professional movies that can fully duplicate the larger professional cameras.

That's all fine and good, but extra features add unnecessary cost, weight, and complexity and increase the chances that the camera will break down under hard field use. What you, as a straightforward outdoor movie photographer, need is a compact, well made camera with very good lenses and a 5-to-1 or longer zoom. One slow-motion speed is plenty, and you probably will find that you seldom ever use that.

Ways that Make a Difference

Pickups. Keep your eyes open for all sorts of interesting and unusual "trophies" and mementos lying around that can just be picked up and taken home.

A bleached-out moose antler or deer antler makes an interesting ornament for the mantelpiece, especially if it is outsized. And it often seems that these antlers are larger than any you see disporting themselves around on the heads of live animals. The antlers often show gnawings of porcupines and rodents, which go after the calcium and salts.

In Alaska I once picked up the jawbone of an enormous old grizzly bear that appeared to have been snared by Indians at least fifty years earlier, from the way the ground read. My son was ecstatic when I gave it to him, and he cherishes it to this day. A handful of dry and odorless moose droppings from British Columbia has been the focal point for some interesting conversation starters around our place for several years. Some of the local housewives have guessed them to be everything from nuts, to berries, to funny rocks.

Smooth or interesting stones always make a good pickup trophy. I'm not a rock hound, but I do enjoy seeing unusual

A guide here poses with a set of caribou antlers the author picked up in British Columbia. The shovel measured 19 inches, and the bez are the largest the author has ever seen. Rodents ate away the top portion, so those measurements remain conjectural. For sure, this rack came from a very large and old bull—too old to survive another winter.

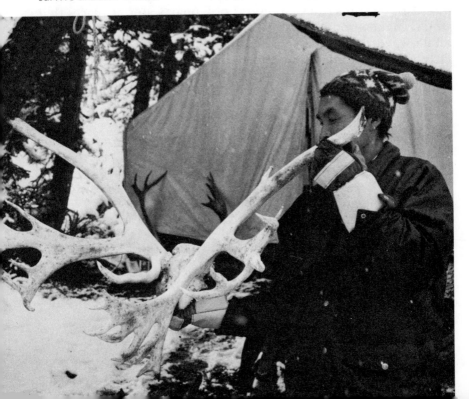

rocks or mineral formations, and from each hunt I try to bring back at least one rock that is either unusually attractive or particularly typical of the area that we were hunting. Riverbeds are good places to keep your eyes open for attractive and unusual stones. There are often good smooth stones, buffed and honed by years of spring floods washing at them. I have picked up a number of these that serve quite well as sharpening stones for my knives, and they have the added advantages of being free for the taking and filled with sentimental value.

Spring bear hunters or those on some of the high-country, late-summer hunts have the added enjoyment of seeing the carpets of exquisite alpine flowers in bloom that the rest of us miss in the fall and winter hunting. Some friends of mine have picked these dainty, colorful little flowers — only taking a few of each type — and pressed them between the leaves of books to preserve them. At home they have framed them or had them embedded in clear plastic to preserve a bit of the color and beauty of the fragile mountaintop world.

Old bottles and various other oddments that turn up, particularly on old trails, can be interesting to pick up and ponder. However, be sure that you are not breaking any relic or antiquary laws that may be in effect where you are hunting. Arrowheads, old pottery shards, bones from long-ago fires, scraps of leather from old saddles or dog harnesses and untold other interesting things can be noted. Look near water at places that would make good campsites, and you'll often find something. Shallow, fordable stretches of larger rivers are often particularly good. Finding these old items, without detracting from your hunting is interesting, and it gives you the satisfaction of feeling that you are learning how to read the country and its history.

Conversation. One of the very best leisure time occupations around camp is the fine old art of conversation. If you are hunting far away from home, the guide, outfitter or local hunters in camp are fascinating sources of information on the country, the game and the ways different people live.

On a fishing trip I took to Lake Athabasca in northern Saskatchewan some ten years ago, it rained for three solid days of my 7-day trip, but talking to the Indian guides made things more than bearable, even worthwhile. I found out how they traveled north into the far Northwest Territories each winter to trap and went for five or six months without seeing another human. Sleeping out in the open with only the most rudimentary camping equipment, in 30- and 40-degree below-zero weather, these men survived by huddling up with their sled dogs. (I wonder if today's snow machines are that warm?) The guides helped me look into another way of life as strange as a Martian's. One had left Yellowknife, N.W.T., the year before with a rusty old .30-30 and five cartridges. How he lived by snaring fish and game and shooting caribou made an epic 7-month saga to me. To him it was just routine. I'm sure that I never would have gotten to know these men as well and learned as much about them if our conversation had been limited to casual fishing conversation in the boat or mealtime talk at night.

You don't have to go far away to do the same thing. Other hunters in camp almost always can furnish new hunting tips that you didn't know about or, at least, interesting anecdotes from their own experiences over the years.

More. There are many other aspects to this broadening and deepening of the hunt and your enjoyment of it. Often you can do a little fishing, sometimes for rare and exotic species not found close to home. There's always the opportunity to pick up new skills: how to sharpen an axe, how to saddle a horse, how to bone out an elk or moose. You can learn new recipes that will make the eating both tastier and more interesting when you return home. You can make new friends and explore new ideas.

The actual kill is over in minutes, often seconds. The serious stalking which gets your adrenaline pumping at full force is usually limited to a few minutes or a few hours, at most. It just makes good sense to do everything possible to extend your enjoyment of the hunt to the utmost during those hours in camp or afield when you are not actually stalking the quarry.

Physical Conditioning

16

Once I did an article for an outdoor magazine for which I contacted over a dozen of the most famous trophy hunters in North America and asked them a number of questions. Their replies were most interesting, especially since they, as a group, had more than 500 years experience. They ranked the grizzly as the top North American trophy, with the bighorn sheep a close second. Their favorite North American hunting ground was Alaska. Some of their other answers surprised me quite a bit, while still others were about what I had expected.

In one of these exercises, I gave them four predetermined considerations and asked them to rank them in order of importance as to which was the biggest problem among trophy hunters. The four "problems" and the way they ranked them were:

1. Lack of knowledge of area and game............... 42 points
2. Poor physical condition..................................... 35 points
3. Poor shooting ability .... 32 points
4. Trouble with guns and gear............................. 21 points

Now all of these are important considerations among trophy hunters. However, I was probably more surprised by this set of answers than any other in my voluminous questionnaire. These men are all rather wealthy chaps who have hunted all over the world. Most have been on a number of safaris in Africa, which is by and large far easier hunting physically than North American trophy hunting. Maybe that accounts for their ranking poor physical condition in second place.

I wouldn't. There isn't a doubt in my mind that, across the board, this is the biggest single problem and pitfall of trophy hunters. This is the one that guides and outfitters who see hundreds of clients over the course of years cry about most

loudly and frequently. Most men, at least among trophy hunters, learn to shoot reasonably well and put in some time on the
range. Most are interested enough in their chosen sport to read
up on it and learn more about the area to be hunted and the
game in question (thus, this book). And outdoor guns and gear
have been engineered to such a high degree of effectiveness
that hardware problems definitely are decreasing.

Most big game hunting is fairly strenuous and almost all
serious trophy hunting is. You, as a trophy hunter, must be
prepared to make great exertions, often during adverse
weather and in the thin, strength-sapping air of high altitudes.
All of this is just common sense, so why is physical conditioning
such a chronic problem? Because most of us have become such
an urban people in the last generation that there are very real
language problems involved with this whole business of physical conditioning. The same words simply don't carry the same
meanings for most of us that they do for our mountain-bred
outdoor cousins.

What's "good shape" for the city-bred desk pilot is pathetic to
the professional hunting guide or seasoned outdoorsman who
lives and works in the outdoors the year round. Chances are
that the average East Coast citizen's idea of a tough outing is
hitting the golf links for eighteen holes rather than nine. And
this in the thick, easy air down near sea level. Eighteen holes
probably wouldn't even get a mountain guide's juices flowing
up in the harsh, thin air at 5,000 or 6,000 feet where most of
the good mountain hunting starts nowadays. The guide is used
to being exposed to bad weather and to exerting himself mightily at high altitudes. The city man's idea of "bad weather" is airconditioning gone on the fritz, and high altitude is the twen-
tieth floor of his sea level office building.

Practically all of us are overweight by serious trophy hunting
standards, especially for high altitude work. What looks to be a
trim outline at the country club is a noticeable burden when the
gasping, wheezing lowland hunter is trying to drag it up a steep
mountainside at 7,000 feet. What looks to be a "little" fat in the
bedroom mirror becomes a grotesque burden when the exhausted hunter is desperately trying to sprint that last 300 feet
around a rugged sidehill after a tough 1,500 foot climb for that
now-or-never shot at his spooked trophy elk or mule deer.

Even in lowland eastern whitetail deer hunting, the difference between the hunter who takes just any deer and the
hunter who takes the big buster is often partially the physical
conditioning. The man who gets up early and is well into the

woods long before daybreak has the edge. The man who goes out and stays out in really rough weather, through sleet and unseasonable cold when most other hunters are back in camp toasting themselves in front of the fire is the fellow who eases up on the big outsized trophy head.

Even though high altitude work isn't called for in the East very often, some surprisingly strenuous climbing is. The hunter who makes it all the way to the top of that big Pennsylvania ridge or that mountain in the Ozarks or the Catskills is the one with the best chance of surprising an old-timer and collecting on him.

Even though great distances aren't a necessary part of most eastern whitetail hunting and, in fact, the canny hunter with a stand or tree stand at the right point may be ahead of the game, good condition is still important. The ability to stand the cold, which is twice as penetrating when you're inactive, and still remain alert and shoot with a steady hand depends upon physical conditioning. Your physical condition largely determines your energy level, your alertness level, your agility and your all-round muscle tone. All of these factors are vitally important to the hunter seeking that outsized, tough-to-get, old mossy back with the hatrack on his head.

If some of these comments have sounded a bit harsh, all I can do is assure you that they are based on experience. Physical conditioning became the name of the game when you traded up to serious trophy hunting. Every season, guides go crazy because of physical condition problems with their hunters. A booking agent I know recently related that one of his clients had written him a long and heart-rending letter after his unsuccessful Montana elk hunt. Not only had this hunter not drawn blood but he felt that his guide, although friendly enough at first, had ended up treating him rather meanly. After the fourth day, the guide had hardly ever smiled or made small talk. The big city hunter was perplexed and hurt. Even his wittiest sallies fell on deaf ears and all the charm he could dredge up came to naught.

My friend the booking agent checked into matters. The guide told him that on the fourth day they had spotted an enormous bull elk early in the morning. The way the ground lay, the guide figured to have the wrangler circle around to give the old bull his wind so that he would spook their way. All the guide and his hunter had to do was to climb a relatively easy 500-foot side hill to shoot. Although they had time to spare when they set out, the overweight and out-of-condition hunter moved as

The good physical condition of these outdoorsmen enables them to hike into brown bear country through water and binding mud. However, one's climbing and hiking ability is important on wilderness horse hunts too.

though he were walking in tar and the clock ticked away relentlessly.

Eventually the wrangler circled around into position, the old bull caught his wind, leaped up and came charging by the guide right on cue. The only problem was that the miserable hunter, badly winded and shaking with fatigue, had collapsed a bare 100 feet below the crest he was to shoot from. The guide had gone on ahead and when he saw the big bull clearly, *he* almost collapsed. It was one of the largest 7-point bulls he had ever seen in over twenty years of professional hunting. When he yelled this down to spur on his prostrate hunter, the poor fellow gasped back, "I think I'll wait here until he comes around again."

The guide didn't know whether to laugh or cry!

An Exercise Program

The best investment you can make for physical conditioning is two small paperback books: *Aerobics* and *The New Aerobics*. Both are by Dr. Kenneth H. Cooper of the U.S. Air Force Medical Corps. They are based on his extensive studies of physical conditioning of thousands of men in the Air Force. These books have been adopted as the official training manuals for the physical conditioning of the armed forces of more than a dozen countries, and they do a peerless job of explaining just what good physical condition is and what it isn't.

Muscular fitness (strength) is of some value according to Dr. Cooper but the real key is endurance fitness. This latter criterion is based on the body's ability to bring in a maximum amount of oxygen and deliver it to the organ or tissue where the energy is needed. Dr. Cooper's sprightly prose does much to clear away some of the time-hallowed misconceptions about physical fitness.

His theory is very instructive, but the really unique value of these books is the point system which he provides. The "chart pack" in *The New Aerobics* lists points for different levels of activity, depending upon speed and duration, and for different types of activity, such as jogging, cycling, swimming, basketball, other sports. He also breaks down the number of points by age groups and by sex to tell you what you should earn to reach differing levels of fitness.

All this data was statistically verified through Air Force studies of large groups of men. The value of this specific, tangible point system can't be over emphasized. For the first time, you know specifically how many points you should be earning to achieve the five different levels of physical conditioning from "Very Poor" through "Excellent," and you can tailor your own program to achieve the desired fitness level. I have personally used the system and recommend it highly.

Physical conditioning and dieting, if necessary, should start four to six *months* before a major hunt. See a doctor first for a checkup. Don't go on a crash program four to six *weeks* before the hunt. You'll just overstrain yourself and probably weaken yourself further, if not actually endanger your health. Incidentally, the Aerobics system is a boon to heart patients and those with other known ailments of a serious nature. Its step-by-step, *controlled* nature enables most of these hunters — under a physician's supervision at all times — to achieve some remarkable results, and do it safely. It just takes them far longer to build up

Good physical condition also helps the body adjust to the dietary changes encountered in the field. Extreme diarrhea or constipation can put you out of action as effectively as a broken leg.

to the desired proficiency level, as it does with older hunters in their sixties and beyond. Age alone doesn't mean that you must give up most trophy hunting or stop being serious about it!

Other Regimens

Don't forget the other requirements on your personal conditioning prehunt countdown. See your dentist and get your teeth cleaned. Do it far enough in advance so that any necessary dental work can be completed before the hunt begins. If there is a Hell on earth, it's being twenty miles from the nearest road with a wracking toothache!

See your optometrist, even if you don't wear glasses. You may find that you need them now. Or, if you do wear them, you may need a prescription change. Again, allow enough time for any necessary work to be completed and for new glasses to be made for you if necessary. If you don't wear glasses, the trip to the optometrist will, at the very least, confirm the old 20-20, and that can be reassuring.

Check your feet. They're the single most important part of your body. If you can't walk, you can't hunt. Chances are, if you're a city dweller, that they're terribly tender. Going bare-footed in the yard helps some, as does limited soaking in an alum-and-water or salt-and-water solution. It's important to avoid those painful, trip ruining blisters.

Personal Hygiene

Be sure that your toenails and fingernails are clipped short. Torn nails are painful, and bad toenails have been known to put hunters out of commission entirely. Change your sox often and keep your sox and feet as clean as possible.

Let's do some serious talking about dirt. Believe it or not, there's something of a science to it. After you get in good physical condition and start your trophy hunt, the important thing is to *stay* in good operating condition so that you can reap the maximum benefit from all that laborious physical conditioning and increase your chances of getting the big trophy.

Your biggest enemy in maintaining yourself at peak operating efficiency is—surprisingly—dirt. Many of us who don't work outside or with our hands for major portions of the year aren't very used to a certain amount of filth in our everyday lives. The year-round outdoorsman is. In a very real sense there are two kinds of dirt. Let's call the first type "cosmetic dirt." This is the readily visible smudges that show up on our face, arms and other exposed body parts—the kind that makes a mother sigh when the children come in after playing out in the yard all day. This type of dirt is the least dangerous, and it's much easier to control because it's visible.

There is, broadly speaking, a second type of dirt. Let's call this one body filth or accumulated perspiration. It comes as a natural by-product of our extreme exertions on arduous hunts. This one *is* dangerous—and deceptive at times. Many hunters don't change and wash their underthings often enough, just as they often don't wash themselves frequently enough—especially on cold weather hunts. And yet I've taken sponge baths in below-zero weather by merely heating the water and working on, and thus uncovering, only a portion of my body at a time.

Often hunters feel an atavistic urge. They want to "get back to nature" when they're on a hunt. So they grow beards and get pretty dirty. Or, they may be just too tired to maintain things as they would prefer. This is all right—up to a point. But, beyond that point, I've seen hunters so galled in the crotch or so chafed under the arms that they could barely walk or function. Ironically, most dudes are far more negligent about these things than the full-time outdoorsman who knows that personal hygiene has a good bit to do with his effectiveness. He knows that he simply must take good care of himself if he is to continue to perform efficiently at a high exertion level.

There's nothing sissy about washing out your sox and underwear and nothing especially manly about smelling bad. I'm not here concerned with the social aspects of being a bit "ripe" but, rather, with the fact that really pronounced body odor is nature's signal that your body is building a big problem for itself. This is worth extra concern if you are placing very high demands on it and most especially if you have the tender skin that comes from spending most of your time indoors.

The seasoned outdoorsman knows all of this. Although he may have some dirt smudges on his arms or face and appear "dirty," chances are his body hygiene is well maintained. He knows that he stays warmer that way and avoids painful chafing and galling. Also, your odor is distinctive enough, anyway, and can spook prey far too easily without your aggravating the situation. I would imagine that, when body odor becomes really pronounced, it at least doubles your scent radius under any given circumstances.

Keep your lips from becoming chapped and cracked. Take two or more chapsticks, in case you lose one, and use them *before* you need them. That way maybe you won't need them later. High wind conditions or cold weather can chap your face and lips amazingly quickly. If you do get stuck with painful, burning lips and no chapstick, use elk or deer fat. I have and it works pretty well.

Make sure you have some good sunglasses along and that you use them when needed. Heavy snow conditions can overstrain your eyes with glare before you know it. So can the penetrating rays of the sun at high altitude when the normal insulating blanket of dust particles and smog is only a fraction of what it may be down lower and in the city. Sunglasses also help to protect your eyes in dust storms or driving snow. I do try to pull mine off when actually stalking an animal because the sun can glint off them and spook the game.

It's surprising how many hunters, and some pretty savvy ones at that, baby their guns, cameras and binoculars and let themselves go, entirely. Many may even train diligently to get into good condition but then not *maintain* that condition once in camp. When you think about it, that doesn't make much sense, does it?

How to Cut Costs

17

Alas, like almost everything else in this life, the cost of top quality trophy hunting is skyrocketing. This applies whether you're talking about a far north outfitted hunt with all the trimmings, a mid-range Montana share-the-chores elk hunt, or a straight do-it-yourself south Texas trophy whitetail hunt. Only the numbers are different, the direction of the costs is the same — straight up.

But there are things the shrewd and knowing trophy hunter can do to minimize many of these staggering costs. Admittedly, using the cost cutters often means that you must pay with things other than money. This can mean that extra time or physical effort is required for the hunt, that there may be more discomfort or inconvenience than on the "country club" hunt, or just that it may take extra time and effort to properly investigate and organize the hunt during that all-important desk work stage, months before the actual hunt.

But, if these sacrifices make the difference between going and not going, they begin to look somewhat less distasteful. This is especially so if you share my view that many of them, such as the additional desk work at home or the time and trouble to get into top physical shape, actually enhance the hunt and add to the total trophy experience rather than detract from it. Anything that adds to your all-round competence and knowledge of this fascinating sport of trophy hunting makes it more enjoyable, not less!

Let's talk about some of the costs so that you know what you're up against. These are general guidelines and there will be exceptions. However, they are accurate in the main as of this writing. Then we'll see what can be done to pare these costs down to more manageable amounts. To a degree, this depends on which animals you want to hunt, where you want to hunt, and how you want to hunt. Sheep and grizzly are very expensive and much less elastic in cost than moose, goat, caribou, deer and pronghorn. Elk run the gamut in cost, from fairly cheap to very expensive. Far northern hunts are much more expensive than most southern and eastern Canadian hunts, while western U.S. hunts run from cheap to very expensive. Horses cost money, as do airplanes and any other mechanical contrivances. It's still cheapest to hunt on shanks mare (afoot).

Costs in Various Hunting Areas

Alaskan Costs. To retain a top-drawer outfitter who operates in a first-class area is a real piggy bank wrecker. A full 18-day "5-animal" hunt for Dall sheep, grizzly, black bear, moose and caribou used to go for $1,500 in the late 1960s. In 1970, these hunts could be had for $2,500. Nowadays you'd better figure on anywhere from $3,200 to $3,500 — to $4,500. And while the "5-animal" hunt of a decade back usually lasted 21 days rather than 18, now it's more often 14 or 15 rather than 18.

A "3-animal" hunt costs something like $2,000 to $2,500. But grizzly is excluded by practically all outfitters now on this type hunt — though some will let you shoot one for $1,000 extra. That puts you right back up over $3,000 as in the case of the 5-animal hunt. True, you didn't have to pay all of it on the front end. You paid only if you got the coveted grizzly. However, you only got an 8- to 10-day chance at it on the 3-animal deal.

Some Alaska outfitters are going to a flat-fee-per-animal basis that usually runs about like this.

Black Bear	$250 – $400
Caribou	$500 – $700
Moose	$750 – $1,000
Sheep	$1,500
Grizzly	$1,500 – $2,500

Ready for more? Many outfitters often add in an "escalator" if you take a Boone and Crockett class trophy. This may occur on any of the bases that the outfitter figures the hunt, but it most often seems to pop up on the last, flat-fee-per-species method and often means a 50 or 100 percent increase for the cost of that animal. To top it off, your airfare will usually run around $600 round trip depending on where in the "southern 48" you're coming from, and bush plane costs could add anything from zero to $300 to $500. For licenses, figure better than $500 for a full bag.

Yukon Territory Costs. The Yukon is a vast, underpopulated land where population has actually declined in the last seventy-five years and it offers the same animals as Alaska and possibly, due to lighter pressure, better hunting. Until recently the hunting was considerably cheaper here than in Alaska, northern British Columbia and the Northwest Territories. Ten-day sheep hunts were still possible, and 12- to 15-day sheep hunts were the rule of the day, most of them costing around $125 per day. All of these mixed-game hunts are for all animals; the "5-animal" and "3-animal" approach is restricted to Alaska. (On a per diem basis, figure Alaskan hunting at around $225 per day with some brown bear hunts running over $300 per day for a ten-day hunt.)

Although still somewhat cheaper than the others, in the last couple of years the twenty-two Yukon outfitters (limited to that number by Territorial Law) have been playing catch up. Ten-day sheep hunts are very rare, with the rule being 15 to 18 days and the per diem average running $150 to $175. While practically all Alaskan hunting is sans horses, except for that offered by a few outfitters in the extreme southeastern part of the state in the Wrangell Mountains by the Yukon border, as well as a few other spots, all Yukon hunting is on horseback. Alaskan outfitters usually rely on bush planes and then a combination of walking and, for extra cost, tracked or 4-WD vehicles.

Northwest Territories Costs. Only a relatively few small portions of the extreme western edge of this giant land are open to nonresident hunting. These MacKenzie Mountain concessions were opened in 1964 and offer the same animals as the Yukon and Alaska. There are practically no goats in the two Canadian territories while Alaska has a burgeoning population of the slab-sided animals, especially in the southern panhandle. Costs in the NWT run about the same as in the Yukon, perhaps slightly more although licenses in both are still cheaper than in Alaska or British Columbia.

Northern British Columbia Costs. This marvelous province, regarded by many as the queen of all North American hunting grounds, must be considered in two aspects because of the great variation between its northern and southern hunting methods and costs. In the far north, the wondrous Stone sheep is still available in goodly numbers in most areas, although a few grounds are beginning to be shot over pretty hard. Quite a few trophy hunters regard the fabled Chadwick Stone ram, shot in the late 1930s in northern B.C., as the finest trophy of any type ever taken on this continent. And many hunters think that Stone sheep are the finest single trophy species. Only in B.C., in all the world, is he available; although a few intergrades (with Dall sheep) do lap over into southern Yukon.

Costs for northern British Columbia hunting have gone right through the roof. A sheep hunt is usually a minimum of 18 days, with 21 being the rule. These hunts are costing $200 to $250 per day. Thus, a sportsman can drop $4,000 to $5,000 on a hunt or considerably more money than levied for many African ranch-shooting type safaris that offer 10 to 15 species rather than 5. The B.C. government recently tripled their hunting license costs to over $1,000 for a full game bag; this puts license costs over those for some African shoots. Furthermore, they scrapped their progressive and intelligent Trophy Fee System, whereby the hunter bought a general game license and tags for each species, all at somewhat nominal costs and then paid the main costs on the back end, only for those trophies that he elected to take.

I always felt that this was a fair way to do things and it had the added benefit of encouraging more selective, discriminating shooting. Evidently the authorities didn't agree with me. I shudder to see some of the "trophies" that will now undoubtedly start coming out as hunters desperately try to insure that they get their "money's worth" for horrendous costs that they have to pay in advance.

The authorities in B.C. have a somewhat cavalier attitude about the whole thing, something reminiscent of all those fellows in bedsheets farther to the east who are roosting on all that oil. The fruits of this political response to the tired old cliché "the Yanks are getting all our game" remain to be seen.

Southern British Columbia Costs (including Alberta). The costs and the hunting vary all over the lot, and are similar to that in the western U.S. Rocky Mountains. Costs can run anywhere from $60 per day on up to $150, depending upon where and what you are hunting. Mule deer, whitetail, elk and a few bighorn sheep now put in an appearance as the Stone and Dall sheep to the north drop out of the picture. The grizzly start getting sparser and are often relegated to spring-only hunting. These hunts may be straight hiking, horseback or 4-WD in nature.

Eastern Canadian Costs (including Prairie Provinces of Saskatchewan and Manitoba). Hunting quality, when compared with that farther north, drops off here both in number of species available and in size. But, much of the country is beautiful, the people are interesting and the costs are lower. Saskatchewan and Manitoba hunting is limited largely to moose for nonresidents. But since the largest whitetail on this continent grow in southeastern Saskatchewan, if the authorities should decide to reopen whitetail hunting to nonresidents, it'll be a unique opportunity to bag the deer of a lifetime. Black bear are also available.

Farther east whitetail are available to U.S. hunters, as are moose and black bear. Some nice whitetail are taken every year in Ontario and Quebec, and they seem to be coming back from a decline in New Brunswick. Newfoundland offers moose and a unique opportunity for woodland caribou, with a herd of some 12,000 to 15,000 on the island.

These eastern moose often run larger than our western U.S. Shiras moose but considerably smaller than the western Canadian and far northern giants. Since many men feel that one moose head, a gigantic corner-filler in all but the largest rooms, is all they'll ever have mounted, that's a comparison to remember.

Hunting in this vast, almost continent-wide region is usually on foot or by canoe, but seldom by horse. Costs are reasonable, running from $50 to $100 per day, possibly more than that when hunting Quebec-Labrador caribou in the northeastern part of this territory. But, though the hunting may well be exciting and memorable, don't expect to often see the game that you would farther west. This is as much due to the fact that much of this hunting east of the prairie provinces is lowland and in thick cover with short-range visibility as it is due to the smaller population of animals per square mile.

Western U.S. Costs. This hunting is so varied that it would take a book in itself to cover it. A very incomplete run-through tells us that the moose get smaller and sparser as you go south and then disappear entirely in Wyoming as do goat. Deer become more plentiful as do elk and pronghorn. Sheep hunting becomes *extremely* limited.

Costs vary a great deal from those for "groupie" elk hunts in which the outfitter packs you and your rig in and then comes in and gets you a week later ($50 per day) to first class, full-accommodation outfitted hunting that runs $100 to $200 per day. Hunting is not cheap here because of the relatively high wage rates for guides and for extra expenses. Hunting license costs are cheaper than farther north, but they are getting more expensive, and more limited each season.

Like all Canadian provinces, practically all western states require nonresident hunters to have a guide. Although you may think of this as a subtle type of graft to unglue you from some of your hard earned *dinero,* there are also some sound reasons for it. Most states get tired of spending expensive time and manpower to rescue all sorts of strangers from their mountains and forests each season. Also, if you're investing that precious once-a-year vacation and a considerable amount of money for transportation, nonresident hunting licenses and your guns and gear, it's best to avoid going into hunting country completely cold.

Of course "guide" may be interpreted many ways, running from the full-time pro who is working with a single hunter; to the part-timer who works with 2, 3 or even 4 hunters at a time; to the obliging rancher who lets you have hunting access to his place, a bunk in the bunkhouse and breakfast, all for a reasonable fee. He points you in the right direction each morning. These options result in the wide variance in prices.

Eastern U.S. Costs. Here we're talking almost strictly whitetail, with black bear being largely bonus trophies, except for those taken in a few spots in North Carolina which, after Washington state, has one of our largest populations of blackies.

Although whitetail abound over much of this swath of countryside, *trophy* hunting for them — with any reasonable chance of success — is largely limited to various specific and rather restricted areas. Some of these such as the Black Hills in northeastern Wyoming or the Rapid City area in South Dakota are "eastern" only in the sense that they're east of the Rockies and have outfitters who cater to strangers.

Most true eastern areas featuring big whitetail offer few or no outfitters catering to nonresidents. These include certain parts of Missouri; the strip of border territory near Laredo, Texas; and the Arkansas Ozarks. Here the hunting can be very expensive even though it doesn't cost you much out-of-pocket money because you may not get or even *see* any game. That's a year's vacation-hunt wasted, not to mention some transportation expense. (Yet I believe more and more eastern states will soon follow the lead of the western states by boosting nonresident license costs and requiring a local guide.)

Trimming the Costs

Although the preceding capsules are so broad as to admit to many exceptions, I assure you that the high costs are representative in the main. Furthermore, the ever-spiraling cost trend is accelerating, not slowing. Unless the economy suddenly belies Adam Smith's centuries-old dictum about supply and demand, chances are that inflation will continue.

Very few hunters are fortunate enough to have had an obliging benefactor leave them with a big stack of chips to cover the necessities of life such as playing the ponies and big-game hunting. So, what can be done about these fearful costs? Surprisingly, there are a number of possibilities, some major and some minor, some rather straightforward and mechanical and others considerably more unorthodox and "far out."

Which possibilities will work best for you depends mostly on your own personality and degree of interest. Some are easy to pull off and others require much more energy and aggressiveness. There are trade-offs ("goods" and "bads") to all of them which you need to think through carefully. Let's explore them.

On the broadest level costs can be broken down into three basic categories, each offering possibilities:
- Transportation
- Equipment and supplies
- Hunt

Transportation Costs. With the rocketing prices of fuel, if you need to travel long distances to reach your hunting field, you'd better give this category some thought.

Obviously, the very cheapest way for several fellows to make a long trip is to crowd into a car and take off. This has some definite disadvantages, though. It's slow and tiring, and the baggage area is limited. Many hunters only have two-week vacations. Thus, even by cheating a day or two on the ends, it often just isn't feasible to make a 10-, 12-, or 14-day hunt and still safely drive the enormous distances involved — especially coming back after a long and tiring hunt.

Air travel offers many advantages. It's easier and you can arrive fresh and ready to hunt hard. It's much safer and faster. But it requires that you carefully edit your baggage, cutting it to a minimum. Check out the rather complex baggage regulations of the different carriers. Sometimes a carry-on bag and one *big* duffle bag (rather than two smaller ones) can hold more of your gear and do it cheaper, depending upon what you have and how it's shaped. Cram as many items into your carry-on bag and pockets as possible. Wear bulky hunting boots, clothing and underwear. Why wear a business suit or even city casuals out to the bush?

Bring your trophies back from the hunt with you as "passenger-accompanied freight" rather than the generally more expensive "air freight." The savings can be considerable, running 30 to 50 percent and more, depending. (Incidentally, overland freight from truly remote areas, if available at all, can be about as expensive as most air freight. Besides overland freight takes longer and your trophies aren't as safe.)

Getting your trophies ready to bring back with you may be a bother at the end of a long, tiring trip, but you'll save big money. As accompanied freight they usually don't need to be crated; you merely tag them and tape all sharp antler points. If sent later by air freight, they generally must be crated at great cost in remote areas. You'd be amazed just how great! Thus, accompanied freight comes at a cheaper basic rate, and it saves you the cost of crating and the additional freight cost of shipping the big crates as well as the trophies. Your precious trophies are back sooner and safer, under your personal care. Think about it.

Hunters usually bring back more baggage than they left with. This is due to souvenirs, trophies, keepsakes and various goodies picked up along the way. If you had a good trip, tip your guide(s), host(s) or whomever with equipment rather than cash. If they're back in a remote area, they'll probably appreciate it more than money. And having given away ammunition, coat, boots, packboard or whatever, you really save a lot of weight and space on the plane back. No, I'm not recommending that you come home clad only in skivvies because you gave everything to your new-found rancher friend or eagle-eyed guide. Just keep this two-way possibility in mind.

Try to plan the trip so that, if a bush plane is required for the last leg into camp, it always brings someone out when it takes you in and vice versa. Bush planes aren't cheap, and this both-way usage cuts the cost way down. On my last major far-north hunt, the flight in from Watson Lake, Yukon Territory, south to the Stikine River country in northern B.C. would have cost me $260 each way by myself. Three other hunters flew in with me and I squeezed in with four hunters coming out. The $117 cost looked downright cheap compared to the $520 that little circuit would have cost me solo!

Don't neglect to check on chartering a plane, rather than flying one of the scheduled airlines. In the right circumstances a charter can work out to be the best of both worlds—both cheaper and more convenient. It usually works better for a party of three or four taking a medium length trip of three-hundred to seven-hundred air miles for a week or so. If the chartered plane can take you all the way to your final destination and save you from chartering an additional bush plane for that last hop, things really do start to get interesting!

A big plus for the charter plane is that it gives you far, far more flexibility as to where and when you go. There are multitudes of variables involved with this one. But since planning the trip is half the fun and there's usually plenty of time to check things out, give it a try.

Equipment and Supplies Costs. A dedicated trophy hunter ends up spending a significant amount of coin on equipment and supplies. If you don't believe it, just inventory your own! Learned outdoor gurus have been admonishing us to buy quality equipment, the best we can afford, for many decades. This guideline is more valuable now than ever before, if you use your gear over a period of years. Buy the best, take care of it, and it'll last a lifetime. And your children may be able to enjoy it after that. In the process it will cost you less than cheap (though probably not inexpensive) shoddy that must be replaced every time it's banged around some. And worse yet, cheap shoddy gives out at just the wrong time in the field.

Take your time and accumulate items over a period of years, even if you have to borrow some things to make the first few big hunts. This brings to mind an interesting point. Possibly you and a similar-size buddy can team up and coordinate your purchases so that you can borrow from each other and thus have access to a complete set of equipment much sooner. Perhaps you can buy the down coat and he the sleeping bag and then you can trade these items back and forth when not hunting together. This is not an ideal solution but an option worth considering.

In some cases you can go in together with friends and bulk-buy purchases of film, reloading components or other items at considerable savings. Speaking of reloading, if you aren't "into it" yet, why not give it a try both for the savings and flexibility it affords you? You can cut your shooting costs 75 percent or more. So if you like to shoot and own several big bores, reloading can save you a considerable sum each year. You can custom-tailor loads to make your rifle, *any* rifle, more accurate. And you can cook up special loads to extend the flexibility of your gun by loading heavier or lighter bullets than available from the factory, and you can load higher- or lower-velocity and differently-shaped or constructed special-purpose bullets. Besides, it's just more fun to take game with ammunition that you have painstakingly developed and proven out in your gun. Here again, several of you could split the cost of a single reloading press, dies and other equipment, as well as the reloading supplies. This cuts down both the start-up costs of reloading and also, the ongoing cost of the ammunition itself.

Some leading mail order houses specializing in outdoor equipment offer best quality kits from which the handy outdoorsman, or his wife, can fashion their own down sleeping bags, down coats, tents, rucksacks and all manner of other goodies at 30 to 60 percent savings. These kits can save you a lot of money, but you should start off with an easy project to see how well you do before going all the way with a sleeping bag or big tent.

Watch for sales, especially at the large discount stores. If you have a buddy overseas, he may be able to get you cameras or guns from their country of origin at real chop-licking savings. However, remember that federal law requires that a firearms dealer with an FFL (Federal Firearms License) actually import the guns and clear them through customs. For film and cameras, be sure to check the big New York camera store ads in the leading photography magazines. Some of their prices are shaved right down to the bone.

Don't rule out entirely the buying of best-quality, well-maintained, second-hand items in some categories. I'm not in love with the idea of buying used optics (binoculars, cameras, riflescopes). But you might pick up guns that you've thoroughly checked over or those you've had checked by a gunsmith in no way involved in the deal. Second-hand saddlebags, gun scabbards, and some other items can be excellent buys. Better to have *good* second-hand equipment than new junk!

Another way to save money is to avoid expensive gimmicks, as you would leprosy. Riflescopes with rangefinder reticules

Doing your own cooking and camp chores saves dollars, but it also costs prime hunting time at the early and late hours of the day.

that are more complex to operate (and easier to damage) than the periscope of an atomic sub are best left in the store. All sorts of exotic and expensive survival and rescue gadgets, optical rangefinders and other paraphernalia aren't really necessary.

All these gizmo-class items cost mucho dinero, and they are the single best way to give your guide an instant case of heartburn and a bad first impression of you. We all have to sing for our supper with one tune or another. And thus the nature of our superb capitalistic economic system being what it is, there will probably be an unending stream of this expensive trivia on the market from now on. That doesn't mean you need it. *Stick to the time-tested essentials!*

Costs of the Hunt Itself. Now let's talk about the cost of the main event, the hunt. Sheep and grizzly are expensive animals. And whatever you do to hunt them, they'll cost a big dollar. Good physical condition is absolutely necessary if you are to save some money on these expensive hunts and still have any sort of decent chance at good trophies. The costs are enormous, but no other animals on this side of the water can quite match the glamor of the sheep and the grizzly. They are usually at the pinnacle of any trophy hunter's growth in the sport.

One possibility is to take a late-season hunt. Although this option more often applies to moose and caribou, even sheep hunts (primarily bighorn) may be available in Canada during the last two weeks of the season in October for up to 25 percent off. Alaska has a much shorter sheep season and offers no finagling on their sheep hunt prices. If you do set up a late season sheep trip at tidy savings, there's a reason. Although the sheep may actually be easier to find if cold weather has begun forcing them down from the heights, you can bet it'll be tougher going for you. Climbing in ice and snow can be very tiring and uncomfortable. And if it gets cold enough, you may find yourself churlishly wishing for those idyllic, sunshiny August days usually described in the magazine sheep hunting stories.

Also, if the outfitter is giving reductions for late-season sheep hunts, you should check to insure that this isn't because he has a bad sheep area in general and thus has trouble filling his sheep hunts, both early and late. You can clear this up by checking with other hunters who have hunted with him in the last couple of years.

Moose and caribou combo hunts (moose-caribou-goat, in some areas) can be far cheaper than the full mixed-game hunt that also features a chance at sheep and grizzly. This is especially true if these more limited hunts are booked late in the season.

These hunts are available in the northern and central regions of British Columbia and Alberta. Several years ago my stepbrother John picked up a fine 60-inch moose and a decent mountain caribou for only a pittance in northern B.C. His guides were tired from having been out in the bush for several hard months; the rigging and equipment were beginning to show the strain of long weeks afield (even in this well run camp); and the mid-November weather was brutal. They had to stop each day to build fires, and John was constantly crying due to the involuntary tear reflex triggered by the intense cold. These tears would immediately freeze and cause more problems. It was an exciting, memorable hunt that he'll treasure forever, but he earned those savings in full!

Sometimes, if you bring four or five hunters with you on a ranch hunt or an outfitted hunt, the outfitter, rancher or booking agent may give you a reduction of as much as 20 to 30 percent on your own hunt for throwing all that business his way. But be sure this won't result in more than four hunters to a single camp or two to a guide if you're serious about your trophy hunting. You can most often collect your reduction from your final payment for the hunt, after you are already in camp, cash in hand. So many feather merchants have tried phoney deals of this type that people are pretty cynical though, and they tend to want to wait to see that all hunters make it to the hunt and pay their money before your cake is iced with a rebate.

If you should arrange a hunt on this basis, be aware that under the wrong conditions it might lead to some resentment among your hunting partners. If you should do far better than one or the other of your friends, they might feel that you received preferential treatment. And that could lead to antagonism and recriminations even if it were totally untrue. Stranger things than that, by far, have happened in trophy hunting camps. So, be careful in several ways on this one. If you should all do badly, including yourself, the others might feel that you "got us into this swindle" and resent it even if you scored no better than they.

If you are booking your hunt through one of the larger hunting consultants or booking agents specializing in outdoor trips, you may be able to save a third or more by stepping in for a last-minute cancellation. This is risky though. You have to wait until it happens and maybe end up high and dry if it doesn't. You also must be ready to take off on short notice. However, occasionally I've seen some very savory deals indeed available on this basis. About six years ago I turned down a hunt in Zambia on which I could have saved almost 50 percent. Watching the prices and conditions change over there since then, I've been everlastingly sorry that I did!

In British Columbia you can hunt good areas and save considerable amounts of money if you are willing to go on a Class B hunt. These are guided but feature fewer amenities than you get on Class A hunts, and offer little or no use of horses or mechanized vehicles that come with Class A. You may even have to help with the chores and meals. All this takes its toll in time and energy spent away from the actual hunting.

Going this austere route may not be a good idea for you, and it should be carefully and coolly considered. But this way you can save lots of money on practically all species except sheep. In 1971 I took a good southeastern B.C. mountain grizzly on a

$600 hunt. When you figure that most grizzly hunts go for $1,500 to $2,500 or more, this was some bargain. Especially since I took a decent 9-inch goat, too.

But, on this hunt I took a chance and went to an area with fewer grizzly than the more expensive hunts featured. It was terribly rough country, mostly too rough to use horses in even if we had had them available. I was in top physical condition and walked into that hunt with my eyes wide open, ready to accept the fact that I might not score. I told the outfitter-guide that I would only spend one day, the first one, on goat and then would pass everything up on my single-minded quest for the big bear.

Not getting greedy and being sidetracked by trying to take other trophies, I passed up a good 6-point bull elk, almost as large as the one I have on the wall, because to stalk and take him and then pack the meat out of there would have cost us three days of the 10-day hunt. I knew exactly why I was there and made sure that my host did.

It was a hard, tough hunt and I was discouraged many times. I saw three grizzlies and finally took one on the morning of the last day. By then I had had enough hunting to last me for a few days. But, it's an unforgettable experience that I'll cherish each winter the rest of my life as I stoke up the fire and settle back to look at that bear skin on the wall. I did not have the money to hunt grizzly any other way that year, so it was that or nothing. Today, I wouldn't take anything for the experience and the friends I made on the hunt. Keep in mind, though, that if you don't enjoy the hunt, it's no bargain even if it's free. So be realistic about your physical condition and your chances of success if you try this route.

These "Class B" guides can save you money. Although they offer fewer luxuries, many are fine hunters and hunt good areas for most game except sheep. The grizzly are sparser too.

Incidentally, lest you think that all guides and outfitters are getting rich as I recounted all those horrendous prices, let me assure you that most aren't. It's a tough, insecure way to make a buck, and although a few have done very well financially, many haven't. They do the work more for the love of the kind of life than because they think they'll get rich. Running a packstring or a plane and several vehicles in the bush, carting in all the food supplies and "necessaries" and providing the services to run a good trophy camp cost phenomenal amounts of money these days.

There is one final category of "savings" which is really more a way of deferring expenses. That's to make sure that you protect your valuable gear to avoid damage or theft and that you are fully protected if the worst does occur. Be sure that you are fully insured. The cost of special three- or four-week coverage under a special "calamity" rider when going on a long hunt is fairly nominal, and it sure brings peace of mind. Check with your insurance agent for full details.

Carry your expensive cameras and optics in hard plastic or metal cases that are foam lined. Do the same with your guns. Lock them up while in transit and make sure that your name is *permanently* attached to these cases. Include several of the "Warning — Do Not X-Ray" stickers on the outside of your container(s) carrying film. Pack all other frangibles in the center of your duffle bags, well protected by down garments and sleeping bags.

Lock up your duffle bags if possible. Affix your name and full address to them permanently. Try to spread out your most precious items among several bags or cases, if feasible, so that if any one of them is lost, you aren't out of business on the hunt until the items are replaced.

It's a grand sport this trophy hunting. You get what you pay for and none of the tips herein contradict that. As I mentioned earlier, some of these savings mean that you pay in ways other than with money. Others mean more organizing, mental effort and risk of failure. But, as long as you are realistic with yourself and those around you, these ideas can save you money and provide exciting ways to hunt some grand trophy species that might otherwise be totally beyond your financial reach.

Getting the Most
out of Your Guides and Outfitter

18

I killed the first sheep that I ever shot at, just about 150 times. That's how often I replayed the $1,500 missed shot in my head for two years afterward. I missed him and in the process bummed up a trip that I had saved two years to make because I didn't know how to "read" my guide and thus didn't know when to listen and when not to.

My intrepid guide, a young fellow whom we'll call Mickey, and I had toiled up the spiny side of an unusually broad shouldered Alaska Range mountain. We finally heaved our palpitating carcasses up onto the small knoll that we had been working toward for the past three bone-rattling hours. Sure enough, the old gentleman was still there, dead across the canyon and chewing his mid-afternoon snack as contentedly as any barnyard woolly.

Not only was this my first sheep but he sported an honest 38-inch-plus set of horns. This is doggoned good when you realize that—in spite of stories to the contrary—the *average* Alaskan Dall sheep being taken by trophy hunters nowadays runs 32 to 33 inches around the curl. I was about as calm as a tourist at a nudist convention!

Quicker than it takes to relate it, I had sucked in a dozen king-size breaths, plumped up the old down jacket into a vise-steady rest under the fore end of the 7mm Magnum and wormed my way into a comfortable prone position. As the crosshairs steadied up on him at 7 power, that ram was already dead and caped out. Visions of hanging that big head in the long saved "sheep space" on my trophy room wall were frisking and frolicking through my head.

Mickey whispered into my shell-like ear: "Make it good, he's over 500 yards away." It sure looked more like an honest 300 yards to me, and I had been planning to hold about two-thirds of the way up his side, figuring that the 3-inch drop at that distance would allow me to nicely lob the 150-grain Core-Lokt into his upper lung area and still give me a good 75-yard safety margin in case I was underestimating the range.

I whispered back that he looked a lot closer than 500 yards to me, but the guide shushed me up and indicated that I had better get on with it before the ram fed his way around the shoulder and out of sight — which he was perilously close to doing. There was no way to cut the distance any because this was a cross-canyon shot. And there was no other feasible stalk route to him. My choices were to make this long shot or wait until the next hunt.

White animals always look far larger than they are just as black animals look smaller. Since this was the first all-white big game that I had ever aimed at, I hurriedly charged off most of the discrepancy in our range estimates to the fact that the ram's stark white was so contrasty against the greenish-brown slope that it was throwing my radar out of joint. Trusting my guide, I dutifully cranked the big 7mm up another 15 inches, sighed, and settled in for a trigger squeeze that would warm the cockles of a Camp Perry man's heart. At the crack of the shot, my prized trophy leaped sideways madly and then hightailed it out of sight, while the echoes were still ping-ponging their way up the big canyon.

Sheep season was ending the next day. I sat down and glumly pondered the chilling fact that I would soon be forking over enough traveler's checks to cover the balance of a hunt whose total cost was then that of a good economy car. And there was no snow-white Dall, the trophy I had my heart set on, to show for it. Two years of scrimping and saving and no sheep! Mickey and I didn't talk much as we made our way down that mountain.

I was mad, sad and exhausted all at the same time — a grim combination at best. It took me a long, long time to get over that little episode. The main reason it did take so long was not that the trophy was a pretty good sheep so much as it was that the whole thing was really more *my* fault than the guide's — as I finally figured out.

In many ways the position of a hunting guide is unique. He's a paid professional. He's expensive and he has to rely on good judgment as well as rote past experience. So far this sounds about like the requirements for any other profession such as those for doctor, lawyer or architect. Now the differences: I know of no other profession in which the client *consistently* knows — or thinks he knows — something about the expertise involved.

Most of us, even in this era of TV doctor-lawyer shows, don't pretend to be able to discuss and analyze a problem on a professional level with our doctor or lawyer, let alone disagree with him. If we do, our man quickly trots out some impressive Latin terms, or sighs and mumbles some medical jargon or something about precedents. That is, this occurs often enough to make 99 percent of us shut up and mind our own business while the pro gets about his — which also happens to be ours for the moment. Any doctor or lawyer will tell you, if you know him well enough, that the worst patient in the world is another physician and that the worst client is another attorney. And these are people who really do have the expertise. They're just over-involved because it's their health or their business affairs that are involved. They don't have the necessary detachment and objectivity to properly handle some situations — even though they're proven professionsls. (Ever hear the old truism that "the attorney who represents himself has a fool for a client"?)

It's different with the guide. He's usually a pro, yet everyone coming up to hunt with him also knows something about the craft of hunting. The hunters sometimes think they know more than the guides. But even accomplished hunters, if they haven't hunted an area or its game, would do well to listen and learn. Even outfitters or guides who hunt an unfamiliar area and new game use a guide or someone to help them get oriented and learn about any regional peculiarities that may be present, though they may not generally be associated with the game.

Furthermore, there is no other profession that so frequently gets its factual, tangible basis clouded up with emotional considerations. Hunting often involves deep emotional considerations that touch on virility and the "self" concept. Other activities do too, even normal business activities do — but not in such a basic, elemental fashion. Trophy hunting especially can fall prey to competitive considerations, and some high-gear hunters turn it into competition. That's unfortunate but it happens. All of these emotional considerations can easily surface and affect the client's relationship with his guide and how well he utilizes the guide's professional skills and knowledge. Far more frequently than you might think, a hunter pays a good buck for a guide's help and then spends the rest of the hunt disagreeing and trying to teach the guide about hunting! I know it sounds silly on paper, but every year it continues to happen.

People in other professions don't have to live in such close personal proximity to their client as the guide does. The hunter and the guide are together night and day, often far away from most other people and distractions, for a highly intense one- to three-week period. They have very little privacy and, in practically every case, the client is in an unfamiliar environment, far removed from his everyday fare.

And this holds true for almost all of us. Even the urban dwellers who have hunted a lot and frequently still need several days to "decompress" and adjust to the entirely different pace in the bush or wilderness. Client and guide will spend their days away from camp alone or perhaps with one other hunter along. If they're hunting seriously, they'll be pushing themselves hard physically in an environment that is potentially dangerous and hostile. All this — the amount of physical activity, the mountains and high country or the deep woods, the solitude — is foreign to the hunter's normal routine and can readily affect his attitude and conduct.

Add to these factors the consideration that the hunter is spending a lot of money and every day, minute by minute, has a chance to evaluate whether he's "getting his money's worth." He doesn't actually see the surgeon operate, the lawyer research the legal precedents or the architect draw up the plans. But every day and every minute he sees his guide in action. This juxtaposition really leads to some cliff-hangers especially if the hunt is lagging due to bad weather or just plain bad luck in sighting game. Then the hunter begins to get nervous and doubt his guide.

So the guide is simultaneously 1) one of the hired hands, 2) an expert professional, 3) a personal companion. That's a patchwork quilt of roles if there ever was one. These are potentially conflicting roles. Add in the intensity and intimacy that are built in, and you really have an interesting situation going. Everything is magnified, sometimes vastly, and it can affect the hunter-guide relationship negatively enough to ruin the hunt — if the hunter lets it.

Every guide-hunter relationship is different. The final tone, and effectiveness, of the relationship varies with the personalities of the individuals involved, how much game they're seeing, the attitude and physical condition of the hunter, how well the hunter is shooting, how good the weather is, and any number of other factors. This always varies, from hunt to hunt, even if you hunt with the same guide the following year. Circumstances can be different enough from the first hunt so that the two bear little resemblance to each other in tone and feeling. That's why so many hunters who had a marvelous hunt one year and book with the same outfitter, specifying that they must have the same guide again, are surprised and sometimes hurt and disappointed on the second go-round.

Perhaps half of their second hunt is rained or weathered out. That's a big disappointment to both. And this can have an insidious, poisoning effect on the whole venture. Perhaps there is just not as much game in the area as there should be, and this has a depressing effect on the hunt. Perhaps the guide has suffered reverses in his private life during the preceding year that are affecting him and his outlook. Perhaps the hunter misses one or even two easy shots at prized trophies. That makes him unhappy and, in its own way, affects the guide just as severely. (Guides don't like to work hard and then have the client blow easy shots. Most good guides are somewhat competitive themselves and they know full well that they will ultimately be judged by their peers, their employer and their paying hunters on how much game they bring in and its quality. All of the other contributing factors, like weather and hunter competence, tend to fade into the background somewhat in the same way that yardage gained, number of first downs and other statistics pale into insignificance when compared to the final score of a football game. Maybe that's not the way it should be, but that's the way it is.)

The point is this: Each individual hunt experience is different from all others due to the multitude of variables involved. Thus, there are few or no ironclad rules that will always apply, no matter what. However, with sensible interpretation, there are some pretty safe generalities that usually do apply.

How to Become a Successful Client

1. Don't rush things, and don't be overfamiliar. Most of the time the client-hunter is so thrilled to be at last taking his dream trip that he tends to be more talkative and ask more questions than he would under any other circumstances. This is especially so if he has never hunted the area or game before. He immediately wants to get acquainted with his guide and strike up a friendly, agreeable relationship with him. These feelings are all perfectly understandable and the guide expects this, particularly if he has been at the game for sometime.

However, it can be overdone. Most guides who spend all or most of the year in the wilderness or semi-wilderness tend to be considerably more reserved than the average paying hunter who deals with more people in a faster-paced environment. The guide is usually not nearly as verbal or outgoing. That doesn't mean that he's unfriendly. Rather, his clock runs on a different time. This is especially true of native or Indian guides and of far-north guides who live a very solitary existence.

Add to this the fact that the guide, if he's been around for awhile, has been stung with his share of boors and deadbeats — hunters who couldn't climb, couldn't walk, couldn't shoot, couldn't ride, and couldn't do much of anything, except chatter a lot and eventually blame most of their "bad luck" on the long-suffering guide. A few of these bad experiences are enough to make any guide want to form his relationship with his new hunters in a gingerly, step-at-a-time fashion, until he sees what he's got to work with.

There's nothing wrong with being excited and enthusiastic and letting some of it show through. But the wise man doesn't overdo things the first day or two. The guide is not the hunter's instant "buddy" and though many guides and hunters do become quite close during a hunt, this happens over a period of time and is based on mutual respect and love of the outdoors. It is *not* the result of instant hale-well-met conviviality. In fact that's one of the quickest ways to turn the guide off.

2. Don't lose your enthusiasm. This is really just the opposite side of the preceding rule. Just as many hunters are too familiar and too verbal at the beginning, many lose *too* much of their buoyancy as the hunt progresses. This happens for a variety of reasons. They begin to tire and become sore as the extreme physical exertion cumulatively takes its toll. Often there's a bit of a letdown or anti-climax now that the long awaited hunt is finally at hand. In some ways I think it similar to a woman's post-partum depression. No matter how well the hunt is going, how beautiful the country, how benign the weather, it's almost impossible for things to measure up to the combined dreams of the last few years. And if the weather isn't good or things aren't going as well as they could, these problems add to the trouble.

About a third of any trophy hunt is luck. Pure raw luck! That's true even if the hunter chooses the outfitter and area well, is a competent hunter and shooter, and is ready physically and mentally for the hunt. He has no control over the weather, over whether the rut is early or late, whether migratory animals are moving early or late, whether there is an abundance of game around but no real trophies, and a host of other things. Most hunts move unevenly. Luck is bad and then it turns. Or it's good and then it sours. You go several days without seeing game and then suddenly the hills come alive.

The trick is for the hunter not to let these ups and downs overly affect him. Though the guide doesn't want an instant, first-day "pal," he does want a hunter who is interested and excited and willing to work for his game. If the hunter won't get up early enough, climb and walk far enough, glass and stalk patiently enough, why should the guide extend himself? On the other hand, if the hunter shows *sustained* interest and enthusiasm, then the guide usually extends himself for the hunter.

And that can make the difference. There are many things a guide can do to greatly improve the hunter's chances. Things "above and beyond" the letter of the guide's obligations. A guide who genuinely likes his hunter and sincerely wants him to do just as well as possible can hunt that vital extra hour or so with him even though it means a long day, a dark ride home, and a cold supper.

A guide extending himself to the utmost for his hunter might decide to cape out and take the head off large game like elk, caribou or moose and then walk back to camp while his horse packs in the meat and trophy. For the hunter that means the next day is spent hunting rather than taking a packhorse or two back to the kill. An enthusiastic, energetic hunter who is also willing to walk back so that both horses pack everything out right then is the type of client who gets this treatment. And the fellow who has lost interest and is not willing to extend himself will lose out here.

Ironically, all too many hunters overdo things to begin with and then lose too much interest as the hunt progresses.

3. Size your guide up, and remember he's human, too. My sad experience with Mickey and the Dall sheep, I related at the beginning of this chapter, was mostly my fault. There were many telltale signs along the way that I should have noticed or put more weight on and thus should have trusted my judgment more than his. For one thing, we never seemed to get out of camp and into gear until about 9:00 or 9:30 in the morning. Even after several hints from me, each successively less subtle, we just couldn't seem to be hunting before 8:30 in the morning, though I was up and ready to go well before that and willingly lent a hand with any necessary morning chores. (At the start of the hunt we were working on moose and caribou, and getting out early was considerably more important than it sometimes is when hunting sheep.)

For another thing, I was spotting too much game before he was. Sure, I had excellent binoculars and wasn't exactly a novice hunter. But I was in unfamiliar country, looking for unfamiliar animals with my short-legged eastern eyes that still hadn't fully acclimated to the mountain vistas and perspective. A really good guide should have outspotted me somewhere between two and three to one, if he had already been hunting this general locale for several weeks, as this fellow had.

It seemed that every moose we saw a long way away on the other side of some rough going was "too small" and every bear that was far up a steep sidehill was "too late" to get to. The same guide was hard pressed to give a good tight estimate of a caribou or moose rack when they were only 200 or 300 yards away, but he sure could tell they were too small when they were a mile or so out.

There were other things. He had practically no equipment. What he did have wasn't much good, and he didn't pretend to take very good care of it. He just didn't seem to be very mountain-wise, that is, able to pick the best route up or down a mountain face almost automatically. Nor did he seem overly interested and involved in the hunt. Rather, he just seemed to be doing a job.

But this was one of my first far-north hunts, and until then I had been very lucky with guides. To me, they were all little cardboard figures who were supposed to be decent chaps (the vast majority are!) and *equally* mountain-smart and game-wise. How naive and how wrong! Hunting guides, like people in every other occupation from chorus girl to cleric, come in all qualities and calibers.

So, size up your guide and notice all the little things. They may start adding up to tell you something about how much you should rely on your own judgment and how much on the guide's when the two come into conflict.

4. Give your guide the benefit of the doubt. This is the counterpoint of the preceding rule. While you're watching your man with gimlet eyes, bend over backwards to give him the benefit of the doubt.

The guide may do things that seem odd to you. Many times, especially if he is the taciturn type, he may not explain the details of a decision to you. He may not want to hunt a particularly "moosey-looking" area because he knows the last trophy was shot out of there a few days ago. Or the ground may have been heavily hunted in recent days and the game disturbed. So he may want to "rest it" momentarily. He may not want to climb a particular mountain until he knows your capabilities better. Or he may know your capabilities and not want to tell you that you couldn't cut it.

He may make an easy first day of it because he's just had a rough week. Remember that guides get tired, too. This is usually most obvious on late-season hunts when the guides have been in camp several weeks, possibly even three or four months if they came in early to cut trails, set up camps, etc. Then they've had to walk and climb with several hunters during the season. This varies a lot. The guide can be fresh as a daisy in late season if he's had only pot-bellied types over 50, or he can be pretty well shot if he's had several athletic lads in their 20s or 30s or some physicians in their 40s who know how to take care of themselves and do so by eating right and jogging a couple of miles a day. The guide's own age, general health and yen for cigarettes have a cumulative effect on his late season get-up-and-go, too. This is something to consider when booking late hunts.

The guide may want to pass up a shot because he thinks you can get a better trophy, but he may not want to put it to you exactly that way because it verges on a commitment. So, until he deserves different, bend over backwards the first few days to give him the benefit of the doubt. You're both still on a shakedown cruise the first two or three days out, and a snap judgment can be as bad or worse than no judgment on your part.

5. Be honest! With him and yourself! This should be engraved on stone tablets. If the guide asks if you can make a certain long shot and you have serious doubts, tell him that you want to get closer. There's no shame in that. If you are on a particularly bad mountain face and start getting scared, tell him before you get into trouble. I've known hunters to force themselves into bad places because they didn't want to be "chicken" and then literally lock up and remain motionless for several hours, literally afraid to move until finally helped or coaxed down. Sure you want to push yourself some, but you should also know and respect the outer limits of your own capabilities, whatever they may be. Getting into a tough situation and then getting scared to death is not only dangerous for you and your guide, it's not much fun. After all, you came to enjoy the hunt!

If your saddle gets uncomfortable or appears to be slipping, ask the guide to look at it for you if you don't know how to adjust it properly. Don't worry about appearing dumb or being taken as a complainer. A saddle with too-short stirrups—the common problem—can begin by being merely awkward and end up causing great pain. It can even put you out of commission for the rest of the day if you cramp up badly enough. The guide may be assuming you will say something or make the adjustments yourself. So he doesn't ask you about it.

When your guide asks you if you can handle a particularly vinegary little horse that makes a habit of showing the whites of his eyes and lashing out at anything behind him, summon up that magic word "No" if you're a novice horseman.

I believe a lot of hunters get into trouble at times because they're not honest with themselves. They may tend to spin a lot of yarns to the guide the first day or two in some misguided attempt to get to know him better or impress him with their feats of woodcraft, shooting, or stamina. A good story seldom loses anything in the telling, especially if it's a hunting yarn. But this is the one instance in which too broad an application of the truth stretcher can directly and immediately cause problems that may cost you game or decrease your enjoyment of the hunt.

If you're not in the kind of physical shape you'd like to be in for rough country work, admit it! Don't dote on it and trade on it, but let the guide know, honestly and objectively, what he's got to work with. That affects his general hunt planning and the routes he chooses when scouting for game.

You want your guide to be honest with you. He probably will be if you don't penalize both him and yourself by being less than truthful with him.

6. Don't try to run things; don't compete; don't brag. Many trophy hunters, especially the tightly-wound, take-charge-type executive or professional man frequently encountered on major hunts, simply can't seem to decompress adequately for the hunt. They are used to a pressure cooker urban environment where things *happen* and people deal with each other much differently than in the back country.

Many westerners, northerners or Indians are polite to the point of misunderstanding some of these hunters. If the hunter suggests very directly that they "try this valley" or "go on up a bit farther" or "stop glassing and start hunting" (which is exactly what glassing is in the truest sense!), the guide may go along with them even though it's against his better judgment. He simply doesn't want a hassle. If the hunter, who after all is paying the bills, *wants* to do something, he'll often let him. Let the guide run things, he's the pro on the hunt.

Usually the hunter doesn't even realize he's intruding and warping decisions. He's used to "hashing things out" back home in his more frenetic, verbal world. While the hunter may think he's just talking things over and investigating possibilities, the guide may well see it as argument and an attempt to take command.

Some hunters seem to feel that they are competing with their guide in some subtle way. Unfortunately, it sometimes works the other way around, too. The fact that the guide is smaller but can pack far larger loads or older but can climb and walk much farther rouses the latent competitiveness in some hunters. It shouldn't. This is the guide's turf. You wouldn't expect him to do as well as you unraveling your freeway system at home or any number of other problems that you deal with all the time.

Don't take umbrage at getting help or advice from the guide. If you do, you'll turn him off and not get the benefit of the services that you're paying for. Many guides are very hesitant about possibly embarrassing their hunter—especially if he is the loud spoken, aggressive type to begin with.

Since your guide can probably match you in spades when the subject is hunting exploits and feats of derring-do, learn from him about some of *his* most interesting experiences. There is much he could probably teach you, and it's doubtful that the reverse would be true. As he gets to know you, and if you're getting along well, he'll probably become interested enough in you to ask about this or that so that he has a better idea of your experience and competence.

7. *Bring plenty of equipment.* It is the fashion in much outdoor writing to overemphasize "going light" and not taking too much gear and duffle when making these longer, guided hunts. It is true that some really ridiculous things occur every fall. I know of one fervent gun nut who showed up in Alaska with eleven guns, all suitably cased up in weighty metal and wooden boxes. The outfitter sighed, gestured toward the Cessana and asked whether the hunter preferred to board the plane himself or send all that artillery because both sure couldn't make it. Another time a well meaning, conservative lad on his first "big" hunt showed up at John Holmes' northern British Columbia

base camp with thirteen substantial duffle bags of gear for a 21-day hunt. The hunter was a whiz-kid computer programmer for the Government who made a living planning for all conceivable contingencies. And that's just the way he'd organized for the dream hunt — to cover every imaginable possibility except the eminently practical one that outfitters aren't set up to allot four or five packhorses to each hunter!

However, aside from such extreme over indulgences, the only thing worse than carrying too much into the bush is not carrying enough! My rule is this: If I'm pretty sure I'll need it, I take it. I don't rely on my guide or outfitter to furnish some things even though the outfitter's brochure, and he himself, may say that they do.

Some for instances? Every guide is supposed to have his own binoculars. But just suppose he doesn't? Or, perhaps he may have broken or lost them the day before your arrival. Gear, even that of the best quality in the hands of a careful user, takes a tremendous pounding in a season of sustained professional hunting day in and day out. What then? You have two very unpleasant choices. You can lend him yours and miss out on all the thrills and excitement of spotting for game; in fact, without binoculars in most big country hunting, you really aren't even *participating!* Or, you can keep them yourself, thus robbing yourself of the use of those paid professional eyes that know the game and the country much better than you do. Either way, the number of eyes helping you find that trophy is two rather than four. So I always carry an extra pair.

Always take a spotting scope on any mountain or open country hunt. I take mine *everywhere* because I know I might need it. Maybe the guide should have his own. Or the outfitter may say he furnishes them. But again, you could come up short. A good spotting scope of 20x-or-better magnification can save you miles of traveling by enabling you to size up heads at far greater distances.

On a horseback hunt, always take your own rifle scabbard. You may end up without one if you rely on the outfitter or, at best, it probably isn't well enough made with a hood to completely enclose that expensive scope sighted rifle of yours to give it the protection it needs. After a hunter loses a coveted trophy because his rifle scope was knocked out of adjustment or fogged because of a flimsy, ill-fitting scabbard that may have been rigged out of canvas, he'll bring his own from then on.

Also, bring your own saddlebags. Many times these will not be available or, if they are, they'll just consist of a single canvas sack slung onto the back of the saddle. That cuts down on the amount of gear you can take afield each day. And because it's a single bag, without any directly offsetting weight on the other side, it unbalances the horse, and it provides scant protection for the expensive camera or other goodies you'd like to carry back there.

So carry everything you reasonably may need. If it's unduly bulky or not needed, you can practically always leave it in base camp or with some reliable person at the town or village that is your jumping-off point for the bushplane flight. But if the gear is a couple of thousand miles away at your home, your options are much more limited!

8. Know your own mind, and let your guide know it too. You should clearly have in mind what trophies you want—in what priority—and how big you feel they should be. Sure, everybody wants "one of each" on a mixed-game hunt, even including those rare and coveted "bonus trophies" like wolverine and wolf. And everyone wants "big" trophies. That's not good enough. To get the maximum mileage out of your guide, and your hunt, you should have the mental discipline to make some hard choices on your preferences and then let your guide know just where you stand. Don't blur things so much that he is just taking you out looking for "big" trophies of "anything" that may come along. Tell him: "I want a sheep and that's what I want to work on until I get him. Everything else is secondary." Or, "I'm far more interested in caribou than moose and would like to concentrate on them first."

Also, try to let him know about what size you have in mind. Admittedly this is a bit arbitrary and subject to adjustment as the actual hunt unfolds and you get a better idea of your chances. But tell him, "I want to work on a 40-inch-or-better sheep and I'm willing to pass everything else up until the last two or three days to get him." Or, "I've got my heart set on a 15-inch pronghorn. And if I can't get one that big, I just won't take one this year." This gives the guide an idea of how hard you have to hunt, where he'll have to take you, how realistic you are, and how much time to put in on a single species or head.

One of the most common mistakes hunters make on guided hunts is in just this area. They either don't do all the mental analysis and self-examination in the months before the hunt begins so that *they* have a clear idea of their priorities, or if they do, they don't bother to let the guide know it.

Also, when some hunters actually hit the game field, they are overcome by temptation. They may have booked a good moose-caribou-goat hunt, in an area where there are very few sheep or grizzly, with the intent of concentrating on one or two of those animals. Then, as they arrive at the jumping-off point and are buying their licenses, they often get carried away with the rapture of the country and the fact that the long-awaited day is finally here. So, they buy grizzly and sheep licenses too, "just in case." Now things change markedly. In this era of very expensive hunting licenses, they may now have several hundred dollars invested in those "just in case" licenses that they have very little chance of filling. Yet, because they have all that money tied up and there's a small chance they might score, they then start out sheep or grizzly hunting.

The upshot usually is that they don't get a sheep or grizzly and have to settle for less game and just second-rate trophies on the species that they did come to hunt. This happens frequently every year, even though the outfitter may have told them all along that he had few or no sheep or big bear. Apparently the chance at a "cheap" grizzly or sheep just overpowers some hunters. (The rates are always lower in the areas without many of these premier animals.)

So, know your own mind and let others know it too. Don't let things get so foggy and confused that you're just rambling around the country here and there in a disjointed fashion. Don't turn a *good* deer hunt into a *bad* elk hunt or a *good* moose-caribou trip into a *bad* sheep hunt. If you want to hunt the more expensive game, then save up for another year and pick a good area and outfitter for *that* game!

Even if you do a good job of selecting your most desirable species, don't stop there. Do the best job you can of working out how big a trophy you'll settle for as the hunt unfolds. As a trophy hunter, this is of prime importance to you. It's sad indeed when a hunter takes a second-rate head in the first two or three days of an extended hunt and then sees numerous better animals in the next two or three weeks. That's worse than setting your standards and, by adhering to them, shooting no game at all.

There are a lot of what I call "first-blush trophy hunters" who look for good trophies the first few days and then, often without even realizing it, alter their objective so that they will shoot about anything if they're still dry after a week or so. Then they're no longer trophy hunting and they should realize it—and let the guide know as well.

The man who kept his powder dry until the 18th day of a 21-

day hunt when he finally did take a big head is a trophy hunter. He knew what he wanted, he stuck to it and he was prepared to go all the way. An amazing amount of game is shot on the last day of the hunt. I shot my biggest bull elk on the morning of the last day and took my best grizzly on the afternoon of the last day. If you panic and fill out on "just anything" too early, then you're foreclosing your chances permanently. Otherwise, the hunt isn't over until your gun is sheathed on the final day. (Sometimes not even then! I took a fine moose due to being weathered in an extra five days up in the Cassiars one year.)

Be as specific as possible with your guide, as specific as this: "I want a caribou with beams about 50 inches long that would score up around 375 or better, and for the first week or 10 days I'm willing to pass up everything else to get him. After that, depending on how much game we're seeing and how the weather is going, I might come down a bit but I just won't take a head under about 350 in score." Let him know your best thinking on what *you* call a trophy (a word with a different meaning for everyone). Then the guide knows what his target is, and as the hunt unfolds, you and he can work out any adjustments that circumstances may dictate, *together.*

You wouldn't try to shop for a house or take a vacation without giving the real estate agent or travel agent a fairly good idea of what you wanted. This is always subject to some adjustment on the spot, of course. The same goes for the guide.

9. Mention the tip. Although the practices may vary a bit from here to there, it is generally not out of line to extend a reasonable gratuity, or tip, to the guide at the end of a successful hunt. I often do so, frequently giving a piece of equipment rather than money. It's more personal and more usable. It cuts down on my luggage going home and goes over better with some guides than money itself.

Mention of the tip before hunt's end should be handled with care to avoid the appearance of trying to "buy" the guide. However, after you get to know each other a bit, it's a good idea to let the guide know that a certain type of trophy is worth "additional consideration" on your part. After they get to know you a bit, guides will often slyly let you know how much they admire one piece or another of your gear with just this in mind. As long as this "consideration" is not all out of proportion to the situation or is not tendered in a heavy-handed fashion by the client-hunter, this practice is okay. Sure, you're both there because you love the outdoors and hunting. But guides don't make a lot of money to begin with, and we all have to live. It's perfectly all right to reward *exceptional* performance or service in other environments with additional consideration, and it's good practice after a hunt, too. Done properly! I do *not* extend a tip for poor or standard performance, however. Guiding is far more elastic than hopping tables. Maybe most waitresses should get some kind of tip no matter what, but not guides.

Incidentally, in my opinion the game brought to bag is not the only way you evaluate a guide's performance. There are many things beyond his control. Hunter's luck can foil the best of guides and hunters — especially trophy hunters who are, by definition, more discriminating in their objectives. How professional is the guide? How hard does he try? How companionable is he? How much did he contribute to your enjoyment of the hunt, as well as your bag? Was he friendly and agreeable throughout the hunt? Was he patient? Guides are asked the same questions over and over again and receive a truly outrageous request every now and again. Was he *sincerely* interested in you and your hunt? All these vital personal considerations are as important to the overall enjoyment of a hunt as anything else.

10. Be enthusiastic! Though I've stressed this earlier, it's so important that it simply can't be overemphasized. Your attitude and enthusiasm are, most times, about as important as your hunting ability and physical condition. Almost all guides work harder for the fellow who is enjoying himself and pushing himself to his own limits, *whatever they are.* A fellow in superb physical condition, who is also a good hunter, won't get much out of his guide if the hunter isn't interested enough to work hard and push himself.

Guides like to work with hunters who are enjoying their outing and who are good sports about the inevitable disappointments and hardships that are a part of the game. They'll make that all-important extra effort for the man who is treasuring the outdoor experience and not just trying to knock over a set of horns or antlers and beat it home as quickly and easily as possible. If the hunter is lackadaisical, why should the guide knock himself out?

11. Know the distinction between an outfitter and a guide. Getting the most out of outfitters requires similar methods to those used with guides. At times the outfitter and guide is one and the same person, or else the outfitter may regularly tour his camps, periodically "turning his hand" by taking out a hunter so he's got his finger on the day-to-day pulse.

The main difference in your dealings with outfitters and guides is that you will be in touch with the outfitter *before* the hunt starts and you will not meet your guide until it actually does begin. To best work with the outfitters, tell them clearly and specifically what you want in the way of trophies, just as we discussed in dealing with guides. The main difference is that this will be handled long-distance, mostly by mail rather than face-to-face. If the hunt appears to be firming up after a couple of letters, it's a good idea to phone the outfitter. Sometimes you can get information this way that doesn't come through on paper, for the outfitter may just be a bad correspondent by nature. Some fine points of discussion just lend themselves to question-and-answer dialogue and can't be handled well by letter, anyway.

Again, be sure to check the outfitter's references. Don't just rely on the three or four names he gives you. Every outfit, however bad, has had a few good hunts. Make sure you get the names of several people that hunted with him last year rather than two or three seasons back.

Try to get the names of some people who hunted at the same time of year that you plan to, so that you can check on general weather conditions and game availability. Try to get the names of people who hunted or took particularly good examples of the species you are most interested in. Maybe late-season hunts are just too cold for your liking. Maybe the "high game," the sheep and goat, you want are often snowed in by a certain time. Maybe the migratory caribou won't be moving by the time you want to go, or maybe most of the elk rut will be over in that area. *Now* is the time to double-check and verify these things, not after you get there and find out the hard way.

Often on western U.S. pronghorn and mule deer hunts, the "outfitter" will actually be a rancher who handles hunts part time. Respect for his gates, fences, stock and all the other basics are certainly important in keeping his good will.

A hunter-guide relationship is strange and unique. Usually brief but intense, it can be the basis for lasting friendship or enmity, not to mention having much to do with your success in bagging game. But it's not all up to the guide to make it work to best advantage. It's strictly a 50-50 proposition. The wise hunter plans and acts accordingly.

Climbing to the Best Hunting

19

The bush plane that had deposited me and my duffle here on this desolate gravel bed in the Alaska Range was now a fast-receding speck in the sky. As my guide lent a hand with the gear and we headed toward the white A-wall tent that was to be home for the next two weeks, we traded pleasantries and sized each other up.

What I saw was a 5-foot 7-inch Aleut Indian who probably weighed about 138 pounds, dripping wet and with a full pocket of change. We'll call him Phillip. By city standards, he would be called scrawny. To me he just looked wiry and whit-leather tough. He also looked more youthful than his 37 years.

What he saw was a fellow who had a few inches and 35 pounds on him, 10 of which weren't needed for mountain work. Since I had only recently passed over to the wintry side of 30 and was somewhat younger than most clients, the outfitter had matched me up with this, his toughest and hardest hunting guide.

I was young enough and tough enough so that I could stay with him even with the extra poundage. On the flats and foothills, that is! We had no horses and we hiked as far as 24 miles in one long day, with very little climbing involved. When we got into steep mountain work, things changed. Whereas before I had always stayed within 20 feet or so of Phillip, now my most common sighting of him was limited to fleeting glimpses of his jean-clad bottom disappearing over the next shoulder of the mountain as I huffed and wheezed along.

Each night I would haul my aching carcass into the down sleeping bag and Phillip would shoot me one of his bland looks and ask gravely, "What's the matter, Tom? Why you slow down so much last few days?" I determined during this agony that there were *several* lessons to be learned here.

As I returned grindingly exhausted but somewhat wiser each night, Phillip and I gradually got to know each other better. Since a little campfire ribbing never hurt anyone and I am basically a good natured chap, we even started getting pretty chummy. At least I was willing, if not always able, and that always goes a long way with any guide.

Bob, the Competitor

As our friendship budded and blossomed, one night he confided to me the story of his last hunter, a young fellow we'll call Bob. Bob had left the day before I came in, and apparently it was just as well. He evidently went out just about on his knees.

Bob was a strapping young 6-foot 2-inch, 28-year-old health-food addict. He ran four miles to and from work each day. And he subsisted mostly on special foods and vitamin pills. But satisfying his huge appetite around camp became a major problem because he steadfastly refused to eat such hunting camp staples as peanut butter, cheese and butter. Most outfitter's larders aren't too well stocked with the blackstrap molasses, brewer's yeast, yogurt and other goodies that Bob craved.

Bob's first few days hunting were largely spent in the lowlands, as is routine. On this turf Bob's long stride and godzilla-like physical condition often left Phillip far behind. That was a mistake. It was not only senseless and bad form, but with a particularly proud native guide such as this one, it was a prime personal insult.

Then Phillip's dark, round face wreathed itself into a smile for a toothpaste commercial as he gleefully told the rest of the story. "I ask Bob if he ready to do some sheep hunting after I spot sheep on roughest mountain around here," he chuckled. "Bob say-um 'yep' so I take him up worst face of mountain fast as we can go. Bob start dropping behind and Phillip tell-um, 'what's the matter, Bob, you feel bad, can't you make it?' That really make Bob mad and him hurry to catch-um up. Phillip go faster. Then Bob get-um way behind and Phillip go back down and offer to carry his gun. A little later Bob start to get-um scared. And finally, we come to bad place and Phillip have to help him down mountain him so scared. Sheep still up there."

There's no doubt that with that little caper Phillip broke every code there is for guides. He shouldn't have done it. He shouldn't have needled his hunter so hard that the fellow overcommitted himself that much. Especially on a bad mountain face. I saw that face later, and it was no place to hold a picnic.

But, in the final sense, the hunter brought much of it on himself by not knowing how to read and work with his guide and, also, by not really understanding a lot of the physical aspects of climbing. Since we talk about getting along with guides elsewhere in this book, I'll skip over those aspects and concentrate on climbing.

Even though Bob was a fanatical physical culture buff, he was also a flatlander with little or no mountain experience. He simply did not understand some basics about the physical and mental considerations involved in climbing. For one thing, obviously he just did not know how much tougher the going is for a fellow used to living at a 500-foot elevation when he gets up into elevations 10 or 15 times that. This bears out for any lowlander, no matter how superb his condition may be!

For another, Bob surely didn't realize that climbing stresses your muscles differently than walking or running and that one of the biggest difficulties climbing poses is the enormous strain that it loads onto a limited number of tendons and muscles. That's why, when you're getting ready for a big hunt and there aren't any steep hills located obligingly nearby, it's vital to condition yourself by running up stairs or stadium seats. However, when stairs are available, most folks make the mistake of running straight up them. I never saw a mountain yet that I could walk straight up, feet nicely pointed to the front and weight distributed on the ball.

Physical Conditioning

When you've been sidehilling around a mountain for some length of time, the massive strain placed on the outside edge of your uphill foot and the inside of your downhill foot will speak to you far more eloquently than any all-day lecture on the unequal physical stresses of climbing. Even if you're U-turning your way back and forth to climb a face, going to the left as often as to the right, you're still putting completely different, and more massive, strains on your feet and legs than those incurred in running or straightforward stair climbing.

Thus, if I'm using stair climbs to train for a hunt, I always jog up them with my feet *to the side* (at about a 45 degree angle) and *canted somewhat*. This is closer to the real thing. It's also far more strenuous and dangerous. You must be careful to avoid twisting an ankle or taking a header after you get good and tired. All this is still a distant cry from the real goods. The wise man knows, even if our friend Bob didn't, that there really isn't anything much like mountain climbing, except more mountain climbing.

Usually I trot up the steps in alternating cycles of five flights facing to the right and then five facing toward the left. That distributes the strain more evenly and allows me to work out longer. Thus I get more physical imprinting, or benefit, from the exercise. Ditto for going *down* the stairs. It's just as important to train by running down as well as up, provided you do it rapidly enough.

If you do have to resort to stair climbing, the best way to do it is to secure permission from the watchman, building owner or other authority to use an office building after hours. Zipping up those steps sideways means that you'll be blocking the whole stairwell and that you'll have to stop if you meet anyone. Also, in the after hours there won't be people around shooting quizzical looks your way and maybe chasing you with big nets.

In this era, going to the best big-game hunting fields usually means a fair amount of climbing. There are some exceptions such as when whitetail hunting and when canoe-hunting for moose in the flatlands of eastern Canada. But getting safely up and down in country turned on its side is what trophy hunting is about these days.

A horse can do much of the climbing for you. Even so, you can often go places that the horse can't. And the final stalk, often a steep climb, is almost always on foot. Also, there's a certain satisfaction to hoisting yourself, mostly unaided, up to the high, clean roof of the world — and in having the skill and strength to do it in a workmanlike fashion.

Up and Down

Yet even though the best hunting is up high and you so often have to climb up to it, lots of otherwise well informed hunters think that climbing is about like walking on level ground that just happens to be slanted. It isn't. And if a stranger in the mountains relies too much on his flatland "common sense," he can get into trouble. Quick!

For instance, it would seem that the most difficult and dangerous aspect of getting around in mountains is climbing them, right? Wrong. By far, the most dangerous part of mountain climbing, is *coming down,* because the hunter is usually very tired and careless by this stage. He's anxious to get back to camp, kick off those boots and wrap himself around a big dinner and some scalding hot coffee. He's not alert and he's operating far below his physical optimum. He just wants to "fall off" that mountain and get back to camp.

Whenever you're on a mountain, going up or coming down, you should always try to walk as flat-footed as possible and keep your weight directly over your feet. Most hunters try to walk straight down off a mountain with few or no switchbacks along the way to reduce the grade. They try to walk down on their heels, thus giving them the least possible bearing surface. This puts their weight *behind* the bearing surface, not over it, practically pushing them off the mountain. They're almost programming their feet to skid out, causing a backside-over-teakettle descent.

Also, most hunters try to pick the "easy" route down. All too often this is a chimney or rock chute full of treacherous loose rock. Not only is the footing chancy, if any other loose rocks or debris are going to come tumbling off the mountain, this is where they'll come!

Many of the truisms for going up hold for going down as well. Most hunters don't use frequent enough or long enough "S" curves or switchbacks to go up a slope. The longer the loop you make on each switchback, the more you are leveling out that grade. Although using switchbacks may take ten times as many steps as going straight up, it makes the job much easier. In the long run you'll get there faster and with less energy expended if you go the "Burma Road" way.

When making those climbing switchbacks, or when sidehilling around a steep shoulder, keep your feet as flat on the ground as possible. This is much safer, and after a while it's much easier. Most inexperienced climbers try to walk on the edges of their feet in order to keep their feet "level" (and hanging out in mid-air!). But this puts tremendous strains on a very small area of the feet and on a few leg tendons. Soon—very, very soon—the legs will begin to shake and cramp up. All the while you will have very little bearing surface on the mountain and your weight will be pushing you down the mountain, not into it. That's not safe! Climbing up it's easier to throw your weight *into* the mountain.

Pacing

One of the most basic mistakes that hunters make in mountain country is in failing to pace themselves—not knowing how. The high altitude plus the unaccustomed strain of steep country throws all their normal gauges way off. Until they get their "mountain sense," they just simply can't do many things that they might feel they can. There's a world of difference between walking three miles with a 3,000-foot climb and sauntering the same distance downtown.

Many times guides don't help much. Sometimes, during the first day or so, they may try to walk their hunter right into the ground. I've had some confide this to me. And it's pretty easy to subdue a hunter if his "radar" is way off while he's acclimating. He'll simply overextend himself unknowingly.

If the guide does this, it may not be as unkind as it sounds. Often it's the quickest and most humane way for the guide to assert himself over his hard-driving executive or professional man. The guide must let the hunter know that on this turf *he's* the pro. Thus, running the dude into the ground is a quick and dirty way of doing it. Unfortunately, there are those bad apples who are unethical about this. They know very well that if they get their man charley-horsed up or scared enough, they'll have it pretty easy for the rest of the hunt. This happens only rarely, but it is something to be aware of.

It's best to try to know yourself and your limitations well enough to strike a pace that will allow you to climb steadily all day. "Pride goeth before a fall" in the mountains like nowhere else on earth. Staying "right up there" with the guide for the first hour or so does the hunter scant good if he's done-in after lunch—or for the next two days. So, pace yourself and climb against yourself and the mountain. It's not a competition with someone else, least of all your guide who's a seasoned native.

Getting over-fatigued not only may knock you out of a day or two of hunting, it's downright dangerous. That's when costly mistakes are made. Exhaustion also leads to fear and mental debilitation. Remember our friend Bob? First he got dead tired, then he got scared. The mountain always looks much higher and more treacherous to the completely exhausted man. And it is!

There should be a loose but definite rhythm to climbing. It's difficult to explain to someone who's never done any extended climbing or backpacking. There's a sort of slow but swinging plod that you want to cultivate, even when you're high up and the going is very, very hard. The rhythm is important because if you stop completely, even momentarily, you've lost that tiny but precious momentum.

Milestones and Climbing Sticks

Another common, but very costly, psychological mistake is to mentally try to climb the whole mountain at once. When the going is really tough and each gain in elevation is coming hard, avoid raising your eyes mournfully skyward and contemplating the impossibility of reaching the top. Such is the food of despair. Rather, pick out a clump of brush, large rock or other prominent landmark some reasonable distance above you and make up your mind to climb to that point. This approach of setting "milestones" and using them to lever yourself up the mountain can be a big help.

By all means, use a climbing stick. I have, in extremes, used my (shudder) rifle butt, a willow stick and various other oddments that came to hand. The rifle is awkward and clumsy, and using it to maintain footing does your stock not one whit of good. The green sticks that can be cut and used are always crooked, and they break at downright inconvenient or dangerous times. A good ski pole is almost ideal for this purpose. The walking stick gives you a third leg to balance on when the going gets tricky. It's a handy probe to test the depth of snow or the dependability of footing on a shale slide. It also provides a handy rifle, camera or binocular rest. A handy, easy-to-carry tool, indeed!

Beware of Handholds!

When you are climbing, *never* rely on your hands and arms to hold you up. If you must climb an almost sheer rock face, support your weight on your feet, and use your hands for balance holds only. Try not to use your knees at all. If you have to use your hands and knees to hold yourself up, get out of there quick!

Give an outdoor writer a typewriter and some fresh paper and he ascends to the pulpit. I've been guilty, at one time or another, of committing just about every one of these no-no's that I'm sermonizing about. But that's how I learned they were no-no's.

Take the time I was hunting a different area of Alaska with another guide. I wasn't feeling well and had been up with a stomach ailment most of the night. Then the guide spotted a real buster Dall, and we climbed steadily all day to get at him. By the time we got up near his street, I was so bushed I couldn't have climbed up on a chair to change a lightbulb, much less the remaining 500 or so feet to where we wanted to go. When you get that tired on a mountain, you'd better stop in your tracks and rest before you have an accident. Prudent sort that I am, that's just what I did. We decided that the guide should go on ahead to see if our white-coated friend was still around. I watched as he steadily climbed higher and angled off to the side to peer around the shoulder of the mountain.

When he finally reached the agreed upon point, he thoroughly scanned the area and then signaled back that nothing was in sight. Then he disappeared around the mountain and was gone for about 15 minutes checking farther ahead. Back he came with another negative signal. Rather than returning directly to me, he wisely decided to drop down that edge of the shoulder more directly to see if the ram was still over there but hidden from him in some pocket or behind a knoll. As he dropped lower, I noticed that he was making a lot of up and down false starts to get there. Soon I was to find out why.

Finally he did work back down to where he was only about 100 feet above me but well around the mountain from me. I could barely see him, but that was enough to tell that he'd either discovered gold or found our sheep. He was bouncing up and down and frantically waving his arms. I had rested up pretty well but was still feeling far below par. More importantly, the situation had left me mad as a grizzly with a toothache. Here I was, about to lose what might be the sheep of several lifetimes because I had the vapors. What a situation. If only I had been able to keep up enough to be sitting over there with the guide and drawing a fine bead on that sheep! But anger doesn't belong up on a mountain, as I would soon find out. As I sidehilled my way directly toward the guide, the going got rougher. I started encountering patches of rotten rock that would give way under foot. Also, the mountain got steeper. Sidehilling is fairly easy up to a certain pitch. After that, it becomes almost impossible to continue and still stay on the mountain.

As I drew ever closer, I was on a pitch with a near "no-go" degree of sharpness. So I had to drop down lower to keep going. The guide was signaling me to head back because of the hazards of all the rotten rock around him. That's why he'd had such a time dropping down. And he'd taken a safer route than I. The closer I got, the more he waved me off. I thought about aborting but, the excitement of that big sheep and my anger at myself for getting into this predicament combined to make me continue.

The worst was yet to come. I finally reached a point only about 75 feet directly below the guide.

Now 75 feet may not sound like much to climb, but it's equivalent to the height of a 7-story building. I started up, pulling myself upward hand over hand half the time. I clung to that face with my toes, my fingers, my knees, my chest, my groin. I was daffy for not descending after the first few feet when it became obvious that this was a hand climb—and a rough one.

About halfway up I hit the worst going. Although I had been thoroughly testing each handhold before committing my weight to it, I finally hit one that broke off in my right hand just as I started shifting my weight. My Adam's apple bounced off my belt buckle as my right hand and foot both lost purchase and I swung crazily out from the mountain. I dropped the 5-pound chunk of rock that I still clutched in my right hand. It bounced once about 40 feet down and then took off for a much longer flight. About this time I was devoutly regretting that I hadn't taken up coin collecting, finger painting or *anything* but big-game hunting. There I was, like a fly on a wall, held there momentarily only by my left hand and foot.

If both holds hadn't stayed firm, this book would be the first successful contact from the other side. Well, I finally did make it on up that cliff because that was easier than going back down. I didn't get the sheep. As soon as I reached enough solid ground to collapse on I suffered the shakes for five minutes. It had been that close. And all my fault!

Let's count up the bad plays on my part. For openers, I shouldn't even have started out after the blasted sheep that morning. A day's rest would have been safer and would have put me on my feet the following day. When I did start climbing and found out just how tough it was on me, I should have turned back. Then, when the guide signaled me to come for the sheep he had spotted, I should have screwed down my anger and impatience and approached him more cautiously. When he started waving me off from that last stretch, I should have aborted and found a longer but safer route. So much for the perfection of those who write books and give advice to others!

General Cautions

Often you must cross extensive slide areas. Shale slides are far safer to traverse than snow slides. Shale, no matter how loose it may be, never slides in front of you. So, if you scamper across it quickly enough to keep ahead of the debris your own feet dislodge, you'll be okay. Snow is different. It can and often does slide ahead of you. You can start and become engulfed in your own avalanche!

The mountains demand constant alertness – especially around rockfalls or rotten rock faces. Always keep your eyes open for these areas. Probably the most dangerous time on a mountain is that idyllic period around 11 a.m. If there has been a hard freeze the night before and moisture has seeped into the rock cracks and frozen, late morning is the time that things thaw out well enough for the rock to slide free and come hurtling down.

Although Homo sapiens may have scuttled around on all fours at sometime in the dim past, we've been upright, two-legged types for the past million years or so. By now we move best upright. Yet each year I see some desperate novice climbers trying to slither across some very steep and scary slopes in a weird, crab-like crawl using their hands, feet and butt at the same time. Although this does lower the center of gravity and somewhat increases the bearing surface, it makes for terrible balance. It doesn't allow you to lean into the mountain as much. So stand up. It's faster and safer.

Boots and Feet

It's important to wear the right boots and clothes for climbing. Top quality 8-inch climbing boots or 6-inch climbing shoes don't come cheap, but they're well worth the cost. With Vibram soles, reenforced heels and toes, sewn-in tongue and scree ring on top, they're the only way to go. Good shoes go for $35 and up. Good boots can easily run $60 and more. They should be heavy and sturdy. Although they might look impossibly heavy and awkward in your family room, up in rough mountains they'll look right in scale and you'll bless them for the heavy duty protection they afford. They're the single most important item of gear for a mountain hunter. If you can't stay on your feet – and do rough work – you simply stop functioning in mountain country.

One simple but significant thing that every climber should do before he leaves home is to toughen his feet up. Even if he is in good condition and wearing the proper boots and sox, chances are if he's from the lower, flatter land, his soles will be tender and unaccustomed to the pounding, wrenching shocks they'll receive in rough rock. Going barefooted while working in the yard or jogging helps. Calluses before the hunt prevent critical blisters later.

Make sure your boots are well broken in. One trick is to wet new boots thoroughly, even filling them completely with water and allowing them to stand for several hours so that the leather absorbs as much water as possible. Then put them on your feet and walk them dry. This molds them to your feet in a fashion somewhat akin to the way fine pistol holsters and rifle scabbards are formed. It's faster than any other method. After that, wear your boots often to finish breaking them in. Make sure your toenails are clipped short to avoid some surprisingly painful mishaps while climbing. Proper sox are a must. Two pair, both wool or the inner of silk or cotton if wool bothers you, help to cushion your feet against the pounding. Boots should be a full size larger and a width wider than your street shoes to allow both for the two pair of bulky sox and also for the swelling of your feet each day as you put them to hard use.

Being in Shape

The critical importance of good general physical condition simply can't be overemphasized. Hunting is a vigorous sport. High-country climbing makes it doubly so. This kind of hunting puts a severe strain on people in good condition, and it's downright dangerous for those in poor shape. Raw physical condition, more than any other single factor, determines how far and how well you can climb. If you're in terrible condition, all the tricks, technique and savvy in the world won't help much.

Lose weight. See your doctor if you need to lose a lot of weight and then, with his approval, get skinny. I don't mean trim. I mean skinny! "Trim" at the country club is "fat" in the mountains. Unless you have some other kind of health problem, you can't be too skinny for mountain work.

If you smoke, don't just cut down or switch to milder brands. Quit! I did after more than fifteen years of chain smoking, and so can you. Most smokers don't need scientific texts to explain the debilitating effects of smoking. They know it from having tried to play ball or run track back in school. Smoking murders "wind" like nothing else.

Even though your faithful guide probably belches smoke like a vintage locomotive and he can still outclimb you, he's doing it in spite of the smoking and not because of it. It's hurting him, too. He can just get away with it somewhat more easily than you can. For a while! Eventually it'll catch up with him.

Clothing

Several other items just about complete your climbing outfit. Although I often wear jeans, they're probably not as good for climbing as top-quality, loose wool trousers. The wool pants are warmer, especially when wet and, being looser, they don't bind as much. Layers of loose, high-quality, 100 percent wool shirts are light and warm and can be shucked on and off in a trice as your own thermostat swings wildly up and down from climbing and resting. I personally prefer to don one or more of the lighter 10- to 14-ounce types rather than a single heavy 20-ounce jac-shirt. The lighter ones don't gall you as readily, and wearing several gives you more temperature options. Also, carry a lightweight down jacket. Cold temperatures and drastic temperature changes are expected up high. Again, I prefer one of the lightweight down shirt types to the heavier parka types. The lighter ones are easier to carry and two of them, one a size larger, will do anything a single big one will do and do it more cheaply and easily.

Anxious Achievers

Another thing that I'm sure our poor benighted friend Bob didn't realize is that dudes in mountain country labor under a mental overhead that isn't affecting their guide. The guide is relaxed and in his element. Whereas, to some degree, the dude is on edge. He's got a lot of money riding on his hunt. And he may feel he's got to get "his money's worth." His money's worth will be in terms of inches of horn or antler, feet of hide, or pounds of meat. So, rather than hunting hard in a relaxed fashion, he builds too much pressure into the situation.

Also, this hunter is usually tense and occasionally scared. He simply is not used to all this. Some of those spectacular bottomless vistas prompt the nagging questions "What if I fall off?" and its concomitant, "How will I ever get down if I get hurt up here?" These considerations affect hunters in different ways. If the hunter truly came to savor the magnificence of the country and the singular excitement of the hunt as a total experience, he'll slough off most of these artificial burdens.

If he came to see and do and learn and not just to kill and collect, it's much easier for him to slip into the rhythm of things and truly enjoy himself. That doesn't mean he doesn't hunt hard. It just means that the trophy is something less than life or death with him.

But the citizen labors under heavy burdens if he is hunting to fill up spaces in his trophy room, or to get something "impressive" to show off to business associates, or to get his "ticket punched" for this mountain range or that animal. The pressure is constantly on him and continues to build as the hunt wears on. He's never doing well enough, no matter what he's shot, and he strains to do better. How sad! He's missing the whole point of the adventure, and he's also adding immensely to the physical strain of the hunt. No wonder he can't enjoy himself.

So, when you're climbing, try to relax. That certainly doesn't mean to drop your alertness and become lackadaisical, it just means don't make it any rougher than it already is.

Climbing Proficiency

Mountain climbing can be intimidating to some hunters, but it shouldn't be. The big-game hunter is not a true mountain climber in the technical sense—requiring ropes, pitons and other specialized equipment. Rather he is climbing as a requirement of his chosen sport—big-game hunting. A good technical hard-rock climber would probably laugh himself off his feet and all the way down the mountain if I showed him mountain faces that I thought were intimidating or impassable.

With his specialized equipment plus his training and technical skills added to a certain unusual bent of mind, these areas would look entirely different to him than to me or other "amateurs." No, the serious big-game hunter isn't a serious climber in the final analysis. He doesn't have to be. It's just not necessary 99 percent of the time, and he can always skip the other 1 percent.

What he *is* is a man dedicated to the sport of hunting who is trying to develop a decent proficiency in climbing in order to add that skill to his battery of others, such as woodsmanship, shooting, and camp savvy, in order to become a better all-round hunter. I would put this hunter about midway between the serious hiker and the serious climber.

Anyone who is relatively vigorous and who is serious about his hunting can learn all he needs to know about climbing if he wants to. I did. I'm not a natural climber nor am I an outstanding one now. But I'm proficient. You can be, too, if you want to.

Getting the Most
out of a Hunting Horse

20

Sooner or later the serious trophy hunter has to become some kind of horseman and learn something about those wondrously perverse and fascinating creatures — horses. Much of the best trophy hunting in North America lies in country so big that horses are the best and most effective way of combing it. This means using riding mounts to hunt from and packhorses to give the camp the mobility and comfort necessary for long stays in the field. Besides, there's just nothing in the world quite like a well run packstring hunt in beautiful, pristine country.

Some years ago I took my first long horseback hunt up in the breathtakingly beautiful White Goat Wilderness Area of Alberta. I'll carry, and relish fondly, those memories forever. I was a heavy smoker back then. And since I lived in the "wilderness" of Long Island at the time, my backsides and legs were subway-rider-soft. I wasn't really ready for the hunt, and the two main things I had going for me were my enthusiasm and a canny old buckskin gelding with the unlikely name of "Maude." He was a seasoned old hand of twenty-nine years in the mountains and was typical of his breed. Short-coupled and chunky, he probably weighed no more than 1,000 or 1,100 heavy-barreled pounds. If you kept your cool, he'd usually keep his.

He vastly extended my out-of-condition hunting radius, and he taught me a lot about himself and his kind, and no little about myself and mine. He was a gentle, steady soul and he added much to my hunt. I got the big 6-point bull elk I had my heart set on in a dramatic, "now or never" last day situation — but only by the grace of a chillingly wild ride down a steep snow slope, through dense spruce "jungles," and across several frigid mountain torrents lined with horse-size boulders.

Only a good horse, inured to the ways of both mountains and men, could have got me through that ride and to the elk in time. On foot I simply could not have gotten close enough to shoot before the elk would have lost himself in one of the innumerable side canyons filled with heavy cover. From where I sit writing this, I can easily glance at that big head hanging on my wall. Every time I do that, I remember old Maude.

Horse Disadvantages

One of the first things that I learned from that old buckskin was that horses, like most good things in life, have their disadvantages. Several of them. For one thing, you'll be ten times colder and stiffer sitting up on a horse than you would be hoofing it on your own — especially if you're on a cold, late-season hunt. You won't be walking and generating body heat and you'll be sitting way up there in the cold wind. That means that you'll have to take more clothes than would otherwise be necessary. It also means that when you do get down, whether to make the last steep climb to shoot or whether just to walk and rest the horse, the agony will be twice as great. When you do suddenly leap from the saddle and straight into a tough climb, your temperature will swing wildly upward and then, when you stop to rest, just as wildly back down.

These temperature swings, if extreme enough, can be dangerous. Over the years, I've been struck by how seldom hunters get sick out in the bush, even though they may strain themselves prodigiously. I think the main reason for this is that everything is so *clean*. The air is pure, the water unpolluted. Better yet, there are few germ-laden humans milling around and spreading whatever new virus is in vogue that season.

Next to accidents, due to carelessness 99 percent of the time, the biggest hazard is getting the vapors from being drastically overheated and then suddenly chilled from honest sweat. You can largely alleviate these wild temperature swings, so prevalent on horseback hunts, by carrying and properly using the right clothing.

The clothing should be of top quality down, wool, and synthetics. And you can use it wisely by constantly venting yourself. This is done by unbuttoning and unzipping whenever you start heating up too much and by not hesitating to shuck whole layers of clothing as you get still hotter. Conversely, you must don them immediately as you start to cool, bearing in mind that these temperature drops, especially if it is windy, usually occur with kamikaze-like swiftness. Yes, I know it's aggravating to be pawing continually through your saddlebags to bring out or put back items of clothing, but you'll be more comfortable and safer for doing it. All this donning and shucking isn't nearly as necessary if you are working consistently on your own two feet throughout the day and maintaining a relatively constant body temperature.

Another problem. Although your four-legged pal can go places that you might not believe possible, there are some places where you can make it and he can't. These spots don't need to be long slopes or large areas. Sometimes, to get where you need to go, you must make a short but almost vertical climb, with or without the aid of a rope. Your horse, not being blessed with hands and opposable thumbs, can't follow. There may be other tight spots where the horse's bulk may preclude his making it.

When your horse can't make it with you, you either have to take the long way around, if there's a way, or you must leave him behind. If you leave him, that means you must come back

Well adjusted stirrups allow you to distribute weight to your feet, giving you "spring" that makes things easier on the horse, and on you. Standing fully erect, you should be able to fit a clenched fist between the saddle and your crotch.

later to pick him up, more or less retracing your steps to do so. Retracing your steps means you can't hunt out a different way, covering new ground. Hunting time is precious. Try calculating the number of *net* hours spent hunting during a 10- to 14-day trip and you'll see what I mean. Retraced steps, covering ground already hunted, don't help improve your odds any.

Then too, there is a more obvious drawback to hunting by horseback. These hunts are necessarily more expensive than most other types. This is due both to the cost of the horses themselves and also to the salary of the one or two wranglers necessary to take them out in the evenings and round them up and saddle them before daylight. A horseback camp without a wrangler, except on very short hunts or in unusual circumstances, is difficult to hunt from. By that I mean that you must choose from two unsatisfactory alternatives. You must either leave too late in the morning and return too early in the evening, thereby eliminating one of the prime reasons for using horses to begin with. Or else you or your guide, whoever is wrangling the horses, will turn into a zombie from lack of sleep.

Another common problem is that several hours in the saddle tends to stiffen up the fellow not used to it and to make him lazy. Once he's up there and gets stiff, he just doesn't want to dismount again. Thus, he usually doesn't get off frequently enough to keep himself warm on cold weather hunts, nor does he get off enough to rest the horse properly in rough country when the horse is doing a lot of steep climbing.

Thus, one of the most frequent gripes of guides and outfitters across the country is that the hunter just won't get off his horse. When easing over a ridge or around a particularly interesting bend, the guide may dismount to glass the area and ease up on it. A tremendous amount of game has been lost because the stiffened-up hunter wouldn't dismount to go with the guide for a look. Often, by the time the guide comes back for the hunter and they both make their way back to the vantage point, the trophy in question has disappeared.

Horse Advantages

Enough bad. Let's talk about good points of horseback hunting. There are so many! Better than any other conveyance known to man, good horses can still get you back into rough country with all the gear necessary to set up a comfortable base camp. The ability to move around the country, setting up comfortable camps along the way, gives you far more flexibility than flying into a permanent base camp and being restricted to hunting out of it.

I'm a firm believer in the old maxim about the work just beginning after the game is down. Pack out a few assorted moose and elk quarters and racks on your own groaning sacroiliac as I have and you'll soon be a convert, too. You can lighten your load by boning out the meat before packing it out on your back, but that also burns up precious time in the field. The best way is to bring horses in. They can pack your trophies and meat out, especially that from the larger animals, and save you a day or more of valuable time and back-breaking toil. And this eliminates waste too.

Another big plus is that horses often wind or spot game before even the sharpest-eyed hunters. It's always good to watch your mount's ears. If he's twitching them around and craning his neck here and yon as though he forgot to mail a letter, chances are he knows something that you don't but should. Horses have put me onto a lot of game that I might not have seen until too late or might have missed entirely.

Horses let you hunt later in the day. You can start that last long climb or stalk at 2 or 3 p.m., or later if all you have to do is to get off the mountain by evening and let your horse carry you the 8 or 10 dark miles back to camp. If you must walk back yourself, especially if it's through strange country at night, it's usually necessary to break off in mid or late afternoon and thus miss that priceless final 60 minutes of evening hunting. Except in the case of sheep and sometimes goat hunting, the last hour at evening is often worth more than the whole 8- or 9-hour day after 8:30 in the morning.

Ditto on getting out early! By sunrise, a horse can have carried you safely and easily in the pre-dawn darkness through miles of unfamiliar country and have you at your hunting ground, well away from the bustle of base camp. Another 60 minutes of *golden* hunting time!

In the right kind of country, a man in superb condition can actually hunt farther on foot than on a horse. But horses are a godsend for older hunters, those with health problems and — let's face it — the 75 percent who just aren't in condition for tough high-country trekking and climbing.

Matching the right hunter to the right horse is an important part of any outfitter's or guide's responsibility. Horses, like the ladies, just naturally seem to warm up to some fellows more than others. I found that out jiffy-quick on that first horse hunt.

After several days up on old Maude, I was getting the hang of things pretty well and feeling a bit cocky. The grass was so sparse around our snowy, high-country camp that the horses were in a somewhat weakened condition. So we had to take it as easy as possible on them. In the interest of resting old Maude, the outfitter suggested that I try out a little horse that was hardly larger than the 700- to 800-pound bull elk we were chasing around those mountains.

Now, most outfitters use geldings for riding and packing. Probably 75 percent of these hunting horses are gelded, the rest being mares. Nobody uses stallions. And about 90 percent of these geldings are "hard gelded." Some few of them are "easy gelded" or cut differently so that they retain more of their spirit and orneriness. Far more! The little fellow I was now hooked up with had been a wild mustang stud until he was caught when he was about seven years old. Then, because the outfitter was a superb horseman and wanted a spirited mount for himself, the horse was "easy gelded"—*very* easy, as I was to find out! We did not exactly become buddies, that horse and I.

He was 800 pounds of pure poison for a greenhorn. He wanted to bite and fight every other horse that got near him and most that didn't. If you didn't watch him, he just might take a nip out of you, too. He was as ornery as a fellow on-the-wagon at a cocktail party. About the best way to get his attention was to belt him in the chops occasionally. The outfitter, a strapping fellow, had done just that a few times. So the little horse was pretty obedient with him.

But I was a different commodity than the outfitter, and the one day I spent with that little hellion on four legs was eminently unforgettable. Looking back, I now see the experience as something rather funny, and I know that things would be different if it occurred now. *Then* it wasn't funny at all, and it cost me a good day of hunting and a lot of aggravation and anxiety. Old Maude looked like money from home when I clambered aboard him, a considerably humbler rider, the following day.

Saddle-wise Tips

There are some tips you should know when dealing with horses of either the riding or packing persuasion. For one thing, always split up your gear, especially your more valuable items, among as many horses as possible. Something could hap-

Good horses can carry you through deep snow. But remember that cold-weather horseback hunting calls for much warmer clothing than hunting on foot.

pen to a horse, such as his falling off a cliff, drowning or getting dunked in a cold mountain stream. Or he could just up and run off. The less gear you stand to lose on any one horse, the better.

Horses dearly love to roll—particularly after a long and chafing ride. This may happen, no matter how alert you, the outfitter, or the guides are. It is awe inspiring to see what a 1,200-pound horse, rolling around like a beagle after a bath, can do to your precious guns, cameras, binoculars and other breakables, no matter how well they are packed. Minimize your risks of a total wipe-out by splitting your gear up.

If you value your shooting irons, watch the horse or horses with your guns stashed on board. If an animal begins to look itchy, as if a good roll would really hit the spot, yank your guns out quick.

Don't pretend that you know more about horses, their ways and their rigging, than you do. Many seasoned and experienced trophy hunters who cut their teeth on whitetail deer and nonhorseback western hunts, don't know a lot about horses. There's no shame in that. If you're green as grass, don't say: "I can get by." Ask for help. A saddle that is only slightly out of adjustment in the morning will be causing you excruciating pain after a hard day's ride. Don't be embarrassed to ask your guide or hunting partner questions or to ask for his help. Otherwise, guides at least, may just let you go, assuming that you're okay. Most guides don't like to embarrass their hunter, especially if the guy is an aggressive, "take-charge" type. And the guides generally assume that if anything is bothering you, you'll tell them. Do so!

Don't overload your saddlebags. One of the most persistent peeves of guides and outfitters across the country is the fact that most dudes blandly assume that their mount can tote them and half their belongings over hill and mountain. Not so! For one thing, the horse is already "overloaded" with your carcass. Don't add unnecessarily to his load. For another, you are live weight and therefore are a self-adjusting, balanced load. Bulky items tied onto the horse here and there are never balanced, and an out-of-plumb horse is about as efficient as your family flivver when the front end is out of line.

Don't abuse your horse and don't overwork him. Sure, he's big and strong. He's also terribly fragile and delicate. Just glance at his ankles; they're smaller than your own! Don't ask him to do all the climbing, and don't push him too hard. Climbing is tough work, even for a horse, when he has over 150 pounds of quivering *Homo sapiens* on his back. And, though you might not think so, it's even tougher on him to come *down* a steep mountain with you on his back than to climb it. His hindquarters are far, far stronger than his front end. When you won't even get off of your mount to come downhill, you're making him strain those much smaller front legs enormously. Remember, he's just like you in that if you wear him out completely in the morning, he's not going to be much good to you that afternoon.

Watch your horse. Be alert to him in general, not only to see if he's spotted any game but just to note how he's doing and how he's feeling. That's no automaton or machine down there underneath you. Far from it, that's a wonderfully quirky, perverse, fascinating live animal. You just never know what he'll do from one moment to the next because *he* never knows either. Riders who daydream their way past certain danger signals or into other sudden emergency situations get themselves, and possibly others, into trouble in the wink of an eye.

Probably the biggest single cause of riding accidents and falls is the horse's being suddenly surprised about something. It doesn't have to be the sight of a grizzly or a dramatic sudden slip on a steep trail. It's not so much *what* surprises him as how *unexpected* the surprise is that determines how strongly the horse will react. For instance, around the ranch or base camp, a horse expects to see a lot of human beings running around jabbering and making a general commotion. Let some fellow sud-

Here a guide carefully weighs duffle before loading a packhorse. A load in excess of 150 pounds would overburden an average horse on a routine hard day in the mountains. Balance and bulk are other key loading concerns.

denly come chattering and yelling around the bend of a high, lonely trail, where the horse doesn't expect anyone to be, and you may quickly feel that your mount decided to audition for a bucking slot in the Rodeo Hall of Fame. If you're woolgathering in the saddle and don't react until too late, you might find yourself hitting the ground. And on many a steep mountain trail that may be 500-feet down!

So, watch your horse. Is he tired? Is he nervous? Is he mad and irritable? Is he being overly stubborn, dawdling to nip at grass along the way, not wanting to follow your lead, or any number of other little things because he thinks you'll let him get

away with it? Your first day up on a strange horse is very important. That's when he can pick up a lot of bad habits. Remember,
he's sizing you up that first day, just as surely as a bevy of subur-
ban matrons checking out the new member in their garden
club. It's important to get started off right. Be firm but fair.
He'll understand both.

Do some sizing up yourself while he's checking out your volt-
age. Horses are about as individualistic as people. Some are
more patient and gentle than others. Some are stronger and in
better physical condition than others. Give him a good going
over to get an idea of what you can expect from him. Don't hesitate to ask your outfitter, guide or anyone else familiar with the
horse to tell you a little about him. He may have some quirks
about him just as some people do. Does it sound as though I'm
overhumanizing the beast? I'm not.

Mules

Although some U.S. outfitters use mules, practically none of
the Canadians do. They're in the minority stateside, probably
peaking out at about 25 percent of the stock in a few spots such
as the Bob Marshall Wilderness Area. But even there they're
used almost solely as pack animals rather than as riding stock or
as combination animals.

Many full-time professional packers do prefer mules.
They're smarter, tougher and can carry bigger loads. Mules
usually last longer in this tough mountain life with a fair number making it past the age of 30. I've even heard rumors of
some 40-year-old patriarchs! On the other hand, the oldest
working mountain horse, that I've verified myself, is a staunch
old mount of John Holmes, the premier northern British
Columbia outfitter who hunts in the Cassiars. This Methuselah
of the mountain horse clan was 34 the last time I heard and still
going strong.

Why do so few outfitters use mules, even though they're
often smarter and tougher? The worn-out old phrase "stubborn as a mule" is worn out simply because it's so true. Mules
are very difficult for greenhorns to handle and they can drive
even seasoned hands to drink at times. Also, there aren't many
in the far West and the North, and most have to be brought in
from the South where they're bred from jacks and mares. All
this costs considerable amounts of money.

The Outfitter's Investment

A good mountain horse doesn't really hit his stride until he's 4 or 5 years old. He's in his prime, toughened by toil and smartened by experience, from about 10 to 15 years of age. Horses are a substantial investment, and they are getting more expensive to maintain every day. At this writing, a good mountain horse for riding will cost around $250 to $350, depending. Figure another $150 a year for hay and $8 and $10 per month for pasturage when needed. And remember that these prices are skyrocketing. To keep a riding horse decently equipped costs around $150 for rigging and this must be replaced every five years or so, even without any undue abuse, because of the tough wear and tear built into hard mountain use. Add another $15 to $20 a year in vet bills and a few bucks for shoes, and you'll see that someone has made a substantial investment — especially if he's running a string of 30 to 50 head.

Don't expect your outfitter to thank you if you abuse his gear or horseflesh. You won't get nearly as much out of the horse if you do that, either. So, which is your hunting horse to be? Boon companion and priceless helper or wary enemy and drag on your hunt? The choice is really more up to you than him!

Do's and Don'ts Around Camp

21

A hunting camp is a little, self-contained world with a reality all its own. Its social circumstances are broadly akin to those which people share on a cruise ship or on cross-country through trains. All feature closed environments. At its best the hunting camp is a place where old friendships meet a new test and emerge stronger and dearer than ever and where new friendships are welded together firmly by shared precious experiences. Priceless memories, that will be talked about and shared among friends for a lifetime, are a natural by-product of a good camp.

At its worst a bad hunting camp, in which the chemistry of the various hunters is at odds, can become a seething caldron of resentment, envy, distrust — or even hate. It can cause things to be said that can never be unsaid. It can break up old friendships and cause potentially fine new ones to be stillborn. In some extreme cases, it can even result in fist fights and lawsuits.

Yet the hunting camp is also quite different from the cruise ship, train or other of the genteel comparisons that come to mind. For one thing, it offers a far more physical, basic existence. For another, around the camp itself, there is far less privacy. More self-reliance and physical stamina are called for. Laziness of a person on the train or ship is hardly noticeable or, at worst, only a bit vexing. In a working hunting camp, especially on hunts without guides or outfitters, it can cause very real discomfort or even hardship. Even on an outfitted hunt, laziness is instantly noticeable.

Many things beyond your control have some influence upon camp happiness. Continual bad weather, causing discomfort and lost hunting time, doesn't help. Bad food, which may be beyond your direct control, can make folks pretty grouchy.

So can leaky tents, overage horses and second-rate gear.

One of the most important factors is Who is actually in camp? Are they good guys or bad? This can be beyond your area of choice in that the outfitter will be booking in total strangers who will share camp with you. So, to a degree, it's a throw of the dice as to the sort they turn out to be. Even on a do-it-yourself hunt, often friends-of-friends will turn up — total strangers to you.

Often, even if you do have a hand in selecting your camp mates, it's a shot in the dark. Unless you have actually made extended stays in the wild with some fellows or hunted seriously with them for top trophies, you just don't know how they'll be. The likeable chap who does eighteen holes with you every Saturday on the local links may turn out to be an irascible boor in the quite different environment of a working hunting camp. On the other hand, someone whom you have never been very drawn to in your day-to-day activities may turn out, under the stimulus of wilderness camping, to have a fine sense of humor and reserves of strength and self-control that you had never noticed before. Like climbing a mountain, you just never really know how living in a particular camp with specific people will be until you've done it. You can be fooled a lot, on both sides of the coin, and that's one thing that keeps the whole business so interesting.

Now, having stated all the things beyond your control in making a good camp and those that even falling within your grasp may be uncertain, let me hasten to say that the majority of things that spell whether you have a good or bad camp are within your direct control, and that of your buddies in camp. Your attitude and your conduct, day by day, have more to do with how well you get along and how much you enjoy the camp and the hunt than anything else. Honest.

I've always felt that the difference between most good and bad hunting camps, like that between good and bad marriages, is generally a lot of little things rather than a few big ones. People tend to rise to the occasion on the big problems and dilemmas, especially out in the wilderness. It's the nagging, grinding little things that "bug" people, sometimes to the point of distraction. And in a hunting camp there's nowhere else to go to get away from whatever is bothering you. No movie theater, no bar, no "elsewhere." You either learn to live with your gripe, or you correct it, or you get mad. That's about all of your options.

I've seen some weird goings-on in hunting camps. This is especially so on extended trophy hunts well "back in" away from civilization. Responsible men in commerce and industry argue furiously over who has the top or bottom bunk or who is snoring how loudly at night. No, things don't often get down to that level. But, when they do they can ruin a whole hunt and, by that time, it is very difficult to correct them. Other things, less noticeable and more subtle occur along the way and lead things to this point. Attitudes are hardened, "minds are made up," and egos may be bruised on the road to this sad state. It's pretty hard to undo all this.

Let's talk about these "little" things that can, often very innocently and almost unnoticeably, get you into trouble. They have varying degrees of relevancy, depending upon whether you are in a camp run by a professional outfitter with hired guides and cooks or whether you are in a straight do-it-yourself camp with a bunch of buddies and acquaintances. However, sooner or later, most of these potential booby traps arise on either type of hunt.

Doing the Chores

This is less of a factor on an outfitted hunt. Supposedly the hired help is there to do all those things. Yet it's really not that way. You'll make more friends and enjoy the camp more if you roll up your sleeves and offer to pitch in and help. By that I don't mean that you should try to shoulder an equal load with the guides, the cook and the wrangler. That can get to the point of cutting into your enjoyment of the outing, and it can be demeaning to you.

But, if you do offer to help and do help, it shows you're a good guy and not above getting your hands a bit dirty. That tends to make the hired help cotton up to you a bit more. So when you need their help, they tend to extend themselves a bit more. Also, aside from showing that you're a nice guy, you can be of very real benefit around camp, at times. It's not so much what you do as when you do it that counts. Keep your eyes open. When things really get rushed and hectic around camp, that's the best time to lend a hand. If several trophies come in at once and the guides are busy caping and salting the heads and hides and rough-butchering the meat, that's the time to help bring in the water and wood, start the fires, help see to the horses, and so on. That's when you're needed.

There are some things to remember when you're doing this, though. Don't offer to do things you don't know how to do. You can just get yourself and others into trouble. Don't offer to chop

Good food goes a long way toward making a happy camp. Since most wilderness cooks are individualistic, avoid imposing too much help on them.

up a lot of wood if you've never done it. Chopping wood is not the simple chore it may appear to be to the uninitiated. Greenhorns tend to hook their axes on overhanging limbs while taking a hefty cut at the wood and brain themselves in the process. Or they tend to hold and hit the wood wrong when they're chopping it into kindling on the ground. Then it flies up into their face and injures them. Or they chop through the wood on the ground and bang the axe into a rock, whereupon it bounces back and hits them or into the earth itself, which doesn't help the edge the guide painstakingly put on the axe the day before. (The rock didn't help things, either!)

So, if you're a complete greenhorn with axes, restrict yourself to carrying wood and maybe chopping it into kindling on the block after it has already been felled and rough-chopped by seasoned axemen.

Don't offer to do all sorts of things with the horses, by yourself, if you don't know a darn thing about horses. That's when you put the saddles on wrong and cause discomfort or even hazard for another rider. Or, you get yourself kicked because you picked the wrong horse and didn't know how to handle him. When you get kicked, the outfitter invariably has to send the best guide or two and the best horses out with you to get you medical attention as soon as possible. That not only ruins your hunt, it messes up things for your buddies. If you don't know much about horses but are willing to learn, tell the guide just that when you offer to help. Then he can show you what to do and not to do and which horses to stay away from.

It's best to avoid being too "helpful" with the cook. Most professional wilderness cooks — men and women — that I have met are highly individualistic people who are very set in their ways and don't like any interference. So, offer to help and do so. But use your head about it so that you don't cause problems for yourself and others.

On a do-it-yourself camp, things are far different. Everyone has to roll up his sleeves and pitch in to make things work. Here again, if you're in camp with some hunters whom you don't know very well, explain your strong points and weak points candidly. Do this, not in an attempt to duck the more strenuous chores but just to help in the most effective assignment of chores. Some men are just better cooks than others and always will be even though all may "know how" to cook. When you're not busy and are lolling around and others are busy, pitch in and help without worrying about whose job it is. Do this consistently, even if there is some goofing off involved by the other party. Sooner or later this will surface and be attended to by all in camp. Meanwhile the camp is continuing to function smoothly and, if you do later deem it necessary to criticize someone, you are putting yourself in a position to do so appropriately because you have demonstrated that you aren't a shirker.

Deciding Who Hunts Where

This usually isn't much of a factor on outfitted hunts. The guides will decide. If you have some question or disagreement about the way the hunting territory is being assigned, give it a few extra days to be sure. There may be all sorts of inputs for those decisions that would be difficult to explain to you. If after several days you're still unhappy, get the matter to the outfitter to decide, rather than doing it yourself directly with the other hunters or guides.

On an unguided hunt, the nearby hunting ground and the lower, easier-to-walk terrain should be reserved for any older hunters in camp, or those with health problems, or those who

Experienced hunters know the importance of firearms safety. This includes unloading upon returning to camp and not reloading until just before departure.

are badly out of condition. The other territory should be discussed thoroughly, assigned by coin toss in the event of competing claims for the same area and rotated regularly among the hunters so that all get a chance to hunt most of the ground. Then it becomes mainly a matter of who hunts where *first*.

Limiting Commotion

This is very important on non-horseback hunts and hunts where you have older or out-of-condition hunters in camp. It just isn't necessary to have a lot of loud horseplay going on, banging on cans, plinking with .22 pistols and a whole host of other things that greatly extend the amount of walking you must do to get into good hunting territory. Remember that any camp, particularly one with several hunters that will be in the same spot for a week or more, is going to disturb the game, especially those canny trophy-sized animals that everyone is after. All you can do is try to minimize the commotion.

Getting Up in the Morning

The truth is, a breakfast before daylight is probably more important to putting trophy game on the meat rack than having the best hunting territory and the best equipment. When heavily hunted, most diurnal animals become far more nocturnal than the average hunter realizes. This especially applies to outsized trophy game that has lived beyond the average span for its species.

On a guided hunt, getting up early can be crucial. If you want to lie around, don't expect your guide to force you out of

As the hunt progresses, you should try to improve your chances by becoming increasingly adept at glassing for game. Here outfitter John Holmes focuses a 20x spotting scope on a slope of the Cassiar Mountains in British Columbia.

bed. If you want to goof off, it's fine with him. In fact, you may have to be sure that you get up first to "encourage" him to do so. This may be a more pronounced problem on a late-season hunt, when the guide has been back in the bush working hard for several weeks. He's tired. And getting up early seven days a week is no fun.

On a nonguided hunt, your oversleeping probably won't hurt anybody but yourself, depending upon how the chores have been set up.

Watching the Alcohol

This one can be very touchy and get out of hand quick. One or two "sundowners" don't hurt in the evening. A ceremonial drink or two when the treasured trophy is taken helps to formalize the occasion. I'll never forget how good that special 21-year-old scotch tasted that I had laboriously packed into the British Columbia wilderness to celebrate my first grizzly. When

Leaving heavy-duty chopping to the camp staff usually lessens abuse to axes and reduces the number of emergency client evacuations.

I finally took him after ten back breaking days and a couple of heartbreaks along the way, the scotch added a nice touch.

But alcohol can cause a lot of problems. Put any large group of men together and you have a good chance of ending up with at least one guy who will abuse the privilege and drink beyond the point of moderation. This is especially true out in the bush. There just seems to be something about the atmosphere and experience that tends to make a lot of otherwise moderate drinkers overdo things. This excess usually arises after some hunters have already taken their game and are "celebrating," and thereby generally make a nuisance of themselves to those who are still hunting.

On guided hunts, watch alcohol carefully. Things can get out of hand quick. I've never seen a guide turn down a free drink, nor as many free drinks as were offered. That doesn't mean all guides are lushes or anything of the sort. It just means that you shouldn't build yourself into a bad situation. Make it a drink or two — *period* — and that's it. More means trouble. Don't stick to these guidelines religiously and then leave the balance of the bottle for the guide as part of the tip, either. It doesn't hurt you any, but it sure screws up things for the pilgrim coming in to hunt after you!

No, I'm not saying don't drink at all and don't take alcohol in with you to the hunting camp. Used with discretion and moderation, it's okay. However, to be honest, I must say that the more I'm out in the bush and the more unfortunate situations I see in which alcohol was the culprit, the more I think that hunting and booze just basically don't mix well.

Keeping Clean

When we get into the wilderness almost all of us feel the deep, atavistic urge to get back to nature and to "get away from the telephone." We grow beards, get dirty and — all too often — stay dirty. That can be overdone. For reasons that I explained earlier in this book, if you let your personal hygiene drop to too low a level, it can and will greatly reduce your hunting effectiveness. The same thing occurs if you let your clothes — your sox, underwear, denim trousers and the like — go too long between washings or at least rinsings.

In addition to reducing your hunting effectiveness, sloppy hygiene also can irritate your hunting partners — especially if you are sleeping several to the tent in cold weather camps where the air can become fetid in hot, closed tents very quickly. Most of us can tolerate some grime and sweat and some rather ripe odors. Hunting isn't a parlor sport, and we don't expect it to be exactly elegant and perfumed. But you can have too much of anything, and tolerances can be stretched. It's no fun to be overwhelmed by the sweaty odor the moment you enter the tent — to have body odor reach the point of downright unpleasantness on the part of one or more of your hunting partners. So keep yourself reasonably clean and your clothes in the same condition. Don't leave your deodorant at home. Remember the old saw: "When you can smell yourself, others have been smelling you for two days."

Snoring

This hilarious device on TV situation comedy shows can be anything but hilarious in the close quarters of a hunting camp. The wrong circumstances occur when you have a very loud snorer or nighttime teeth-grinder sleeping in the same tent with one or more light sleepers. Lost sleep makes anyone grouchy. And the hard-working hunter desperately needs all that he can get.

Unfortunately, there isn't a lot you can do about this one. If you're the snorer, don't discount the seriousness of the problem to those who are complaining. It may sound funny to you, but I assure you it isn't the least bit comical to them. If you have more than one tent in camp, sometimes you can switch sleeping arrangements so that the heavy sleepers are all quartered with the heavy snorers and loud teeth-grinders, and that will cure the problem. Otherwise, you can make sure that the snorer is the last one to go to sleep, and be sure to let the complainers get to sleep first. If things are bad enough so that the log-sawing is actually waking the men up out of a sound slumber, then about all that's left is for the snorer to sleep outside or, if only one person is bothered by it, for the snorer and "snoree" to toss a coin to see who sleeps outside. I have seen some real arguments develop over snoring in camps in which hunters were thrown together for two or three weeks.

Putting It All Together

Hunting is, or should be, a pastime in which the total experience is savored and enjoyed, like a fine wine. If we reduce it

The condition of the cape or hide determines the difficulty of the taxidermist's task, particularly the amount of repair work required. This will affect your taxidermy bill and probably your ultimate satisfaction with the mount. So for fine-skinning of facial features, you're well off to rely on the pros.

only to the climactic moment of the kill, or even the few hours spent actually stalking the animals, we're missing the majority of the fun. In fact, those intense moments, alone, just aren't worth all the expense or bother.

All of this is doubly true for the dedicated trophy hunter. Chances are you have spent more time, money and energy on your hunt — whether it be for Montana elk or Missouri whitetail — than an occasional or casual hunter would have. Also, chances are you are a more experienced hunter and you know these things. The camp life is a key factor in determining how pleasant and memorable the nonhunting aspects of your hunt are. The camaraderie and fun, the feeling of well being and "all's right with the world" that a good camp inspires are the foundation for an unforgettable hunt. This is especially so for trophy hunters who often camp together, farther away from civilization and for longer periods of time to get those outstanding antlers and horns.

But, good camps, again like good marriages, don't just happen. All the partners have to work at it to make it happen. And that's mostly a matter of being considerate and constantly alert to all the little things. Make sure that you are, and this will improve chances that everyone else will be, too.

Basic Cameras

22

In recent years, an interesting and accelerating trend has broken out among hunters. They've discovered photography, the single most popular hobby in the world, and they've taken it up with a vehemence. And why not? What better way for the hunter to capture and hold forever the golden moments spent afield? And what better arena for the photographer than the outdoors with all its color, drama and excitement?

If the hunter-photographer is a trophy hunter, then the chances are even greater that photography will make his trips more memorable and his game more interesting. Best of all, even when you're not hunting, you can be afield with camera in hand extending your enjoyment of the outdoors. If archery is termed the "second season" sport, then photography with absolutely no seasons or bag limits is truly the "unlimited sport."

Photography expands your horizons as a hunter and naturalist. The good photographer *sees,* not "looks," with a keener vision than most non-shutter snappers. He has to in order to take good pictures. The colors around him, the types of light at different hours of the day, the trees and plants, camp goings-on, wildlife and wildlife signs, landscape features — all these and more are grist for his mill.

Incidentally, another often overlooked bonus of photography is that there is no better way to introduce a youngster to the outdoors than through picture taking. It will teach him to appreciate the outdoors with that special brand of sensitivity that comes from looking at things through photographer's eyes.

Camera Essentials

Let's talk about the basic still cameras that you can choose and use. (We'll stick to basics in this chapter and then address advanced amateurs and professionals in the next chapter.) All cameras have their advantages and disadvantages. There are zillions of different cameras around, all with enticing features of one sort or another and some not-so-enticing price tags. I'm going to be slightly arbitrary here and assume that you, as a straightforward trophy hunter and outdoorsman first and a shutter-snapper second, want a flexible, lightweight, durable rig that is *reasonably* priced. Notice I didn't say cheaply priced but reasonably priced. Quality does cost money, even with the fads and frills trimmed off.

Here are the four basic camera types that you should consider.

1. 35mm Compact Rangefinder
2. 35mm Single Lens Reflex
3. Cartridge-loading Cameras (such as Kodak Instamatic)
4. Polaroid Cameras

Each of these camera types has its partisans, and nobody should categorically say that any one of them is better or worse than any other. Determining which is best for you depends upon how much money you want to spend, how many pictures you'll be taking, how flexible you'll want your camera to be, and how much rough treatment it may receive.

Terminology. Before we talk about each of the four basic types of cameras, let's define some general terms and then set the criteria for features that constitute a good hunter's camera.

BUILT-IN LIGHT METER. Your camera should have one. Without light meter, you will take too many bad pictures. A separate light meter is generally expensive, easy to lose and not really necessary for this level of photography.

LENS SPEED. The lower the number on the lens, the faster the speed and, generally, the more expensive the lens. A faster lens means that you need less light to take a good picture and that you can freeze faster action without a blur. Your lens should be at least an f2.8, but f1.8 would be better. (The lower the *F. number,* the faster the lens.)

SHUTTER SPEED. Besides lens speed, this is the other factor affecting how much light you need to take a good picture or what speed of action your camera can freeze without blur. A faster shutter speed will require more light but it will freeze faster action.

For instance, 1/500th of a second, shown simply as "500" on the shutter speed dial, is twice as fast as "250" (1/250th of a second). Thus, the shutter is open only for half as long at 1/500th as at 1/250th, and it admits only half as much light to the film. This means you need either a brighter day or a lower-light (faster) film for similar results when shooting at 1/500th rather than at 1/250th. However, shooting at 1/500th enables you to freeze motion or movement that is twice as fast as that you can freeze at 1/250th. This is because the shutter is open only half as long at the faster speed and the moving object can move only half as far in the shorter time the film is exposed. (Here we won't get into a discussion of real motion versus apparent motion and how they differ depending upon your angle of incidence to the moving object. But these factors exist.)

Although 1/250th will generally freeze a walking hunter or a slowly trotting dog, 1/500th is necessary to fully stop a running animal or leaping fish and 1/1000th or even 1/2000th is necessary for the fastest moving animals and birds. All these comments apply to "normal" focal length lenses, that is those that see approximately as the eye sees. A telephoto lens magnifies motion just as it magnifies everything else, so some of the above recommended shutter speeds should be increased for powerful "tele" lenses.

As a minimum, your camera should have shutter speeds running from a full second through 1/500th. Without using a telephoto you can, if you're careful, shoot as slow as 1/60th without a blur while hand-holding the camera, but below that you had better use a steady rest and squeeze the shutter button off as carefully as you do the trigger of old Betsy at the shooting range. That's not a bad technique to use no matter what speed you're shooting at. Good breath control, eye coordination, trigger squeezing and all the other ingredients for a good marksman are similarly valuable for a good photographer who wants to hand-hold his cameras, without help from a tripod.

WEIGHT. This is a highly personal consideration. I don't like to carry more than about twenty-four ounces hanging on my neck for extended periods, although I occasionally drape as many as three cameras there, sometimes one of them being a rather heavy, bulky motor-driven rig.

The first thing I do is replace the abominable, standard, thin leather straps that most camera companies provide with a wide "pro" strap. This makes carrying the camera much more comfortable. Actually the neck isn't the best place to carry a camera. Often roomy jacket or hunting coat pockets or game bag areas can carry the more compact rigs. I also use knapsacks or back-packs to carry mine.

MISCELLANEOUS. Your camera should have a self-timer. Often you may be caught in a situation in which you are alone with your recently downed trophy deer and have no one to take those precious pictures. Later will be too late because the animal will have stiffened up. Only the self-timer, easy to use and capable of taking surprisingly good pictures if you're careful, can help you here.

Your camera should have a shoe to which you can attach either a flashbulb holder or an electronic strobe unit to enable you to take pictures at night or inside a tent or house. Your light meter should be coupled to the lens for ease of adjustment.

You should buy a skylight filter, put it on your lens and leave it there permanently. It serves to protect the more expensive lens that it covers, plus it will filter out the excess blue that shows up frequently when you take pictures around water or snow, or at high altitude. And there's absolutely no disadvantage to leaving it on permanently.

Use a lens shade on each and every lens. I prefer the flexible rubber type that can be folded back and left permanently attached to most cameras, even in the case. This shade protects your pictures from "flare" (light streaks) that may show up when shooting color film toward the sun or even in strong side-light. Since water won't cut the grease that inevitably accumulates on a lens, you'll need a little bottle of lens-cleaning fluid, some lintless lens-cleaning tissue, and a soft camel's hair brush to complete your basic accessories. Use the brush to lightly flick dust and particles off the lens (or skylight filter, I should say). Never tissue-wipe a lens or filter dry, for you may scratch the surface. *KEEP YOUR LENSES AND FILTERS CLEAN*. The best camera in the world takes second-rate pictures if it's shooting them through a dirty window.

The Four Basic Cameras. Now back to the four basic types of cameras you should consider.

1. 35MM COMPACT RANGEFINDER CAMERA. This is the best choice for many trophy hunters, and it makes a good back-up camera if the sportsman is carrying a more expensive 35mm single lens reflex (SLR) camera as his main camera.

These compacts are just that: small and light enough to

The two "workhorse" cameras for the outdoorsman are the 35mm single lens reflex (SLR), shown left, and the less expensive, top-quality 35mm rangefinder. Many hunters start with the rangefinder and then trade up to the SLR, continuing to carry the rangefinder as a backup and all-weather camera.

carry and store easily, yet they shoot the superb 35mm film (which, like the .22 rimfire, is the most highly engineered product in its field). The film is available anywhere in the world. It comes in a staggering variety of types, and it makes slides from which prints can be made to 11x14 inches or larger; this can be very important. You may want to blow-up that trophy picture of a lifetime to large size and hang it in your trophy room. The 35 mm format not only enables you to do that, but it also produces slides that project brilliantly. Slides are generally a better choice than prints when you're shooting outdoor color pictures, as we'll see in the next chapter.

These compact rangefinder cameras differ from their larger, more expensive 35mm single lens reflex cousins in that they do not offer interchangeable lenses (with only one or two enormously expensive exceptions, that is). And when you look through the viewfinder, you don't see exactly what you will get in the picture.

A rangefinder camera is designed so that you look through a viewfinder, rather than through the actual picture-taking lens, as in the case of the SLR's, and you see an outlined, rectangular area which indicates your approximate picture-taking area. This approximation is generally pretty accurate except at very short ranges, where there is more divergence of view because the viewfinder and the picture-taking lens "see" the subject from different points. There are usually additional corner markers within the rectangular area which define the "sure" picture taking area, no matter what the range.

Also, the rangefinder camera, if it has a built-in light meter — and it should, for our purposes — will not meter the light through the actual picture-taking lens. The higher-priced 35mm SLR's usually feature this Through The Lens (TTL) light metering, and obviously it is both the most accurate and most expensive way of doing it.

The advantages of the better grade 35mm rangefinders are that they are lightweight and compact, and that helps. The most expensive camera in the world isn't worth anything if you leave it back in camp when you may need it in the field. Yet these cameras still have enough weight and "hand" so that most people can hand-hold them with rock steadiness. The new generation of super-small cartridge-loading cameras, such as Kodak Instamatics, are *so* small and lightweight that many people have difficulty hand-holding them properly.

Rangefinder cameras are sturdy and reliable, built to take rough field use — provided you buy quality and take reasonable care. Remember that any camera is still a somewhat delicate, precision optical instrument. There's no heavy, though delicate, mirror swinging up and down inside them as there is in the SLR's, and they are much less complex instruments, by and large, than the SLR's. Durability is probably more important to hunters than to any other type of amateur photographers because it's doubtful that many other people would submit their instruments to rougher use or to more varied weather conditions. Cameras and water don't mix well at all! No matter how careful you are with them, cameras inevitably get banged around some in the field, and there always seems to be plenty of dust and moisture about.

Rangefinders are usually considerably less expensive, even if you buy finest quality models, than the top-of-the-line 35mm SLR's or Polaroid's new SX-70. They're about the same price as top-grade cartridge-loading cameras. A good rangefinder will set you back $80 to $120, depending upon which brand or model you purchase and where you buy it. Camera shops usually give up to 10 percent discounts of "list" price while the discount palaces often go 15 to 20 percent off.

The huge camera "supermarkets" in New York City and a few other major cities across the country will sometimes go 25 to 28.5 percent off depending upon the item — and no sales tax for out of staters. Some items have a bit more profit built in than others. So there's more running room for the retailers to work in. Buying from these huge stores can net you considerable savings, but there are disadvantages. Unfortunately, in the camera business as in any other, there are some unscrupulous speed merchants who advertise items they don't have in stock at prices lower than they intend to sell them for. I'm told that a few have even been known to try to substitute reconditioned used cameras for new ones and fool their long-distance customers. This has never happened to me, though.

However, the vast majority of these firms are honest and upright. Just exercise the care that you would when making any substantial purchase. Buying long-distance you also sacrifice the service that should be built into a face-to-face relationship that you establish when you buy locally. I buy some items locally so that I have that relationship to fall back on when I need it. And for other, more expensive items, I often buy from the major stores in New York, Chicago or Los Angeles. These stores advertise regularly in the photo magazines, and two good ones to check are *Modern Photography* and *Popular Photography*. All the discounts percentages I cited here are general rules and may vary. If you want to check out a firm that you plan to purchase from, consult with the Better Business Bureau in that city to check their track record, or meet some other more advanced photographers through the local stores and ask their opinion of the firm in question. Chances are these more experienced photographers have some idea as to the firm's reliability, based on experience or hearsay.

2. 35MM SINGLE LENS REFLEX CAMERAS (SLRs). These "system cameras" are the queens of the modern camera makers art and, with more money tied up in them than I like to count up, I must admit that here is where my heart lies. The better-grade SLRs actually are the centerpieces of complete systems of lenses, accessories and special-purpose attachments that allow the photographer to do about anything that his mind and pocketbook can conjure up.

This is the type of camera that has almost completely superseded all others for most professional-level photographers who do substantial amounts of work out of the studio and on their

hind legs. Photojournalists and fashion and advertising pho-
togs who must go on location to shoot pictures, and — of course
— we outdoor photographers, all regard this camera as the
primary right arm, with all others being somewhat secondary
or in backup roles.

Want to take pictures of running deer, flying birds, scamper-
ing rabbits? Want to show the whole room or scene? Want to
get lovely wildlife shots requiring a telephoto lens that can
reach out and capture the animals on film? Want to hook a
motor onto your camera so that you can shoot a whole series of
pictures at the rate of four or five per second to best stop the action on a running animal or a flushing covey of quail? Want to
take pictures through a microscope or automatically from an
unmanned blind? Then the SLR is the camera for you. It will
do all these things and more, if you spend the money for one of
the better grade models that is part of a broad-based "system."

All of these special-purpose capabilities cost money though,
in times when ferociously high prices are the rule of the day.
But, if you want pictures of unrivaled clarity, beauty and
drama, these are the cameras that enable you, with some goodly
portions of sweat and imagination, to take them.

There are some moderately expensive, but still good quality,
SLRs in the $200 to $250 range that more than meet all of my
basic criteria. That price gets you the camera and the basic 50
or 55mm lens that sees approximately as your eyes see. However, it really doesn't make much sense to go into 35mm SLR
system photography unless you plan to avail yourself of the
benefits of the system by purchasing additional, interchangeable lenses. This is the biggest single feature of these system
cameras.

Two additional lenses, a wide-angle and a moderate telephoto, might well be your first purchases toward this end. In
decent quality glass these could well run you $100 to $200 each
and top-level professional quality lenses could be twice that expensive. So, to get into business with a 35mm SLR and a couple
of additional lenses could easily total to an initial nut of $400 to
$500. That's considerably more than $80 to $120 for the
rangefinder or top grade cartridge cameras, or the $120 to
$150 for the Polaroid SX-70. Only you can decide if the extra
features are worth the extra cost.

3. CARTRIDGE-LOADING CAMERAS. These are small, highly-
engineered cameras, such as Kodak Instamatic, that have
evolved from rather simple cameras to those which, at the top
of the line anyway, take very good pictures indeed. They are

Inexpensive cartridge-loading cameras made by numerous manufacturers take satisfactory pictures when properly used. Though the more expensive models offer a regular and a short telephoto lens, most offer only the regular lens. This limitation is sorely felt when there's need to reach out to photograph distant animals or get a wide angle of view, such as when inside a tent.

Miniature cartridge-loading cameras use film in small, rectangular format. They are ultra-lightweight and fit easily into a shirt pocket.

easy to use, and as long as you don't want to take anything but candids and up-close people pictures, they do a fine job. The cheaper models run from about $20 to $50, but seldom do these offer adequate lens speed or general picture-taking flexibility. The best models will run over $100.

The cartridge film load is a convenience feature of interest to some people. However, the 35mm cassettes used with other types of cameras are so easy to load that there isn't much difference. On the bad side, the lenses and shutter speeds are often slower than I recommend, and they don't have the range that they should. I don't feel that these cameras have quite the flexibility of the comparably priced 35mm rangefinder, but some photographers would probably disagree.

Right now there are two different film formats, or sizes, available for cartridge cameras. The larger and older is the 126 size, which has a format that is roughly an inch square. The new pocket cameras feature size 110 film, which has a rectangular format with only one-fourth the area of the 126 size.

But even though the 110 has a far smaller format than the 126, and though smaller films generally will not blow-up as sharply either in print enlargements or on the projection screen, I would choose the 110 myself for three reasons.

• The 110 film's rectangular format allows you to make shots in either vertical or horizontal frames and thus compose more thoughtful and pleasing pictures.

• Kodak has done wonders with 110 film, which makes high quality pictures, indeed, for its small size.

• In photography in general and in this cartridge-loading end in particular, when Kodak sneezes, the other camera and film makers catch cold. Kodak brought out the 110 size fairly recently. And huge budgets for promotion and product-development seem to be going that way. So that's the team I'd want to be on. And with Kodak continually upgrading the 110, I believe the 126 size could be eclipsed and eventually discontinued.

4. POLAROID. I do not favor the older, wet technology Polaroids for general outdoor use. They're heavy, bulky, easy to damage. You can't snap pictures quickly due to having to stop and "dress" each one. The wet dressing is sloppy, hard to apply in the cold, and it collects grit and grime with marvelous efficiency.

The film is expensive, and careless people litter the outdoors with the discarded outer papers. There is no negative to make copies or enlargements from easily, and the camera is not usable for fast-action shots. Worst of all, slide or transparency film is not available.

The dry technology Polaroid SX-70 is a fantastic design and production accomplishment for both Dr. Land and American technology. The camera is small, compact and offers reflex viewing (you see what you photograph). However, it's still rather expensive, especially the film, which, at about a buck a shot when you use the flash bar, is almost prohibitive. There still is no slide film available for this camera either. This type of camera may well be the way of the future, but at the current time and for the foreseeable future, I'll stick to the 35mm's for all-round outdoor use.

Although my own notions of which camera types are better for general outdoor use are obvious in the preceding pages, now I'll venture right out on that shaky limb with specific opinions. If there is any one group of people who can argue as long and strong over hardware as gun nuts and hunters, it's photographers. With many a photographer, contradicting his cherished opinions on photography and cameras is something akin to telling him his wife is running around on him and expecting him to thank you!

Thus, I'm identifying the following as just that—opinions, not holy writ. Also, they are honest, independent judgments I've formed by using all the camera types mentioned and by shooting a fair amount of pictures. (One memorable day I shot 55 rolls of 36-exposure film, or 1980 pictures, probably impossible to do without a motor drive.)

If you have a fair amount of experience in photography or if you are pretty sure you'll be serious about it, I'd recommend that you try the 35mm SLR system approach. If you don't have much experience picture-taking and money is a significant factor, you could start with the 35mm rangefinder with the possibility in mind of trading up to the SLR later if your interest in photography continues to grow. Yes, the cartridge-loading types, such as the Kodak Instamatics, would also be a good way to start, but I prefer the rangefinder route. The rangefinder is more similar to the SLR in functioning. Thus, familiarity with it would be better training for the more advanced camera. Also, since it uses the same 35mm film, it would be a better back-up camera later. That film, due to its availability and variety is also a big plus for the 35mm rangefinder over the cartridge-loading type.

The Polaroid SX-70 is a marvelous camera but, even though the new dry-technology model brings it far closer to my outdoor requirements, I still wouldn't choose it at this time. I might, possibly later when and if slide film comes available and the price of the film comes down considerably.

Whichever camera you choose, use it! Frequent use makes the whole process become easy and automatic. The easier it is to take pictures, the more you take. And the more you take, the more you enhance your hunting adventures with treasured photos that can be viewed again and again to help you or your family and friends recall moments of high drama and excitement.

Films

23

Choosing the right films for different situations is often the most confusing single task for the beginning photographer.

Film is to the camera what ammunition is to the rifle. Shoot a grizzly bear with your trusty .270 loaded with a lightly constructed 100-grain woodchuck pill and you're going to have one very mad, un-killed bruin on your hands. Shoot a chuck with the same gun and a stoutly constructed 150-grain pellet and you will only succeed in ventilating the old fellow with a clean hole exactly .277 of an inch in diameter. And he'll probably get away to die in his den. Switch these .270 rounds around in the chuck and grizzly situations, and you're in business.

Shoot a picture in black-and-white that calls for color and you lose the brilliance and beauty that only color can fully realize. Shoot a picture in color that calls for black-and-white and at best you end up with a bad color picture rather than a good black-and-white shot. And at worst, you may lose the picture entirely. Shoot color prints when you should be shooting slides, and you spend extra dough plus you lose the slide's sizzling brilliance and luminosity that no print, however correctly exposed and developed, can ever hope to achieve.

Color vs. Black-and-White

Like about everything else from caviar to crab apples, the choice between color and black-and-white should depend on many factors. If it's a bright day, color is generally better for outdoor shots. This is especially true if there are colorful objects in the pictures such as orange tents, blue backpack rigs, red canoes, bright clothes, colorful birds or animals. If you have a bright blue sky filled to overflowing with fleecy white clouds, it's a mortal sin not to shoot color and use a low angle in order to cleverly get that big beautiful sky backing up and brightening up the object that you're photographing. Color brings an extra beauty and definition to pictures that black-and-white can't match.

So, throw out all the black-and-white film, right? Dead wrong! Black-and-white most definitely has its uses, and they are not all limited to the substitute-by-necessity-for-color category either. For one thing, if it's a cold, dank day — a monochromatic, no-color day — then shoot black-and-white to convey the proper mood and atmosphere. Black-and-white pictures, at their best, can convey a certain stark beauty and intensity that color can't match.

Black and white is the film for low-light situations. But it is possible to "push" Ektachrome color film by presetting the camera's ASA dial so the entire role receives a uniformly lighter exposure than it would with normal settings. Then the film must be specially processed. But technically this doesn't yield true color because, to oversimplify, color is a product of reflected light. No light, no color. And color film can't handle contrast with the definition of good black-and-white. So why shoot a broken-legged color shot that just ends up being colorless color, washed out and muddy looking, when you could get a nice, snappy black-and-white print?

Even when you do have ample light, color can cost you a priceless picture in some situations. This is because color has less latitude than black-and-white. That means that you must expose it much more accurately, and, even if you do, if you shoot into a contrasty-enough situation (say, a ruffed grouse sitting on white snow under a dark bush), your light meter will probably be "fooled" enough so that even if you do your part and adjust the camera properly for the meter reading, the color film won't handle the mis-metered situation properly. Chances are that black-and-white would have.

Good old black-and-white is your workhorse film for those tough situations in which you want to be *sure*. Far more forgiving of bad exposure setting on the photog's part and in tough lighting conditions in general, black-and-white is your safest bet.

What to do? Carry both films afield. Take a moment before you shoot to decide which type of film you want to use or, if it's a special picture that lends itself to such treatment, shoot it both ways to be sure. Shoot a lot of both so you can "learn" the two types and what they can and can't do for you. This learning process comes very quickly.

I am going to limit most of my remarks to 35mm film for several reasons. As a serious trophy hunter, you are probably shooting that format camera, or else you will be in the future. Also, since 35mm film is the broadest category imaginable, most of my comments will also apply to other film formats.

Exposures Per Roll

Most films come in long or short roll options. With 35mm film the option is between the 20 exposure roll and the 36 exposure type. As a professional I wouldn't think of using anything but the longer 36 exposure roll. It saves me time because I'm reloading less and I'm less likely to miss a critical shot due to being out of film at the wrong time.

But it also saves me money to shoot the long roll. So, even if I were an amateur, I wouldn't use the shorter one. Here are some figures I recently gathered from a retail camera store near my home in Pennsylvania.

Color prints in 3½×5-inch size — this is for everything, film, developing and final-prints returned to me.

- 36 exposure roll — 32.3¢ per picture
- 20 exposure roll — 36.7¢ per picture

That may not sound like much, but it amounts to a savings of about 12 percent on processing costs that aren't exactly cheap to begin with. Over the course of a year that margin, for the very same pictures in each case, can be substantial.

On color slides, the difference in cost per shot between short and long rolls is even greater! This also includes film, developing and final slides.

- 36 exposure roll — 18.6¢ per slide
- 20 exposure roll — 22.0¢ per slide

That amounts to over 15 percent difference, slide for slide. Mere pennies on the surface but, again, they add up.

The above prices can vary all over the lot. At some discount stores and other outlets, they might be cheaper. By the time you read this, they might be more expensive. The point is, all of the above prices were taken at the same store at the same time and the *relationship* of the prices — small roll to long roll — will remain pretty constant, no matter what the circumstances.

Color Slides Vs. Prints

By now you know that I prefer the slides for many reasons. As a professional photographer, I know that magazines want slides for color reproduction. And maybe something for you to remember: You might someday sell some of your pictures. I started as an amateur and so did all other professionals. No one is born a pro.

But, I would shoot slides (and did), even if I weren't a professional — for two reasons: beauty and cost. Slides are just prettier than prints. It's inherent in the different physical properties of the two modes.

Here's how the two stack up on the cost side of the ledger.

- 36 exposure slide roll, fully processed...................... 18.6¢
- 36 exposure print roll, fully processed...................... 32.3¢

That's a whopping 73 percent difference in cost! Assuming that you shoot a roll each month for all occasions, you would save $59.18 per year.

As a trophy hunter, you're likely to shoot twice or three times that much film, maybe taking 10 to 20 rolls of it on a single 2-week trip. So you could save the equivalent of a $200-plus camera in a year or two. That's food for contemplation.

Of course everyone needs some prints to give away or to show to friends and neighbors. These can easily be pulled from slides. The cost is slightly more for each print than if prints had been originally shot but you are only pulling those expensive prints on the edited shots that you know you want printed, not on every shot taken. You can afford to pay a few more cents per picture to pull 10 or 15 prints rather than making prints for 200 or 300 pictures that you shot during the entire trip.

Frankly, the beauty of the slides is as important to me as the savings. Shoot some pictures of both types, especially of the more colorful outdoor scenes and see if you don't agree. The slides can be viewed either by inexpensive hand viewer or by various sorts of projectors.

Brands of Film

This is a tough one. Almost all the major brands are top quality and very close to each other in quality nowadays. Kodak film and processing is somewhat more expensive than the others in this "Snow White and Seven Dwarfs Industry." However, it is readily available and it is the standard against which all others are judged. Whichever color slide film that I do use, I always buy the mailer from that brand and have them process it rather than letting the local or drugstore outlet do it. It costs a little more, but the results are more consistent and are well worth the extra cost.

Types of Slide Film

For purposes of discussion and since it's in the widest usage the world over, I'll use Kodak film to describe the different types available. If you want to use another brand, all you need to do is ask for the equivalent of the Kodak film that I describe.

Kodak makes a number of outdoor slide films. They vary in "speed," with the slower film requiring more light but yielding better results as far as being less grainy and affording brighter, smoother color tints. The faster the film, the less light you need to drive it and the faster action you can stop without blur — but the grainier it will be. Photography, as you have no doubt learned by now, is mainly a series of balancing acts requiring that you try to match the right camera, lens, shutter speed and film speed to get the overall results you're trying to achieve.

Let's talk about the major outdoor films, and some new developments among them, one at a time.

Kodachrome 25 (KM). This is the slowest basic outdoor slide film that Kodak markets, and it has only recently replaced the famed Kodachrome II. The latter was the standard by which all films were judged. Grain, smoothness, color rendition were magnificent. Although KM-25 has only been out a short time as this is written and Kodak will no doubt continue to perfect it, there is some doubt as to how much of an improvement it is over the older Kodachrome. In fact, initial lots of the film did not seem to handle whites and lighter tones as well as K-II, but Kodak has moved to correct that. KM-25 is a fine film that gives excellent results but some (myself among them) wonder if the new KR-64, also released onto the market in mid-1974, won't do everything that KM-25 will and then some.

Kodachrome 64 (KR). This is a superb new film that is the delight of every outdoor photographer using telephoto lenses which require more light and faster films than standard length lenses. The American Standards Association (ASA) rating of 64 rather than 25 for the slower film we just discussed means that this film is faster and needs less than half as much light. It replaces the old Kodachrome-X which, though I shot enough of it to send more than one kid to college, was not close to the old Kodachrome II in quality. The KR-64 is about as good as KII or KM-25 in grain and color rendition, and it requires far less light. It is a dream come true for outdoor photographers or those using telephoto or slower lenses of any type. This is by far my favorite or lead film, whether I'm shooting candids for myself or pictures for publication.

Ektachrome X (EX). This fine old standard has been with us for some years now. Although it used to be debatable as to which was "better," the old Kodachrome-X or Ektachrome-X since both were rated at ASA 64, I usually opted for the KX preferring its somewhat warmer skin tones and colors to the cooler, bluer colors of EX. A good case could be made for either one over the other, depending upon what you were using the film for and your own individual preferences. Many professionals in the outdoor field swear by this fine film.

However, I feel that the new KR-64 is so manifestly superior to both KX and EX (though some pros may disagree with me) that I could not recommend EX for shooting at ASA 64.

High Speed Ektachrome (EH). This marvelous film can be rated at either ASA 160 or ASA 400. The basic film is at 160 (requiring less than half the light of an ASA 64 film). But by the simple expedient of buying a special Kodak film mailer (the ESP-1 at about $1.25 to $1.50 each) and using it in *addition* to the regular mailer, you can set your camera on a speed of 400 and require less than half the light as at 160.

This film has its limitations. I shoot it when needed in low-light situations requiring a fast shutter speed and color. But you pay a price for this. Put your slide under an 8x glass, or project it, and you'll definitely see that it's grainier.

It seems to me that the results from this film are considerably less consistent than from the two "mediums" at ASA 64. At times I am as happy with my color fidelity (at 160 not at 400) as I am with EX colors. At other times I'm not. Of all the really fast color films on the market that I am familiar with, High Speed EK (EH) is by far the best.

Which color slide film should you use? In a magazine article I once recommended KII and a few rolls of High Speed EK in reserve for special situations. Now I would recommend KR-64 with a few rolls of EH in reserve. Shoot some film of all types around the house and see which you like best. Don't take my word for it. Your "eye" may see things differently than mine. On things like color preferences people differ. Shoot some EH at both 160 and 400 to check the difference. Then carry as few different films as possible. This will help avoid mix-ups which cost you pictures due to incorrect exposure settings. And be sure that all film is clearly labeled as to type and speed.

This is a "conversion" from a 35mm color slide to a b&w print. Because many publications use both color slides and b&w prints, and because slides can be converted this well, many outdoors photojournalists shoot slides almost exclusively. Thus, they can provide editors the color and b&w option while using only one camera and one film. B&w conversions cost over twice as much as prints from b&w film, and they lack some of the tonal gradations that well-exposed b&w film would produce. But the average reader seldom notices this subtle loss of quality in the published photo.

Here even the fastest color film would have been too slow without flash or strobe lighting. But such artificial light would have left the background too dark and the tent interior too bright. Fast black-and-white film allowed the author to take this shot in available light at dusk, while inside the tent the hunter needed a flashlight to help him locate his gear.

A few final words on color slide film. The suffix "chrome," as in Kodachrome, always means a slide film. Whereas the suffix "color," as in Kodacolor, always denotes print film. Slide film usually comes in both indoor and outdoor types. You should always use the outdoor type. Slide film is correctly color balanced for natural light or sunlight and can readily be used indoors with either an electronic strobe light or the proper flashbulbs.

Black-and-White Print Film

When shooting black-and-white film, always shoot prints because black-and-white slides are really rather limited, special purpose items that don't make much sense for us and our purposes. Again, I'll discuss Kodak films, and you can ask for equivalents in other brands when you buy.

Kodak makes three basic 35mm black-and-white films, just as they make "slow," "medium" and "fast" films for 35mm color slides. The three are Panatomic-X (the "slow" film rated at ASA 32); Plus-X (the "medium" rated at ASA 125) and the Tri-X (the "fast" film rated at ASA 400). All have their uses and purposes, but Tri-X is such a great, fast and "forgiving" film with good grain that most outdoor pros, let alone amateurs, limit their black-and-white shooting to it. Probably 95 percent of my black-and-white work is done with this fine film, and I suggest that you do 100 percent of your black-and-white work with it.

Color Print Film

As mentioned earlier, I wouldn't and don't, use any. However, if you must go this way, the new Kodacolor II (ASA 80) is a fine film.

Film Processors

For Color. For color films you have three basic routes to go:

1. Kodak labs (or other "mainframe" film maker labs)
2. Specialty labs doing high volume work
3. Local or "drugstore" processing

The three options are listed above in roughly the descending cost versions. To me, whether I were an amateur or pro, it would be worth the extra money to have the film maker (Kodak or otherwise) process their own color film with its more exacting requirements, as compared to black-and-white.

The mainframe lab route generally insures the most consistent results, though there certainly are good volume labs doing color-only work, as advertised in the leading photo magazines, and decent local processors. Whether you want to go the cheaper routes is something that you should check out and determine for yourself. If you do have a roll of color slides with some special pictures on it, I urge you to send it to the lab of its maker.

In many low-light situations, fast black-and-white film can record details without the need for bothersome electronic flash. Shooting from available light here, the author captured the mood and avoided unwanted flash reflections.

For Black-and-White. For b&w there are also three routes:

1. Home developing
2. Custom labs
3. Local drugstore processing

Although home developing is a fascinating hobby in its own right, I'll assume you're not into it for our purposes here. On black-and-white processing, "custom" labs are really that. They do fine, expensive processing on a professional quality level. This isn't necessary for most people.

Since black-and-white *is* so much more tolerant and forgiving than color film, good drugstore processing will suffice. I'd suggest that you first shoot some black-and-white film in the outdoors and then test the local drugstore for results. A tip: You can often have a single 8 x 10-inch "contact print" pulled showing all 36 pictures on the roll at actual negative size (1 x 1½-inches for 35 mm) and then select those pictures that you want to have printed. Depending upon what your processor charges and how many prints you might want to have pulled and at what size, this could be cheaper than just having the whole roll automatically printed up in "wallet size" prints. It's something to check out anyway. You could often save money by pulling the one 8 x 10-inch print and then printing the three or four prints you want rather than having all 36 shots printed a full size to begin with.

The main thing with film is the same as with cameras. Use it! If you don't shoot a picture you won't have it. Nor will you learn, from your mistakes, as I still do every time I go out. That's what keeps this fascinating adjunct to our basic sport of trophy hunting so fascinating!

How to Take Better Pictures

24

Now that we've talked cameras and film, let's put them together and take some pictures. The difference between good pictures and bad pictures is usually surprisingly slight. And the simple guidelines here should help you get good pictures from about any situation you may encounter on hunting trips.

1. Think pictures! This is the base on which all the other steps are built. Don't let good pictures just be after-thoughts — thoughts that come so long *after*, that you miss the shots entirely. *Think pictures!* Before you leave on the hunt, make sure you take plenty of film and a few flashbulbs or flash-cubes to handle those inside the lodge or tent scenes that help round out your photo coverage. Take along a few of the inex-pensive heavy-duty plastic bags you can buy at any supermarket so you have a waterproof protector for your camera in damp or rainy weather. You don't want to have to choose between leav-ing your camera in camp all day where you can't use it and perhaps ruining it by taking it with you.

Make some informal lists of the various shots you want to take to properly show the whole trip. Do this before you leave. (More on this a little later.) Let the people in camp know that you plan to take some pictures and that you may be asking their help along the way. Most folks are happy to oblige. Provide some safe place to keep your exposed film after you shoot it. The worst thing of all is to take some irreplaceable pictures and then lose them or have them damaged by water. I keep mine in a bright crimson canvas bag with a drawstring top (hard to lose that! and roll it in my mattress or sleeping bag when I'm not around.

2. Avoid posed pictures. Like poison! Be sneaky. Follow folks around and catch them doing things, not posing "at" doing things. Catch them in natural, relaxed poses when they are "loose" and their actions are authentic. When you go to pose people, nine out of ten will get stiff and adopt unnatural movements and facial expressions. The natural picture is by far the best one.

3. Achieve a candid look in those necessarily posed pictures. Okay, there are times when you must pose a picture to recreate a certain scene or to insure that you don't miss a particular facet of the trip in your pictorial coverage. Even here, there are things you can do to "loosen up" the pictures. Don't let the person or persons look directly at you or the camera. Even though they know they're "on candid camera," you'll usually get a good picture if you have them looking at each other and talking, indulging in some horseplay or doing one of the myriad "bits of business" that are part of any good hunting trip—such as lighting a fire, cleaning a gun, packing a duffle bag, or sharpening a knife. When your subject is occupied and not sure exactly when the camera is going off, he begins to loosen up and "natural" up. The minute he's looking directly into that camera, he begins to stiffen up again.

Even if the hunter is solo and there's not much for him to do but look in your general direction, at least have him look over your shoulder and never directly at you or the camera. I have even been known to make an occasional crack bordering on the lewd in order to "crack up" the subject and get him laughing and relaxed before snapping the shutter.

4. Feature people in your pictures. People are ultimately the most interesting pictorial subjects. Yep, strange to say, but even the most spectacular scenics soon pale to boredom if completely empty.

Use people to show what's happening, to give perspective to the "long" scenic, to give scale to the camp shot or to keep your shots just plain interesting. The more colorful and outlandish the peoples' garb, the better. The more animated and excited their positions and expressions, the better.

Never have your subjects looking out of a picture, they should always be facing into it. Don't have too many people in a picture, it just confuses things. Generally include no more than three or four at most—one or two are usually better. If several people are in the picture, it's usually better to have one person

If you always keep a camera ready, you'll be able to capture unposed scenes like this one in which the hunter, at right, and the camp staff relive the recent stalk and taking of the moose trophy shown.

in the foreground rather than have all of them about the same size and "lost" in the background. Be careful that you don't take pictures with trees, telephone poles or similar oddments growing out of the tops of peoples' heads.

Hunters use all sorts of fascinating gear and paraphernalia. Take full advantage of it in your people shots. Show folks with hunting knives, backpack rigs, canoes, scope-sighted rifles, red shirts and outsized woodsman's suspenders. No use presenting them as though they're attending the local Rotary meeting!

5. Use interesting and offbeat camera angles. To capture interest don't just stand up on your hind legs and snap every picture from the normal, anticipated eye-level height. That's the "look" and the perspective everyone expects to see and it isn't as fresh and interesting as some other angles.

Lie down or kneel down to look up into some scenes. This also lets you put some of that gorgeous blue sky and those fleecy white clouds into your pictures. Nothing is so beautiful as a nice blue sky, and the general lower angle heightens and dramatizes practically any scene.

This obviously posed photo may not win any photo awards. But if you're in such a shot, it's sure to make a hit with family and friends.

Or climb a tree, a fence or a slight hill and look down into a scene to photograph it. It only takes a few added feet to change the look of a picture and give it an entirely different point of view. If you're using the 35mm rectangular picture format, take some verticals as well as the more common horizontals. Your 35mm film is half again as long as it is high. So when you want to emphasize a "high" shot with tall trees or a mountain peak behind a hunter, tilt the camera around and get the extra sky and elevation into the shot. This definitely adds drama and excitement to certain scenes. It's a shame that most hunters don't take more of these verticals.

6. Feature yourself in many pictures. If I had to pick the single most frequent mistake made by hunter-photographers, this would undoubtedly be it. They just don't get enough pictures of themselves. There are a variety of reasons for this. Both ways of getting yourself in your pictures are awkward and clumsy. You either have to set up the camera and then ask someone else who doesn't understand how to use it to snap your picture. Or else you have to use the self-timer, if your camera is blessed with one.

Another reason that many hunters don't get the pictures of themselves that they should is that they're afraid others will think them a bit conceited or self-centered. Nonsense! Your family and friends are most interested in seeing you in pictures. They know you, and your being in the shots brings home the drama and the interest far better than pictures of all sorts of anonymous characters. They're interested in seeing *you* in those pictures. And, let's face it, so are you. If that makes you "conceited," well you're not any more or less so than the rest of us. These pictures will mean far more to you and your family as the years go by if you're in them, participating in the hunt and all its aspects to the fullest! Show your buddy how to work the camera and then get yourself into those pictures.

7. Take plenty of film and use it. Another frequent mistake that most hunters make is that they simply don't shoot enough pictures. On a big trip, one shouldn't be stingy with film. Shoot those important pictures, especially the trophy shots, from different distances and angles to insure getting good ones. Take duplicates of major shots so that you have "insurance" against a bad exposure by varying your exposure readings to "bracket" the shot. Remember, the picture you don't take is the one lost to you forever!

8. Shoot from long, medium, and short ranges. Take a tip from the Hollywood cinematographers. When they film major movie scenes, they shoot them simultaneously with a number of different cameras at close, medium and long range. This gives them the flexibility to later edit the scene from maximum effectiveness and impact. You can do somewhat the same thing. On those important "basic" shots around camp, don't shoot the same picture 100 times and think you have 100 different pictures. You don't. You have 100 replicas of the first shot. And while it's a good idea to repeat shots at times, enough is enough.

Rather, shoot these basic shots from different distances to get them long, medium and short. And shoot them from different angles and elevations, as we've already discussed. Then later you have a good selection from which to edit out the very best group of slides or prints.

9. Have a "reason" for each picture. All of us know better than to flock-shoot a gaggle of geese or a rising covey of quail or a group of running trophy animals. To do so either means a total miss or, worse yet, wounding the wrong animal. Don't "flock-shoot" your pictures. Know what you are photographing and why. Each picture should have a focal point or center of interest.

Often this is someone doing something such as skinning out a head, glassing for game, sighting-in a rifle or sharpening a hunting knife. But it can also be inanimate things, such as meat cooking over an open fire, the "frame" furnished by the door-way in a tent or cabin, or just a prominent landmark such as a beautifully gnarled old tree.

When you know what your focal point or "reason" for a picture is, then you should roughly, but never exactly, center it in your viewfinder. Whenever you just grab the camera and point it out into space because of the feeling that "it's time to take a picture," you'll practically always come up with a disjointed picture that has no interest because it has no "reason."

10. Improve on the typical trophy shot. These are so important and yet so easy to do badly. Remember, many of your nonhunting friends will see these pictures. And to them, the shots may look unsightly and attest to your cruelty, even though to you they seem just fine. Have some regard for their sensibilities, and be sure that you aren't assisting in the birth of another anti-hunter. Those persons, incidentally, could even be your wife and children, though they might not mention those feelings to you. Just a bit of extra care will help you get better trophy shots — ones that you, and all those around you, will enjoy viewing.

The first thing to do is to be sure to take your pictures rather quickly after the kill, before the animal has a chance to stiffen up and get that "dead" look that no one, not even hunters, find particularly attractive. I usually smooth the hair or fur back on the animal if it has been disturbed, brushing all dirt and blood off while I'm at it. If an exit hole or two have left gaping wounds, then it's usually better to photograph the other side of the animal, from another angle that doesn't show the wounds. Or as a last resort, pile up a rock or two in front or lay the gun or saddlebags or something else over wounds to obscure them.

Note the animal's mouth and tongue. Those shots in which the mouth gapes open and the tongue hangs crazily out aren't too enticing. Close the mouth and either hold it shut or prop the animal's head so that it will stay shut. The eyes should be open, and you should not obscure too much of the horns or

It's sometimes a mistake to comply with the old box-camera edict that the sun be at the photographer's back. In this instance the low sun throws the photographer's shadow into the picture and forces the subject to squint markedly. Subtler trophy pictures can be made with the hunter either examining or measuring the trophy.

antlers by holding them with your hands or otherwise covering them up. You're a trophy hunter and a good view of those horns or antlers is one of the prime ingredients of a good trophy picture.

I usually photograph the animal a few times where it falls, just for the record, so to speak. Then, if I can move it, I do so I can take better pictures. Often by moving the animal you can greatly improve the background so that the snow-clad peak or the small mountain lake, shimmering like a spray of jewels, shows and adds much to the backdrop.

Or, perhaps by moving the animal you can get it out of the shadows and into better light where the picture will be brighter and clearer. Possibly you can get it over near a weathered old stump or piece of driftwood or some other appropriate, but not unduly competitive, "piece" for foreground interest.

When you are taking the trophy pictures, as in other types of shots, get the long, medium and short shots at differing elevations and angles. Don't worry about taking too many shots. This is what you came for. You can't overdo the photographic coverage of it! If it's a bright, clear day, try to get some shots from a low angle to include the blue sky. Be sure you have your gun in some of the pictures. With your rifle in hand, pose yourself differently ways: kneeling beside the animal, sitting behind it, standing, crouching, and any other reasonable postures depending upon the size of the animal and how he lies. In some pictures you may want to lean the rifle against the animal. Be looking at the animal in many of the pictures, rather than looking toward —never *at*— the photographer in all of them.

If a buddy or a guide was with you on the hunt, by all means get some pictures of you with him, shaking hands, congratulating each other and pounding each other on the back. This is usually a joyful moment, capture it to the fullest.

If you are wearing a cap or hat, especially a wide-brimmed western-type hat as is often the case, be sure to take some pictures with it on and some with it off. In the right shot, the big hat adds an extra note of color and realism. On the other hand it often casts shadows, sometimes hardly noticeable in the excitement of picture taking, especially if you're relying on the self-timer. And these shadows can almost totally obscure your face. The result may be that you end up with a rather bland picture of "someone"—not particularly you—and the animal.

Though it is common practice to take shots of the hunter "riding" or "bulldogging" or otherwise manhandling his trophy, I don't much like them. This is a matter of personal taste, but it can so easily smack of disrespect for the animal that it can ruin the priceless atmosphere of that special moment when you have, at last, taken your treasured trophy after a long, hard and fair chase. I believe that this type of shot also tends to offend many of the nonhunters who may see it, though they might not mention it to you directly.

If there is a large puddle of blood that has collected on the ground or is staining the snow, then it is a good idea to move the animal to a cleaner spot. The main idea here is to use just a bit of forethought in order to present a vibrant and lifelike looking trophy and the proud and excited hunter (you) to best advantage.

11. Follow a scenario. This goes back to what I said earlier in this chapter about planning, in advance, to get those better pictures. Sit down on some evening when you have nothing to do and dope out the different elements of your hunt. Break them into any set of categories that you want to. You could use such general headings as going to camp, camp scenes, field scenes, trophy shots, returning home from camp. Or, you could break them down far finer, depending upon how long and complex the trip will be and how many pictures you want. Then, under each category, list all the shots that you can think of. This checklist or "scenario" approach helps you to know how much film to take. It also insures that you get all the key shots and that

Be sure to take either an electronic strobe or a flash attachment on your trips. This allows valuable indoor shots, such as this one of the cook.

you return with a more *balanced* array of pictures. (Most of us seem to shoot pictures in rashes, rather than all throughout a trip. Thus, on a ten-day trip, we might only shoot pictures on the first and last days and one day in between. This happens because the hunter shoots only when it's convenient or when he "remembers to." What a shame! Think of all the good times and memorable events that he'll miss by doing it that way.)

A final word. Good pictures, like anything else of value, don't come easy. A bit of extra mental and physical effort is needed. You can't expect good pictures just to happen — not anymore than you'd expect to just stumble onto a big trophy without any prior thought to its food, cover, or water or to how it might be moving.

Some hunters do rely on sheer luck, but I wouldn't. Ditto on the good picture. That's not to say that taking pictures should become enormous drudgery that interferes with the basic hunt itself. Not so. Good planning and forethought reduces much of the "work" of getting good pictures. All you then need to do is keep your camera and film handy, stay alert to good photo opportunities and, when they come, be prepared to expend just a tad of extra energy to get the distinctive elevation or angle.

Extra effort isn't really much of a price to pay to insure that you get exciting, "telling" photos that you and your family will treasure more and more as the years go by. The alternative is ho-hums that make you mumble sheepishly, "Well, you had to *be* there."

Serious Wildlife Photography

25

It is a normal pattern for the general meat hunter and sport hunter to evolve to be a more selective and competent trophy hunter, and then to be a trophy hunter who does as much work with a camera as with a gun. The reasons for this progression are many.

After a man has killed a head or two of a particular species, he generally wants to devote himself to securing better and better heads of that species rather than merely duplicating his achievement. As he becomes a better hunter he rises to the challenge of securing the older heads of game that have lived long enough to grow their outsize antlers and horns by being cannier than their brothers.

Also, naturally, the larger heads with their more sweeping antlers or more massive horns make far more attractive trophies. But, as a hunter becomes more selective in the size of the quarry, that also means that he is rejecting more killing opportunities. Thus, the result is that he picks up the camera to get some good out of these opportunities that often involve long stalks and difficult climbs.

Usually, by this stage of his evolution, the trophy hunter is a reasonably accomplished still photographer in the sense that he knows how to thoroughly photograph a trip without leaving out key elements. And he often knows how to compose and shutter more interesting and provocative camp and in-field candids showing himself and all the other people on the trip doing all the things that are part of any major big-game hunt.

But, when our hunter steps into the new dimension of serious wildlife photography, which essentially means telephoto photography, he is in for some surprises and often some rude shocks. From reading the general outdoor press, it is all

Serious wildlife photography often calls for a back and legs that are a least equal to one's technical knowledge and creative ability. Here photographers, each packing over 100 lbs., are escorted by a gun toting guide through muddy tidal flats and inlets of the Alaska Peninsula.

too easy to get the impression that a 135mm lens is a "long" lens and that a 200mm lens can accomplish long-distance miracles. Alas, such is not the case my friends. (Throughout this chapter, unless I indicate differently, I'll be talking about 35mm cameras with interchangeable lenses.)

Our budding wildlife photographer's first experience with this new aspect of his sport often begins when he has stalked to within easy gun-shooting range of a potential trophy but then rejects taking it and decides to take a picture instead. He views the quarry through his camera, usually equipped with a 135mm or 200mm lens, and is astonished at how far away the animal *still* appears in the viewfinder. He decides to work closer. Stealthily he moves in closer and closer, with the tension mounting geometrically as he approaches. He stops several times to view the animal through his camera, but each time he is dissatisfied, so he continues to move in. Finally, at less than 50 yards, which is practically like staring down the tonsils of the animal in normal gun-shooting terms, he's satisfied. He cranks off the rest of the film roll then in his camera — maybe 6 or 8 shots — and stops when it runs out, well satisfied with his efforts.

When color slides return from the film processor, the photographer excitedly unwraps them and holds them up to the light for a quick informal viewing with the naked eye. Nothing. The animal is a mere dot. Oh well, surely he'll come out fine when projected onto the viewing screen in much larger size. Then still another disappointment. The animal is now visible when projected but is still rather small and unclear, and the few poses he took are rather uninteresting. And worse yet, the pictures that seemed to the photographer to offer such extensive coverage, when he carefully clicked them off one by one in the field, now supply only a disappointingly brief and incomplete coverage of the interesting event.

This first, typically disappointing exposure to wildlife photography has driven home a number of useful lessons to our neophyte. Here are some of them:

1. Take many pictures! Film is widely available and relatively cheap. Opportunities to photograph beautiful wild animals at close range aren't. It's simply amazing how lengthy a process the actual taking of a roll or two of 36 exposure 35mm film can seem to be during the shooting. Yet when these same pictures are viewed later at home, they seem too few. This is especially so after all the culls are thrown out. For every time that I have regretted taking quite so many pictures of a particular subject, there have been at least twenty or thirty other times that I have (sometimes bitterly!) regretted not taking enough.

There are a number of reasons for this. Many pictures must be thrown away because they are badly exposed (too dark or too light) or because they are fuzzy and unclear due to camera-shake or bad focusing. Then there are a number of other shots that, though they may be technically acceptable, just aren't interesting or exciting because of dull postures or static poses of the animal or animals. A good wild animal portrait should transmit a certain dynamism and excitement and not portray the animal grazing as contentedly as any barnyard animal.

To minimize camera shake, put into practice all the good rifle shooting techniques that you have practiced over the years. Shoot your camera from an informal rest of some sort whenever possible rather than firing it offhand. When using the rest, try to put a bit of soft padding (hat, gloves, scarf, etc.) between the camera and the surface of the rest, especially if the rest is rather hard and unyielding. Good breath control is important, as is s-q-u-e-e-z-i-n-g off the shutter rather than punching or jerking it.

On especially important shots, it's a good idea to bracket the exposure readings on your meter, shooting off one or two shots on the "minus" side and one or two on the "plus" reading as well as centering your light meter needle. This provides extra insurance against badly exposed pictures in case the meter is "fooled" by the light conditions. And any light meter, whether it is a separate unit or is located inside the camera, no matter how well designed and expensively made, will occasionally be fooled in some lighting situations. However, this occurs very seldom when you properly use the best meters.

Some portion of the animal photographic subject, especially on the larger animals, will almost always be partially out of focus in even professionally shot pictures. To insure that you always have the most important area in sharp focus, always focus on the animal's near eye.

The soul of an animal — or human for that matter — resides in the eyes. Most of the time, if you can't see the eye, you shouldn't take the picture. Focus as sharply as possible on the eye so that the head and all facial features are in sharpest focus. (The head is the first part of the animal that the photo viewer's attention is drawn to.)

If at all possible, try to get a highlight in the eye — that is, light glinting off the eye. You need to be rather close to the animal and/or using the longer lenses to do this, but it isn't as difficult as it may sound. Animals are constantly cocking their heads at differing angles and swinging them to and fro. And wild animals must do this while constantly working to scent the changing, eddying wind or to swing their heads around to glance this way and that. A slight change of angle is often all it takes to bring out eye highlight. This highlight is easily visible because most big-game animals have considerably larger eyes than man, and their eyes seem to catch and reflect this light more than the human eye. In color shots, eye highlight adds that all important "snap" of life and animation.

2. Select the Right Equipment. The best all-around type of camera for the vast majority of us is the higher grade 35mm SLR (single lens reflex). This camera features mirrors that allow you to see through the picture-taking lens, rather than through a separate viewfinder. Thus you see exactly what you will photograph.

Your SLR should be one of the so-called "system" cameras, meaning that a wide assortment of lenses, accessories and attachments is available. This way, no matter how sophisticated your camera and photography needs might become in the future, you will never outgrow your initial equipment, and thus you avoid an expensive reinvestment in another brand.

Lens selection for wildlife photography is a thorny subject, much like selecting differing rifle calibers for different species

The motor drive and cordless battery pack mounted under this Nikon F-2 lets you take up to five pictures per second. Shown also is an Intervalometer (remote timer) that fires shots at preset intervals. Similar options are offered by other makers such as Leica, Canon, Minolta, and Pentax.

Large zoom lenses of the best quality produce excellent results but cost upwards of $1,000. This f8 180mm-600mm Zoom-Nikkor by Nikon weighs about 10 lbs.

The Bronica, shown here, and other large professional cameras such as the Hasselblad and Rolleiflex use film with a 2¼x2¼-inch format, which is about four times larger than 35mm. However, color transparency film for them is limited to the Ektachrome type films. Whereas 35mm's can also use the improved, almost grainless Kodachromes and thereby challenge the low-grain and sharpness advantages formerly attributed to 2¼'s.

of game or for differing hunting situations. There are as many different opinions as there are "experts." All I can give to you are personal opinions, based on extensive field experience, as to what works best for me.

Most newly interested wildlife photographers start off with the idea of buying a 135mm lens. The arguments in photography are endless and one of the oldest of the lot is whether a 135mm lens is actually a "portrait" lens for photographing people or a short telephoto. (To determine the power of any lens for a 35mm camera, divide its focal length by the factor 50. Thus, a 135mm lens is slightly more than $2\frac{1}{2}$ power.)

I have never liked the 135mm focal length, finding it too short for just about any kind of serious wildlife work. Rather, I much prefer the 200mm lens for my "short" glass. This "4-power" lens does enable you to photograph some particularly large or tame animals and, its 4-power size does enable you to readily hand-hold it and still get sharp pictures under most circumstances.

The workhorse focal length for myself and most other serious outdoor photographers that I know is the 400mm (8-power) lens. As a telephoto lens becomes longer and more powerful, the problems associated with keeping its quality up and its weight and bulk down multiply geometrically. Generally speaking, it is more than twice as difficult to produce a 400mm lens of top brilliance and sharpness as it is a 200mm lens. Also, the longer the focal length of the lens, the more difficult is its use in the field: The long lens is harder to hold steady, and it demands more light. This restricts its use to certain days or certain periods of the day.

The 400mm seems to be the best all-round compromise of a focal length that is long enough to enable you to photograph animals some distance away and yet short enough so that you can carry it and use it afield without undue bulk and light requirements. Very few lenses over 400mm in focal length will, at any price, deliver professional-quality fidelity.

My basic outfit recommendation for beginning wildlife photography would be to equip yourself with a high-quality 35mm SLR system camera and a 200mm lens (around f3.5 to f4.5) and a 400mm lens (around f5.6 to f6.3). This will get you into business pretty well.

There are other focal length lenses that also play their part. For years I shied away from the 300mm (6-power) lens as being "too long to be short and too short to be long." But in recent years I have found it handy to use when I am on a horsehunt

Good wildlife shots of the "herd" can be taken with the standard lenses, in the 50mm range. Here a 50mm captured large Alaska browns fishing for salmon.

and it is difficult, or next to impossible, to carry a 400mm lens and tripod around with me. The 300mm lens gives me a bit of desperately needed additional power over the 200mm lens, and yet it is relatively compact and easy to carry around. And, with a bit of extra care, it can usually be hand-held under good light conditions, still giving sharp pictures.

There is also a fair number of serious outdoor photographers that have put the 500mm (10-power) cadiotropic or "mirror" lenses to good use. These lenses are of a completely different design than the basic telephoto lens, and they are considerably shorter, lighter and more compact than their telephoto counterpart would be. They offer some advantages and disadvantages when compared to telephotos. So the debate as to whether they are "as good" or "better" is endless. Suffice to say that I own one of best quality (made by Nikon, an f8) and use it occasionally. Its small size is a godsend in certain highly restrictive situations, yet I have never regarded it as a basic, primary lens but always merely as a supplementary special-purpose lens. I do not feel that its quality is quite up to the very best 400mm telephotos, and it is very difficult to hold steady and shoot due to its very compactness. Also, its rather "slow" f8 speed demands twice as much light as the normal f5.6 speed of the quality 400mm telephoto. And this light requirement becomes highly restrictive when you are shooting color film early or late in the day.

No survey of lenses would be complete without mentioning the various zoom types. Zoom lenses, of multiple powers, or focal lengths, are inherently not quite as sharp as fixed focal length lenses. However, in recent years the very best zooms have reached a very high level of quality indeed. So when I need to, I don't hesitate to use them professionally.

Zoom lenses give the photographer options in framing shots that simply are not available with any other type of lens. In some instances such as a particularly difficult mountain climb when weight I can pack is minimal, the zoom lens gets the nod. With one zoom lens I can take close, medium and long shots. These include facial portraits, full animal portraits and herd or group shots. And, because I'm not burdened down with several heavy lenses, I can carry more film with me.

There are three basic ranges of zoom lenses:

1. Wide angle to near telephoto (*35mm to 100mm; 43mm to 86mm; etc.*)
2. Near telephoto to mid-telephoto (*70mm to 210mm; 80mm to 200mm; 80mm to 240mm; 50mm to 300mm*)
3. Long range to ultra-long range telephoto (*180mm to 640mm; 400mm to 1200mm*)

I own and use several lenses in the first two categories and have found them to be invaluable.

The 43mm to 86mm Nikon zoom is very handy when making candids around the hunting camp or shooting packstring pictures. For near range shooting, it's surprising how much the rather conservative zoom range helps (approximately .85 "power" to 1.7 power) in being able to frame up subjects and activities for maximum effectiveness. I also use the superb Vivitar Series-I 70mm to 210mm Macro-zoom and the enormously flexible Nikon 50mm to 300mm zoom. The new generation of macro-zooms, such as the Series I, not only afford marvelous quality when used as a conventional telephoto zoom but, with a very minor click-type adjustment, they also enable the photographer to focus ultra close for small subjects like flowers, insects, animal tracks, etc. For most purposes, and in a pinch, these macro-zooms can replace three or even four lenses.

The 50mm to 300mm Nikon zoom, though a relatively old lens design, affords good sharpness and clarity but is not quite as needle sharp as Series I in the case of my own two lenses. And its almost unparalleled 6 to 1 zooming range is a marvelous addition to any photographer's arsenal. It is also, albeit a rather heavy and very expensive lens, rather "fast" at f4.5. Zoom lenses should be seriously considered by any relatively

This 400mm Novoflex with squeeze-focus pistol grip can be mounted on a skeleton gunstock. The integral bellows between the camera and lens allows ultra-close focusing on small objects.

As a minimum, the serious wildlife/outdoor photographer should have these three basic lenses: 1) the 400mm long telephoto, shown leftmost, for wildlife portraits, 2) the 200mm close-range telephoto for herd or group shots and for close-in handheld work, and 3) the standard 50mm lens for panoramas and "normal" candid shooting.

serious wildlife and outdoor photographer because of their flexibility. However, beware of most cheap zooms. They can be an abomination or, even if relatively sharp initially, they can quickly go out of adjustment, since they are inherently somewhat less durable than most fixed focal length lenses.

Incidentally, the old rule-of-thumb as to when you can safely hand-hold a telephoto states that the shutter speed should equal or exceed the millimeters of focal length of the lens. In other words, a 200mm lens requires (*on average*) a shutter speed of about $\frac{1}{250}$th of a second, while a 400mm requires at least $\frac{1}{400}$th and is better with $\frac{1}{500}$th. This is subject to all sorts of variables, of course. As with some gunners, some photographers are far steadier shooters than others and can get away with slower shutter speeds. Also, a motionless subject is easier to photograph than a moving one. In this case, subject movement may cause the photographer to move and thus make the photographer betray his presence. And some photographers are just more demanding about quality than others. There is no strict line of demarcation between a "fuzzy" picture and a "clear" one. Rather, there is a great gradual continuum along which two photographers might each regard the same picture as being "sharp" in one case and "soft" in the other, depending upon the standards they set and the uses they will put the picture to.

I feel that, in most cases, lenses over 500mm in focal length cannot yield high quality pictures except under the most controlled of circumstances, which usually aren't possible to achieve in the field.

3. Buy the very highest quality equipment and lenses that you can afford. There is a regrettable tendency, fostered by many camera store promotions, to buy quality cameras with the "mainframe" or same brand basic lens (50mm or 55mm) and then fill in the "outfit" with one or two second-rate telephoto lenses. This doesn't mean that all of the "independents" (people who supply lenses-only to fit various brands of cameras) make bad glass. For the money, some of these lenses are quite good. But many aren't. And the worst place in the world to "save" money is on a long 400mm lens that is far more difficult to design and produce than the "basic" 50mm lens!

It's better to buy your outfit one lens at a time and buy the best. Better to have fewer lenses but of top quality. When you use the best in equipment and you take a bad picture, at least you have the consolation of knowing that you were most proba-

Here nature photographers are shooting a mule deer buck in Yellowstone National Park. Such opportunities come after Labor Day when most tourists have departed, and cold weather is forcing big game down from the heights.

bly at fault and not the equipment itself. It's a shame for a photographer to work hard for some really outstanding pictures, take them, and then find that they simply don't measure up because of basic lack of lens quality.

For my own use I prefer the Nikon system for 35mm format. This is a marvelously broad and powerful system enabling the photographer to meet practically any photographic challenge that he can conjure up—and his pocketbook can cope with. There are also several other fine system cameras in the 35mm format, but my Nikons have never let me down and I have never regretted choosing them for professional use. They are not cheap.

I also shoot the 2¼-inch format since some clients and photographic markets still demand this larger size. Here I have chosen the fine Swedish Hasselblad, with German optics. And like the Nikon, it is the standard against which all others of its type are judged. It too is a "system" camera with a surprisingly broad list of options available for this large-format size camera.

There is one special lens that is dear to my heart. For wildlife photography, I use it more than all others put together. And it is one of only two non-Nikon lenses that I will use for 35mm

Jim Balog (left), a professional movie photographer, focuses his 16mm Bolex while noted wildlife still photographer Leonard Lee Rue III adjusts his Nikon F2 mounted on a 400mm Novoflex. These pros were preparing to photograph brown bears along the McNeil River on the Alaska Peninsula.

photography. This is the superlative, German-produced Novoflex "follow-focus" lens system that is imported by Burleigh Brooks Optics, Inc., 44 Burlews Court, Hackensack, New Jersey 07601.

The quality of these lenses is fantastic. If the photographer does his part, these lenses yield needle-sharp pictures that are far sharper than any 400mm lens has a right to produce—the limits of optical-glass lens technology being what they are. This is actually a lens *system* built around three basic focal lengths (280mm f5.6, 400mm f5.6, 600mm f8). The one that I am particularly acquainted with and use so much is the marvelous 400mm. In addition to its peerless quality, this lens offers several unique features of special interest to the bird and wildlife photographer that are found on no other equipment at any price.

Practically all camera lenses focus as you twist a circular dial around the lens housing itself. The Novoflex utilizes the squeeze ("follow-focus") method. This greatly expands the photographer's flexibility, especially in photographing any moving subject up to and including animals at a full run or birds in full flight.

The Novoflex rig of most interest to the wildlife photographer is the complete kit that they call their "Naturalist and Surveillance" unit. (A lot of law enforcement agencies also use these high quality, flexible units.) The Novoflex comes complete with a lightweight, highly usable gunstock. The unit, when mounted on the stock, somewhat resembles an old fashioned Thompson submachine gun and can be used in left-hand or right-hand position. The rear pistol grip contains the control for the follow-focus feature. Here a squeeze-controlled focusing trigger is under slight but constant pressure, thus allowing the photographer to *continuously adjust focus* without disturbing his camera aim or operation and without moving the trigger hand in any way. The front grip has the cable-type shutter release. There's nothing to twist. No requirement for any upsetting movement, just handy squeeze controls.

This means that, either hand-held or on a tripod, the Novoflex rig can be swung through on a running animal or flying bird while you continuously adjust the focus by gently squeezing the rear grip to keep the subject in good focus all the while. Actually it's much like shotgunning in the swing-and-followthrough mode. Thus it now becomes possible to get the most exciting of all wildlife shots, those galvanized by the subject's being in motion or even in full flight.

The Novoflex has still another unique feature. It has an integral bellows attachment that comes as a part of the Naturalist and Surveillance rig and remains on the unit at all times. This little jewel is not delicate at all and can take all the punishment inherent in consistent field use of such a rig. The normal minimum focusing distance of this 400mm lens is about 21 feet, which is about average for this size telephoto lens. However, with the bellows racked out you can pull this minimum range down to as close as a mere six feet. This means that if you are photographing a small- to medium-size subject that would be disappointingly small even at 21 feet, you can about fill up the frame with him at under ten feet. I have laboriously gotten to

To be sure you get those once-in-a-lifetime photos, carry your camera whenever you go afield. Here in the full flush of the rut, two bucks — with spreads of over 20 inches — do some heavy hooking. It's wise to keep in practice by using your camera outdoors throughout the year.

within almost 10 feet of jaunty green-wing teals, and at that close distance was nearly able to fill the whole picture with a little 11- or 12-inch long drake. At 21 feet he would have been far smaller and the picture much less dramatic.

4. Working with animals. A prime ingredient in successful wildlife photography is that the photographer have both a thorough knowledge of the quarry and that he be patient and willing to work hard. Wildlife photography is much like hunting. The photographer must know his game and its habits — know where, when and how to locate and approach it. He must be patient because all too often he cannot get close enough. Or, sometimes when he does, the light may be too subdued for good color shots, or else the animal may have a defect, such as a bad horn or antler or a rubbed spot on its hide that somewhat spoils the picture.

Serious wildlife photography is fascinating and demanding. Animals must be approached far more closely than in gun hunting. In various national parks this is often fairly easy to do at certain times of the year, but not all photography can be done in these sanctuaries.

The photographer must be especially careful when working with large, potentially dangerous animals. And bull elk or moose at the height of the rut can be very dangerous indeed, if you approach too close. Also, when climbing to photograph the high-altitude types like goat and sheep, you can be concentrating on the picture requirements at hand and get yourself into a dangerous mountaineering situation.

I cannot think of a more soul-satisfying hobby than wildlife photography. It gives one the opportunity to be out observing and photographing animals and birds the year round with no closed seasons. It has its own special brand of fascination and challenge. It is, perhaps, the ultimate level of trophy hunting for the hunter who has evolved through all its successive stages.

The End of the Hunt

26

Chances are that you will have spent so much time and energy getting "up" for your trophy hunt that you'll begin to take things easy as the hunt nears its end and, most especially, after you return home. This is natural. You may have worked hard planning, organizing, and saving for the trip. You probably will have worked hard during the first stages of the hunt. With the end in sight, especially on highly successful trips, the natural tendency is to just relax completely. After all, you'll feel you've earned it.

Well, there's nothing wrong with relaxing a bit. And this letup does often allow you to enjoy certain less dramatic but equally fulfilling nuances of the total experience. But it's best not to relax completely. Not yet. Not even when you get home. There are still some important details that will need your attention just to make sure that your highly successful trip doesn't end with unfortunate happenings, which occur all too commonly, sad to say.

What are these things that you should attend to? Well, it's impossible to list all of them because they will vary considerably. They depend upon you and the exact nature of your hunt. However, I'll sketch in some of the basic ones that generally apply, whether you've been on a guided or an unguided hunt. Let's divide these concerns into two broad classes: those that bear watching before you leave camp and those that should be checked on as soon as you return home.

Before You Leave Camp

Get everyone's name, address, and phone number. This includes the other hunters, the guides, the cook, the wrangler and anyone else in camp. You may want to swap pictures with them later, contact them about another hunt or something that occurred on this one, or just ask their advice. This address can be of value, even if it's used on a "Please Forward, If Necessary" basis several years later. Get telephone numbers because you may need to call on some matter too urgent for the mails, or you may be asking for considerable information that you feel would be too much of a burden or imposition to handle by mail. Yet you know these acquaintances would be glad to furnish the info over the telephone. Sometimes people have unlisted numbers. So, if you don't get them in camp, you won't get them through telephone information services.

The names of all the people you hunt with in different parts of the country over the years add up to a valuable network of contacts for information and help on planning future hunts or in helping your friends plan hunts. You can use all the help you can get, including these contacts.

Take those pictures you need to round out your coverage of the trip. Earlier in this book I suggested planning and actually listing a "scenario" to insure that you don't miss any key photos of the trip. Now is the time to haul that list out and double-check to make sure that you've taken all the shots you want and to get those that you haven't. Also, you may want to get double or even triple coverage on some of the key posed shots — such as you with your guide, your guide with your trophy, etc. — to make *sure* that they come out well.

Now is the time to do all this. Once you've gone home, the opportunity is lost. No matter how many more hunts you go on, even in the same country or with the same people, you will have forever lost the chance to capture *that one hunt* on film. So do some checking to make sure you get home with the shots you want. Also, this is the last chance to add any original shots, that weren't listed on your scenario. That scenario, no matter how well thought out and complete, was put together in your head before you actually got to camp. There is always a good picture-taking opportunity or two that you can think up after most of the hunt is under your belt.

Check over your duffle and gear. Now's the time to round up all of your gear and make sure that it's there and in good condition. Things really get tossed around in a lived-in camp.

People borrow things, sometimes without bothering, or being able, to ask. Things get thrown about and out of order. Sometimes, fortunately very rarely, there is some petty thievery. Now is the time to check. After you reach home, it's either too late completely because the camp will have split up and the hunters will have scattered to the four winds, or, at best, it's difficult.

Take care of that trophy and ship it yourself. See to that precious trophy. Don't let it be ruined or lost now. Make sure it is well salted, especially around the eyes, ears, nose, mouth and paws. Use fine-grain table salt, not coarse rock salt. And remember, there's no such thing as putting too much salt on, but you sure can put too little on. Hang or spread the trophy to dry, flesh side out, in the shade. Direct contact with the sunlight can cause it to "burn" and may ruin it.

Ship it to the taxidermist as soon as possible. Of course, if this isn't a guided hunt, you must handle the shipping anyway. But, if you're on an outfitted and guided hunt, do *not* leave the trophy in camp for the outfitter to ship. Even though he does it for other hunters and letting him ship it would be easier, make sure that the most dependable person you know is attending to that all-important detail. That person is you!

How do you ship trophies and why do you ship them? Capes or hides, well salted and dried, should be shipped in burlap bags. The antlers or horns can be shipped loose, but I always pad the points with cardboard taped on because some carriers require this. Ship by air and fully insure everything. You want those precious trophies to get to the taxidermist as quickly and safely as possible. In addition to attaching the normal tag on the outside of each bag or carton that shows my name and address and that of a cosignatory, I also whittle out wooden tags and letter-in my name and address. I attach these wooden tags to the actual trophy inside the bag or carton. It's best to attach them with heavy string or cord because wire can rust and stain some light colored capes.

Why do all this yourself? Well, the outfitter has a million things on this mind, and running an operation out in the bush is not exactly like having three secretaries at your beck and call to get coffee and take dictation. Usually, it will take several weeks or months for the outfitter to send the trophies out. Why wait? Also, as long as the trophies are sitting around, even though the outfitter will try to take care of them, something could happen. Accidents or worse! It pains me no end to say that I have seen some men (I won't call them hunters) offering money, and lots of it, to guides and outfitters to switch their tag with another one in camp or on a bigger or better trophy.

In some cases these "sports" may not have even shot a sheep or grizzly. Yet they want the person they are trying to bribe to affix their tag to someone else's trophy and tell the hunter that his trophy was lost while coming out of the bush. The overwhelming majority of guides and outfitters are honest and upright. But, as in any other calling, there are a few bad ones. Why take the chance that someone may take advantage of you? And even an honest fellow may have to think twice if he has a sick wife at home or bills piling up when some lout offers him more than a year's wages to perform one simple, and totally dishonorable, act.

The bad thing is that the more outstanding your trophy, the more liable you are for this kind of betrayal. And there would be little if anything that you could ever do to prove it or even ascertain just what did happen. It grieves me to say that with the growing demand for some trophies and with increasing numbers of hunters, that inevitable (but small) percentage of bad characters cause this heinous practice to occur more frequently. This is a special problem on sheep, grizzly or record-book size trophies of any species.

So, ship your trophy yourself. Then it's safely on its way and cannot be feloniously lost or switched. Write your taxidermist, *immediately,* before you leave for home. Tell him exactly what you shipped and when. Give him all the flight numbers, shipment numbers and other data so he can trace the shipment, if necessary.

Give the taxidermist the exact measurements of your trophies so that he can verify that he received *your* rack or horns and so that you have a copy of these measurements yourself to check the trophy when it comes in to you from the taxidermist months later. (Allow from 5 to 10 percent for shrinkage of both hides, horns, and antlers during that time.) Keep a copy of this letter for your records, and ask the taxidermist to telephone you collect at your home to immediately confirm his receipt of your trophies.

Don't leave any gear to be shipped. Guides and outfitters are not valets or administrative assistants. Their strong points lie elsewhere. Don't leave, purposefully or accidentally, things for them to ship to you. That is bothersome for them to handle and, often, downright expensive. Guides, especially, don't make much money. A $20 or $25 shipping cost, plus trying to pack it or pay for having it crated, is a substantial investment. If, in spite of everything the guide has to ship you something, give him the money to do so before you leave camp. Or, if you discover you forgot something in camp when you reach home, send him the money to cover the expenses and a couple of bucks extra for his trouble.

Mark up your map. You should have carried a good map of the area into camp with you. You can certainly use it when you hunt to familiarize yourself with the country.

Before you leave camp, get someone more familiar with the countryside to help you mark in neatly the location of all the significant events of the hunt and all the camps. You'll want to know locations such as base camp, any spike camps, the place where you shot your trophy, the high rimrock where you got a little scared on the climb up, that special little alpine valley with the meadow that you'll always remember as the most beautiful spot you ever set eyes on, and anything else important to you.

A map like this, with all things of importance slotted in, from each hunt becomes a prized memento. These maps can be framed and, backed with colorful burlap or sailcloth and possibly edged with the hunting licenses. some Canadian money from a Canadian hunt, a handwritten note or rough map scrawled by the guide, a few snapshots or any number of other things. Such a mounting becomes both an attractive "talking piece" to be hung on any wall and a great memory prodder.

Square up all money matters. Misunderstandings over money have been known to set brother against brother since the dawn of recorded history. Don't leave camp owing anyone money or with anyone owing you money. Take care of all loans, tips, purchases or whatever right before you depart.

Anything Else? So, while you're savoring those final moments of the successful hunt, try to think of any of these important details that you may have let slip. You'll learn by trial and error. I certainly have. Though I have never had a trophy lost, switched or damaged on me, I have neglected to get names or addresses that later I desperately wanted. Most of these omissions came about because I kept putting off this simple chore until, finally, it was too late.

There was one brief but memorable hunt in the parched, starkly beautiful South Texas countryside several years ago that I didn't photograph properly. In fact, I took practically no pictures. It was mid-May and the mercury was sizzling and steaming at over 100 degrees. We ran several miles behind the pack of hounds before we finally bayed up and got our javelina. Along the way I lost my breakfast and became mortally ill. All I wanted to do was lie down and drink a quart of cold tea. (I drank nearly a gallon later!). And I just didn't bother to capture the ugly-beautiful countryside on film, nor did I film many elements of the hunt.

Admittedly this was not a "trophy hunt" in the proper sense of the word nor was it my preferred way of hunting. However, it was an unforgettable experience that I'll probably never repeat, and I've always been sorry that I didn't take the time to film it properly. It serves as a good example of the trap you can fall into on your trophy hunt.

The moral of the story? The time to attend to all loose ends is when you get your chance at hunt's end. Later may be too late.

As Soon As You Get Home

Home at last. But before you relax completely, there are still several items you should take care of. These are especially important if your hunt has been a lengthy, difficult one. And if the hunt has been in very cold or wet weather, the tasks are urgent.

First, you should check your duffle thoroughly, even though you did that right before you left camp. Check to see that nothing is missing. And if you picked up any breakable souvenirs, check to see whether they arrived safely.

Sort through your clothing right away. All damp clothes should be washed or taken to the cleaners right away to avoid mildew and ruin. Dirty items should be similarly sorted and not allowed to sit around for days or weeks until all the dirt and grime "sets" thoroughly and is difficult to remove.

Film should be sent in immediately for developing. You went to so much trouble to take pictures, and they are priceless in that they can't be duplicated. So why take the chance that they may become misplaced or lost. Also, the dyes on color film can fade if it is left around too long after it has been exposed without developing. This is especially so in warm weather.

Confirm arrival of your trophies at the taxidermist's. Give him two days to contact you, as you instructed him. If he does not do this, you should contact him. If the trophies haven't reached him yet, you should then initiate a tracer immediately. The sooner you do this, the better chance you have of locating that stray shipment.

After you have rested a day or two and your clothes have been cleaned, get them all hung up and organized, ready for the next hunt. Your wife will appreciate your help, and that's the best way to insure that you get maximum wear from the garments. Clean and saddle soap those dirty boots and leather goods. Oil them if they're dry but don't overdo it.

If you booked your hunt through a hunting consultant or booking agent, write him a brief note, telling the results of your hunt and your opinion of the service you received. If you had a good hunt, you'll be giving credit where credit is due. In that case, send a copy of the letter to the outfitter, rancher or whoever was your host on the hunt. If you had a bad hunt and you are unhappy with the service, your note will help get the word out and help to protect some other hunters from being duped. (In this case, you'll regret that no one had done that for *you*.) Either way, contact your middleman to let him know how things turned out.

If you said you would write to other hunters you met in camp and/or send them pictures, this is a good time for it.

Clean your gun thoroughly and check over your binoculars, spotting scope and cameras to make sure that they weathered the trip okay. Now's the time to discover any damages so that you can collect on the catastrophe insurance or whatever coverage that you did carry. Later it may be awkward or impossible to recover. And repair of equipment can run into real money.

With these few tasks done, you can begin savoring memories from the trip and start planning next year's hunt!

How to Choose and
Use a Good Taxidermist

27

It is simply amazing that many trophy hunters spend hours deciding where and how they will hunt, when to go, and what gear to take—and then select their taxidermist as casually as they do their sox. And then, just as often, these hunters don't follow up with specific directions to the taxidermist. Thus, even if they were fortunate enough to blindly choose a good pro, their trophy may be returned to them as a well done mount or rug but not in the exact fashion desired. This happens to hunters each year, even to many a conscientious and otherwise canny trophy hunter.

Even though there is far more to trophy hunting than the mere trophy itself, it does make sense to take every reasonable precaution to insure that the trophy is well mounted. To do all this takes hardly 5 percent of the time and effort that it takes to plan, arrange and make the hunt. Yet probably most of today's sportsmen don't make that all-important 5 percent investment.

Selecting the Taxidermist

The first thing you must do, before checking his prices and delivery dates, is to insure that his quality is adequate. A mount that returns to you with a bizarre, grotesque look rather than the vibrant, "alive" look that you want is one that you are ashamed to hang and display. And it's too expensive at any price. The mount that lasts a lifetime and with each passing year becomes an ever more cherished memento of a priceless experience is well worth the money, whatever the price. Quality costs money in taxidermy as in anything else. But either the trophy is worth top quality artistic treatment or you shouldn't have it mounted to begin with.

Proper field care is essential, but it alone won't guarantee a satisfactory mount. Handsome capes can be ruined in shipping. And if you don't tell your taxidermist which pose you want, you might be unhappy with his choice.

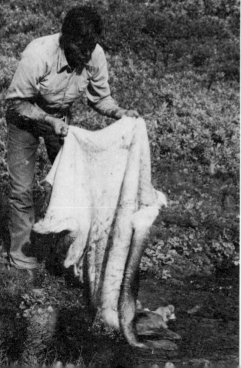

Soaking of the hide in clean mountain water helps remove blood stains and dirt before they "set." This field cleaning often reduces the amount of cleaning and bleaching required of the taxidermist, and thus it may reduce your bill.

So, check your potential taxidermist's quality. Do this by looking over as much of his work firsthand as possible. Concentrate especially on the species that you are interested in. Just because a man does an exceptional job capturing the look and spirit of sheep and bear doesn't mean he's necessarily as proficient on elk and whitetail.

Look at as many of his mounts as possible and try to do this in the company of other experienced hunters so that you have the combined evaluations of several pairs of knowledgeable eyes. If possible, compare his mounts firsthand with other mounts. If those other mounts are of the same species for more direct comparison, all the better. Like the rabbit coat that looks good by itself until you hold the mink up beside it, almost any mount looks better isolated. Comparing the work of several men directly lends more perspective.

Check your potential taxidermist's references. Do it thoroughly, just as you would those of a potential guide or outfitter. Call the references who are nearby. You'll get more information over the phone than through a letter. And if the trophies are close enough it might be worth driving over in your car to see them and check how they're standing up to the test of time.

On those more distant references, it's a good idea to enclose a stamped self-addressed envelope for the fellow's convenience. Also, you might even include most of your questions in the form of a convenient fill-in-the-blank or multiple choice questionnaire that the fellow can fill out with a minimum of time and energy. After all, he's doing you a big favor by furnishing the information, why not make it easy on him?

When checking those references, in addition to reviewing the general references that the taxidermist gives to you, it's also a good idea to check on some of the same species that the man has recently completed. That way you can get a better idea of the kind of work the man's shop is currently turning out on *your* kind of trophy. Also, I'd specifically ask for some references that are several years old so that you can verify that the man's work is holding up well over the long haul. (If you do get a negative report, be sure to find out whether the trophy is hung in direct sunlight, or over a frequently used fireplace, or whether it is in some other fashion adversely displayed. Many times the owner himself, not the taxidermist, is responsible for the rapid deterioration of his prized trophy mount.)

After you find a man whose work is satisfactory, check his business terms. Review his prices to insure that, although they may be on the expensive side (the best work usually is), they are not too overpriced when compared with comparable quality work. Also, find out what his delivery time is. Six to eight months is normal, and one year isn't too unusual these days. Because most of the work comes in late fall, taxidermy is a very uneven business. And good work takes time to complete. However, much over a year is a bit long. And no matter what the man tells you, two- to three-year deliveries are ridiculous.

Normal deposit when you send the work in is from 25 to 33 percent down. I would not plunk down 50 percent, even if it is requested. Also, if the work is to take over a year, I would begin reducing the amount of my deposit proportionally. Find out if packing and crating are included in the basic price. (Usually they aren't.) Then ask the taxidermist to give you some "for instances" as to how much it might cost to pack and crate varying size shipments. Ask what his packing and crating practices are and how he builds his crate. (More than one hard-won trophy has been lost on the way home, after a hard and expensive hunt and a long wait at the taxidermist's, because it wasn't sufficiently protected from the elements and the inevitable rough handling it received.)

Also, confirm that you will be charged at the price in effect when you send the trophies to the taxidermist and that you will not have to pay any price increases that occur while your work is being completed. More than one unhappy hunter hasn't covered this point and has found that he owed more money than he anticipated. Find out if there are any other "extras" that aren't covered in the basic cost.

How to Work With the Taxidermist

Once you have selected your taxidermist and sent the trophies to him, you should follow up with him to insure that you get the most benefit from his craft. If you are having a basic shoulder mount made of your deer, pronghorn or whatever, tell him specifically if you want it facing straight ahead or to which side you want the head turned.

Determining if you want the trophy facing front or to the side at a specific angle depends on what species the trophy is and on where you want to hang it. Generally, moose (due to their large size), sheep (due to tradition), and goat (due to having no neck) are faced front while the others may be faced either directly front or to a side. I find that turning the heads adds a bit of variety and liveliness to the poses. However, the

Here a guide removes a small piece of moose headskin that will be shipped with the antlers to the taxidermist for an antler-only mounting.

large antlered trophies like elk or caribou cannot be turned at extreme angles, as deer and antelope can be, because beyond a certain point, their antlers would collide with the wall.

You should decide where you will hang your trophy before having it mounted. Then you can tell the taxidermist which way you want the head turned. The trophy should face out into the room and, the farther toward one corner of the room or the other that you display the head, the more extreme the angle at which you will probably want to turn the head. By using the word "extreme" angle I don't mean overdoing it to the point of making the mount look artificial or bizarre, of course. But if you don't give specific instructions to the taxidermist initially and the head returns facing the "wrong" way, then you have no one to blame but yourself.

After you have several whitetail, or mule deer mounted, it's nice to add variety by putting one up in the "sneak" pose: neck

Wilderness trips can yield many kinds of souvenir pickups, such as these bleached-out antlers that belonged to a winter-killed moose. Here, a good taxidermist can come up with interesting mounts.

outstretched, head down with chin up. But, again, you must tell this to the taxidermist before he begins his work.

Often it is necessary for the taxidermist to do repair work on a hide or cape. And this usually costs a bit extra. I control this by telling the taxidermist, in writing at the beginning, that he is authorized to perform up to $25 in repair work on any given trophy. But beyond that amount, I ask that he contact me and explain the situation so that I may decide on any further expenditures.

If I am having a rug mount made, I always tell the taxidermist which two colors of felt he should use when edging the mount and whether I want an open-mouth or a closed-mouth mount.

As I've mentioned earlier, when I ship the trophies to the taxidermist, I ask that he have someone call me collect when they arrive at his place to confirm their safe arrival. It's well worth a couple of bucks for a 3-minute phone call to get this assurance.

Once you have located a good taxidermist who does quality work at a fair price, it's usually a good idea to stick with him in the future. Often these fellows are sources of good hunting in-

408

formation because of all the trophies coming in, and a taxidermist is more apt to forward nuggets of good information to his better clients, the way of the world being what it is.

While I'm giving the taxidermist all these specific instructions, to avoid any confusion later and to protect both of us, I always ask his advice and opinions. The taxidermist is the pro in the field; he may well have a better idea or a new twist that you haven't thought of for your mount. To get the full benefit of his professionsl background, be sure that he feels free to make suggestions.

The taxidermist is an important, though expensive, member of your hunting "team." And your trophy hunt isn't really over until you get the prized trophy back from your taxidermist, mounted as you want it to be. Make sure you've done your part in choosing the right man to do your work and in giving him explicit directions. You'll get more for your money that way!

The Trophy Room

28

A good trophy room will be both striking and tasteful in appearance. It will project a unique yet traditional masculine character that is attractive to both men and women of varied backgrounds. A bad trophy room will have an appearance that ranges from the cluttered and confused to the bizarre and grotesque.

What separates the good from the bad in trophy rooms is that elusive quality of good taste. There is general agreement on the elements that make a good trophy room and even agreement as to what is "good" and "bad" for each element. But when the elements are combined to produce the final ambience of the room, the room may meet with disagreeing responses.

Basic Elements

1. Room Location. It is a good idea to locate the room "off in the corner" of the house, so to speak, out of the primary traffic pattern. This is especially important if there are several youngsters in the family who are often in the house with their friends or if there are frequent young visitors such as grandchildren. Without meaning to, unsupervised children can wreak havoc in a trophy room by touching mounts with sticky, dirty hands; breaking feathers or fins on mounted birds or fish; or walking on rug mounts.

Keeping the room tucked out of the way is also a good idea if a number of rug mounts are displayed on the floor. The term "rug" is highly misleading because *no* animal hides should be walked on repeatedly. They simply will not stand up to it. Since

Secondary trophies add interest to any collection. This grizzly skull is neatly lettered with kill data. And it shows a bullet hole between the eyes, the only shot the author needed to fire.

bright sunlight is not good for mounts and since exposure over a long period will dry and fade mounts, it's often a good idea to locate trophy rooms on the north or west side of the house, especially in the southerly parts of the country. Of course, although any trophy room with windows should be provided with lined drapes for protection, location of the room on the less sunny sides of the house does give the option of opening those drapes occasionally.

2. Room Size. A trophy room can be attractive or unattractive, no matter how large or small it is. However, care must be taken in the case of extremely small rooms, or areas within rooms to avoid the overcrowded or "busy" look. Depending on factors such as windows, doors, and partitions, doubling the size of a very small trophy area often means that three times as many trophies may be attractively displayed. All this gets into subjective judgments, but most people agree that the cluttered look is not attractive.

The very large, high-ceilinged room also poses problems. These large rooms can easily take on a cold, austere and uninviting look. Also, they can end up with a "museum" or exhibition look that lacks the personal touch and the mellow feeling that a good trophy room should convey.

Of the two, the very small room or area is probably the easier to deal with. The main consideration is to keep the room clean and uncluttered even if this means not being able to display some prized pictures or mementos. The large room is more difficult to set up and requires a thoughtful hand in its furnishings, lighting and general layout.

3. Layout of the Room. A rectangular rather than a square room is better because it provides more options. In a rectangular room, you can space the trophies differently on two long walls and two short walls, rather than being limited to four walls of nearly equal size. Also, because of its greater number of grouping options, a rectangular room yields more display space than does a square room with equal perimeter. This means that you can hang more trophies in a smaller room; which will probably be less expensive to build.

However, the exact proportions you may need for your room are somewhat determined by other things. If your ceiling is less than 9-feet high, the large heads of trophies such as elk, caribou and moose will stick out *into* the room rather than above the head height of people who are in the room. Thus, the room suddenly seems to constrict into a narrow-corridor type space. This can be overcome to a degree by putting all the large heads down one side of the room, but a narrow low-ceilinged room can be a problem.

If the ceiling is at least 9½-feet tall or taller, the actual living space is unaffected because the heads project, more or less, above the living space. Of course all this depends upon how large the heads are and the pose they are mounted in. They can be placed to take up space above head level, thus requiring a high ceiling.

4. Furnishings and Appointments. I prefer wood paneling on the walls, and favor the darker tones of walnut. Because of its role in the making of gunstocks, walnut seems most fitting. And it is also very attractive. To me, the darker tones seem to convey the masculine, mellow look a good room should have. However, lighting is always a bit of a challenge in medium-large to larger rooms, and the darker walls aggravate this a bit. They can all too easily lead to a cave atmosphere if the room isn't well lit.

There are many other attractive possibilities for wall coverings. Many hunters prefer the lighter-toned woods, and quite a few trophy rooms aren't paneled in wood at all. I have seen some very attractive rooms with walls of stone or plaster. This is standard in the Southwest where a Spanish motif is appropriate. However, the stone becomes rather expensive and both types of walls can easily look cold. The plaster walls also catch and show dirt.

Tastes in floor coverings range widely. Mine tends to run toward crimson or maroon carpet. But here again, this darkens the room and can demand counteracting lighting. The crimson carpeting does add a bit more brightness. There are many other possibilities in carpeting, though I would tend to stay away from white and pastels because they show dirt and are difficult to clean. Also they tend to weaken the character of the room. Tweeds are often attractive, if not too "busy."

Some of the Spanish-type trophy rooms are very handsome, with their stone or stone-veneer floors covered here and there by area rugs or animal rugs. However, a stone floor without wall-to-wall carpeting will tend to throw up more of the inevitable dust and dirt that collects, rather than absorbing it. Thus, the trophies tend to get dirtier in a short time.

Lighting is very important — to the point that it may be advisable to get professional consultation. Avoid dark spots and "holes." And to anticipate the various uses the room may be put to, you can install dimmer switches, which offer brightness control. Indirect lighting is often helpful. And multiple ceiling lights may be needed to augment floor or wall lamps in the higher ceilinged room. Warm-tone fluorescent lights are more pleasing to most eyes than incandescent lights because the former are daylight balanced. Also, the fluorescent lights don't have to be replaced as often. Though fluorescents are more expensive initially, they help you avoid the pesky chore of changing those high ceilinged light bulbs so frequently.

Furniture for the trophy room depends on which part of the country you are located in, as well as your own tastes and the general "look" you may be trying to project. I have seen very at-

Animal rugs enhance any collection. The author took this winter-furred coyote as a bonus on a Wyoming big-game hunt.

tractive rooms furnished in all styles from "traditional" to "contemporary" to "modern." Good taste in selecting and arranging the individual pieces seems far more important in determining whether a room "comes together" rather than what style or period furniture is used.

Many nice trophy rooms in Texas and southern California tend toward the modern in furnishings, while rooms I've seen in Texas and other southwestern states lean toward a Spanish look. In the East and New England there are many rooms in the traditional vein, and quite a few lean toward the look that I call "the New England pine look." In the South and the Midwest many rooms are in the contemporary style. It's all a matter of preference. If care and discrimination are used, an attractive and livable room will result.

Windows and doors play an important role. It's usually not a good idea to include too many draft encouraging doors that keep the dust stirred up and thus transport dirt up to the trophies themselves. Some people prefer a trophy room with no windows at all. This does afford more wall space and also makes the room more secure against burglary.

Many sportsmen like to have a door open from their trophy room onto a patio for entertaining or just for general convenience on warm still evenings. This does create an agreeable option but it also has some disadvantages. Often if both inside and outside doors in the trophy room are open at the same time, a draft is set up that may stir up the dirt and dust or even pull some into the room. Also, since many hunters do like to build their trophy room in such a way that their guns and other valuables may be stored in a secure area, the exterior door weakens this intention.

Airconditioning with a humidifier can reduce trophy maintenance and extend trophy life. If you have central airconditioning that also affords one of the various types of static-electricity atmosphere cleaners, so much the better. The humidifier keeps the heads from becoming too dried-out during the winter heating period. And in summer airconditioning keeps the room agreeably cool and comfortable for you without stirring up the dust. The "atmosphere cleaner" can filter out significant amounts of dust and dirt.

A trophy room almost seems out of kilter without a fireplace of some sort. And yet, an open fire is one of the worst enemies of your mounts. The fire may throw out sparks or soot to damage or dirty mounts or rugs. The soot especially may be so light that it is invisible to the eye most of the time, yet over a long period, it can coat your mounts with a gummy, greasy patina that discolors them and detracts from their appearance. This patina can cause expensive cleaning and repair work in some cases, and in other instances it may even ruin the trophies. Just look at some of those heads that have been displayed for years in various saloons or taverns with open fireplaces.

A fireplace will wreak heavy damage to those heads hung near or immediately over it. This is most apparent on white sheep and goat, and on most of the delicate-haired pronghorn. Bird mounts are particularly susceptible to this kind of damage, too. The answer is to provide the fireplace with glass doors which can be closed to prevent any soot from entering the room.

It's a good idea to group smaller trophies. This provides balance in relation to larger trophies, and it makes optimum use of limited wall space.

Another bad effect from a frequently used fireplace is its heat. Without the glass doors, a fireplace dries out the surrounding atmosphere. A dry atmosphere is bad for the hair and feathers on your mounts, robbing them of their natural oils and causing them to fade and to become dry and brittle. Thus they become much more susceptible to breakage when handled, however carefully.

So, though a fireplace can add much to the character of a trophy room, be careful when using one. It's a good idea to provide the glass doors and keep them closed at all times. If you feel you must open them, at least keep them closed when the fire first starts to burn. This helps to avoid the occasional sparking and sooting prevalent at the start and also enables you to let the "roaring" fire burn down to one of more modest proportions so that it does not dry the room air so drastically.

5. *Trophy Grouping.* I do think that a few bird and fish mounts can add an interesting note of variety and color to the basic big-game trophies. Usually I group my fish or birds

together so that they are not interspersed throughout the room, creating a rather busy soup of big-game heads with all sorts of birds and fish flying and swimming through them from all angles.

Depending upon the size of the room, it is often a good idea to loosely group smaller heads, such as pronghorn or deer, together. This makes comparisons easy and takes up less wall space than required for spacing out all the heads. It also provides interesting focal points that somewhat offset the "weights" of really large heads like moose or elk. In many rooms the center area of one end of the room is occupied by a big moose head. Then other heads are arrayed around the big moose which "ties down" the whole area. Often the other end of the room is focused on a center head of particular merit — perhaps a sheep or an outstanding head of any species. The side walls will then often be focused on a large head or two (elk, caribou) surrounded by smaller heads or "groupings."

Large rugs can be displayed on the floor, well out of the traffic pattern so they are not walked on frequently, or they can be hung on the walls. The larger rugs take up a surprising amount of wall space but they do have the advantage that they can often be appropriately displayed in other rooms, or even hallways, through the house. Of course a big brown bear that stretches more than 8 feet between the front paws must be displayed in a high ceilinged room if he is to be hung on the wall. (This 8-feet measurement is rather common, for it will occur on most animals squaring 7 feet and over.)

All of these comments are just general guidelines, and much depends upon which species the hunter has taken and what his most outstanding trophies are.

6. *Other Considerations.* Though it is in perfectly good taste to display bear, cat or wolf mounts with mouths open and teeth showing, I get the vapors when I see the overly "ferocious" poses. The teeth can be displayed without the rabid leer that some over-zealous taxidermists put out. Plastic teeth are good because most real teeth eventually split and also because this enables you to keep the skull with the teeth intact as a prized secondary trophy.

I am not particularly excited about much of the furniture that I see made from various animal parts. Some furniture is pleasing when covered with certain animal hides; though these might wear and scuff rather readily if the furniture is used much. And I have seen some interesting cocktail tables that used antlers in their construction. Of course all sorts of small items can be made such as ashtrays and gun racks, from hoofs; hide-covered picture frames, desk sets, cigarette holder and lighter sets; and a number of other things. However, it is well to watch the fashioning of furniture from animal parts with a particularly keen eye. Disrespect for the animal is often just a step away. Also, much of this furniture just isn't comfortable. And, since I see a trophy room as a *lived-in* part of the house and not an exhibition hall, this is an important factor.

Most of the tableaus involving several animals or birds and animals are not attractive to me. Many are just too contrived and those that aren't usually look as if they belonged in a museum rather than in a sportsman's trophy room. Also, these tableaus are damnably expensive.

The whole sport of trophy hunting has many highly subjective elements and probably none more so than the most tangible manifestation of the sport, the trophy room itself. Many of my comments in this chapter might be debated by hunters of taste and discernment. But I offer them as general guides so that you may pick and choose among them as you build the trophy collection and room that suits you.

One thing doesn't vary though. No matter how large or small the room, no matter how extensive or limited the trophy collection, the single most important item on display is *you*. Undoubtedly, many nonhunters will pass through your room. Many of these people will be of the large "middle" group of voters who are neither for nor against hunting. Their votes will ultimately decide the fate of gun ownership and sport hunting in this country. How tasteful your trophy collection is and how well you represent your sport will have a lot to do with the opinions they form about hunting. That's something to remember.

The Boone and Crockett Club

29

In its relatively brief history, American sport and trophy hunting has not had time to develop all the traditions and ritual of the sport in Europe, and most notably in Germany. But more than time is involved. The vast differences in the cultures plus the differences between a sport open to the masses and a sport for an elite group would also imply that the American traditions may never become quite as elaborate. However, America is very well on its way to evolving and adding to its own trophy-hunting traditions. And this is all to the good.

A knowledge of what has gone before and a perspective on the contributions of hunters from an earlier day add much to the sport. This can help produce better and more agreeable hunters. There is, or should be, much more to the sport than merely striving to kill a particular specimen of a certain size. This is especially important here in America where hunting, both on sport and subsistence levels is so inextricably entwined with the settlement and development of our country and even with mores of today.

A knowledgeable hunter, who becomes ever more competent in his sport, finds himself inevitably becoming a student of all sorts of things from ecology and wildlife sciences to the exploration and development of the West and the evolution of the American rifle. (And there is definitely a distinctly *American* long gun.)

The Boone and Crockett Club is a leader among the institutions that have given form and substance to these hunting traditions. Over many years of trial and through the contributions of some remarkable men, the Club has evolved a very sophisticated and reasonable scoring system for evaluation of trophies. In 1973, the Club and the National Rifle Association of America (NRA) entered into a joint sponsorship the Awards Program. In this association, the Club continues to determine policy and standards, and the NRA handles the basic administrative duties. Together they sponsor the awards programs, which sum up trophy entries for continuing three year periods. And they update and republish the *North American Big Game* records book about every six years.

Theodore Roosevelt, an innovator in many fields, started the Boone and Crockett Club nearly a century ago. On a bleak December evening in 1887 Roosevelt, then just 29 years old, gave a dinner at his residence at which he proposed the formation of a club of American hunting riflemen. He also suggested the name. And his fellow organizers, mostly young men too, enthusiastically entered into the project. The precepts of the Club have changed very little since its inception, though practically everything else in the world of sport has.

The Club is involved in many activities other than the awards programs and the publication of the related record books. Throughout its long and venerable history, the Club has played an active role in the setting up and preservation of many game refuges, including such major ones as Yellowstone Park, McKinley Park and the Sheldon Antelope Refuge in Nevada (named for that fine old sheep hunter and distinguished Club member, Charles Sheldon). The Club has also given direct financial grants to many constructive wildlife research studies which have done much to add to our knowledge of wildlife and promote better game management principles throughout the country.

The Club has published a number of hardcover books, including six different record books (1932, 1939, 1952, 1958, 1964, 1971) and nine other titles between 1893 and 1961 in the general area of hunting and conservation. The Club plans to continue publishing books, and I recommend highly all of their titles. Since most of these are out of print, they fetch prices that range from high to stratospheric and usually can be got only from antiquarian bookdealers specializing in the search and sale of out-of-print titles in this subject area. Many hunters have begun to collect old sporting books, especially the Boone and Crockett titles. They furnish enjoyable reading and greatly broaden the hunter's view of his sport. Many of the old illustrations are "priceless."

To its undying credit, the Club has also aggressively helped to formulate and encourage the "fair chase" approach to the sport. By declining to admit for trophy consideration certain species or specific trophies taken in unsporting ways, the Club has helped discourage the widespread use of bushplanes, snow-mobiles, electronic communication devices and other technology that easily affords the unscrupulous hunter an unfair advantage in the chase.

The point is that though the Club is often equated almost solely with the trophy competitions and the publication of the attendant record books, they are actually involved with many additional constructive aspects of the sport. They have never been the parochial "inch counters" that some have implied.

However, the trophy competitions, and the basic scoring system upon which the Club is predicated, remain by far its best known achievement. The scoring system, which does a remarkably able job of evaluating many factors, evolved in a rather interesting fashion. The first two record books (1932 and 1939) did not utilize today's comprehensive system. And due to the fact that the early scoring did not credit certain substantial trophy factors of some species, great controversy arose. This controversy sparked reconsideration of the whole trophy scoring matter.

Dr. James L. Clark has originated and copyrighted a formula system in 1935. A second system was devised by Grancel Fitz in 1939. Dr. Clark was a well known taxidermist and sculptor at the American Museum of Natural History, and Fitz was a well known outdoor writer. Both had hunted extensively and given much thought to trophy evaluation and ranking.

In 1949 the Boone and Crockett Club established a committee that was to develop a standardized trophy scoring system. Clark and Fitz were among the committee members. The chairman was Samuel B. Webb, long an influential voice in the Club's affairs. The current Official Scoring System is basically a consolidation of the best points of the Clark and Fitz systems, and incorporates a few additional points and some simplifications along the way.

The Boone and Crockett Club has long played a constructive role in the affairs of American trophy hunting and, through its new association with the NRA, it should continue to do so in the years to come.

To request score charts, lists of current minimum qualifying scores, other publications and general info, write North American Big Game Awards Program, c/o Hunting Activities Department, National Rifle Association of America, 1600 Rhode Island Avenue, N.W., Washington, D. C. 20036. If you kill and score a trophy that appears to approach or exceed the minimum qualifying score, you should then request an up-to-date list of official scorers in your area.

Bibliography

Baillie-Grohman, W. A. *Sport in the Alps in the Past and Present.* Charles Scribner's Sons, New York, 1896.

Barclay, Edgar N. *Big Game Shooting Records.* H.F. & G. Witherly, London, 1932.

Boone and Crockett Club. *North American Big Game.* Charles Scribner's Sons, New York and London, 1939.

Boone and Crockett Club. *Records of North American Big Game.* Holt, Rhinehart and Winston, New York, 1964.

Boone and Crockett Club. *North American Big Game.* The Boone and Crockett Club, Pittsburgh, Pennsylvania, 1971.

Brakefield, Tom. *The Sportsman's Complete Book of Trophy and Meat Care.* Stackpole Company, Harrisburg, Pennsylvania, 1975.

Clark, James L. *The Great Arc of the Wild Sheep.* University of Oklahoma Press, Norman, 1964.

Clark, James L. *Good Hunting.* University of Oklahoma Press, Norman, 1966.

Hall, E. Raymond and Keith R. Kelson. *The Mammals of North America, Vols. I and II.* Ronald Press Company, New York, 1959.

Kelsall, John P. *The Migratory Barren-Ground Caribou of Canada.* Queens Printer, Ottawa, 1968.

Moyle, John B., Ed. *Big Game in Minnesota,* Technical Bulletin No. 9. Minnesota Department of Conservation, 1965.

Murie, Olaus J. *The Elk in North America.* Stackpole Company, Harrisburg, Pennsylvania, and the Wildlife Management Institute, Washington, D. C., 1951.

Mussehl, Thomas W. and F. W. Howell. *Game Management in Montana.* Montana Fish and Game Department, Helena, Montana, 1971.

O'Connor, Jack. *The Art of Hunting Big Game in North America.* Outdoor Life, New York, 1967.

Roosevelt, Theodore, and George Bird Grinnell. *American Big Game Hunting: The Book of the Boone and Crockett Club,* Forest & Stream Publishing Company, New York, 1893.

Roosevelt, Theodore and others. *The Deer Family.* The Macmillan Company, New York, 1903.

Rue, Leonard Lee III. *Sportsman's Guide to Game Animals.* Outdoor Life Books/Harper & Row, New York, 1968.

Sheldon, Charles. *The Wilderness of the Upper Yukon.* Charles Scribner's Sons, New York, 1919.

Sievers, Ruth, Ed. *1975 N.R.A. Hunting Annual.* National Rifle Association of America, Washington, D. C., 1975.

Taylor, Walter P., Ed. *The Deer of North America.* Stackpole Company, Harrisburg, Pennsylvania, and the Wildlife Management Institute, Washington, D. C., 1956.

Wright, Wm. H. *The Grizzly Bear.* Charles Scribner's Sons, New York, 1915.

Sources for Additional Hunting Information

U.S. Government Publications. Begin by requesting that you be placed on the mailing lists for two monthly indexes: *Selected U.S. Government Publications,* a magazine that lists and describes over 100 popular government titles each issue; and *Monthly Catalog of U.S. Government Publications,* which lists between 1200 and 2000 new publications each month. Write Superintendent of Documents, U.S. Government Printing Office, Washington, DC 20402.

Topographic Maps

U.S. Topo Maps. First request free index maps on the states of interest. These indexes will show areas covered by quadrangular maps in several scales: 7½-minute (1 inch = 2000 ft.), 15-minute (1 inch = about 1 mile), and others. To order maps east of the Mississippi River, including Minnesota, write Branch of Distribution, U.S. Geological Survey, 1200 South Eads St., Arlington, VA 22202. For maps west of the Mississippi, including Alaska and Louisiana, write Branch of Distribution, U.S. Geological Survey, Federal Center, Denver, CO 80225. Alaska residents may request Alaska maps from Distribution Section, U.S. Geological Survey, 310 First Ave., Fairbanks, AK 99701.

Canadian Topo Maps. To order maps in various scales from 1: 50,000 (1 inch = ¾ mile) to 1: 250,000 (1 inch = about 4 miles), request instructions from Canada Map Office, 615 Booth St., Ottawa, Ontario, Canada K1A OE9.

Appendix

Mail-order Houses

Abercrombie & Fitch, 45th & Madison Avenue, New York, NY 10017.

Charles F. Orvis Co., Manchester, VT 05254. (Offers mostly fishing gear, but also has some clothing and interesting nick-nacks.)

Eddie Bauer, 1737 Airport Way So., Seattle, WA 98134.

Gander Mountain, Inc., Wilmot, WI 53192.

Gerry Mountain Sports, 5450 N. Valley Highway, Denver, CO 80216.

Gokey, 94 E. 4th Street, St. Paul, MN 55101.

Herters Inc., Waseca, MN 56093.

L. L. Bean, Freeport, ME 04032.

Norm Thompson, 1805 N. W. Thurman, Portland, OR 97209.

Woods Bag & Canvas Co., Ltd., 16 Lake St., Ogdensburg, NY 13669.

General Hunting Info

(These are also the addresses to write with complaints about hunts that were misrepresented or were otherwise unsatisfactory.)

IN THE UNITED STATES

Alabama Dept. of Conservation and Natural Resources; Game & Fish Div.; 64 N. Union St.; Montgomery, AL 36104.

Alaska Dept. of Fish & Game; Subport Bldg.; Juneau, AK 99801. Also Alaska Professional Hunters Assn.; Box 4-1932; Anchorage, AK 99509.

Arizona Game & Fish Dept.; 2222 W. Greenway Rd.; Phoenix, AZ 85023.

Arkansas Game & Fish Commission; 2 Capitol Mall; Little Rock, AR 77201.

California Dept. of Fish & Game; 1416 Ninth St.; Sacramento, CA 95814.

Colorado Div. of Wildlife; 6060 North Broadway; Denver, CO 80216. Also Colorado Guides & Outfitters Assn.; Sweetwater Route; CO 81637.

Connecticut Dept. of Environmental Protection; State Office Bldg.; 165 Capitol Ave.; Hartford, CT 06115.

Delaware Dept. of Natural Resources and Environmental Control; Div. of Fish & Wildlife; D St.; Dover, DE 19901.

Florida Game & Fresh Water Fish Commission; 620 S. Meridian; Tallahassee, FL 32304.

Georgia Dept. of Natural Resources; Trinity-Washington Bldg.; 270 Washington St. S.W.; Atlanta, GA 30334.

Hawaii Div. of Fish & Game; 1179 Punchbowl St.; Honolulu, HI 96813.

Idaho Fish & Game Dept.; 600 S. Walnut; Box 25; Boise, ID 83707. Idaho Outfitters & Guides Assn.; P.O. Box 95; Boise, ID 83701.

Illinois Dept. of Conservation; Div. of Wildlife Resources; 605 State Office Bldg.; Springfield, IL 62706.

Indiana Div. of Fish & Wildlife; 607 State Office Bldg.; Indianapolis, IN 46204.

Iowa Conservation Commission; Information & Education; 300 4th St.; Des Moines, IA 50319.

Kansas Forestry; Fish & Game Commission; Box 1028; Pratt, KS 67124.

Kentucky Dept. of Fish & Wildlife Resources; Capital Plaza; Frankfort, KY 40601.

Louisiana Wildlife & Fisheries Commission; 400 Royal St.; New Orleans, LA 70130.

Maine Dept. of Inland Fisheries and Game; State Office Bldg.; Augusta, ME 04330.

Maryland Dept. of Natural Resources; Natural Resources Bldg.; Rowe Blvd. & Taylor Ave.; Annapolis, MD 21401.

Massachusetts Div. of Fisheries & Game; State Office Bldg.; Government Center; 100 Cambridge St.; Boston, MA 02202.

Michigan Dept. of Natural Resources; Mason Bldg.; Lansing, MI 48926.

Minnesota Div. of Game & Fish; 390 Centennial Bldg.; 658 Cedar St.; St. Paul, MN 55155.

Mississippi Game & Fish Commission; Box 451; Jackson, MS 39205.

Missouri Dept. of Conservation; North Ten Mile Dr.; Jefferson City, MO 65101.

Montana Dept. of Fish & Game; Helena, MT 59601. Also Montana Outfitters & Dude Ranchers (MODR); P.O. Box 382; Bozeman, MT 59715. Also Montana Wilderness Guides Assn.; Ovando, MT 59639.

Nebraska Game & Parks Commission; P.O. Box 30370; Lincoln, NB 68503.

Nevada Dept. of Fish & Game; Box 10678; Reno, NV 89510.

New Hampshire Fish & Game Dept.; 34 Bridge St.; Concord, NH 03301.

New Jersey Div. of Fish, Game and Shellfisheries; P.O. Box 1809; Trenton, NJ 08625.

New Mexico Dept. of Game and Fish; State Capitol; Santa Fe, NM 87801. Also Professional Guides & Outfitters Assn. of New Mexico; P.O. Box 455; Albuquerque, NM 87103.

New York Dept. of Environmental Conservation; Div. of Fish & Wildlife; 50 Wolf Rd.; Albany, NY 12201.

North Carolina Wildlife Resources Commission; Albemarle Bldg.; 325 N. Salisbury St.; Raleigh, NC 27611.

North Dakota State Game & Fish Dept.; 2121 Lovett Ave.; Bismark, ND 58501.

Ohio Div. of Wildlife; Dept. of Natural Resources; 1500 Dublin Rd.; Columbus, OH 43212.

Oklahoma Dept. of Wildlife Conservation; 1801 North Lincoln; Box 53465; Oklahoma City, OK 73105.

Oregon State Game Commission; 1634 SW Alder St.; P.O. Box 3503; Portland, OR 97208. For current address of Oregon Guides & Packers, Inc., write the Game Commission.

Pennsylvania Game Commission; P.O. Box 1567; Harrisburg, PA 17120.

Rhode Island Dept. of Natural Resources; Veteran's Memorial Bldg.; Providence, RI 02903.

South Carolina Wildlife & Marine Resources Dept., Div. of Game; 1015 Main St.; P.O. Box 167; Columbia, SC 29202.

South Dakota Dept. of Game, Fish and Parks; State Office Bldg.; Pierre, SD 57501.

Tennessee Game & Fish Commission; P.O. Box 40747; Ellington Agricultural Center; Nashville, TN 37220.

Texas Parks & Wildlife Commission; John H. Reagan Bldg.; Austin, TX 78701.

Utah Div. of Wildlife Resources; 1596 W. N. Temple; Salt Lake, City, UT 84116.

Vermont Fish & Game Dept.; Montpelier, VT 05602.

Virginia Commission of Game and Inland Fisheries; P.O. Box 11104; Richmond, VA 23230.

Washington Game Dept.; 600 N. Capital Way; Olympia, WA 98501.

West Virginia Dept. of Natural Resources; 1800 Washington St.; East Charleston, WV 25305.

Wisconsin Dept. of Natural Resources; Div. of Fish & Game; Box 450; Madison, WI 43701.

Wyoming Game & Fish Commission; Box 1589; Cheyenne, WY 82001. Also Wyoming Outfitters Assn.; Triangle C Ranch; Dubois, WY 82513.

CANADA

Alberta Dept. of Lands & Forests; Natural Resources Bldg.; 109th St. & 99th Ave.; Edmonton, Alberta, Canada T5K2E1.

British Columbia Fish & Wildlife Branch; Dept. of Recreation & Conservation; Parliament Bldgs.; Victoria, B. C., Canada. Also Western Guides & Outfitters Assn.; c/o Mr. Larry Prevost, Sec'y/Manager; 1717 Third Ave., #213; Prince George, B. C., Canada.

Manitoba Tourist Branch; Dept. of Tourism; Recreation and Cultural Affairs; 408 Norquay Bldg.; Winnipeg, Manitoba, Canada.

New Brunswick Dept. of Natural Resources; Fish & Wildlife Branch; Centennial Bldg.; Fredericton, N. B., Canada.

Newfoundland & Labrador Wildlife Dept.; Dept. of Tourism; Confederation Bldg.; St. John's, Newfoundland, Canada.

Northwest Territories Supt. of Game; Gov. of the Northwest Territories; Yellowknife, Northwest Territories, Canada.

Nova Scotia Div. of Wildlife Conservation; Box 516; Kentville, Nova Scotia, Canada.

Ontario Ministry of National Resources; Parliament Bldgs.; Toronto, Ontario, Canada. Also Northern Ontario Tourist; Outfitters Association (NOTO); R. R. #1; Alban, Ontario, Canada.

Prince Edward Island Fish & Wildlife   Div.; Environmental Control Commission; Charlottetown, Prince Edward Island, Canada.

Quebec Dept. of Tourism, Fish & Game; Parliament Bldgs.; Quebec City, Quebec, Canada. Also Quebec Outfitters Assn.; 2860 Chemin des Quatre Bourgeois; Quebec, Canada G1V IY3.

Saskatchewan Wildlife Branch; Dept. of Natural Resources; Gov. Administration Bldg.; Regina, Saskatchewan, Canada.

Yukon Territory Dept. of Travel and Information; Box 2703; Whitehorse, Yukon Territory, Canada. Also Yukon Territory Game Dept.; Box 2703; Whitehorse, Yukon Territory, Canada.

MEXICO

Director General de Gauna Silvestre, S.A.G.; Aquiles Serdan No. 28-7°; Piso, Mexico 3, D. F., Mexico.

The Pope and Young Club

The Pope and Young Club is the North American authority on big-game trophies taken with bow and arrow It is the bowhunter's counterpart to the firearms hunter's Boone and Crockett Club.

The Pope and Young Club is dedicated to selective hunting, good conservation practices, and fair chase. In addition to serving as the bowhunter's voice throughout North America, the Club conducts periodic award programs for the recognition of record-book trophies and conservation achievement Trophies are measured and scored in accord with the system developed by the Boone and Crockett Club.

Incorporated in 1963, the Club takes its name from Dr. Saxton Pope and Art Young, who during the early 1900s learned the bow-hunting art from Ishi, the last surviving member of California's Yana Indian tribe. Pope and Young went on to take many big-game trophies both in North America and in Africa.

The Club's first record book was published in 1975. It contains a history of the Club, profiles on big game, field savvy, a listing of record trophies, sample score charts, and a listing of official measurers. Price: $17.50, postpaid.

Bowhunters can enter a trophy for recognition by arranging to have an official measurer score it.

Correspondence should be directed to Carl M. Hulbert, Executive Secretary, Pope and Young Club, 600 E. High St., Milton, WI 53563.

Illustration and Photo Credits

Index